THE OFFENCES AGAINST PUBLIC ORDER

INCLUDING THE PUBLIC ORDER ACT 1986

AUSTRALIA AND NEW ZEALAND
The Law Book Company Ltd.
Sydney : Melbourne : Perth

CANADA AND U.S.A.
The Carswell Company Ltd.
Agincourt, Ontario

INDIA
N. M. Tripathi Private Ltd.
Bombay
and
Eastern Law House Private Ltd.
Calcutta and Delhi
M.P.P. House
Bangalore

ISRAEL
Steimatzky's Agency Ltd.
Jerusalem : Tel Aviv : Haifa

MALAYSIA : SINGAPORE : BRUNEI
Malayan Law Journal (Pte.) Ltd.
Singapore and Kuala Lumpur

THE OFFENCES AGAINST PUBLIC ORDER

INCLUDING THE PUBLIC ORDER ACT 1986

By

A. T. H. SMITH, LL.M., PH.D.

Barrister and Solicitor of the
High Court of New Zealand
Professor of Law in the
University of Reading

LONDON
SWEET & MAXWELL
POLICE REVIEW PUBLISHING COMPANY
1987

Published in 1987
by Sweet & Maxwell Ltd. of
11 New Fetter Lane, London
Computerset by Promenade Graphics Ltd., Cheltenham
Printed in Great Britain
by Adlard & Son Ltd.
Garden City Press
Letchworth

British Library Cataloguing in Publication Data

Smith A.T.H.
   The Offences Against Public Order including the
Public Order Act 1986.
   1. Breach of the peace—Great Britain
   I. Title   II. Great Britain [Public Order Act 1986]
   Public Order Act 1986
   334. 104,53   KD 8035

ISBN 0-421-36580-3

For Timothy Guy, Gill, Benca
and my parents

PREFACE

My reasons for producing a book devoted to public order law are several. The principal catalyst for the work, obviously enough, was Parliament's passing of the Public Order Act 1986. The book seeks to provide a guide to the contents and application of the Act for whose who will have to implement and operate it; the police, lawyers (be they prosecutors, defenders, or Justices Clerks), students of law and the courts. First and foremost, I have sought to give an account of the law, pointing out the areas of difficulty and doubt that seem to me to arise, and suggesting solutions. I have not tried slavishly to follow the Act, and comment in detail on each and every section. For reasons elaborated upon in the text, the Act cannot be regarded as a code, and I have therefore included in my treatment other important offences encountered in the field of public order, seeking to explain how the new and the old combine.

Public order law is unlike other areas of the criminal law such as theft, homicide and criminal damage, or the offences against the person. For all that it is so understudied a branch of the law, it can touch upon areas of our social existence of quite fundamental political and constitutional importance, especially where the disorder is occasioned or accompanied by the activities of those who are exercising rights of freedom of speech in public. To put it altogether too crudely, society has not much option but to penalise theft, criminal damage or the various offences against the person. Public order is different. The extent to which any society sees the need to penalise those who challenge its prevailing mores, assumptions and constitutional arrangements is much more a matter of political judgment. Although this book is principally a technical exposition of the criminal law, then, it is written with an eye to these wider considerations. In the first chapter, I have addressed some of these issues directly: elsewhere in the discussion, they obtrude less overtly. Whether or not we should continue to have a law of riot, for example, is a policy question with which Parliament's policy advisers were forced to grapple and the issues *pro* and *contra* can usefully be canvassed as a way of highlighting the rationale for the continued existence of the offence. These and other issues may be expected to recur. Should we resurrect some sort of dispersal power, enabling the police to scatter large crowds? Should the police be given a power to ban marches selectively, rather than by the imposition of blanket bans, as the Act permits? Although these questions have been resolved for the time being, they cannot in their nature have been settled for all time, and I have therefore commented on them but where space has permitted.

Public order law is, like many of the categories that an expounder of the law is forced to adopt, a field whose boundaries are artificially set. The decision about what to include and exclude in the treatment was influenced by my intended audience. Affray is frequently treated in some works as an aggravated offence against the person. In this respect, I have taken my cue from the Law Commission and the Home Office. Treason and sedition have been omitted because, although historically they were of great importance, they are today of marginal practical significance (which is not, of course, to say that they will always remain so, as the example of the resurrection of affray graphically demonstrates). Criminal libel and blasphemy have also been left out, although the public order credentials of both (not to mention their revival at the hands of Sir James Goldsmith and Mrs Whitehouse respectively) might warrant their discussion in a book such as this. Principally for reasons of space, I have not tried to deal in any depth with the Prevention of Terrorism Acts, nor with the provisions of the Aviation Act 1982 proscribing hijacking, although again the social menaces dealt with by both would quite properly bring them within the covers of a book such as this one. The space between the covers would be significantly enlarged were I to attempt such a task, and there is in Clive Walker's recently published book *The Prevention of Terrorism in British Law* (1986) a more rounded account of the problem than a writer on the substantive criminal law could hope to present. Readers may wish to disagree with the extent of the coverage, but I hope they will be pursuaded that the selection is not eccentric.

For the most part, the book follows the ordering adopted by the Act, with the exception that violent disorder is dealt with before riot. This format has been adopted because of the likelihood that violent disorder will become the principal offence relating to public disorder. If this is so, a good many of the problems over the scope of the law will arise in the context of trials for that offence rather than in trials for riot (although it seems likely that riot will be prosecuted more frequently in the past, in cases of large pitched battles hitherto charged as affrays).

Some of my colleagues read and commented upon one or more chapters. I should particularly like to thank Mrs. P Leopold, Dr P.A.J. Waddington and Dr. H. Beynon for their help. The pressures of time have been such that I did not think it fair to inflict the bulk of the book on colleagues, however willing, so the errors are more than usual all my own responsibility.

I have read in other prefaces what might appear to be ritual thanks to publishers. Sweets have been extremely supportive, patient and helpful, and my gratitude to them is anything but ritual, not simply for their ready help in preparing the index and table of cases, but for the many ways in which they have helped the process of authorship and encouraged the author.

June 1987

ABBREVIATIONS

References to law reports, journals and periodicals employ standard citations and notations.

"The Act," unless the context otherwise indicates, refers to the Public Order Act 1986, and references to sections and schedules are also references to that Act. In addition,

"The Bill" refers to the Public Order Bill introduced into the House of Commons in December 1985. The Bill became the Public Order Act 1986.

"The draft Bill" refers to the Bill annexed to the Law Commission's "Report," *Criminal Law: The Offences Relating to Public Order* (1983) H.C 85.

"PACE" refers to the Police and Criminal Evidence Act 1984

"The Commission" refers to the Law Commission.

"CLRC" refers to the Criminal Law Revision Committee.

Official Reports

"Working Paper"–Law Commission Working Paper No. 82 *Offences Against Public Order* (1982).

"White Paper—The Home Office and Scottish Office, *Review of Public Order Law* Cmnd. 9510 (1985).

"Report"—Law Commission Report *Offences Relating to Public Order* (1983) Law Com. No. 123.

"Brixton"—Report of an Inquiry by the Rt. Hon the Lord Scarman, *The Brixton Disorders 10–12 April 1981* Cmnd. 8427 (1981).

"Red Lion Square"—Report of an Inquiry by the Rt. Hon. Lord Justice Scarman, *The Red Lion Square Disorders of 15 June 1974* Cmnd 5919 (1975).

Reference will also frequently be made to the following works:

"Archbold"—Archbold, *Criminal Practice and Pleadings* (42nd ed., 1985).

"Supperstone"—M. Supperstone, *Brownlie's Law of Public Order and National Security* (1981).

"Smith and Hogan"—J. C. Smith and B. Hogan *Criminal Law* (5th ed., 1983).

"Williams, *Text*" Glanville Williams, *Textbook of Criminal Law* (2nd ed., 1983).

"Williams, *C.L.G.P.*"—Glanville Williams, *Criminal Law: The General Part* (2nd ed., 1961).

CONTENTS

9. Racial Hatred Offences

10. ASSAULTING OR OBSTRUCTING A CONSTABLE IN THE EXECUTION OF HIS DUTY

11. OFFENCES ON THE HIGHWAY

14. MISCELLANEOUS OFFENCES

TABLE OF CASES

TABLE OF CASES

TABLE OF CASES

TABLE OF CASES

TABLE OF STATUTES

TABLE OF STATUTES

CHAPTER 1

PUBLIC ORDER LAW—THE CONSTITUTIONAL FRAMEWORK

1. THE NATURE OF PUBLIC ORDER LAW

The protected interests

As a general principle, we employ the criminal law to prevent harm to **1–01** certain social interests such as personal safety and physical integrity, and rights in property. The deliberate infliction of harm that the criminal sanction entails is justified as being designed to protect one or other of those interests, or because (to adopt a retributive justification) the offender has harmed such an interest. What is the comparable value in public order that we seek to preserve through the laws of riot, affray, violent disorder and the other, more minor, offences? Our physical integrity and safety are protected by the offences against the person, and the offences against property are designed to safeguard private property from those who would deprive us of it by stealth or violence.

By comparison with these clearly visible social needs, the interests protected by public order law are much more diffuse and indeterminate. Public order law ranges in its extent from the preservation of mere peace and tranquility as between rowing neighbours or the prevention of unreasonable street exhibitionism—nuisances on the outer margins of criminality—to threats of an altogether different magnitude. When public order and stability are jeopardised as they are in cases of affray and violent disorder, public fear is aroused in the minds of bystanders and witnesses that the conduct impugned may lead to physical harm to persons and property. The interests to be protected are therefore, in a sense, inchoate. In cases of really serious outbreaks of public disorder amounting to riot, the constitutional stability of the country itself may seem to be threatened. There is in such situations a visible threat to the rule of law which may lead to a loss of public confidence in the ability of society to regulate itself. When the head that wore the Crown was more uneasy than it is today, the crimes of sedition[1] and treason[2] were employed to preserve society from (or punish after the event) widespread outbreaks of disorder. Here, we are at the bor-

---

[1] Principally for reasons of space, sedition will not be considered in this work. It is rarely if ever prosecuted in modern Britain, the modern form of it being incitement to racial hatred, which is dealt with in Chap. 9. The Law Commission has issued a working paper on the reform of this area of the law; *Treason, Sedition and Allied Offences* (1977) Working Paper No. 72. And see L. H. Leigh, "Law Reform and the Law of Treason and Sedition" [1977] P.L. 128. E. Barendt *Freedom of Speech* (1985) 155. On May 19, 1986, the Attorney-General explained to Parliament the legal difficulties of employing the charge of treason in modern conditions in response to a question demanding to know why treason was not employed in cases of terrorism; see H.C.Deb, vol. 98, col. 14. And see A. Wharam, (1976) 126 New Law J. 428.

[2] *Messenger* (1668) Kel. 70, 84 E.R. 1087; *Dammaree* (1709) 15 St.Tr. 521; *Frost* (1839) 9 C. & P. 129, 173 E.R. 771. Foster's *Crown Cases and Discourses*, p. 210. Riot was initially limited to situations where the rioting was for a private purpose, the reason being that riots with a public purpose were punishable as treason; *Vincent* (1839) 9 C. & P. 91, 173 E.R.

derline between riots and revolutions. But as Professor Dahrendorf points out, many of these severe forms of disorder somehow defy a sanctioning process which is essentially geared to individuals and identifiable small groups.[3] The implications of this insight were not, perhaps, fully appreciated by those responsible for framing the law that has become the Public Order Act 1986.

Historically, the offences of group disorder (riot, unlawful assembly and affray[4]) were most unusual in English criminal jurisprudence. In principle, criminal responsibility was (and is) individual and personal. Criminal liability attaches only where the individual himself brings about a proscribed harm or encourages another to do so. A person is only rarely liable for what others have done, and then only derivatively.[5] Furthermore, mere presence at the scene of an offence is not sufficient to attract liability; proof is required of encouragement and an intention to encourage.[6] Failure to dissociate oneself from what is happening is apt to be regarded indulgently by the common law, which is reluctant to punish omissions.

The conduct struck at by the group disorder offences is at variance with these principles, or at least places them under strain; the very essence of these offences is that the offender is one of a group of persons whose conduct together is such as to cause public fear and alarm. The law could respond to this in two quite distinct ways; it could compromise with the individualistic principles outlined, and regard presence at the scene of a disorder without more as being in itself reprehensible, but not very serious. Proof of the offender's presence at the scene would suffice. Historically, it is suggested, the common law preferred this course. Riot was regarded as a particularly heinous offence only when it became a challenge to authority after those responsible for preserving order had tried to do so, and the Riot Act had been read. Until then, it was a misdemeanour only.[7]

Alternatively, the law could regard participation in one of the offences of group disorder as being very serious, and seek to build into the defi-

---

754. The nineteenth century Criminal Code Commissioners were highly critical of this, saying that the distinction between public and private purposes was "wholly inapplicable to the present state of society." It was founded on a "fundamentally erroneous" principle of "constructive treason in its most obnoxious shape" in a way that was "repugnant to all just notions of criminal law"; 5th Report (1840), p. 90. See Lord Leary C.J. in *O'Brien* v. *Friel* [1974] N.I.L.R. 29 at 43.

[3] *Law and Order* (1985) at p. 33.

[4] Technically, affray might not be classified as a group disorder offence, since it can be committed by one person attacking another. But it will usually be committed by groups fighting in public.

[5] See S. H. Kadish, "Complicity, Cause and Blame: a Study in the Interpretation of Doctrine" (1985) 72 Cal. L.R. 324; K. J. M. Smith, "Complicity and Causation" [1986] Crim.LR 663.

[6] *Coney* (1882) 8 Q.B.D. 534.

[7] Which is not to deny that the penalties for misdemeanour were not savage, by modern day standards. Some evidence for the opinion offered in the text is to be found in the Commonwealth Codes, which were based on the English common law, and which tended to regard riot as punishable with relatively light penalties; Australian States tended to select three years' imprisonment, Canada two years' and New Zealand two years'. See the Report, Appendix C.

nitions of the offences the elements of individual participation of which Professor Dahrendorf speaks. It might then be justifiable to regard the commission of the offence as particularly serious. Several reasons may be offered for adopting the second course. A person who is part of a group will draw courage from the conduct of others in the group, and may well behave in ways that he would not act when alone. His chances of detection are, in the nature of things, rather lower when he can hide in the rabble. Another justification for the second alternative is that where several people are present together acting violently, their weight of numbers in itself increases the dangers to public order inherent in their conduct.[8] A mob is not merely a collection of individuals, but a collective entity. Even though the participants cannot be proved individually to have caused any injury or damage, there is some justification in treating members of a group whose conduct causes such damage as being jointly responsible for what has happened.

The framers of the Act have adopted this second course. Riot and violent disorder are treated by the Act as being offences of considerable seriousness. The first course would require the resurrection of a dispersal power similar to that contained in the Riot Act 1714. This possibility had been rejected by Lord Scarman, whose opinion on the matter seems to have been decisive.[9] Where it cannot be proved that a particular participant has caused damage to persons or property, but was merely part of a group that did so, the scale of his offending is not demonstrably as great as that entailed when the offender can be proved to have been personally responsible. For that reason, the range of penalties available for the group disorder offences is set at a lower limit than is available for the most serious offences against the person,[10] and is at the same level as simple criminal damage.[11]

The "political" character of public order law

In former times it was possible to identify certain crimes as being political in character.[12] For example, the offences of treason and sedition were explicitly and overtly political in nature in so far as they were designed to prevent the undermining of the established constitutional order. It has **1–02**

---

[8] *Caird* (1970) 54 Cr.App.R. 499.

[9] Scarman, *Brixton*, paras. 7.31–7.40; White Paper, paras. 6.14–6.15. There is some scope for the new power to impose conditions on public assemblies conferred by s.14, which supplements the common law powers of dispersal, to develop into something like a much modified Riot Act. This very much depends on the way in which the Act is implemented by the police.

[10] Homicide is, of course, punishable with life imprisonment, mandatorily in the case of murder. Wounding with intent, contrary to the O.A.P.A. s.18 is also punishable with life.

[11] Criminal Damage Act 1971, s.4(2). Where fire is the damaging agent and the offender commits arson, the available penalty is life imprisonment; *ibid.* s.4(1).

[12] The characterisation is of course problematic, as the legal experience of the "political offence" exception in the law of extradition illustrates. See G. S. Gilbert, "Terrorism and the Political Offence Exception Re-Appraised" (1985) 34 I.C.L.Q. 659. And see C. Walker, *The Prevention of Terrorism in British Law* (1986).

become much more the practice these days to use the "ordinary" criminal
law such as the offences against the person and property or the explosives
offences to deal with outbreaks of disorder. Riot and unlawful assembly
were, at least until they were brought back into use following the miners'
strike,[13] falling into desuetude. A corollary of this is that the law used
against political demonstrators, those exercising rights to freedom of
speech in public, is formally at least the same as that for football hooligans,
people brawling outside pubs and others whose conduct can make no colourable pretence to being an attempt to express a political point of view in
public. Where violence has been used, the courts are understandably reluctant to acknowledge the political dimensions of what has occurred. In
Caird[14] Sachs L.J. summarised the traditional attitude of the courts as follows:

> "Any suggestion that a section of the community strongly holding one
> set of views is justified in banding together to disrupt the lawful activi-
> ties of a section that does not hold the same views so strongly or which
> hold different views cannot be tolerated and must unhesitatingly be
> rejected by the courts. When there is wanton and vicious violence of
> gross degree the court is not concerned with whether it originates from
> gang rivalry or from political motives. It is the degree of mob violence
> that matters and the extent to which the public peace is being
> broken."

This is sometimes generalised by saying that we have no special law for
protesters,[15] and the reasons offered are that the law is insufficiently precise to distinguish a good motive from a bad one, even if we should wish to
do so.[16] As a description of how public order law works in practice, however, this account is simplistic, and may well obscure more than it reveals
about the way in which the law actually operates to secure freedom of
speech. Prosecution and sentencing[17] policy and policing tactics undoubtedly reflect the fact that persons who may be nominally infringing the law
are seeking to exercise rights of freedom of speech in public. The theoreti-
cal restrictions imposed by the law are often at some remove from what the
public and the police are prepared to tolerate. How much can be permitted
at any particular time is inevitably a matter for political judgment, the
making of which will depend on complex assessments of the relationship
between the law and police effectiveness, public support for the police and
matters of that sort. These in turn may well depend on the extent to which
the person (or institution) making the assessment adheres to the demo-

---

[13] See 1–11.
[14] (1970) 54 Cr.App.R. 499.
[15] Defenders of the decision in *Moss* v. *M'Lachlan* [1985] I.R.L.R. 76, 149 J.P. 167 (stopping
   would-be picketing miners from proceeding to their chosen sites on the grounds that this
   might lead to breaches of the peace) pointed out that the breach of the peace power being
   employed was precisely the same as that used every Saturday throughout the winter to herd
   crowds of unruly football supporters through the streets.
[16] Law Commission Report, para. 2. 3.
[17] Foley (1969) 52 Cr.App.R. 123.

cratic as opposed to the anti-disruptive view of the nature of social disorder.[18]

The role of the law in the preservation of public order

The principal subject of this book is the substantive criminal law.[19]   **1–03**
Although this branch of the law has a role to play in defending the public peace, lawyers are aware that there are other socially inhibiting factors besides the law—civil and criminal—which preserve public order, and that the law may have a limited sphere of influence in the control of public disorder. If ill-disposed persons are determined to cause disorder, there is little that the law can do to stop them, any more than the law can prevent persons from killing, robbing and raping.[20] What role does the law play? Lord Scarman put the point as follows[21]:

> "The sombre lesson of recent British history is that the balance between public order and individual liberty, though its *existence* is protected by an alert and independent judiciary and an enlightened law, is in its operation the business of the police. At the end of the day standards of police conduct and the proper use by the police of their powers means more to society than the theoretical state of the law."

The widespread acceptance of this insight into the relative importance of the position of the police has been responsible for a mushrooming of interest in the study of police policies, technology, and tactics, and the role of the law governing them.[22] But Lord Scarman's view may be unduly dismissive of the part that the law can play, and perhaps understates the contribution that the state of the law actually makes to the preservation of public order. Even if it is not possible to explore such questions very fully in a book devoted to the exposition of the substantive criminal law, we can explore some of the implications of the fact that the law establishes a framework by which the standards of police conduct are guided and

---

[18] See D. G. T. Williams, "Processions, Assemblies and the Freedom of the Individual" [1987] Crim.LR 167.

[19] Even after the Public Order Act 1986 has taken effect, "the law" refers to "an ill assorted collection of common law offences, statutory offences, administrative powers, police powers, political pronouncements and official and unofficial reports." D. G. T. Williams, "The Principle of Beatty v. Gilbanks: A Reappraisal" in A N Doob and E. L. Greenspan, (eds.) *Perspectives in Criminal Law* (1984), p. 105. The impact of these other influences is referred to where possible.

[20] As the Government points out in its White Paper, "no amount of tightening the law, short of draconian measures which would be quite unacceptable, can guarantee the prevention of all disorder"; para. 1.9. See Chap. 1 of the White Paper generally for a discussion of the role of the law in this sphere.

[21] "The Conflict in Society; Public Order and Individual Liberty" in *Papers of the 7th Commonwealth Law Conference, Hong Kong 18–23 Sept* (1983).

[22] In the context of public order, see in particular D. G. T. Williams, "The Accountability of the Police: Two Studies" in *The Cambridge-Tilburg Law Lectures* First Series (1978); D. Cowell, T. Jones and J. Young, (eds.) *Policing the Riots* (1982); J. Alderson, *Law and Disorder* (1984). And see 1–10 for further discussion of the role of the police in the preservation of order.

shaped, and against which they are measured. Might it not be possible to say that the law does rather more than establish a permissive framework within which discretion is paramount? Especially when the law is reformed, it should be with a view to making those whose business is the implementation of the law responsive to the need to balance various civil liberties with the demands of public order. The law should also afford some guidance as to how the balance should be struck. What subsidiary aims might the reformers have? English lawyers are by tradition and training reluctant to generalise and speculate about the aims of the law, and what it should be seeking to achieve. American lawyers, more accustomed to thinking in terms of constitutionality, have less difficulty in formulating abstract propositions. For example, the introduction to Article 250 of the Model Penal Code characterises the aims of the reform of this area of the law as being:

(i) "To systematise the chaotic provisions of prior law penalising a wide variety of petty misbehaviour under such vague headings as 'disorderly behaviour' or 'vagrancy.'

(ii) to provide a rational grading of penalties and especially to limit the discretion of minor judiciary to impose substantial imprisonment for petty infractions;

(iii) to safeguard civil liberty by careful definition of offences so that they do not cover, for example, arguing with a policeman, peaceful picketing, or disseminating religious or political views" etc.

It is, of course, possible to disagree with those aims, or at least to phrase some of them differently. They do however provide a defensible critical starting point, and it is proposed briefly to examine English law and its recent reform in the Public Order Act 1986 in the light of these aspirations.

2. THE AIMS OF PUBLIC ORDER LAW

Systematising offences

1–04   Although the Public Order Act reduces the common law offences to statutory form and abolishes some anachronistic older statutes, it is not a comprehensive systematisation of the law, and is in no real sense an attempt to create a code of public order law.[23] The first five sections of the Act create a simpler and better structured scheme of offences than the common law had evolved, both in terms of the gradation of penalties available and in selection of the mode of trial.[24] But the Act does not touch the common law offence of public nuisance, and leaves in place a number of measures such as the Town Police Clauses Act 1847, section 28 and the Metropolitan Police Act 1839, section 54 which continue to govern minor

---

[23] See further 2–12.
[24] See 2–01 and 2–07.

obstructions and nuisances in public.[25] Partly because much of the local legislation that had in the past been used in the preservation of order were progressively repealed by the Local Government Act 1972, section 262, the Government was prompted to enact in substitution section 5, penalising offensive behaviour. Even after these reforms, there are still a considerable number of byelaws in force having a bearing on public order.[26]

More seriously, perhaps, the Act makes no attempt to subject to legislative confinement the common law power of the police to prevent breaches of the peace, and the associated offence of obstructing a constable in the execution of his duty.[27] In practice, this power, as interpreted in the cases such as *Duncan* v. *Jones*,[28] *Piddington* v. *Bates*[29] and *Moss* v. *M'Lachlan*,[30] is of immense practical significance in the preservation of public order, and the law remains open to the criticism that in this respect, no real attempt at systematisation has been made or even attempted. It can be argued that until these powers are reviewed, real reform of this constitutionally significant area of the law is chimerical.[31] The provisional conclusion must therefore be that, although the rationalisation effected by the Acts of 1972 and 1986 is to be applauded, the process is by no means complete.

Limiting the power of the minor judiciary

In England, justices deal with the bulk of public order cases, and can be **1–05** expected to do so under the new Act. The justices' incarcerating powers are limited by the Magistrates' Courts Act 1980 to imprisonment for six months,[32] and the exercise of their powers is subject to rights of appeal to and judicial review by the higher courts. The availability of appeals in criminal cases, and the development of powers of judicial review by the higher courts is an evolving process. To what extent this might be expected to lead to the more orderly development of a public order law is perhaps debatable. Writing in 1967, David Williams made the point that because of the historically limited powers of appeal in criminal cases, some of our most important public order law has never been the subject of consideration by the higher judiciary; appeals tended to stop at Divisional Court

[25] Section 54(13), which closely resembled s.4 of the Act is repealed, but the rest of the section remains intact.
[26] Especially those regulating the use of public spaces such as parks and squares, or semi-public property. See for example Heathrow Airport—London Byelaws 1972, reg. 5(58) of which protesting employees fell foul in *British Airports Authority* v. *Ashton* [1983] 1 W.L.R. 1079, 3 All E.R. 6.
[27] This is dealt with in Chap. 10. Section 40(4) expressly preserves the common law powers to deal with or prevent a breach of the peace.
[28] [1936] K.B. 218.
[29] [1961] 1 W.L.R. 162, [1960] 3 All E.R. 660.
[30] [1985] I.R.L.R. 76, 149 J.P. 167.
[31] See Glanville Williams, "Evading Justice" [1975] Crim.L.R. 430, who expresses the view that "no progress can be made in clarifying and confining the law until the obstruction offences are themselves dealt with."
[32] Section 31(1).

level.[33] But since the Administration of Justice Act removed the requirement of the Attorney-General's fiat in 1960 for appeals to the House of
Lords, the potential has existed for that body to contribute to the rational
development of the law relating to public order. Ironically, by its decision
in *Brutus* v. *Cozens*[34] the House gave to the magistrates an even greater
power to control the shape of the law than had hitherto existed; it decided
that the meaning of "ordinary words" (in this case "threatening, abusive
and insulting" behaviour) was the province of the tribunal of fact, making
it more difficult for a person convicted by the magistrates to appeal against
his conviction, and more difficult for the superior courts to exercise their
supervisory jurisdiction.

By the very nature of its subject matter, public order law relies more
than usually on police evidence for its efficacy, and there is a perceived
danger that police evidence is difficult to challenge successfully before the
justices and magistrates. The lower courts are constantly involved in making judgments about the reliability of a policeman's account of the incident
giving rise to a charge of obstruction or (now) offensive behaviour. It is a
problem for the superior courts to ensure that the lower courts are
approaching their task with a degree of scepticism balanced against the
need for police officers to arrive at spontaneous, on the spot decisions
which can be made to appear incorrect with all the benefit that hindsight
confers. Whether or not what the policeman did was "reasonable" must be
assessed by the magistrates, guided by the superior courts as to what is or is
not acceptable within that most general of formulae.[35]

The preservation of civil liberties

1–06   One of the tasks that the law can perform, and one of its guiding principles in this area, is the clarification of the individual's rights and obligations.[36] The principal liberties in danger from an overinclusive public
order law are, perhaps, freedom of speech and freedom from arbitrary
arrest. But if the law is underinclusive, it will not afford proper protection
to those whose interests are threatened by public disorder. The task for
public order law is frequently seen as being to achieve a balance between
the needs of those who wish to present their case in the public arena as
against the rights of others to go about their business (which might well

---

[33] *Keeping the Peace* (1967), p. 19. When *Duncan* v. *Jones* [1936] K.B. 218 was decided, for
example, there was no appeal from the Divisional Court to the House of Lords. No appeal
could be brought from binding over orders until the Magistrates' Court (Appeal from Binding Over Orders) Act 1956.

[34] [1973] A.C. 854; 2–014.

[35] *G* v. *Chief Superintendent of Stroud* [1987] Crim.L.R. 269.

[36] White Paper, para. 1.9. In the Law Commission Report, the claim is made that "in so far as
the offences are concerned with civil liberties, they are essentially intended to penalise the
use of violence or intimidation by groups of people because such violence or intimidation
goes beyond legitimate means of a public expression of views and becomes conduct which
stifles such expression of views. The offences may be regarded as upholding the liberties of
the subject by penalising those who would infringe his liberty by violence or intimidation";
para. 2.3.

include the freedom to go to work) unmolested.[37] Central to the preservation of this balance is the role of the police, which will be examined presently. But what "balance" are the police and the law seeking to strike? Sir Leslie Scarman (as he then was) stated the traditional view with his customary elegance of expression[38]:

> "Civilised living collapses—it is obvious—if public protest becomes violent protest or public order degenerates into the quietism imposed by successful oppression. But the problem is more complex than a choice between two extremes—one, a right to protest whenever and wherever you will and the other, a right to continuous calm upon our streets unruffled by the noise and obstructive pressure of the protesting procession. A balance has to be struck, a compromise found that will accommodate the exercise of the right to protest within a framework of public order which enables ordinary citizens, who are not protesting, to go about their business and pleasure without obstruction or inconvenience."

The reference to "inconvenience" represents a judgment with which not all would agree. Different views can be and are held as to the extent that the law—and especially the criminal law—should seek to protect us from that which is inconvenient or offensive without being harmful. A great deal of social change has come about through protest, sometimes violent protest. Even those who would not wish to advocate violence or anything like it might well wish to argue that disruption to the life of the community is a proper part of the give and take that democracy entails.[39] In cases of protest, then, "there is the underlying constitutional problem of determining how far the right of protest ought to be tolerated."[40] When the issue is posed in those terms, the potential for conflict is more readily apparent. Who decides what is to be tolerated, and what legal mechanisms should be employed to ensure that the decisions are fairly and impartially given effect? How does the law ensure that minority voices and unpopular views are heard, or not suppressed? These matters too must be the subject of legal regulation, and the task for the law, then, is not so much the striking of a single balance or compromise, but of establishing a framework of checks and balances within which the competing interests are legally accommodated. The criminal law will not always be the most satisfactory mechanism for accomplishing this objective; the civil law, and extra-legal processes all have a part to play. The Act deals with the regulation of processions, for example, as being an essentially administrative matter, at least in the first instance.[41] The criminal law is here being used as an administrative adjunct, to be used only in the event of a failure to comply with reasonably imposed conditions.

---

[37] V. Bevan, "Protest and Public Order" [1979] P.L. 163.
[38] *Red Lion Square*, para. 5.
[39] See, *e.g.* P. Hewitt, *The Abuse of Power* (1982) Chap. 5.
[40] D. G. T. Williams, "Protest and Public Order" (1970) 28 Camb. L.J. 96, at 98.
[41] Chap. 8.

A right to demonstrate?

1–07   The claim is sometimes made that there should be a constitutionally guaranteed right to demonstrate[42] or to picket,[43] and it is not uncommon for the courts to speak, loosely perhaps, of the existence of such rights.[44] The explicit legislative protection of "rights" is foreign to the common law tradition, which sees "rights" as being interstitial liberties, rather than rights in any strict sense. This view, associated with the great Victorian jurist Dicey,[45] is nowadays subjected to challenge on two fronts.

In so far as the Diceyan analysis is accurate, the critics would argue that the law thus described does not adequately protect interests in freedom of speech from those whose obligation it is to preserve public order. In particular, it is said, the police have an obligation to preserve the peace[46] but no corresponding obligation to permit or protect freedom of speech, and that it is therefore necessary that freedom of speech in public should be guaranteed by statute or a Bill of Rights. It is true that English law does not give clear and coherent answers to these objections; the courts and Parliament have evolved a complex and sometimes inconsistent structure of rules and principles that do not amount to a right to freedom of speech in public, and certainly not an unfettered right. But it does begin with the presump-

---

[42] See, *e.g.* Peter Wallington, "Injunctions and the 'Right to Demonstrate' " (1976) 35 Camb. L.J. 82; and see the "cautious support" expressed in favour of the legislative creation of such a right by A. G. Nicol, *The Public Order Act 1936 and Related Legislation* (1980), which Sir Leslie Scarman rejected in his Red Lion Square Report, para. 134(6). A comparison is commonly made between English and American laws on the subject; see Note, "Public Order and the Right of Assembly in England and the United States: A comparative Study" (1938) 47 Yale L.J. 404; Richard E. Stewart, "Public Speech and Public Order in Great Britain and the United States" (1960) 13 Vand. L.J. 625; David G. Barnum, "The Constitutional Status of Public Protest Activity in Britain and the United States" [1977] P.L. 310. And see Supperstone, Chap. 4. For New Zealand, see I. L. M. Richardson, "The Right of Assembly in New Zealand" (1956) 256 N.Z.L.J. 256 and 278, and Canada, R. Stoykewych, "Street Legal: Constitutional Protection of Public Demonstration in Canada" (1985) 43 U. of Tor. Fac. Review 43.

[43] Lord Wedderburn, *The Worker and the Law* (3rd ed., 1986) 541. See Guy S. Goodwin-Gill (1975) 91 L.Q.R. 173, for a measured discussion of the jurisprudential status of such "rights." Ss.12 and 14 of the Act (power to impose conditions on processions and assemblies) employ the terminology of rights. See Chap. 8.

[44] See for example Lord Denning M.R. in *Hubbard* v. *Pitt* [1976] Q.B. 142; Roskill and Cumming-Bruce L.JJ. in *Verrall* v. *Great Yarmouth Borough Council* [1981] Q.B. 202; Otton J. in *Hirst* v. *Chief Constable of West Yorkshire* (1987) 151 J.P. 304. The more traditional view was taken by Lord Hewart C.J. in *Duncan* v. *Jones* [1936] K.B. 218, who speaks rather dismissively of the "called right of public meeting. I say called because English law does not recognise any special right of public meeting for political or other purposes." And see O. Hood Phillips (1970) 86 L.Q.R. 1 and 543. A candidate in an election is given a "right" to a room in which to hold a meeting by the Representation of the People Act 1983, s.95(1), which he can enforce by way of action in the High Court rather than by application for judicial review; *Ettridge* v. *Morrell* [1987] L.G.R. 100. And see *Webster* v. *Southwark L.B.C.* [1983] Q.B. 698. By virtue of the Education (No. 2) Act 1986, s.43, university authorities are under an obligation to afford a platform for speakers.

[45] There has been an upsurge of interest in the writings and jurisprudential significance of Dicey's work following the centenary of the publication of his *Introduction to the Study of the Law of the Constitution* (1885); see the symposium "All Souls—*Public Law* Seminar: Dicey and the Constitution" [1985] P.L. 583, especially E. Barendt, 596 *et seq.*

[46] Examined further below, Chap. 10.

tion that freedom of speech in public is permissible, however odious or distasteful the speech in question might be for others of a different persuasion. Leading cases such as *Beatty* v. *Gillbanks*[47] establish that, except in cases of exceptional difficulty, there is a strong presumption that lawful conduct will be protected.

The second challenge to the Diceyan view is of a different legal order, and maintains that any account of the rights of citizens of the United Kingdom must acknowledge the potential impact of the European Convention on Human Rights.[48] Article 11 of the Convention provides that everyone has the right to freedom of peaceful assembly and to freedom of association with others. The Article also provides that no restrictions shall be placed on the exercise of these rights other than such as are prescribed by law and are necessary in a democratic society in the interests of national security or public safety, for the prevention of disorder or crime, for the protection of health or morals or for the protection of the rights and freedoms of others. It is true that the Convention is not directly applicable in the domestic law of the United Kingdom,[49] but it does provide a yardstick against which that law is measured internationally. Although there is ample scope for the law to impose restrictions upon the freedoms in question, it must do so only where these are "necessary in a democratic society," and then only where the limits are "prescribed by law." Where limits are set that are too vague in their application, the European Court of Human Rights will hold that these conditions are not met, and that the municipal law should be changed to reflect this objection.[50] Might it not be argued that the common law powers of the police to prevent breaches of the peace fall within this category? Are powers to impose conditions on marches and assemblies to prevent "serious disruption to the life of the community"[51] strictly necessary to preserve order in a democratic society? Are they then "necessary to preserve the rights and freedoms of others," as the Convention permits? Whatever the answers to these questions may be, it is clear that any description of the law of the United Kingdom that fails to take account of the European dimension is inaccurate and incomplete.[52]

---

[47] (1882) 9 O.B.D. 308.

[48] See generally, S. H. Bailey, D. J. Harris and B. L. Jones, *Civil Liberties: Cases and Materials* (2nd ed., 1985) Chap. 1, "The Method of Protecting Civil Liberties in English Law." In *Application No. 8440/78 Christians Against Rascism and Fascism* v. *U.K.* (1981) 24 Y.B.E.C.H.R. the Commission ruled inadmissible a claim that a ban under the Public Order Act 1936 was contrary to *inter alia* Article 11. That Article permits an exception for the preservation of public order, but not necessarily for the preservation of public convenience.

[49] See Forbes J. in *Hubbard* v. *Pitt* [1976] Q.B. 142, 156–157.

[50] In *The Sunday Times Case* (1979) E.C.H.R. Series A, vol. 30, *e.g.* three members of the European Court ruled that the United Kingdom's law of contempt was insufficiently certain in its scope to be acceptable as a restriction "prescribed by law."

[51] See Chap. 8.

[52] The Law Commission expressed itself confident that none of its recommendations were in breach of Article 11; Report, para. 2.15. Since its recommendations were entirely concerned with the prevention of disorder, it is simple enough to agree. In the White Paper, the Government expressed rather less confidence, saying only (without being specific) that

The hostile audience problem

1–08   One of the most intractable problems for those involved in the preservation of public order arises where there is a clash (or potential clash) of groups with opposing views. In so far as it is the case that persons should be at liberty to express opinions in public—even distasteful ones—a corollary ought to be that the exercise of that right should not be frustrated by the interference of those with opposing attitudes. At common law, the basic premise was that an assembly was not necessarily unlawful merely because a breach of the peace was threatened by those opposed to the meeting. In the leading case in this area, *Beatty* v. *Gillbanks*,[53] Field J. rejected the proposition that a man may be punished for acts lawfully done because he knows that in so doing he may induce another man to act unlawfully. If it were otherwise, the law would be supplanted by the power of the mob.[54] A practical conclusion to be drawn from this is that where a danger arises that the lawful exercise of rights might result in a breach of the peace, the proper remedy is the presence of the police in sufficient numbers to preserve the peace, and not the legal condemnation of those exercising their rights.[55] To avoid any charges of political partiality, the police can operate a first come, first served policy, protecting those who first indicate an intention to hold their meeting or march, irrespective of their political persuasion. An ideal law would enjoin them to observe this principle, subject to some limited exceptions. Much of the relevant law was elaborated around the old offence of unlawful assembly, now abolished, and the extent to which that legal situation prevails must now be considered.[56]

So far as the new offences are concerned, persons who initiate an assembly do not commit riot, violent disorder or affray if others commit violence as a result of what is done or said. Those offences might be committed by counter demonstrators who themselves use violence, or put bystanders in fear that they are about to do so. But where the conduct or language used by those who initiate the gathering is threatening, abusive or insulting to those who witness it, the offence under section 4 may be committed, since that applies where one person causes another to fear violence, or provokes another into the use of unlawful violence. On its face, this seems to be a reasonable point at which to strike a balance between the

---

it had "borne the obligations of being a signatory to the European Convention and the International Covenant in mind during the review," and made reference to protecting the rights and freedoms of others; paras. 1.8, 2.1 and 2.15.

[53] *Beatty* v. *Gillbanks* (1882) 9 Q.B.D. 308. The case is more specifically concerned with a provocative march, as to which see 1–09, but the underlying principles are the same in each context. For a reassessment of this decision in the light of modern conditions, see D. G. T. Williams, *op. cit. supra*, n. 19. And see *O'Kelly* v. *Harvey* (1883) 15 Cox C.C. 435.

[54] *Humphries* v. *O'Connor* (1864) 17 Ir. C.L.R. 1.

[55] *R.* v. *The Justices of Londonderry* (1891) 28 L.R. Ir. 440 at 450, *per* O'Brien J. And see the forceful remarks of Lord Denning M.R. in *Verrall* v. *Great Yarmouth Borough Council* [1981] Q.B. 202.

[56] The decisions are critically reviewed by W. Birtles, "The Common Law Power of the Police to Control Public Meetings" (1973) 36 M.L.R. 587. And see David G. Barnum, "Freedom of Assembly and the Hostile Audience in Anglo-American Law" (1981) 29 Am.Jo.Comp. Law 59; Note, "Hostile-Audience Confrontations: Police Conduct and First Amendment Rights" (1976) 75 Mich. L.R. 180.

claims of free speech and the need to prevent disorder. It is strikingly similar in its formulation to the "fighting words" doctrine devised by the Supreme Court of the United States to reconcile the competing demands of public order and the First Amendment guarantees of freedom of speech.[57]

Unfortunately, English law does not provide quite so clear-cut a solution. Suppose that those who witness the speech or conduct are themselves acting unreasonably? It was said by Lord Parker C.J. in *Jordan* v. *Burgoyne*[58] that the speaker must "take his audience as he finds it," an aphoristic dictum that has dire consequences for those who would seek to exercise freedom of speech in public. Effectively it confers on those who seek to disrupt a "heckler's veto," and the occasion upon which the Chief Justice coined it bears further examination. A preliminary point should be made. It is an offence for a person to seek to disrupt a meeting being lawfully held.[59] Since the offence carries only a limited power of arrest, it is seldom prosecuted, but its very existence affords some legal argument to the speaker who asserts that the police should not seek to silence him but should proceed against the disrupters. Otherwise, the disrupters are given in effect a heckler's veto on freedom of speech, and that is to return to mob rule deprecated by Fitzgerald J. in *Humphries* v. *O'Connor*.[60]

The speaker who uttered the words complained of in *Jordan* v. *Burgoyne* was a well-known leader of the National Socialist movement. He was addressing a rally in Trafalgar Square, which he knew to contain a number of Jewish people and members of the Communist Party opposed to his views. He made highly provocative remarks, claiming that "more and more people every day . . . are opening their eyes and coming to say with us; Hitler was right. They are coming to say that our real enemies, the people we should have fought, were not Hitler and the National Socialists of Germany but world Jewry and its associates in this country." The London Sessions Appeals Committee allowed the appeals against conviction under the Public Order Act 1936, section 5 of using insulting language whereby a breach of the peace was likely to be occasioned, taking the view that although the words were "highly insulting," they were not of a kind sufficient to make ordinary reasonable people present at the scene likely to commit breaches of the peace. The likelihood that there might be a breach of the peace was to be assessed by the standard of the hypothetical reasonable man. The Divisional Court reversed this decision, and refused leave to appeal further, as did the House of Lords. In allowing the prosecutor's appeal, Lord Parker C.J. said:

> "I cannot myself, having read the speech, imagine any reasonable citizen, certainly one who was a Jew, not being provoked beyond endurance, and not only a Jew but a coloured man and quite a number of

---

[57] *Chaplinski* v. *U.S.* 315 U.S. 568 (1942). See G. Marshall, *Constitutional Theory* (1971), Chap. VIII.

[58] [1963] 2 Q.B. 744.

[59] Public Meetings Act 1908, s.1. At election meetings, the relevant provision is the Representation of the People Act 1983, s.97, discussed further below, Chap. 7–12.

[60] See n.54.

people in this country who were told that they were merely tools of the Jews and that they had fought in the war on the wrong side."

That would in itself have been a sufficient basis on which to restore the convictions, but unhappily the Chief Justice elaborated as follows:

> "If in fact it is apparent that a body of persons are present—and let me assume in the defendant's favour that they are a body of hooligans—yet if words are used which threaten, abuse or insult—all very strong words—then that person must take his audience as he finds them, and if those words to that audience or that part of the audience are likely to provoke a breach of the peace, then the speaker is guilty of an offence."

Even if hooligans came with a "preconceived idea of preventing him from speaking" an offence is committed if the speaker uses threats, abuse or insults. Lord Parker denied that this made inroads into the doctrine of free speech, and asserted that there was no place in the application of the law for any test as to whether any member of the audience is a reasonable man or ordinary citizen. This perhaps puts the issue too strongly; freedom of speech plainly is involved in the decision, and there is some scope for the reasonable man test in the application of the law in deciding what is insulting in the first place. Suppose, for example, that a Cabinet Minister were to speak on a university campus[61] about some matter on which his views were unpopular with a segment of his audience. Even if the audience were to assert that they found his remarks abusive or insulting (Jordan had also said, apparently, "let them howl, these multi-racial warriors of the left. It is a sound that comes natural [*sic*] to them, it saves them from the strain of thinking for themselves," so let us have our Cabinet Minister make these same remarks), the question whether they were insulting must be assessed objectively, by the standards of ordinary people. If they were not insulting by these standards, then even if they give rise to violence, the Cabinet Minister commits no offence.

Two further problems of principle arise; the first is where the language and conduct of the speaker are below the threshold of that which is threatening, abusive or insulting—as the Cabinet Minister's would no doubt in reality be—but is nevertheless likely to provoke the audience to react violently. To what extent then can the police require the speaker to desist, and what sanctions are available should the speaker disobey? The short answer is that it is open to the police, if they fear a breach of the peace on reasonable grounds, to require the speaker to desist, and a failure to do so amounts to the offence of obstructing the constable in the exercise of his duty.[62] The decision of the constable must be a reasonable one, in the sense that there were no steps other than the one that he decided to take that he could reasonably have been expected to adopt. A court will be slow to disagree with the judgment of a policeman on the spot, especially if he is

---

[61] See now the Education (No. 2) Act 1986, s.43, which places a duty on university authorities to provide a platform for freedom of speech.
[62] Below, Chap. 10.

an experienced officer, and will take into account the speed with which decisions have to be taken in the face of such incidents. But if the speaker has not exceeded the threshold set by Parliament, and has not engaged in conduct or used language that is threatening, abusive or insulting, and there are other steps that the constable could have adopted, it is arguable that the speaker should not be guilty of an offence of obstruction, and the decision of *Duncan* v. *Jones* should be regarded as subject to those qualifications.[63]

The second problem of principle arises where the language and conduct of the speaker is threatening, abusive or insulting, but the circumstances are such that the audience is not likely to engage in violence by way of response, but is nevertheless distressed by what it hears. This situation would potentially at least call into play section 5 of the Act, which specifically empowers the constable present to require the speaker to desist from his "offensive conduct."[64] That offence is subject to the defence, of extraordinary width, that the conduct in which the defendant was at the time engaging was "reasonable," and presumably the policeman on the spot must therefore take the reasonableness or otherwise of the defendant's conduct into account in deciding how to proceed. One of the factors that he should take into account, difficult though it may be, is that the defendant is exercising a freedom that is in many other legal systems regarded as a fundamental right to freedom of speech.

The result would seem to be that the law leaves the policeman on the spot with an enormous amount of discretion as to how he will police the situation by which he is confronted. He may ask the speaker to desist; he may call for reinforcements (and modern technology makes the possibilities of his doing that far greater than they were when many of the landmark cases were decided); he may decide to proceed against the hecklers, or advise those who find the language distressing to depart. It is unsatisfactory that so important a freedom should depend on such a slender thread. But it may be suggested that the principles expressed in *Beatty* v. *Gillbanks*[65] and the principle of freedom of speech underlying the Public Meetings Act 1908 ought to have (and do in fact have) practical repercussions in the tactics of policing, and decisions taken that override or ignore them are, in principle, open to challenge as being unreasonable.

Provocative marches

Historically, a good deal of our public order law has evolved in connec- **1–09** tion with provocative marches, that is, processions conducted by persons into areas where they know their sympathies are not shared by the local

---

[63] This would accord with the principle expressed by the Supreme Court of Illinois in *Chicago* v. *Gregory* (1968) 39 Ill. 2d 47, 60, 233 N.E. 2d 422, 429: "It is only where there is an imminent threat of violence, the police have made all reasonable efforts to protect the demonstrators, the police have requested that the demonstration be stopped, and explained the request, if there be time, and there is a refusal of the police request, that an arrest for an otherwise lawful act may be made."

[64] Below, Chap. 7.

[65] Above, n. 53.

inhabitants. The initial response of the courts was that such marches are not *ipso facto* unlawful,[66] in accordance with the principle that a person should not be held to commit an unlawful act merely because those who witness what he is doing respond with violence. That principle remains valid but limited in its operation by countervailing considerations. The usual principle of the criminal law is that, where a person foresees that something is virtually certain to result from what he is doing, it is open to the tribunal of fact to infer that he intends that result. If a person intends to provoke violence, he cannot expect to shelter his conduct behind the banners of freedom of speech.[67] There is here an almost irreconcilable conflict of two apparently equally weighty principles; freedom of speech on the one hand, weighed against the freedom of individuals to proceed with their ordinary lives without harassment, intimidation and provocation. In balancing them, the law has tended to err on the side of caution, preferring the preservation of order to the protection of speech.[68]

How the law should apply when violence is less certain as an outcome of a provocative march is more problematic, but the law has tended to adopt two strategies. First, it relies on the fact that the law affords the policeman on the spot considerable powers to head off trouble when it starts or is about to. The constable is well armed with the power to arrest for breach of the peace and the associated sanctions of binding over[69] or a prosecution for obstructing the constable in the execution of his duty. In the light of those, and in view of the fact that marches are prima facie lawful, the practice was initially to permit the marches to go ahead, dealing with trouble as it arose.

The second legal response was to impose administrative controls on marches and processions; the provocative marches of Sir Oswald Moseley in the East End of London led to the enactment of the Public Order Act 1936, empowering the police to impose conditions and ultimately if necessary to seek bans on such events. With the enactment of Part II of the Public Order Act 1986, it may be thought that the process of ensuring legal control of provocative marches has been completed. That question will be examined in Chapter 8.

The role of the police in the preservation of public order

1–10   Given the diverse social interests protected by public order law, it is scarcely surprising that the role of the police is correspondingly multi-faceted, complex and rapidly evolving. The overriding duty of the police is

---

[66] *Beatty* v. *Gillbanks*, n. 53. A proposed march by American Nazis, the National Socialist Party of America, generated a flood of litigation, and a great amount of public controversy. See D. Barnum (1981) 29 Am.Jo.Com. Law 59 for an excellent comparative discussion of the constitutional issues at stake.

[67] See *O'Kelly* v. *Harvey* (1883) 14 L.R. Ir. 105; *Goodall* v. *Te Kooti* (1890) 9 N.Z.L.R. 26; *R.* v. *Londonderry JJ.* (1891) 28 L.R. Ir. 440, in each of which doubts are expressed about the correctness of the *Beatty* v. *Gillbanks* principle.

[68] The point is made with considerable force by V. Bevan, [1979] P.L. 163. And see G. J. Zellick, "Public Order Law: Principles, Purposes and Problems" [1986] P.L. 137.

[69] *Wise* v. *Dunning* [1902] 1 K.B. 167. Binding over orders are discussed further in 2–10.

to enforce the law and to preserve the peace[70]; of that there can be no doubt. In the course of the last hundred years or so, police forces throughout the country have inherited from the military and magistrates the task of preserving order in the face of all but the most dire threats to public peace.[71] The police have the task of preserving order at industrial disputes, inner city riots, football matches, rock festivals and occasions of religious or political celebration or protest. As the existing arrangements have proved inadequate or deficient, police tactics, equipment, training and organisation, locally and nationally, have all changed radically in the space of the last ten years.[72] C.S. gas, plastic bullets ("baton rounds"), long shields and truncheons are equipment that is readily available, if not standard issue. Police Support Units and—in the Metropolitan Police area—Territorial Support Groups, whose deployment throughout the country can be facilitated where necessary by a National Reporting Centre[73] make the mutual aid policy contemplated by the Police Act 1964, section 14 a tactical reality.

Constitutionally, the organisation of the police is locally rather than nationally based, and in the conduct of their duties, Chief Constables are independent of but supported by local authorities.[74] The Home Secretary also has a broad constitutional oversight of the policing system. The result

---

[70] See M. D. A. Freeman, "Law and Order in 1984" (1984) 37 C. L. P. 175 at 208. For a discussion of the scope of this duty, see Chap. 10. The seriousness with which the constable's obligation is regarded is strikingly illustrated by *Dytham* [1979] Q.B. 722, in which a policeman was successfully prosecuted for the common law offence of misconduct in public office when he failed to intervene to prevent a fatal brawl.

[71] D. G. T. Williams, *Keeping the Peace* (1967), Chap. 1; R. Mark, *Policing a Perplexed Society* (1977) Chap. 7; J. Alderson, *Law and Disorder* (1984). A. Grunis, "Police Control of Demonstrations" (1978) 56 Can. Bar Rev. 393. The classic study of the history of the British police forces is T. Critchley, *A History of the Police in England and Wales* (revd ed., 1978). And see F. Gregory, "The British Police System—With Special Reference to Public Order Problems" in eds. J. Roach and J. Thomaneck, *Police and Public Order in Europe* (1985). The use of the army in the event of a major disturbance cannot, even now, be ruled out entirely. For a discussion of the legal implications, see S. Greer, "Military Intervention in Civil Disturbances: the Legal Basis Reconsidered" [1983] P.L. 573. And see G. Marshall, *Constitutional Conventions* (1984), Chap. IX.

[72] See the Metropolitan Police Report, *Public Order Review: Civil Disturbances 1981–1985* (1986).

[73] The National Reporting Centre was established in 1972, to process requests for mutual aid, and to collate and disseminate information. For the text of the Home Office Statement issued in July 1984 on the role and functions of the Centre, see Appendix D of the Report *Policing the Coal Industry Dispute in South Yorkshire*. See M. Kettle in Fine and Millar, *Policing the Miner's Strike* (1985), pp. 23–33.

[74] For a brief but authoritative description of the constitutional position of the police, see G. Marshall, *Constitutional Conventions* (1984) Chap. VIII. And see H. W. R. Wade, *Administrative Law* (5th ed., 1982), Chap. 5; ed. P. Hain, *Policing the Police* (1979), Vol. 1; B. Whittaker, *The Police in Society* (1979); R. Baldwin and R. Kinsey, *Police Powers and Politics* (1982); S. Manwaring-White, *The Policing Revolution* (1983); R. Reiner, *The Politics of the Police* (1985); G. Marshall, "The Police: Independence and Accountability" in J. Jowell and D. Oliver eds. *The Changing Constitution* (1985), 250; J. Baxter and L. Koffman, *Police, The Constitution and the Community* (1985); L. Lusgarten, *The Governance of Police* (1986); J. L. Lambert, *Police Powers and Accountability* (1986); J. Benyon and C. Bourn, *The Police—Powers, Procedures and Proprieties* (1986) esp. Chaps. 1 and 2; Ian Oliver, *Police, Government and Accountability* (1987).

of this somewhat unweildy structure is that there is a delicate balance to be struck between the operational responsibilities of Chief Constables and the relative responsibilities of politicians, local and national. To illustrate, neither the Home Secretary or the local authority has power to initiate moves to impose conditions or bans on processions—the law makes that a matter for the Chief Constable in each region.[75] The Home Secretary has in effect a power of veto. Again, the local authority provides at least some of the funding for the equipment that the Chief Constable believes to be necessary to enable him to carry out his task of preserving public order. There is clearly considerable scope for disagreement as to what resources should or should not be made available to enable him to carry out his obligation; ultimately, it would appear, the decision of the Chief Constable must prevail.[76]

It is said that the police force is responsible to the law, and to the law alone,[77] by which it is meant that if the Chief Constable fails in his duty to preserve the peace or to enforce the law, the courts have jurisdiction to intervene. In practical terms, however, this means that Chief Constables have very considerable latitude to decide for themselves how they will implement policing policies within their own districts. In *R. v. Oxford, Ex. p Levey*[78] for example, the victim of a burglary sought to complain that the police had failed in their duty in not pursuing his burglars into the Toxteth area of Liverpool. It was admitted that this had occurred because the Chief Constable had concluded that special policing methods were appropriate to that district, so that traffic division and operational support patrols were excluded from routinely patrolling that area of Liverpool, and officers not posted to Toxteth were required to obtain authorisation to enter the area. The Court of Appeal refused to interfere, saying that the Chief Constable had the widest possible discretion in the choice of methods from which he could select in the discharge of his duty.

The problem with discretionary authority is that, although inevitable, it needs to be supervised, if not by judicial review, then by other processes— a system of complaints, or through political channels. Without such checks (and to some extent even with them) wide discretion is open to charges of political partiality. The very existence of broad discretion offers convenient legal weapons for curbing the activities of unpopular minorities. In his Report on the Red Lion Square Disorders, Sir Leslie (later Lord) Scarman claimed:

> "The police are not to be required in any circumstances to exercise political judgment. Their role is the maintenance of public order—no more, and no less. . . . It is vital, if the police are to be kept out of

---

[75] See Chap. 8 for further discussion.

[76] *R. v. Secretary of State for the Home Department, ex p. Northumbria Police Authority* [1987] 2 W.L.R. 998, 2 All E.R. 282.

[77] *R. v. Metropolitan Police Commissioner ex p. Blackburn* [1968] 2 Q.B. 118 at 135, *per* Lord Denning. In *Coxhead* [1986] R.T.R. 411, it was held that a police officer committed an offence in failing (for improper reasons) to enforce the law sufficiently rigorously. On the question whether there is adequate judicial supervision of police powers to ban processions and impose conditions on public meetings, see Chap. 8.

[78] *The Times*, October 30, 1986.

political controversy, that in a public order situation their sole immediate concern is, and is seen to be, with public order."[79]

Vital it may be, but the police are engaged in making political judgments, whether they like it or not.[80] What is critical is that the police should not permit party political considerations to influence their judgment about the proper steps to be taken, as Lord Scarman makes clear. Whether the views to be expressed at a demonstration are of the left wing or the right, the police should seek not to take sides, and to regard their primary task as the preservation of order, and so far as is compatible with that, the preservation of freedom of speech. This is by no means a simple balance to preserve, or to be seen to be preserving. Public protest is regarded by many as the politics of the street, and the means by which those without access to newspapers and television can force issues into the public eye.[81] Where controls have been imposed, it is altogether too easy to depict the police as being the opponents of the cause in favour of which the demonstration is being conducted. In industrial conflict, the political features of the assembly are heightened even further, and when police escort those wishing to work across picket lines, they are readily portrayed as strike breakers, and as siding with one party to the dispute.

So long as the police can counter that it is their overriding constitutional duty to preserve public order, there is a solid point of departure to which none but the most extreme could object. But this traditional description of the police role in cases of conflict requires modification in the light of the new powers conferred by the Act, which represent a subtle but important shift in the constitutional responsibilities of the police. It is for the first time open to the police to impose in advance conditions on marches and assemblies to prevent "serious disruption to the life of the community," as opposed to the prevention of serious disorder.[82] To what extent this accords formal recognition to pre-existing policing practice is a matter of speculation. Serious disruption to the life of the community can lead to disorder, and previous policing practice and policy in the conduct of marches and demonstrations before the Act may well have reflected this fact. When powers are conferred for the purposes of preventing disorder, the scope for the exercise of discretion and political judgment is not as great as when "serious disruption" to the life of the community is to be stopped. What represents "serious disruption to the life of the community" is bound to

---

[79] *Red Lion Square*, para. 7.

[80] Although the police may well seek to avoid being placed in positions where the exercise of political judgement is called for. The suggestion in the White Paper that the police should be given powers to ban selected marches was not proceeded with since, in the words of the Minister of State for the Home Office "the police felt that if they had power to apply for a ban on a single march—for example by the militant tendency or the C.N.D.—it would lay them open to accusations of political bias in an area where they already have to tread very carefully." H.C.Deb., vol. 89, col. 861 January 13, 1986.

[81] See P. A. J. Waddington and P. M. Leopold, *Protest, Policing and the Law* (1985) (Conflict Studies No. 175).

[82] See Chap. 8.

depend to some extent on the view that the judge of the issue holds as to the nature of social existence, and this is inevitably a political judgment.

In the case of minor street nuisances and disturbances, it is possible to level the charge against English law that it does not meet the aspirations of those who would wish to frame a law that ensures that arguing with a policeman cannot constitute a criminal offence. Indeed, there is some evidence that it is only when those who are engaged in such disturbances challenge the authority of the policeman that they run the risk of being arrested[83]; if order can be restored without the need to effect an arrest, the chances are that it will be. There is, however, a danger that the laws will generate oppressive policing. The reality of this possibility has frequently been recognised, as when Parliament abolished the notorious "sus" law.[84] Fears were expressed in the House of Lords by Lords Scarman and Elwyn-Jones that the "disorderly conduct" offence in the Bill would give rise to precisely the old and offensive situation,[85] and some changes were made in the course of the passage of the measure through Parliament to reduce this possibility. But obstructing a constable in the execution of his duty[86] and obstructing the highway[87] are of such breadth that they may both give rise to these objections. Even if a person is not convicted of any offence, his arrest will have precluded his exercise of a right of free speech. Against this, there is a widespread view that the police must have the power to deal with minor nuisances.[88] The application of the law in this area is therefore a matter of considerable concern, and its deployment in practice will continue to be a matter of great sensitivity.

3. THE BACKGROUND TO THE ACT

The social background

1–11   Behind the flurry of official activity that culminated in the Public Order Act 1986, there was a persistent series of sporadic outbreaks of public disorder reflecting industrial, racial and other social tensions. Race riots in

---

[83] M. R. Chatterton, "The Police in Social Control" in J. F. S King, (ed.) *Control Without Custody* (1976). For an excellent overview and analysis of the sociological writings in this area, see Robert Reiner, *The Politics of the Police* (1985), Chap. 4. And see A. Sanders, "Prosecution Decisions and the Attorney-General's Guidelines" [1985] Crim.L.R. 4 at 11, on the use of "resource charging."

[84] Criminal Attempts Act 1981, s.8. This gave effect to the recommendations of the House of Commons Select Committee on Home Office Affairs, Second Report, *Race Relations and the 'Sus' Law* (1980). "Sus" was an abbreviation of "suspected person" in the Vagrancy Act 1824, s.4.

[85] H.L.Deb., vol. 478, col. 934 (Lord Elwyn Jones) and col. 937. July 16, 1986 (Lord Scarman).

[86] Below, Chap. 10. For a discussion of the constitutional implications of this "vague and uncertain" offence, see R. C. Austin, "Obstruction—The Policeman's Best Friend?" (1982) 35 C.L.P. 187.

[87] See below, Chap. 11.

[88] Lord Denning, in the House of Lords, was in favour of the clause; vol. 478, col. 935. And see Glanville Williams, (1982) 146 J.P. at 199; "the police need specific powers to deal with people who make thundering nuisances of themselves, particularly at night."

Notting Hill in the 1950s,[89] C.N.D. and anti-Vietnam demonstrations and student unrest in the 1960s[90] were prominent features of the social scene. In the 1970s there were National Front and anti-rascist confrontations at Lewisham, Ladywood, Southall.[91] More recently, there were serious inner city riots in Bristol in 1980,[92] Brixton in 1981[93] and the Toxteth district of Liverpool.[94] In the summer before the Bill was introduced, outbreaks of rioting and looting in the Handsworth district of Birmingham[95] and, in September 1985 occurred in Brixton and in the Broadwater Farm Estate in Tottenham the following month.[96] This depressing list is by no means exhaustive of the upheavals to which the nation was subjected.

Industrial unrest first manifested itself in mass picketing at Saltley Coal depot in 1972.[97] The tactic was repeated at Grunwick in 1977[98] and subsequently at Warrington[99] and Orgreave.[1] Even as the Bill was becoming law, the Wapping dispute continued to cause concern to those responsible for keeping order.[2] Most traumatically of all, throughout much of 1984 and the early months of 1985, the coal miners were engaged in a bitterly divi-

---

[89] "Race Riots in London" [1958] Crim.LR 709.

[90] For an excellent historical perspective, see D. G. T. Williams, Keeping the Peace (1967). Those who suppose that social unrest and disorder is a particularly modern phenomenon will find this work a revelation. And see the same author's "Protest and Public Order" (1970) 28 Camb. L.J. 96 and "Freedom of Assembly and Free Speech; Changes and Reforms in England" (1975) 1 N.S.W.L.J. 97. And see M. D. A. Freeman, "Law and Order in 1984" (1984) 37 C.L.P. 175.

[91] See M. Kettle and L. Hodges, Uprising; The Police, the People and the Riots in Britain's Cities (1982). See also R. Clutterbuck, Britain in Agony; the Growth of Political Violence (revd. ed., (1980).

[92] See the works mentioned in the last note.

[93] Report, The Brixton Disorders 10–12 April 1981 Cmnd. 8427 (1981). The Report was published by Penguin, and is now available in a 2nd ed., August 1986. For comment on the original Report see G. Zellick, [1982] P.L. 1; S. Saeed, [1982] P.L. 519; J. Beynon (ed.), Scarman and After (1984).

[94] M. Jefferson, "The Toxteth Riots: A Select Bibliography" [1983] Liverpool L.R. 203.

[95] See the Report of the Chief Constable of the West Midlands Police, G. Dear, Handsworth/Lozells September 1985.

[96] For an account of the disturbances at Tottenham and Brixton see the Metropolitan Police study, Public Order Review—Civil Disturbances 1981–1985 (1986). See also the Annual Report of the Commission for Racial Equality for 1985.

[97] The events at Saltley are described by K. Jeffery and P. Hennessy, States of Emergency (1983) pp. 234–236.

[98] Report of a Court of Inquiry into the Grunwick Dispute Cmnd. 6922 (1977).

[99] The mass picketing at Warrington was singled out in the White Paper as being an example of the serious public order problems associated with static demonstrations; para. 5.1. See Messenger Group Newspapers v. N.G.A. [1984] I.R.L.R. 397, [1984] I.C.R. 345.

[1] In addition to the material referred to in n. 3 below, see the Report by the Chief Constable, P. Wright, Policing the Coal Industry Dispute in South Yorkshire (1985).

[2] Wapping was the subject of discussion in Parliament on numerous occasions; on October 17, 1986 a Home Office spokesman informed the House of Lords that 900 people had been convicted of offences in connection with the dispute; H.L. vol. 481, col. 1020. On January 26, 1987, after serious disturbances on the anniversary of the beginning of the dispute, the Home Secretary informed Parliament that 1462 people had been arrested in the course of the picketing, and that 572 policemen had been injured; H.C.Deb., Col. 109, col. 21. See News Group Newspapers Ltd. v. Society of Graphical and Allied Trades [1986] I.R.L.R. 33.

sive strike,[3] and there were frequent violent clashes involving police, striking miners and working miners which took place outside collieries[4] and elsewhere.[5]

Quite apart from these occasions of serious disorder, the police have increasingly been called upon to supervise marches, meetings and demonstrations. In London, in particular, the Metropolitan Police are called upon to police huge numbers of such gatherings.[6] The great majority of these occasions pass off with relatively little incident as a result of cooperation between demonstration organisers and the police. But this is not always so; the Red Lion Square disorders (in which one of the participants was killed) arose out of a demonstration that went wrong because some of the demonstrators failed to understand and follow the police instructions,[7] and there were provocative and rascist marches in Southall which resulted in the death of one of the participants.[8]

Inevitably, this turbulent social background meant that the Bill was the subject of intense political controversy in the course of its passage through Parliament,[9] and clearly affected the character of the measure that became the law, sometimes explicitly so. It was plain, for example, that the offence created by the Public Order Act 1936, section 4, (which had hitherto been section 5) was reframed so that it could be committed in either a public or a private place because of incidents that had occurred during the strike. Striking miners had successfully pleaded that they were not guilty of the old offence because they had been standing on Coal Board (private) property at the time they engaged in the acts complained of, and the Government took the view that this should not afford a defence.[10]

One further aspect of social disorder needs particular mention. Groups attending football matches continued a pattern of social disruption which had begun to get seriously out of hand as early as the mid 1960s.[11] In the aftermath of a disastrous fire at the Bradford City football ground and a riot in the Heysel stadium in Brussels involving British football "fans," Mr

---

[3] For a bibliography, see A. Green, "Research Bibliography of Published Materials Relating to the Coal Dispute 1984–85" (1985) 12 Jo. L. & S. 405; University College London, Working Papers No. 1, *Some Legal Issues Arising Out of the Miners' Strike (1985)*.

[4] *Thomas* v. *National Union of Mineworkers (South Wales Area)* [1986] Chap. 20; see S. Lee and S. Whittaker, (1986) 101 L.Q.R. 35; H. Carty, [1985] P.L. 542.

[5] *Moss* v. *McLachlan* [1985] I.R.L.R. 76; R. East and P. Thomas, "Stopping the Miners" (1985) 135 New L.J. 63 and "Freedom of Movement" (1985) 12 J. Law and Soc. 77; A. L. Newbold, [1985] P.L. 30. See further below, Chap. 10.

[6] This was the subject of the Report of the Home Affairs Committee of the House of Commons, *The Law Relating to Public Order (1979–80)*, H.C. 756–I and II.

[7] *The Red Lion Square Disorders of 16 June 1974* Cmnd. 5919 (1975).

[8] *Southall, 23 April 1979* (1980) N.C.C.L.

[9] Much of the literature is tendentious, ephemeral and partisan. To some extent the debate simply carried on the controversy from the entrenched positions that had been adopted during the enactment of PACE in 1984.

[10] White Paper, para. 3.8.

[11] *Football Spectator Violence* Report of the Official Working Group (1984) H.M.S.O. And see R. Ingram, "A Social Analysis of Football Hooliganism" (1985) 25 Med.Sci. Law 53; E. Trivizas, "Disturbances Associated With Football Matches" (1984) 24 B.J.Crim. 361.

Justice Popplewell was asked by the Government to look into the problems that football hooliganism poses for public order.[12]

The existing law

Until the Public Order Act 1986 was enacted, public order criminal law **1–12**
in England[13] was to be found in a variety of sources, both common law and statute. The principal serious offences, riot, rout, affray and unlawful assembly were the products of the common law, and had never been reduced to a statutory form. To ascertain the essence of these ancient offences it was often necessary to turn to the old institutional writers such as Coke, Blackstone, Hale and Hawkins.[14] Much of this law was developed in social conditions very different from those prevailing in 1986; public order was historically a concern of the magistrates assisted if necessary by troops rather than the police, for example, and ease of travel and communication between different parts of the country were wholly different. As a result, the offences were ill-defined, over-inclusive, full of technicalities, in many respects of uncertain ambit and almost wholly out of tune with modern conditions. According to the strict definition, for example, riot was defined in such a way that it caught robberies (or even lesser outbreaks of hooliganism) where three people were involved.[15] Affray had, by the middle of the twentieth century, virtually disappeared from the prosecutor's armoury, only to be revived in the mid 1950s,[16] since when it had become a particularly useful weapon against pitched battles between rival

---

[12] *Committee of Inquiry into Crowd Safety and Control at Sports Grounds: Final Report* Cmnd. 9710 (1986). This was the last in a long line of similar previous enquiries, beginning with the Shortt Report in 1923, (Cd. 2088) arising from disturbances at the F.A. Cup Final on April 28 of that year. Not one of the eight Reports, including Popplewell itself, recommends exclusion orders (2–09) as a solution to the problem. And see E. Grayson, "Popplewell in Perspective" (1985) 135 New L.J. 881.

[13] Scotland has a separate system of criminal law; the Scottish Law Commission has recently published a Consultative Memorandum no. 62, *Mobbing and Rioting* (1984). Northern Ireland presents public order problems of a kind different from those encountered on the mainland. Insofar as the bulk of this book is concerned with the Public Order Act 1986, which applies mainly to England and Wales, it does not deal with either of those jurisdictions.

[14] *Archbold*, for example, continues to cite Hawkins for its definition of riot. And see *Sharpe and Johnson* (1957) Cr.App.R. 86; *Button and Swain* [1966] A.C. 591; para. 25–13.

[15] *London and Lancashire Fire Insurance Co.* v. *Boland* [1924] A.C. 836. The leading authority on the definition of the offence of riot was a civil action brought under the Riot (Damages) Act 1886, *Field* v. *Metropolitan Police Receiver* [1907] 2 K.B. 853. In *Athens Maritime Enterprises* v. *Hellenic Mutual War Risks* [1983] Q.B. 647, Staughton J. adopted the definition given in *Field* for the purposes of construing an insurance contract, pointing out that "if one takes the word in its current and popular meaning, nobody but a Sloane Ranger would say of this casualty, (thieves armed with knives boarding a ship off the coast of Bangladesh) 'it was a riot'." Even if the offence of riot is more frequently prosecuted under the Act, the precise scope of the offence will be of considerable importance in connection with claims brought under the Riot (Damages) Act 1886. And see s.10 (construction of other instruments).

[16] In *Sharpe and Johnson* above n. 4. The process was continued in *Button and Swain* v. *D.P.P.* above n. 2, and the existence of the offence was affirmed by the House of Lords in *Taylor* v. *D.P.P.* [1973] A.C. 964. The process is described by I. D. Brownlie, "The Renovation of Affray" [1965] Crim.L.R. 479.

23

gangs and spontaneous brawls. Although not technically an offence of group disorder after the decision of the House of Lords in *Taylor*[17] it was in effect a device for setting the courts free from the limitations of proof surrounding the offences against person and as such difficult to justify in principle when the penalty available was life imprisonment.[18] In the common law scheme of things, rout seemed to have no identifiable purpose; it was in effect a dead letter.[19]

Perhaps as a result of these shortcomings, the common law offences tended to be overlooked in the operational preservation of public order (at least in political disturbances) in favour of minor statutory offences and associated police powers to preserve the peace. They were revived during the violence that erupted in the course of the miners' strike in 1985.[20] Although over 100 charges of riot were brought as a result of these disturbances,[21] there were no convictions. A number of explanations can be offered for this. Since the trials were on indictment, their preparation for trial took some considerable time, and the evidence had become stale by the time prosecutions were ready to be heard by the courts. The strike was policed in a quite unprecedented way, in the sense that groups of policemen were lent from forces throughout the country to the areas where the trouble was occurring, coordinated from a National Reporting Centre.[22] The subsequent logistic difficulties of producing evidence may have lead to juries being reluctant to convict. Whatever the causes, many charges were ultimately withdrawn or laid on the file.

The Public Order Act 1936, enacted as a response to the Mosleyite blackshirt marches of the British Union of Fascists through the East End of London,[23] was the principal legislative intervention in the area of public order law. But even this relied upon the rather elusive common law concept of a breach of the peace, and was consequently of uncertain ambit.[24] The Tumultuous Petitioning Act 1661, the Shipping Offences Act 1793 and the Seditious Meetings Act 1817 had fallen completely into desuetude,[25] their origins largely forgotten. Other relatively minor statutory offences such as obstructing a constable in the execution of his duty[26] and obstruction of the highway contrary to the Highways Act 1980, section 137[27]

---

[17] Last note.
[18] See [1982] Crim.LR 485 at 487.
[19] In E. Wise, *The Law Relating to Riot and Unlawful Assembly* (4th ed., 1907), it is said that "the offence of rout, though mentioned in the books, is but rarely the subject of enquiry in courts of law, and when its relation to riot on the one hand, and unlawful assembly on the other, is recollected, any further notice of it appears unnecessary."
[20] See P. Wallington, "Policing the Miners' Strike" (1985) 14 Industrial Law J. 145.
[21] The figures were given in Parliament on January 31, 1986; H.C. vol. 90, col. 232. There were 137 charges of riot, 509 of unlawful assembly and 4107 charges under the Public Order Act 1936, s.5.
[22] See 1–10.
[23] See R. Kidd, *British Liberty in Danger* (1940); D. G. T. Williams, *Keeping the Peace* (1967).
[24] *Howell* [1981] 2 Q.B. 416. See further below, Chap. 10.
[25] They are repealed by the Act, s.9(2).
[26] Below, Chap. 10.
[27] See further below, Chap. 11.

became mainstays of public order law. In addition to these, there existed a miscellany of statutory offences in local legislation similar to the Metropolitan Police Act 1839, sections 54(13) and the City of London Police Act 1839, section 35(13) that were employed throughout the country. These gave the police powers to deal with relatively minor nuisances and disturbances, but they were (with the exception of the separate London provisions) due to lapse as a result of the Local Government Act 1972, section 262.

Statutory law relating to the control of processions and assemblies was selective and sketchy. Only the Public Order Act 1936, section 3 conferred on the police any advance powers of imposing controls, and this was only in connection with processions rather than assemblies. To control a procession, the police commonly relied on cooperation with the organisers and, in the event that trouble ensued in the course of the procession, on their common law powers. There was no national advance notice requirement that a procession was planned, and no power to impose in advance conditions on the holding of an assembly. In view of the increasing demands placed upon finite police resources, the law governing police powers to insist that the arrangements be complied with was seen by 1985 to be sporadic and outdated. This results in some of the amendments to the arrangements established in the 1936 Public Order Act by Part II of the Act.

Racial hatred was originally proscribed by legislation in the Race Relations Act 1965. This made the use of threatening, abusive or insulting behaviour with intent to stir up racial hatred an offence, and the distribution of such material with like intent an offence similarly. This legislation was supplemented by the Theatres Act 1968, and altered in 1976 by putting it into the Public Order Act 1936, section 5A, and by substituting for the requirement of an intention to stir up racial hatred liability where racial hatred was in the circumstances likely to ensue. This change caused its own difficulties[28]; charges were dismissed when it was plain that an intention to stir up racial hatred existed, but in circumstances where it might be said that there was no likelihood that racial hatred would be stirred. Prosecutions required the consent of the Attorney-General, and there were constant complaints that this was given insufficiently frequently.[29]

Law reform proposals

On June 27, 1979, in the course of a parliamentary statement following   **1–13** disturbances in the London Borough of Southall, the Home Secretary announced that the Government intended to conduct a major overhaul of public order law.[30] This review culminated in a White Paper outlining the Government's intentions for reform, published in 1985.[31] In the interven-

---

[28] See 9–09.
[29] See 9–01, n. 5.
[30] Mr Whitelaw, H.C.Deb., vol. 969, col. 441.
[31] *Review of Public Order* Cmnd. 9510 (1985); see A. T. H. Smith [1985] P.L. 533. See also the series of articles by G. Broadbent and M. Williams, "The Public Order Bill" (1986) 150 J.P.N. 229, 247, 264, 393, 407, 424, 442.

ing years, a good deal of preliminary study was given to the problems of public order law by a variety of different bodies. The Home Office produced a Green Paper on the relevant police powers legislation[32]; the Home Affairs Committee of the House of Commons, being particularly concerned with the Home Office responsibility for the problems of policing,[33] reported on public meetings, marches, pickets and demonstrations. The Law Commission, as part of its continuing project of codifying the criminal law relating to the common law offences[34] produced a Working Paper[35] and then a Report[36] devoted principally to the common law public order offences of riot, rout, unlawful assembly and affray.

There were also a number of ad hoc inquiries, three of them chaired by Lord Scarman into a National Front and anti-rascist confrontation,[37] a mass picket,[38] and an inner city riot.[39] Mr. Justice Popplewell produced the latest of a long series of reports into problems of disorder and crowd safety associated with football grounds and the people who attend such gatherings.[40]

The White Paper borrowed heavily from the conclusions arrived at in these studies, but it also effected a number of changes to them. Several significant alterations were made to the Bill in the course of its passage through Parliament, especially to Part III dealing with the offences relating to racial hatred. The result, the Public Order Act 1986, is in many respects a far more radical revision of the law than was envisaged by the Law Commission in its working paper.

The Public Order Act 1986—an overview

1–14   The legislation that resulted was the Public Order Act 1986,[41] which effects a considerable number of changes in the law. For the first time it puts into statutory form the major public order offences, and abolishes the

---

[32] *Review of the Public Order Act 1936 and Related Legislation* Cmnd. 7891 (1980).

[33] Fifth Report of the Home Affairs Committee, *The Law Relating to Public Order* H.C. 756–I & II (1980).

[34] Set up in 1965, the Law Commission has the statutory remit of keeping the law under review with a view to its systematic development and reform, including in particular its codification. It initiated this process in 1968. See the Report to the Law Commission, *Codification of the Criminal Law* (1985) Law Com. No. 143; [1986] Crim.LR 285.

[35] Working Paper No. 82, *Offences Against Public Order* (1982); see A. T. H. Smith, [1982] Crim.L.R. 485; D. M. Morgan and C. Wells, (1982) 132 New L.J. 541; M. Supperstone, [1982] P.L. 354.

[36] Report No. 123, *Criminal Law—Offences Relating to Public Order* (1983) H.C. 85. See D. G. T. Williams, [1984] P.L. 12; Gillian S. Morris (1984) 47 M.L.R. 324.

[37] *Red Lion Square.*

[38] *Report of a Court of Inquiry into the Grunwick Dispute* Cmnd. 6922 (1977).

[39] *Brixton.*

[40] *Final Report* Cmnd. 9710 (1986).

[41] The Act comes into force on a day or days to be appointed; s.41(1). By virtue of the Public Order Act 1986 (Commencement No. 1) Order 1986, ss.11, 16,, 38, 40 to 43, Sched. 1 and certain parts of Scheds. 2 and 3 came into effect on January 1, 1987. And see S.I. 1987/198; S.I. 1987/852; S.I. 1987/853. With the exception of s.38 (contamination of goods) the Act does not extend to Northern Ireland. Ss.12, and 14 to 16 apply to Scotland, as does the whole of Part III (racial hatred); see s.42.

common law offences of riot, rout, unlawful assembly and affray.[42] In their place, the statute creates the offences of riot,[43] violent disorder[44] and affray.[45] These new offences differ from their common law predecessors in their constituent ingredients in many important respects. One very important change effected by the Act is to make the new offences (with the exception of riot) triable summarily, whereas hitherto, they had been triable on indictment only. The Act also abolishes a number of anachronistic statutory offences.[46] and the opportunity was taken to amend the Public Order Act 1936 by abolishing section 5, and replacing it with two new offences, causing fear of or provoking violence[47] and offensive conduct.[48]

Part II of the Act amends and extends police powers of control in relation to meeting and processions. It creates for the first time a national (as opposed to local) requirement that the organisers of a procession (but not of an assembly) should notify the police of their intentions, and empowers the police to impose conditions on the procession (and for the first time on an assembly) both in advance and in the course of the procession or assembly. The grounds on which such conditions can be made are extended so that the police may take into account "serious damage to property and serious disruption to the life of the community"[49] in addition to the power to prevent serious disorder that was conferred by the 1936 Act. The new Act also empowers the imposition of conditions where the senior police officer reasonably believes that the purpose of the persons organising is "the intimidation of others with a view to compelling them not to do an act that they have a right to do, or to do an act that they have a right not to do."[50]

Part III of the Act now contains what is in effect a code of the offences relating to racial hatred. It consolidates much of the previous law that was scattered throughout the statute book in such places as the Public Order Act 1936 (as amended), the Theatres Act 1968 and the Cable and Broadcasting Act 1984. It extends the law to video recordings,[51] removes from the existing offences of publication and distribution of racially inflammatory material the defence that the material was circulated to members of a club or association of which the defendant was a member, creates a new

---

[42] Section 9(1).
[43] Section 1, Chap. 4.
[44] Section 2, Chap. 3.
[45] Section 3, Chap. 5.
[46] Section 9(2)(a) The Tumultuous Petitioning Act 1661, s.1; (b) The Shipping Offences Act 1793, s.1; (c) Seditious Meetings Act 1817. The Act does not unequivocally abolish the vague common law offence of going armed to terrify the Queen's subjects. This was sometimes regarded as an aspect of affray, and at other times as an independent misdemeanour; Brownlie, [1965] Crim.LR 480. The continued vitality of the common law was affirmed in the American decision of *State of North Carolina* v. *Dawson* 272 N.C. 535, 159 S.E. 2d 1 (1968). Since such conduct can now be proceeded against as an offence under the Prevention of Crime Act 1953 (Chap. 13), the courts should say that the common law does not survive. Only a code abolishing all common law offences could make certain of getting rid of it and any other dormant common law offences.
[47] Section 4, Chap. 6.
[48] Section 5, Chap. 7.
[49] Sections 12(1)(a) and 14(1)(a) respectively. Below, Chap. 8.
[50] Sections 12(1) and (b) and 14(1)(b) respectively.
[51] Section 21. The racial hatred offences in Part III are dealt with in Chap. 9.

offence of possessing racially inflammatory material,[52] and confers powers of entry, search and seizure in respect of it.[53] Although prosecutions still require the consent of the Attorney-General, these changes strengthen the hand of those who call for action to be taken under the racial hatred laws.

Part IV of the Act empowers magistrates to exclude persons from football grounds, and makes elaborate provision for the extension by order of the exclusion powers to other sporting facilities should the need ever arise.

As so often seems to happen in the course of legislation proceeding through Parliament, an event will occur that makes it seem appropriate to add another clause to legislation currently before Parliament.[54] In June 1986, a so called "peace convoy" trespassed on the land of an unfortunate farmer who was put to a good deal of trouble and expense to rid himself of their unwelcome presence. The police were apparently reluctant to intervene to compel the intruders to move on.[55] As a result, section 39 was added, giving the police explicit power to require trespassers to vacate land which they intend to occupy. Whether such a power was legally absolutely necessary, in view of such powers as arrest for breach of the peace[56] is, perhaps, debatable. At an even later stage in the proceedings, it was decided to add a further clause proscribing the contamination of or interference with goods with the intention of causing public alarm or anxiety. This was undoubtedly a response to the activities of the so-called animal rights groups, who adopt these tactics against organisations which have any connection with animal experimentation. Reprehensible though such conduct may well be, the connection with public order is, to say the least, tenuous.[57]

---

[52] Section 23.

[53] Section 24.

[54] A previous example is to be found in the so-called "Goya clause" in the Theft Act 1968, s.11. See J. C. Smith, *The Law of Theft* (5th ed., 1984), Chap. VII.

[55] See P. Vincent-Jones, "Private Property and Public Order: The Hippy Convoy and Criminal Trespass" (1986) 13 J. Law and Soc. 343.

[56] But see the discussion of the decision in *R. v. Chief Constable of Devon and Cornwall ex p. C.E.G.B.* [1982] Q.B. 458 in 10–06.

[57] A bomb hoaxer was held to commit a public nuisance in *Norbury* [1978] Crim.L.R. 435, and the activities of the animal rights protesters are not dissimilar to this. But in principle, specific legislation is preferable to the moulding of the common law offences by a process of what is in effect judicial crime creation. Bomb hoaxing is now an offence under the Criminal Law Act 1977, s.51.

CHAPTER 2

PRELIMINARY AND MISCELLANEOUS

1. EVIDENCE AND PROCEDURE

Mode of trial

Of the offences created by the Act, riot alone is triable only on indict- **2–01**
ment by a jury[1]: violent disorder and affray, and the racial hatred offences
in Part III are triable either way,[2] at the election of the defendant. This
effects a considerable change from the previous law. Affray and the predecessor of violent disorder (unlawful assembly) were triable on indictment
only. The offences created by sections 4 and 5 are triable summarily only.[3]
All the offences created by Part II relating to processions and assemblies
are again only summary offences, with varying penalties.

Alternative verdicts

Since the ingredients of the offences created by Part I are in many **2–02**
respects similar, there is a good deal of overlap between them, and consequently the question of alternative verdicts must be considered. An express
provision for alternative verdicts applies to two of the indictable offences.
Section 7(3) states that:

> "If on the trial on indictment of a person charged with violent disorder
> or affray the jury find him not guilty of the offence charged, they may
> (without prejudice to section 6(3) of the Criminal Law Act 1967) find
> him guilty of an offence under section 4."

The reason for the subsection is that the offence under section 4 (fear or
provocation of violence) is triable summarily only.[4] In the absence of some
such provision, therefore, it would be necessary for a person found not
guilty on indictment in the Crown Court of one of the more serious
offences to be tried separately and at a later stage in the magistrates' court
for a lesser offence arising out of the same incident, and this would reflect
adversely on the efficiency of the criminal process. The subsection has the
considerable advantage for the prosecutor that he can charge a more
serious offence in the knowledge that, if the defendant elects jury trial, he
may still be held guilty of the lesser offence by the jury. The words "without prejudice to section 6(3) of the Criminal Law Act 1967" are included
since that makes provision for alternative convictions in general terms, but
only as between offences "falling within the jurisdiction of the court of

---

[1] Section 1(6).
[2] Sections 2(5), 3(7) and 27(3) respectively.
[3] Sections 4(4) and 5(6) respectively, subject to the exception created by s.7(3), which permits a conviction on indictment of the s.4 offence as an alternative to a conviction of violent
disorder or affray. See below, 2–02.
[4] And punishable with a maximum of imprisonment for six months or a level five fine or
both; s.4(4).

trial"[5] and the section 4 offence would not ordinarily be within the jurisdiction of the Crown Court. Of course, there can be no conviction of the lesser offence unless the jury are satisfied that the elements of the offence under section 4 have been proved, and that the defendant did actually cause violence or provoke its unlawful use.

Where there is a finding by the jury of guilt under section 4 under the substitute procedure, the Crown Court's powers of punishment are limited to those that would have been available to the magistrates' court had the defendant been convicted on summary trial.[6]

The application of section 6(3) of the Criminal Law Act 1967

2–03   Where a person is charged with riot, a question arises as to whether he can be convicted of violent disorder, and if charged with the latter, whether he can be convicted of affray (and vice versa). The answers to these questions will depend on the operation of the somewhat unsatisfactory section 6(3) of the Criminal Law Act 1967, as interpreted in the even less satisfactory decision of the House of Lords in *R. v. Wilson, R. v. Jenkins.*[7] The section provides:

> "Where, on a trial on indictment for any offence except treason or murder, the jury find him not guilty of the offence specifically charged in the indictment, but the allegations in the indictment amount to or include (expressly or by implication) an allegation of another offence falling within the jurisdiction of the court of trial, the jury may find him guilty of that other offence or of an offence of which he could be found guilty on an indictment specifically charging that other offence."

Because of some uncertainties surrounding the operation of this section, the Law Commission in its Report recommended that specific provisions should be enacted to deal with the problems of alternative verdicts,[8] and the Bill included draft clauses to give effect to the recommendation. But the proposed clauses were not proceeded with on the Government's initiative,[9] so the general law obtains.

According to the decision of the House, the gist of the section is that there can be alternative convictions where the allegations in the indictment expressly amount to allegations of the other offence; or, they expressly

---

[5] For the text and discussion of s.6(3), see 2–03.

[6] Section 7(4); six months, or a level five fine.

[7] [1984] A.C. 242. For extensive critical comment, see Glanville Williams, "Alternative Elements and Included Offences" (1984) 43 C.L.J. 290; Christopher Emmins, "The House of Lords and Alternative Verdicts" [1984] Crim.L.R. 152; see also J. C. Smith, [1984] Crim.L.R. 37; Archbold, paras. 4.462–463. And see *Whiting The Times*, January 27, 1987.

[8] Paras. 7.5–7.9. This, it might be noted, was before the decision in the House referred to in the text.

[9] Clause 7(4). According to the Government spokesman, Mr. Giles Shaw, "on reflection we felt that it would be wrong to invite judges in public order cases to sum up to the jury on a number of different possible alternatives, which might simply confuse"; Standing Committee G, col. 328.

include allegations of the other offence; or they impliedly amount to an allegation of the other offence; or, they impliedly include an allegation of another offence. This widened the law considerably, since it had been previously thought that an alternative conviction was available only where the allegations in the indictment necessarily included allegations of the other offence (which gave rise to some wholly unmeritorious acquittals), and was thought to apply to lesser included offences only. In both respects, the House has held that the previous understandings were incorrect, with the result that, depending on what the prosecutor alleges in the indictment, or the court is prepared to allow that he has impliedly alleged,[10] the possibilities for alternative convictions are in theory dauntingly wide. The availability of an alternative verdict is subject to judicial discretion in every case, and the basic starting point for the exercise of that discretion is that the defendant has come to court to answer the particular charge or charges in the indictment, and may well be disadvantaged to find half way through the trial that he is expected to meet a different charge.[11]

Perhaps the wisest course for a prosecutor to adopt will be to include expressly separate alternative counts for each offence alleged, as he is entitled to do.[12] Failing that, however, the law would seem to be that on a charge of riot, a conviction of violent disorder is permissible where one or other of the allegations in the riot charge cannot be sustained but the other ingredients of violent disorder are made out. If the prosecutor fails to prove the existence of the common purpose, for example, or it cannot be shown that there were 12 present using or threatening unlawful violence (because some of those present had a defence of self-defence, or something of the sort),[13] there can be a conviction of violent disorder. This can be stated with some confidence, since the particulars in the indictment ought to contain allegations relating to all the ingredients of the offence of riot, which is really an aggravated offence of violent disorder. Whether there can be a conviction of affray on a charge of violent disorder is perhaps more problematic, since violence for the purposes of affray means violence in relation to persons only, whereas violent disorder can be committed by violence towards persons or property. Under the previous law, this would in itself have been a fatal objection to an alternative conviction. Since *Wilson*, however, it would seem that so long as the indictment alleges that the defendant used or threatened violence towards a person, a conviction of affray would be proper. There are further difficulties. If the particulars in the charge of violent disorder are that the defendants were threatening by words alone, they do not include within any of the formulae adopted in *Wilson* an allegation of affray, since that offence cannot be committed by words alone.[14]

---

[10] As to the circumstances when the court should consider directing the jury on the availability of alternative verdicts, see *Fairbanks* [1986] 1 W.L.R. 1202.

[11] *Wilson, Jenkins*, above, n. 7; see Lord Roskill at 261.

[12] As in *O'Brien* (1911) 6 Cr.App.R. 108.

[13] But not, it will be noted, where some of the participants in the events are not guilty by virtue of the fact that they lacked *mens rea*; s.6(7) 3–03.

[14] Section 3(3).

31

Alternative convictions in summary trials

2–04   Magistrates' courts do not have the power to enter alternative convictions comparable to those given to Crown Courts by section 6(3).[15] However, the House of Lords has held[16] that, even without the defendant's consent, a magistrates' court may try more than one information alleging one offence at any one time. Where a prosecutor is in any doubt, therefore, he should include separate informations alleging violent disorder, affray or causing or provoking violence as appropriate, and if the justices conclude that it would be fair and just to the defendant to do so, they should order a joint trial even if the defendant does not consent. Similarly where the prosecutor wishes to charge both the section 4 offence and offensive conduct under section 5.

Duplicity

2–05   The rule against duplicity states, in essence, that no more than one offence may charged in each separate count of an indictment or in a single information.[17] This is greatly complicated by Rule 7 of the Indictment Rules 1971, which provides that when an offence is stated in the form of doing acts in the alternative, or with different intentions, the alternatives may be stated in the same indictment. It then becomes very difficult to say, for the purposes of the rule against duplicity, whether a particular statute creates a single offence that is capable of being committed in a number of different ways, or whether, by contrast, it creates a number of quite separate offences. In the Act, for example, section 4 (Chapter 6) creates what appear to be the two quite separate offences of putting a person in fear that violence is about to be used against him or acting in such a way as to provoke another to use violence.[18] There is scope here for unnecessary technical complexity and meritless defences, and section 7(2) seeks to avoid this by providing that each of the offences created by sections 1 to 5 is to be regarded as only one offence for the purposes of the rules charging more than one offence in the same count or information. A similar provision is to be found in connection with the racial hatred offences in section 27(2).

     The impact of these provisions would seem to be that it is sufficient to charge a defendant in general terms with an offence under one of the relevant sections, and no objection can then be taken on the grounds of duplicity that the particulars charge the defendant with committing the offence by a different means than is proved by the evidence. Whether this wholesale abrogation of a rule that had as its basis the avoidance of embarrassment to the defendant in the conduct of his defence because of the failure to know the nature of the allegations against him will prove to be a wise

---

[15] *Lawrence* v. *Same* [1968] 2 Q.B. 93.
[16] *Chief Constable of Norfolk* v. *Clayton* [1983] 2 A.C. 473.
[17] Glanville Williams, "The Count System and the Duplicity Rule" [1966] Crim.L.R. 255.
[18] *John* [1971] Crim.L.R. 283; *Garfield* v. *Maddocks* [1974] Q.B. 7. The Public Order Act 1936, s.5, which provided that the offence could be committed by "threatening, abusive or insulting behaviour" could have been be interpreted as creating three offences, although the courts ruled otherwise; *Vernon* v. *Paddon* [1973] 1 W.L.R. 663; *Gedge* [1978] Crim.L.R. 167. Section 7(2) puts the point beyond doubt.

development remains to be seen. The courts have an overriding duty to the defendant to ensure that he is given a fair trial, and can permit the appropriate amendments to be made. If necessary the court can adjourn the proceedings or direct that they be started afresh if the defendant has not been given a fair opportunity to meet the charges actually levelled against him.[19]

The Act does not solve all problems that duplicity might cause; it is sometimes difficult to know, for example, whether a series of fights should be charged as one affray, or several.[20] Riot, violent disorder and affray are all continuing offences, but they continue only for as long as the violence or threat of it continues, and if there is a break of real significance between one incident and another, a single count might well be duplicitous. Suppose, for example, that a group of rowdies were to go from one pub to another, fighting and threatening bystanders in each place. It might be better to charge each as a separate affray or offence of violent disorder, rather than treat the incidents as a continuing and single event.[21]

The obtaining of evidence

Securing evidence at the scene of a disorder with a view to subsequent **2–06** prosecution is generally of secondary importance to the more immediate business of restoring or preserving order. For all that riot, violent disorder and affray are highly visible offences, there are logistical difficulties in securing proof of their commission. Even effecting an arrest at the scene of a major disturbance, for example, may require a number of policemen. Although there are no particular rules regulating the collection of evidence of public order offences, certain court decisions and statutory provisions facilitating the police task of policing public disorder may be noted. In *Kajala* v. *Noble*[22] it was held that evidence on video recorder is admissible to identify the participants in a group disorder. The BBC had declined to make available the original film of the news programme recording the incident, but the court held that a video cassette recording, which the court was satisfied as being an authentic copy of the original, could be admitted in any event.

By virtue of the powers conferred by PACE, journalistic material can now be mandatorily obtained in certain circumstances,[23] and it seems quite possible that the BBC and other news-gathering agencies could be obliged to make available to the police any recordings made of the scenes of disorder when these are required for the purposes of identifying the partici-

---

[19] Indictments Act 1915, s.5(4) which permits the court to grant an adjournment. See generally *Archbold*, paras. 1–57 *et seq*. In summary proceedings, see the Magistrates' Courts Act 1980, s.123. In *Garfield* v. *Maddocks* [1974] Q.B. 7, Lord Widgery C.J. explained that the courts have restrictively construed the predecessor of s.123 (stating that defects in the form of the information should not give rise to objection) as requiring the courts to amend informations if what is alleged in the information is greatly at variance with the proof, granting adjournments if necessary.

[20] *Woodrow* (1959) 43 Cr.App.R. 105.

[21] *Jones and Others* (1974) 59 Cr.App.R. 120.

[22] (1985) 75 Cr.App.R. 149. And see *Howe* [1982] 1 N.Z.L.R. 618 as to the propriety of prosecution comment on the evidence thus secured.

[23] Sections 8 to 13. *Bristol in Court ex p. Bristol Press and Picture Agency* [1987] Crim.L.R. 329. And see *Zurcher* v. *Standford* 436 U.S. 547 (1978).

pants. In *Harrington* v. *North London Polytechnic*[24] it was held that persons able to identify members of a demonstration that had been assembled in breach of a court order could be obliged to do so under pain of conviction for contempt of court. It has been argued that decisions such as these may very well make journalists (including photographic journalists) at the scene of any disorder more vulnerable to attack by rioters than they would hitherto have been, and this (if true) may have repercussions on the news coverage of scenes of disorder in the future.

The identification of persons engaged in large group disorders may frequently cause difficulty to the individual policeman. In *Allen* v. *Ireland*[25] it was held that where a person is arrested as part of a group engaging in group disorder, there is at least prima facie evidence of identification against such a person if he has appeared in the magistrates' court and pleaded to the charge in his own name after his earlier arrest and bail as part of the group.

2. SENTENCE

The sentencing structure

2–07   Most of the offences created by the Act are punishable with a period of imprisonment stipulated in the Act itself. Riot is the most serious of the offences, punishable with ten years, violent disorder with five, affray with three. Where the trial is by way of indictment, each of these offences may be visited with an unlimited fine in addition to any sentence of imprisonment. Section 4 carries imprisonment for a period of six months and a fine to level five, whereas section 5 carries a level three fine and nothing more.[26] The Act also makes specific provision for forfeiture orders in the case of racially inflammatory material.[27] In addition, the Act fits into a background of the general sentencing options that are available to the courts.[28] These may include such non-custodial measures as probation and community service orders and, where the use of custodial measures is thought to be desirable, the suspended or partly suspended sentence.

Two species of sentence require particular mention. The Act introduces the exclusion order, designed to keep so-called "football hooligans" away from football grounds. These will be briefly described. Second, the binding over order, that peculiar phenomenon of public order law, requires specific treatment.

---

[24] [1984] 1 W.L.R. 1293, 3 All E.R. 666.
[25] [1984] 1 W.L.R. 903, (1984) 79 Cr.App.R. 206.
[26] The fine structure is explained in 2–08.
[27] Section 25. Forfeiture is an option that appeals increasingly to the legislature as a sentencing option; Drug Trafficking Offences Act 1986.
[28] For an overall view of the sentences available to the courts, see A. J. Ashworth (ed.), Cross, *The English Sentencing System* (3rd ed., 1981); D. A. Thomas *Principles of Sentencing* (2nd ed., 1979); C. Emmins, *A Practical Approach to Sentencing* (1985); C. K. Boyle and Michael Allen, *Sentencing Law and Practice* (1985).

Fines: the standard scale[29]

The Criminal Justice Act 1982[30] establishes a standard scale of fines   2–08
(ranging from scale one to the maximum five) for summary offences, which
can be periodically adjusted by Order.[31] At the time of writing, the statutory maximum penalty is £2,000, and the other present levels are:

level 1—£50
level 2—£100
level 3—£400
level 4—£1,000
level 5—£2,000.

Exclusion orders

Where a person is guilty of an offence connected with football as defined   2–09
by section 31,[32] the court may in addition to any other sentence[33] impose
an exclusion order upon him preventing that person from entering any
premises for the purpose of attending any prescribed football match
there.[34] The full text of the Act may be found in the Appendix, but its
general features will be described here.

A number of conditions must be satisfied before such an order can be
imposed. There is an overriding condition that the court must be satisfied
that making such an order would help to prevent violence or disorder at or
in connection with football matches.[35] The other conditions are alternatives.

1. An order may be imposed if the offence is committed while the
accused was at, or was entering or leaving, or trying to enter or leave a
football ground within two hours before and one hour after the match.[36] It
would seem that a conviction of any offence will trigger the operation of

---

[29] The standard account of how the courts sentence in practice is D. A. Thomas, *Current Sentencing Practice*, and for the public order offences in particular, see B3–1. With the creation
of new offences such as violent disorder, and the reduction of the maximum sentence available for affray (three years, by comparison with life currently), it will be necessary for the
courts to establish new sentencing patterns in the public order offences.

[30] Sections 37, 46.

[31] Magistrates' Courts Act 1980, s.32(9); Criminal Justice Act 1982, s.74. The current order is
S.I. 1984, No. 447.

[32] Section 30(1).

[33] Which may include a probation order or an absolute or conditional discharge; s.30(3)(b),
but not it would seem, a binding over order, which is not a conviction; see *R. v. County of
London Quarter Sessions Appeals Committee, ex p. Metropolitan Police Commissioner*
[1948] 1 K.B. 670; *R. v. London Quarter Sessions, ex p. Beaumont* [1951] 1 K.B. 557.

[34] "Prescribed football match" is defined in s.36 as being that which is prescribed by order
made by the Secretary of State. This is similar to the power of prescription conferred by the
Sporting Events (Control of Alcohol) Act 1985. See the (Designation) Order, 1985 S.I.
No. 1151. There is also provision for the Secretary of State to extend the operation of the
exclusion order sections to other sporting events by order; s.37. For a similar use of exclusion orders, see the Licensed Premises (Exclusion of Certain Persons) Act 1980.

[35] Section 30(2). It is difficult to know how much evidence (if any) must be produced to satisfy
this condition. Can the absence of one person really help prevent disorder in a crowd of
perhaps 50,000 people?

[36] Sections 31(2) and (6). Where the match is postponed or cancelled, the period on the
advertised day is also covered.

this power, subject always to the requirement that the court must be satisfied that the imposition of the order will help to prevent violence or disorder; a pickpocket in the crowd would not come within such a requirement.

2. If the offence is one of violence towards a person, and either the victim or the accused was on a journey[37] to or from a football ground; or
if the accused was on such a journey, and he used violence towards property; or if the accused committed an offence under section 5 (offensive conduct) or Part III of the Act (racial hatred).[38]

3. Where the accused commits an offence under the Sporting Events (Control of Alcohol etc.) Act 1985, section 1(3) or (4) of 1A(3) or (4) on a journey to the designated football match.[39]

The period specified in the order shall be not less than three months, or cumulatively in addition to a previous or the most recent order.[40] There is a power of arrest where a person has entered in breach of the order,[41] and the person entering the ground in breach commits an offence.[42]

The Act makes provision for a person to apply to the court to have the order terminated,[43] and requires the court to inform the person to whom it relates, the police and any other prescribed person that an order has been made.[44] The court also has power (on application by the prosecutor) to order that a photograph be taken of the person to whom the exclusion order relates.[45] The purposes for which this is done, and the use to which the photograph may be put, are not specified in the Act, by contrast with the notification provisions of the exclusion order itself, but it is presumably implicit that the photograph may accompany the information given under section 34.

Binding over orders

2–10   These orders, the origins of which are hopelessly obscure, are of two kinds. There is a common law power to bind a person over to come up for judgment after conviction,[46] and a power to bind over a person to keep the peace and be of good behaviour, which may be imposed whether a person

---

[37] The term includes breaks in the journey, including overnight breaks; s.31(5).
[38] Section 31(3)(a), (b) (c). The offences in s.5 and Part III are fully described in Chaps. 7 and 9.
[39] Section 31(4). The alcohol offences are dealt with in Chap. 13.
[40] Section 32(1), (2).
[41] Section 32(4).
[42] Section 32(3), punishable with imprisonment for one month, or a level three fine or both.
[43] Section 33.
[44] Section 34.
[45] Section 35. Although the Act does not say so, the power should probably be exercised in accordance with the Code of Practice for the Identification of Persons by Police Officers, s.4, issued under the Police and Criminal Evidence Act 1984.
[46] *Goodlad* v. *Chief Constable of South Yorkshire* [1979] Crim.L.R. 51. Conditions (such as that the subject must stay away from a particular place) may be attached under the common law power, but not, it would seem, when the order is imposed under the 1361 or 1980 Acts; *Ayu* [1958] 1 W.L.R. 1264, 3 All E.R. 636. It seems difficult to defend the continued existence of the common law power in the light of modern sentencing powers such as conditional discharge and suspended sentence; see A. J. Ashworth, *Sentencing and Penal Policy* (1983) pp. 381–382.

has been convicted of an offence or not.[47] The orders are a peculiar feature of public order law which present difficult issues of principle because they are used in furtherance of preventive justice.[48] That is, the power enables the courts[49] to bind over a person "who or whose case is before the court"[50] to enter into a recognisance, with or without sureties, to keep the peace and/or be of good behaviour for a specified period. The orders may be made against individuals who have not been charged with any offence,[51] those who have been acquitted[52] or whose convictions are quashed,[53] and persons who appear before the courts as witnesses.[54]

The rationale is that the order is imposed for fear of what those made subject to them might do in the future rather than by way of punishment for wrongs that have already been committed.[55] The power is used extensively in connection with domestic disputes, but also in relation to public protest.[56] A refusal on the part of the person in respect of whom such an order is to be made to agree to it or its terms may lead to a term of imprisonment for a period of up to six months.[57] Where a court is minded to impose a relatively large sum by way of recognisance, or to impose a substantial period of imprisonment in lieu, it must observe the dictates of natural justice, and give the defendant or his representative an opportunity

---

[47] The power is conferred by the Justices of the Peace Act 1361. The Magistrates' Court Act 1980, s.115(1) provides that the power must be exercised by order on complaint. The Crown Prosecution Service has a duty to take over the conduct of all binding over proceedings instituted on behalf of a police force; Prosecution of Offences Act 1985, s.3(2)(c). See generally *Stone's Justices' Manual* (1986), para. 3.131; Supperstone, pp. 312–315; A. D. Grunis, "Binding Over to Keep the Peace and Be of Good Behaviour in England and Canada" [1976] Public Law 16.

[48] Glanville Williams, "Preventive Justice and the Rule of Law" (1953) 16 M.L.R. 417; D. G. T. Williams, *Keeping the Peace* (1967) Chap. 4 and "Preventive Justice and the Courts" [1977] Crim.L.R. 703; G. A. Flick, *Civil Liberties in Australia* (1981) p. 113. They have for some time been under review by the Law Commission, in conjunction with the Home Office; see 15th *Annual Report 1979–80* (1981) Law Com. no. 107, para. 2.15.

[49] Every court of record in England with criminal jurisdiction has the power; Justices of the Peace Act 1968, s.1(7).

[50] As to when a person is "before the court," see *R.* v. *Swindon Crown Court, ex p. Singh* [1984] 1 W.L.R. 449, 79 Cr.App.R. 137; *R.* v. *Kingston Crown Court, ex p. Guarino* [1986] Crim.L.R. 325.

[51] Glanville Williams, "Arrest for Breach of the Peace" [1954] Crim.L.R. 578, citing *Davies* v. *Griffith* [1937] 2 All E.R. 671. According to Supperstone, p. 1, n. 2, the case does not carry the point, since there was no actual breach of the peace in that case, and the Magistrates therefore had a binding over power only. The courts have never settled the dispute.

[52] *R.* v. *Woking JJ. ex p. Gosage* [1973] Q.B. 448. But the exercise of this power is subject to judicial review; *R.* v. *Inner London Crown Court ex p. Benjamin* [1987] *The Times*, January 5.

[53] As in *Sharp* (1957) 41 Cr.App.R. 86; *Younis* [1965] Crim.L.R. 305.

[54] *Sheldon* v. *Bromfield JJ.* [1964] 2 Q.B. 573.

[55] *R.* v. *County of London Quarter Sessions Appeals Committee* [1948] 1 K.B. 670; *Veater* v. *Glennon* [1981] 1 W.L.R. 567, 2 All E.R. 304.

[56] *Wise* v. *Dunning* [1902] 1 K.B. 167; *Lansbury* v. *Riley* [1914] 3 K.B. 329. See D. G. T. Williams, "Protest and Public Order" [1970] C.L.J. 104–106.

[57] Magistrates' Courts Act 1980, s.115(3). Juveniles may not be imprisoned in lieu of refusing to agree to be bound over; *Veater* v. *Glennon* (n. 55), although they may agree to be so bound; *Conlan* v. *Oxford* (1983) 5 Cr.App.R.(S) 237. See G. Norman, "Refusal to be Bound Over" (1977) 141 J.P. Jo. 138.

of addressing the court on the matter.[58] Where the sanctions that it has in mind to impose are less serious, it is desirable that it should do so.[59]

The conditions for the imposition of such an order were laid down by Denning L.J. in *Everett* v. *Ribbands*,[60] where it was said that

> "an order can only be made against the man if two things exist: first, a threat by words or conduct to break the law of the land or to do something which is likely to result in such a breach; secondly, a reasonable fear that this threat will be carried into effect."

There must be a real apprehension that a breach of the peace is likely to be committed.[61] The evidence upon which the order is based must be admissible, and not the assertions of an advocate or the evidence of a policeman on matters of which he did not have personal knowledge.[62]

The major constitutional objections to the orders would seem to be that they can be imposed on a person who has committed no criminal offence, and the scope of what they ordain a defendant to do or not do is most uncertain. He must desist from the activity that gave rise to the order in the first place; but can he, for example, go on a march when he has been the subject of such an order? As a New Zealand judge has put it, "restraints of that kind inherent in a binding over order . . . may have a chilling effect on the exercise of civil liberties given the difficulty of determining in advance the boundaries of legitimate protest and of other exercises of personal freedoms under the law."[63] In *Boulding*[64] the Court said that "a binding over order must not be in such terms as effectively to inhibit a convicted person from exercising his right to free speech within the law."

Discretion as to enforcement and prosecution

2–11   Given the diverse nature of public order law, it is inevitable that discretion will play a significant part at all levels of its implementation. There are also difficult discretionary decisions to be taken by the prosecutor, and the Act contains two specific provisions dealing with the power to prosecute for the offences that it creates. Section 7(1) provides that no prosecution for an offence of riot or incitement to riot may be instituted except

---

[58] *R.* v. *Keithley JJ. ex p. Stoyles* [1976] Crim.L.R. 573; *R.* v. *Central Criminal Court, ex p. Boulding* [1984] 1 Q.B. 813.

[59] *R.* v. *Woking JJ. ex p. Gossage* [1973] Q.B. 448 at 451.

[60] [1952] 2 Q.B. 198.

[61] *Aubrey-Fletcher ex p. Thompson* [1969] 1 W.L.R. 872, 2 All E.R. 836, 53 Cr.App.R. 380; *Lister* v. *Morgan* [1978] Crim.L.R. 292; but see *Hughes* v. *Hughes* (1987) 151 J.P. 304 (kerb crawling).

[62] *Brooks and Breen* v. *Nottinghamshire Police* [1984] Crim.L.R. 677; *R.* v. *Swindon Crown Court ex p. Singh* [1984] 1 All E.R. 941.

[63] *Per* Richardson J. in *Bradford* [1982] N.Z.L.R. 611. The New Zealand Crimes Act permits the imposition of such an order only where there has been a conviction, and the order may be imposed "in addition to any other punishment." This emphasises the slightly ambiguous nature of the order.

[64] Above, n. 58.

with the consent of the Director of Public Prosecutions. The practical impact of this provision is to prevent private prosecutions,[65] since the functions of the D.P.P. are in practice to be exercised by the Crown Prosecution Service.[66] In connection with the racial hatred offences, section 27(1) provides, by contrast, that no prosecution can be brought under Part III of the Act except with by or with the consent of the Attorney-General, and this requires the personal approval of the Law Officer himself. Provisions such as these are met with increasing frequency in the criminal law, especially in politically sensitive areas of the law.[67] The power is not subject to judicial review, and it cannot be circumvented by a private individual's obtaining an injunction.[68]

The consent to a prosecution for a racial hatred offence under Part III may be couched in general terms, without the need to specify the section under which the prosecutor should proceed.[69] But a separate and specific consent is required for a conspiracy charge.[70]

Quite apart from these specific statutory provisions, the public order offences are hedged about with extremely delicate questions of prosecution policy that require to be taken into account by prosecution agencies[71]; the desirability of speed in the suppression of an incipient widespread disorder must be balanced against the majestic progress of justice and its attendant heavy penalties if it is decided to employ the more serious offences. Too hasty a use of relatively minor offences (such as obstruction of a constable or the highway), whose use may be difficult to challenge before magistrates[72] gives rise to allegations of repressive behaviour on the part of the prosecuting agencies. The use of serious offences, affording an opportunity for a jury to assess the true state of public feeling is equally readily characterised as vindictive by critics because of the heavy penalties associated

---

[65] Although the individual can bring a claim for compensation under the Riot (Damages) Act 1886 even though no prosecutions for riot have been brought in respect of the incident for which he wishes to claim. See 4–12.

[66] Prosecution of Offences Act 1985, s.1(6). Even where the D.P.P. has no specific statutory power to veto a prosecution, he has a general power to take over prosecutions and discontinue them; *Raymond* v. *Attorney-General* [1982] Q.B. 839. See now the 1985 Act, s.2(*b*).

[67] For a discussion of the subject in a wider context, see J.I.I.J. Edwards, *The Attorney-General, Politics and the Public Interest* (1984), Chap. 13. In the context of the racial hatred offences, the requirement is said to be an inhibiting factor in the effectiveness of the law; see further 9–03.

[68] *Thorne* v. *B.B.C.* [1967] 1 W.L.R. 1104, 2 All E.R. 1225.

[69] *Cain and Schollick* [1976] Q.B. 496.

[70] Criminal Law Act 1977, s.4(3); *Pearce* (1980) 72 Cr.App.R. 295. And see *McLaughlin* (1982) 76 Cr.App.R. 42 (explosive substances).

[71] See D. G. T. Williams, *Keeping the Peace* at p. 13 on the importance and pervasiveness of discretion in this area of the law. The propriety of taking such factors into account was recognised by Lord Lane C.J. in *R.* v. *Canterbury JJ., ex p. Klisiak* [1982] 1 Q.B. 398 at 415.

[72] Challenging decisions made by the police before magistrates can be difficult for a variety of reasons. Although the decisions of police are generally speaking subject to tests of reasonableness, magistrates are permitted to take into account such factors as the speed with which the policeman was required to act in deciding what was or was not reasonable; *G* v. *Chief Superintendent of Police, Stroud* [1987] Crim.L.R. 269.

with the serious offences.[73] Evidence goes stale, and after the heat has departed from the battle, a jury might well prefer to forget an event (such as the miners' strike) that had hitherto disrupted the community. The use of the serious offences may also give an impression of selectivity. These are sensitive issues of judgment that are frequently absent when the use of other areas of the criminal law is under consideration. Public order law is in this respect very much unlike other areas of the law, where by and large the criminal law is required to be utilised.[74] But the prevalence of discretion in this area might be an indication that the law suffers from what the Americans would term overbreadth.[75]

It remains to be seen what impact will be made by the new Crown Prosecution Service upon the exercise of the police discretion to arrest and prosecute. The hope has been expressed that the Service will "act as a useful filter in preventing the police bringing unnecessarily severe charges against people who should more appropriately be charged with a lesser offence."[76] Although the Code for Crown Prosecutors[77] makes no specific reference to the public order offences, it refers to a number of factors that are relevant to the public order offences. In the case of domestic disputes, the attitude of the complainant will be significant (and in the case of warring neighbours one that the prosecutor may need to resist rather than humour). Considerations such as whether the facts of the case are such that the public would consider a prosecution oppressive, the likely penalty, staleness of the evidence and the peripheral contribution of the defendant on the fringe will continue to influence the prosecutor's choice of charge in cases of group disorder.

3. INTERPRETATION

The Act as a Code

2–12   Contrary to what was said in the Queen's Speech at the opening of Parliament, the Act is not a Code of offences relating to public order law,[78] in the sense that it does not purport to constitute a complete statement of the

---

[73] At common law, riot, unlawful assembly and affray carried (in theory) life imprisonment. Now that there is a clearly structured sentencing pattern, the objections of severity will not bulk quite so large.

[74] See Glanville Williams, "Letting off the Guilty and Prosecuting the Innocent" [1985] Crim.L.R. 115, and the reply by P. Worboys, *ibid.* at 764.

[75] In the particular context of freedom of speech, see the note, "The First Amendment Overbreadth Doctrine" (1970) 88 Harv.L.R. 844. And see P. W. Low, J. C. Jeffries and R. J. Bonnie, *Criminal Law: Cases and Materials* (2nd ed., 1986), Chap. 1 for an excellent discussion of the problem.

[76] *The Times*, July 26, 1985. The new service, established under the Crown Prosecution Act 1985, is considered at length in a series of articles in the [1986] Crim.L.R. 3 *et seq.* The D.P.P. is empowered "to give, to such an extent as he considers appropriate, advice to police forces on all matters relating to police forces"; Prosecution of Offences Act 1985, s.3(2)(e).

[77] Issued under the Prosecution of Offences Act 1985, s.10. For the full text of the Code, see the L.S. Gaz. (1986) 2302.

[78] *Hansard*, H.C.Deb, November 6, 1985, vol. 86, col. 5.

law relating to this area.[79] For example, the principal offences of riot, violent disorder and affray can all be committed only by the use of "unlawful" violence, and the question whether any particular act of violence is lawful or otherwise is a matter of the general law governing self-defence, the apprehension of offenders and the prevention of crime.[80] One of the most intractable questions in public order law concerns the status of the decision in *Beatty* v. *Gillbanks*[81] as to whether or not a person commits a wrong when he does a lawful act knowing that it might cause another to commit an unlawful one. This question remains problematic even after the Act has become law, although it is clear that one of the limits to what is permissible is crossed when the actor's conduct is threatening, abusive or insulting, and amounts to an offence under section 4. The common law offence of nuisance[82] and the statutory ones of assaulting and obstructing the police in the execution of their duty[83] are not included in the Act, yet the latter of these in particular is of central importance in the maintenance of the public peace and the prevention of disorder. The opportunity was not taken to consolidate and restate large areas of public order law such as that relating to the wearing of uniforms created by the Public Order Act 1936,[84] or the offence of disruption created by the Public Meetings Act 1908. Intimidatory picketing is still dealt with in the tendentiously titled Conspiracy and Protection of Property Act 1875,[85] rather than in the new Act where (if the Act were a true code) it would more properly belong. Perhaps most significantly, the Act preserves intact the amorphous power of the constable to take action to preserve the peace as part of his constitutional duty,[86] and leaves untouched the powers of the court to impose orders binding persons over to keep the peace and be of good behaviour.[87] Untrammelled powers such as these are quite inconsistent with the spirit of codification. The new law is superimposed on the common law, rather than replacing it as a code should.

Some principles of interpretation

Even if the Act has at best weak claims to be called a code, it does seek **2–13** to make a fresh start with some of the offences, and it has a scheme of penalties wholly different from those that were available at common law.

---

[79] On what constitutes a code, see F. A. R. Bennion, *Statute Law* (2nd ed., 1983), pp. 81–84 and *Statutory Interpretation* (1984), s.233. See also A. T. H. Smith, "The Case for a Code" [1986] Crim.L.R. 285.

[80] See further below 3–10 to 3–14.

[81] (1882) 9 Q.B.D. 308.

[82] See Chap. 11; the Law Commission expressed the hope that prosecutors would not in the future use this unexpired portion of the common law; Report, para. 1.8. But this cannot, of course, bind prosecutors.

[83] See Chap. 10.

[84] Section 1; see Chap. 14.

[85] Although the opportunity was taken to extend the sentence from three months' imprisonment to six, and to confer a power of arrest; s.40(2), Sched. 2.

[86] Section 40(4).

[87] 2–10.

As it states in the preamble, it is an Act "to create new offences relating to public order." It abolishes unlawful assembly and substitutes violent disorder, thereby ridding this area of the law of the vague concept of breach of the peace; riot is in certain important respects different from the common law offence, but it retains the notion of "common purpose" from the earlier law. In one important respect, the new law is not quite like the Theft Acts 1968 and 1978, the Criminal Damage Act 1971 or the Forgery and Counterfeiting Act 1981, since the law in each of those areas had been the subject of Parliament's attention on previous occasions. Whereas the Act breaks new ground by putting the new offences into statutory form for the first time, most of the public order offences were the creatures of the courts alone.

In approaching the Act for the purpose of interpreting it, as a first step the courts should look to the words of the new statute.[88] Where there is a lack of clarity in the natural meaning of the expressions, it is permissible to turn to the old cases for guidance as to the scope of the new law, but only for the purposes of establishing the mischief at which the legislation was aimed.[89] A similar rule obtains in relation to the use of *travaux preparatoires*. The Act was proceeded by a considerable number of official studies and Reports,[90] and these may be used to ascertain the mischief at which the statute was directed where the statute is itself unclear. Where the statute merely reproduces the terminology of the old law, as it largely does with sections 4 and 5 (in the repetition of threatening, abusive or insulting, taken from the Public Order Act 1936, section 5), there is no point in relitigating unnecessarily all the issues that have previously been settled.

The respective functions of judge and jury

2–14   The respective roles of judge and jury (and in summary cases magistrates) in interpreting and applying statutes were considered by the House of Lords in the decision *Brutus* v. *Cozens*,[91] a prosecution for insulting behaviour contrary to the Public Order Act 1936, section 5. The House laid it down that where a statute uses an "ordinary" word, its meaning is a matter of fact for the magistrate or the jury. There are a number of words used in the Act that might qualify as "ordinary" words[92]; "present together" and "common purpose"[93] in the law of riot, "disorderly" in section 5, and "violence" which, although a central feature of many of the offences

---

[88] *Bank of England* v. *Vagliano Bros* [1891] A.C. 107.
[89] *Black-Clawson International* v. *Papierwerke Waldhoff-Aschaffenburg AG* [1975] A.C. 591.
[90] Discussed in para. 1–13.
[91] [1973] A.C. 854. When the case was decided, s.5 was triable either way, but was made summary only by the Criminal Law Act 1977. See Glanville Williams, "Law and Fact" [1976] Crim.L.R. 472, 532; *Text* 59. A. Briggs, "Judges, Juries and the meaning of Words" (1985) 5 L.S. 314.
[92] In *Brutus* v. *Cozens*, last note, the House gives no guidance on the question whether a particular word is to be regarded as ordinary word.
[93] Although this term, taken from the common law, might also be seen as a term of art. It is considered in 4–10.

created by the Act is not further defined.[94] If the power of the jury and magistrates to determine the scope and application of these terms were completely unfettered, there would be legal chaos; different magistrates and juries could reach different conclusions on facts that were in all material respects the same, and this offends one of the fundamental precepts of justice that like cases should be treated alike.

The potential for the mischief of uneven application that such a doctrine opens up is well illustrated by the comparison of two cases on the meaning of "insulting" decided not ten years apart. In *Williams*[95] the defendant stood outside a club for United States servicemen and handed people entering a leaflet inviting the reader to consider deserting. Some of the recipients of the leaflet appeared annoyed. In dismissing the appeal, the Divisional Court said that "it was difficult to imagine anything more likely to be insulting and to occasion a breach of the peace than an invitation to a member of the armed forces to desert." But in *Arrowsmith*[96] where the appellant had handed out leaflets outside an army centre inviting soldiers who were engaged in Northern Ireland to consider deserting, the charge of insulting behaviour was dismissed even though distribution of the leaflets amounted to an offence under the Incitement to Disaffection Act 1934. In the Court of Appeal, Lawton L.J. observed that "having regard to the decision of the House of Lords in *Brutus* v. *Cozens* it was not surprising that the justices had judged that merely handing a leaflet of this kind to a soldier did not amount to insulting behaviour under the 1936 Act." But what had the House of Lords said that could effect such a remarkable transformation? Lord Reid had said that "an ordinary sensible man knows an insult when he sees or hears it." It is more important so far as the law is concerned, to ensure that ordinary sensible men arrive at the same answer when asked the same question, and this can be achieved only if the higher courts give more guidance than they are currently prepared to offer on the meaning and application of statutory terms.

There are some constraints and controls that curb the untrammelled power of the tribunal of fact, or lend it some guidance. Even though they cannot completely obviate the risk that like cases will be not necessarily be treated the same, they go some way to reduce its likelihood.

There is a rule that magistrates may not find particular conduct to be insulting unless, in the judgment of the Divisional Court, a reasonable bench could so find.[97] But the converse is also the case, namely, that if a reasonable bench could so find, the higher court should not disrupt the

---

[94] The definition in s.8 is not really a definition at all; it extends the concept of violence to conduct that might not otherwise be encompassed. In *R.* v. *Criminal Injuries Compensation Board ex p. Clowes* [1977] 1 W.L.R. 1353, Lord Widgery C.J. says that the meaning of the expression "crime of violence" is "very much a jury point." In *R.* v. *Compensation Board ex p. Webb* [1986] Q.B. 184, this passage is cited with approval, Lawton L.J. also making express reference to *Brutus* v. *Cozens*.

[95] [1968] Crim.L.R. 563.

[96] [1975] Q.B. 678.

[97] *Bryan* v. *Robinson* [1960] 1 W.L.R. 506; *Ambrose* (1973) 57 Cr.App.R. 538. The same principle applies to "threatening" conduct; *Hudson* v. *Chief Constable, Avon and Somerset Constabulary* [1976] Crim.L.R. 451.

finding. In *Brutus* v. *Cozens* itself, the magistrates had come to the conclusion that the conduct of the defendant, who had disrupted a tennis match at Wimbledon by trespassing on the court, blowing a whistle and distributing leaflets was annoying but not insulting. The Divisional Court referred this decision back to the Magistrates with a direction to convict, but the House of Lords said that it was wrong to have done so, since the application of the statute to the facts was a question for the magistrates. In the course of his speech, Lord Reid said:

> "If it is alleged that the tribunal has reached a wrong decision there can be a question of law but only of a limited character. The question would normally be whether their decision was unreasonable in the sense that no tribunal acquainted with the ordinary use of language could reasonably reach such a decision."

If applied too literally, this might mean that the decision of the magistrates on a question of fact will be upset only where it is one that no reasonable bench of magistrates could reach. There is, however, a countervailing principle of interpretation, which is that although the meaning of ordinary words is a question of fact:

> "the meaning to be attributed to enacted words is a question of law, being a matter of statutory interpretation."[98]

If it is plain from the decision at which they have arrived that they must have proceeded on an incorrect understanding of the law, therefore, it is open to the higher court to intervene and supervise. As a general rule, for example, a word should bear the same meaning wherever it appears in the same part of the same statute. "Violence" appears in the first four sections of the Act, and if it appears that the magistrates have given the word a meaning (for example in connection with section 4) that it would be unable to bear in the context of section 2 or 3, the higher court should intervene.

When making the determination as to whether or not the magistrate's understanding of the use of language was improper for the purposes of determining whether any reasonable bench could have arrived at the result achieved, the Divisional Court is able to give guidance as to the meaning of terms. In *Parkin* v. *Norman*[99] the question was whether the conduct of a man masturbating in a public lavatory within sight of another man (who turned out to be a plain clothes policeman looking out for precisely such conduct) could be said to have insulted the other. Although it disclaimed any intention of giving a definition of "insulting," the court pointed out that an insult requires a human object, but that it does not require an intention to insult,[1] so long as the conduct in question is actually insulting. A

---

[98] *Per* Lord Scarman in *Shah* v. *Barnet London Borough Council* [1983] 2 A.C. 309 at 341. For a discussion seeking to reconcile the "ordinary words" doctrine and Lord Scarman's words, see C. T. Emery and B. Smythe, *Judicial Review* (1986) at p. 105.

[99] [1983] Q.B. 92.

[1] *Cf.* the offences under ss.4 and 5 of the Act, which appear to differ in this respect by virtue of s.6(3) 6–18 and (4) 7–09.

distinction was drawn between insulting behaviour, on the one hand, and offensive or disgusting behaviour that might cause annoyance or anger. However, the court held that the behaviour in which the defendant had engaged was "tantamount to a statement" to the effect that the defendant believed the other to be a homosexual, which the average heterosexual would regard as insulting. This test was applied in *Masterson and Another* v. *Holden*,[2] where the defendants were engaged in acts of a homosexual nature in Oxford Street in the early hours of the morning. Their conduct was witnessed and objected to by a small group of passers-by. It was held that such behaviour could be insulting because it might well be regarded by another person as conduct which insults by suggesting that the person who witnesses it would find such conduct in public acceptable. Since this may have been the Magistrates' reasoning, the court declined to interfere with the conclusion that the conduct in question was insulting.

In the Crown Court, it is open to a judge to withdraw an issue from the jury if he comes to the conclusion that, on the evidence advanced by the prosecution, a conviction would be improper. The issue might well arise under the Act over the meaning of "violence." In *Dawson*,[3] the Court of Appeal held that the meaning of the word "force" in the definition of robbery under the Theft Act 1968, section 8 had been properly left by the judge to the jury. The defendant with two others had surrounded their victim, and one of them had nudged him so that he lost his balance, and while he was unbalanced, one of the group stole the victim's wallet. Had the issue been whether or not the defendants' conduct amounted to "violence," it would have been open to the trial judge to rule that such a minor degree of force did not amount to violence. Alternatively (and this is perhaps the more likely course for the judge to adopt), he could leave the jury to say whether or not they considered that the proven force amounted to violence, and point out to them that the force must be such as would satisfy the objective tests of being such as would cause a person of reasonable firmness present to fear for his personal safety. But in appropriate cases, it would be open to the judge to rule that the degree of force proved could not amount to violence. He might, for example, hold that mere congregating in numbers is not, without more, sufficient to constitute violence.[4]

4. POWERS OF ARREST

Arrestable offences

Police powers of arrest have recently undergone a transformation in   **2–15** England and Wales as a result of the Police and Criminal Evidence Act 1984. These are vital powers in the preservation of public order, especially

---

[2] [1986] 1 W.L.R. 1017, 3 All E.R. 39 (a prosecution under s.54(13) of the Metropolitan Police Act 1839, now repealed).
[3] (1976) 64 Cr.App.R. 170.
[4] For further discussion, see 3–06.

those relating to arrest without warrant, and they will be explained here briefly.[5]

PACE creates three categories of powers of arrest. Some specified offences[6] are made arrestable either by PACE itself, or by virtue of the fact that they satisfy the conditions stipulated for being arrestable offences. The most important of these is section 24(1)(*b*), which provides that an offence is arrestable if it is such that a person over 21 could be liable to imprisonment for a period of five years or more. For this reason, riot, violent disorder and the contamination offence created by section 38 are arrestable offences by virtue of PACE.

Non-arrestable offences, for which specific provision is made

2–16   Where offences are not arrestable by virtue of PACE, they may nevertheless be made specifically arrestable by virtue of some other Parliamentary enactment. Several of the less serious offences created by the Act fall into this category; they are not arrestable by virtue of PACE, and are therefore made so by supplementary sections of the Act itself where appropriate. Arrest powers are thus provided for affray,[7] the section 4 offence,[8] and offensive conduct in certain limited circumstances.[9] For the first time, a power of arrest is conferred for the offence of using threatening words or behaviour intended or likely to stir up racial hatred.[10] Certain powers of arrest are conferred in respect of the processions offences.[11] These may be exercised only by a constable in uniform.

It should be noted that in most instances, the power of arrest is available to the constable only where he reasonably suspects that a person "is committing" the offence concerned, and this means that there is no power of arrest when the offence has been completed. But several of the offences are continuing ones—for example, failing to comply with conditions imposed on a public procession or assembly. It may also be noted that there may still be a power of arrest under the general arrest conditions provided for by PACE where the summons procedure is for one reason or another inadequate. These powers are considered in the following section.

---

[5] The leading commentaries on PACE are M. D. A. Freeman, *The Police and Criminal Evidence Act 1984* (1985), M. Zander, *The Police and Criminal Evidence Act 1984* (1985); V. Bevan and K. W. Lidstone, *A Guide to the Police and Criminal Evidence Act 1984* (1985). See also L. H. Leigh, *Police Powers in England and Wales* (2nd ed., 1985) Chaps. 2, 3 and 10; St. J. Robilliard and J. MacEwan, *Police Powers and the Individual* (1986).

[6] PACE, s.24(2) provides for powers of arrest in respect of Customs Acts offences, offences under the Official Secrets Acts 1911 and 1920, certain offences under the Sexual Offences Act 1956, the Theft Act 1968, ss.12 and 25 (taking conveyances and going equipped to steal respectively), and offences under the Public Bodies Corrupt Practices Act 1889 and Prevention of Corruption Act 1906. Other powers of arrest enumerated in sched. 2 of PACE are preserved in force by virtue of s.26(2).

[7] Section 3(6).

[8] Section 4(3).

[9] Section 5(4). See further 7–11.

[10] Section 18(3). No such power was contained in the Bill, but the Opposition pointed out the anomaly that a power was given for the very similar offence under s.4, which carried a much lighter penalty.

[11] Sections 12(7), 13(10) and 14(7).

General arrest conditions

Cases of relatively minor street disorder may trigger the operation of the 2–17 provisions of s.25 of PACE, which creates the so called "general arrest conditions." The gist of the section is that if a person is seen by a constable committing a non-arrestable offence, or one for which he has no express statutory power of arrest, and the police officer comes to the conclusion that the service of a summons would be an impracticable means of getting the offender before a court, he may rely upon the general arrest conditions. These are of such importance in the context of minor acts of public disorder that they warrant statement in full. The relevant part of the section reads:

"(3) The general arrest conditions are—
    (a) that the name of the relevant person is unknown to, and cannot be readily ascertained by, the constable;
    (b) that the constable has reasonable grounds for doubting whether a name furnished by the relevant person as his name is his real name;
    (c) that—
        (i) the relevant person has failed to furnish a satisfactory address for service; or
        (ii) the constable has reasonable grounds for doubting whether an address furnished by the relevant person is a satisfactory address for service;
    (d) that the constable has reasonable grounds for believing that arrest is necessary to prevent the relevant person—
        (i) causing physical harm to himself or any other person;
        (ii) suffering physical injury;
        (iii) causing loss of or damage to property;
        (iv) committing an offence against public decency; or
        (v) causing an unlawful obstruction of the highway;
    (e) that the constable has reasonable grounds for believing that arrest is necessary to protect a child or some other vulnerable person from the relevant person."

It may be anticipated that in practice, the power of arrest conferred under the offensive conduct provision[12] will overlap with the powers conferred by this section.

The conditions specified in paragraph (d) do not necessarily require a belief on the constable's part that the person to be arrested is about to commit an offence. Thus, for example, it would be enough that he is about to damage his own property (in the course of a matrimonial dispute, for example). The phraseology "suffering physical injury" clearly covers a great deal more than the infliction of harm upon oneself, and the section does not say (cf. Paragraph (d)(iv)) "committing an offence" of unlawful

---

[12] Section 5(4); considered in Chap. 7.

obstruction of the highway, although an unlawful obstruction will usually amount to such an offence.

Arrest for breach of the peace

2–18   In addition to the foregoing powers, the police (and citizens) have a somewhat uncertain power to arrest for breach of the peace.[13] One authority has suggested that these powers are "in eclipse"[14] because of the powers now afforded by the general arrest conditions of PACE. Section 40(4) of the Act expressly provides that nothing in the Act affects the common law powers in England and Wales to deal with or prevent a breach of the peace, and these must include the powers of arrest.[15] It may be anticipated, therefore, that the police will continue to use these powers. It must be said, however, that the conditions referred to in section 25(3)(*d*)(i), (ii) and (iii) are remarkably similar to the concept of breach of the peace as recently refined by the courts. In *Howell*[16] Watkins L.J. in the Court of Appeal defined that slippery notion as follows:

> "even in these days when affrays, riotous behaviour and other disturbances happen all too frequently, we cannot accept that there can be a breach of the peace unless there has been an act done or threatened to be done which either actually harms a person, or in his presence his property, or is likely to cause such harm, or which puts someone in fear of such harm being done."

Using that as a working definition,[17] the powers of arrest may be stated as follows: any person may arrest for a breach of the peace committed in his presence.[18] He may also arrest where, although no breach has actually taken place, he fears and has reasonable cause to believe that a breach of the peace will be committed in the immediate future.[19] He may also arrest where a breach of the peace has been committed, and where he has reasonable grounds to believe that it will be renewed if no arrest is made.[20] No

---

[13] Glanville Williams, "Arrest for Breach of the Peace" [1954] Crim.L.R. 578; "Dealing With Breaches of the Peace" (1982) 146 J.P.N. 199, 217; St. J. Robilliard and J. McEwan, *Police Powers and the Individual* (1986) p. 37; L. H. Leigh, *Police Powers in England and Wales* (2nd ed., 1985), Chap. IX.

[14] L. H. Leigh, *op. cit.* at p. 86. S.25(6) says that the section "shall not prejudice any power of arrest conferred apart from this section," which Professor Leigh interprets to mean "conferred by statute." But if it simply means "conferred by law, from whatever source" the powers are clearly preserved intact, whatever they might be.

[15] [1982] Q.B. 416, at 426.

[16] In *Richards and Leeming* (1985) 81 Cr.App.R., the Court of Appeal left open the question whether Archbold was correct in saying that the Criminal Law Act 1967 abolished all common law powers of arrest. The better view, it is submitted, is that it did that; *Podger* [1979] Crim.L.R. 524.

[17] The question of what sort of conduct constitutes a breach of the peace is further explored in 10–06.

[18] *Howell* [1982] QB. 416.

[19] *Albert* v. *Lavin* [1982] A.C. 546; *G* v. *Chief Superintendent for Stroud* [1987] Crim.L.R. 269. This may be so, even where the breach of the peace that is anticipated would not occur in the presence of the person arresting, as in *Moss* v. *McLachlan* [1985] I.R.L.R. 75.

[20] *Howell*, n. 18.

power of arrest is available where the breach of the peace has taken place, and there is no reason to believe that it will be renewed.[21]

The power is a preventive one, and the appropriate course for the arrester where no offence has been committed is to take the person arrested before the magistrates to have him bound over to keep the peace in future.[22] But there is nothing to prevent a prosecution under sections 4 or 5 of the Act, merely because the arrest was initially effected at common law, if the defendant has in addition, committed one of those offences.

[21] *Baynes* v. *Brewster* (1841) 2 Q.B. 375.
[22] See 2–10.

CHAPTER 3

VIOLENT DISORDER

1. BASIC DEFINITION OF VIOLENT DISORDER

Background to the offence

3–01   Violent disorder is a new offence, the creation of which was recommended by the Law Commission as a partial replacement for unlawful assembly.[1] The offence may be expected to become the mainstay of public order law in cases of group disorder,[2] and may now be charged where hitherto unlawful assembly and affray were employed. It may also be used in serious cases of threatening conduct involving groups, formerly prosecuted under the Public Order Act 1936, section 5, although that offence carried a much lower penalty. In its essential features, violent disorder is similar to but less serious than riot which, although it precedes violent disorder in the Act, is now an aggravated form of the new offence. The offence is intended to deal with groups of persons participating in public disorder whose conduct has gone beyond the stage of mere insults or abuse, and amounts to threats or use of violence. It covers some types of affray, but is different in that it can be committed by violence towards property as well as towards persons and is an offence of group violence, whereas affray (which can technically be committed by a single person) need not be. Serious pitched battles between rival gangs that had previously been prosecuted as affrays must now be proceeded against as violent disorder (or riot in extremely bad cases), or one of the offences against the person or property, since the penalty for affray is no longer life imprisonment but three years. Violent disorder is punishable with imprisonment for a term not exceeding five years, or on summary conviction to a term of imprisonment not exceeding six months or a fine not exceeding the statutory maximum.[3]

The offence defined

3–02   Section 2(1) provides as follows:

> "Where 3 or more persons who are present together use or threaten unlawful violence and the conduct of them (taken together) is such as would cause a person of reasonable firmness present at the scene to fear for his personal safety, each of the persons using or threatening unlawful violence is guilty of violent disorder."

Although the section defining the offence says nothing about the mental element with which it is committed, this is provided for in section 6(2) which states that

---

[1] Report, para. 5.23. The additional offence completing the replacement is created by s.4.
[2] In introducing the Bill, the Home Secretary Mr. Hurd said that "violent disorder will be used in the future as the normal charge for serious outbreaks of disorder"; H.C.Deb., vol. 89, col. 795, January 13, 1986.
[3] Section 2(5).

"A person is guilty of violent disorder or affray only if he intends to use or threaten violence or is aware that his conduct may be violent or threaten violence."

It is obvious that there will be a significant overlap between this offence and various offences against the person, especially assaults[4] and threats to property,[5] since if it can be shown that the defendant actually used or threatened violence,[6] he is almost certainly guilty of one of those offences. If it cannot be proved that he either used or threatened violence,[7] he cannot be convicted of the offence under consideration either. That being so, it is not immediately obvious that the new offence adds a great deal to the prosecutor's armoury, and the offence is more tightly defined than it needs to be in terms of the rationale just offered. The difference, as will be seen, is that whereas those specific offences require proof that the defendant intended to cause harm to a particular person or piece of property (as extensively understood in conjunction with the doctrine of transferred malice),[8] the new offence does not, because of the extended definition of violence, but can be committed by using or threatening violence towards persons or property generally.[9]

Three or more

To give effect to the element of combination that is the essence of violent   **3–03** disorder, the Act provides that there must be three or more persons present together using or threatening unlawful violence before the offence can be committed. They need not have a common purpose, or be doing acts directed at accomplishing the same object, although by virtue of section 2(1) it is their conduct "taken together" that must be assessed as being the cause of fear to bystanders. This emphasises the point that the three in combination are not simply disparate individuals, but a collective entity, acting in concert.[10]

It is not necessary that three or more should be prosecuted for the offence, so long as the court is satisfied that three or more were present together at the relevant time. If some of the participants have managed to

---

[4] See generally, Williams, *Text*, Chap. 8 on assaults by threats alone.
[5] Threats to destroy or damage property are specifically punishable under the Criminal Damage Act 1971, s.2 with ten years' imprisonment.
[6] Violence is defined in s.8 (3–07) more widely than would suffice for either assault or criminal damage, and in that sense violent disorder might have a wider ambit of application.
[7] The draft Bill differentiated between offences involving actual use of violence and the threat of it, the latter being punishable with two years' imprisonment only. But the government took the view that this created too many public order offences, and amalgamated the two proposals; White Paper, para. 3.4.
[8] *Pembliton* (1874) L.R. 2 C.C.R. 119 decided that where a person who threw a stone at his adversaries and broke a window, he was not guilty of malicious damage, and *Latimer* (1886) 17 Q.B.D 359, that if he aims a blow at one person and hits another, he would be guilty of malicious wounding. The point is discussed further below 3–15.
[9] 3–07.
[10] This mirrors the pre-Act law in cases of group violence; see *McMahon* v. *Dollard* [1965] Crim.L.R. 238; *Simcock* v. *Rhodes* (1977) 66 Cr.App.R. 192; *R* v. *Mansfield JJ. ex p. Sharkey* [1985] Q.B. 613. It must also be shown that the three were "present together"; 3–04.

escape capture or detection, the others can still be convicted.[11] However, where one or more of the group has the defence that his conduct is for one reason or another not unlawful,[12] no offence is committed if the result is that the numbers who are using or threatening the unlawful violence are reduced to two.[13] For example, if there were a street brawl involving four persons, and it emerges at the trial that two of the participants were set upon by the other two in a way that gives rise to the defence of self-defence, the two attackers are not guilty of violent disorder, although they would be guilty of affray.[14] But if there is evidence that there were other persons present using or threatening unlawful violence who are not before the court, making the total three or more, a conviction of violent disorder would be proper.

Section 6(7), requires some explanation, since it provides an apparent exception to the rule that there must be three persons present using or threatening the unlawful violence. This provides that the subsections describing the intention required for the offence "do not affect the determination for the purposes of riot or violent disorder of the number of persons who use or threaten violence." The subsection is meant to put beyond doubt the point that where a person is charged with riot or violent disorder, the mental element of the other participants is irrelevant to the question whether there were three or more using or threatening violence. So long as the court is satisfied that there were three actually using or threatening unlawful violence, the offence is committed. This seems unexceptionable, but it has the slightly odd (and complicating) effect that where the numbers are reduced because some of the participants lack the mental element for the offence, they can still count towards the quorum for these purposes, whereas if the violence that they are using is lawful, they cannot.

2. THE ESSENTIAL ELEMENTS OF GROUP DISORDER

Present together

3–04   Whether or not a group is sufficiently coherent to satisfy the requirement of presence together (which is an essential element of violent disorder and riot) is, no doubt, a mixed question of fact and law.[15] It is not wholly clear how it would apply in a case such as *Summers*,[16] a prosecution for affray. The defendant was one of a group of three men who made a revenge attack on a man in his own house. The defendant remained in his car while the other two made the attack. He was convicted of affray, and the question arises as to whether he might now be convicted of violent disorder.

---

[11] *Beach and Morris* (1909) 2 Cr.App.R. 189 at 191. The indictment could allege that the defendant engaged in violent disorder "with a person or persons unknown."

[12] Below, 3–11 to 3–14.

[13] This would seem to follow from the wording of the Act. See *Sudbury* (1700) 1 Ld. Raym. 484, 91 E.R. 1222, an old decision to the same effect.

[14] As to whether, in the absence of a separate count, there can be a conviction of affray in these circumstances, see 2–03. There certainly can be a conviction of the s.4 offence. S.7(4) (above 2–02).

[15] See 2–14 on the respective roles of judge and jury.

[16] (1972) 56 Cr.App.R. 604.

Undoubtedly, he was present together with the others in so far as he was participating in the concerted plan which they had concocted. But his presence in the car might not even have been known to the victims (the common law wife of the man attacked, and the child). It is suggested that he is not guilty of the offence of violent disorder, because of the absence of the requisite element of three who are present together. The argument is that if the actors are so well dispersed that they are not within the sight or hearing of the same hypothetical witness, no offence is committed. Another way of putting the same point might be to say that "present together" must mean present together in the same place as the others who are using or threatening the violence. However, had the defendant driven three men to the victim's house, he could have been convicted as an aider and abettor of their offence of violent disorder by virtue of the ordinary principles of complicity.

The expression appears to imply an awareness of the presence of the others using the violence, although clearly no preconceived plan is required. Nothing is said in the Act about the point, but the rationale of the group disorder offences is that it is the conduct of the group together that causes fear, and it should be a defence for the actor to say that he was unaware that he was part of a group.[17] It would certainly seem odd if the offence were to be regarded as imposing strict liability in respect of this circumstance.

The dramatic unities of time and place are clearly relevant to the question whether the actors are "present together," although they are qualified by section 2(2) which provides that "it is immaterial whether or not the 3 or more use or threaten violence simultaneously." The point of the subsection is that violent disorder (and riot), unlike many offences, are committed by single acts of violence or the utterance of a threat or series of threats within the context of a continuing event. To confine it by insisting on proof of absolute simultaneity would make the offences (especially riot) virtually impossible to prove. Rather, it is suggested, the prosecutor must show that although the threats or violence of the other participants were not committed at precisely the same time as the defendant's acts of violence, they are part of the same set of circumstances; they form part of the background against which it must be shown that the defendant acts. The element of unity is reinforced by the fact that the offence is couched in the present tense, and requires that there should be three or more present using or threatening violence at the time when the defendant does the act complained of. The purpose behind subsection 2 is simply to make it clear that the defendant's act of violence need not coincide precisely with the threats of violence of the rest of the group. Suppose that a person were to arrive at a picket line and hurl a brick over the heads of others on the picket line in the general direction of the police. It should not suffice to establish liability in him that other members of the picket line had been arrested for violent

---

[17] This point is more important in connection with the offence of riot, which requires that there should be 12 people present together.

disorder half an hour earlier, if peace and calm had been restored in the interim.

Public or private place

3–05   Although the offences created by the Act are said to be public order offences, this does not imply that they must occur in public; there is a sub-section in each of the definitions of riot,[18] violent disorder[19] and affray[20] to the effect that the respective offence "may be committed in private as well as in public places."

The justification for this is that the gist of the offence in each case consists in causing alarm to bystanders, and these may be present whether the offence is committed in a public or a private place. This certainly clarifies and simplifies the law, but when it is taken in conjunction with the point that, in respect of each offence there is also a provision that "no person of reasonableness need actually be, or be likely to be, present at the scene,"[21] it will be apparent that the public order character of the offences is greatly diminished, and may be almost entirely absent in some of its applications.

That said, however, there is much to be said for getting rid of the distinction between offences in public and private places where the essence of the offence is the use or threat of violence. There is no very good case for saying that people should be free to use or threaten violence merely because they happen to be on private premises, or even in a dwelling. Drawing a line between public and private places has in different contexts proved to be troublesome and technical.[22] Clearly riots at private clubs, or caused by gatecrashers at a private party should come within the scope of offences against public order. Yet such persons might be exempt if it were to be provided that the offences could take place in public only. The Law Commission did not spell out its policy in its draft Bill, taking the view that further definition was unnecessary once it had been decided that the offences could be committed in any place. But to foreclose any argument that might be based on the old common law offences, the point is made explicitly in the Act.

Different considerations arise where the conduct challenged does not consist of the use of violence, but is threatening, abusive or insulting. Such conduct does not usually pose a major threat to public order, and if it takes place in a domestic situation, there are grounds for saying that it ought to be excluded from liability.[23]

---

[18] Section 1(5).
[19] Section 2(4).
[20] Section 3(5).
[21] Sections 1(4), 2(3) and 3(4) respectively. This element of the offence is considered further below 3–09, 4–05.
[22] See *e.g.* Chap. 13, offensive weapons.
[23] Notwithstanding the argument in the text, the Act does in fact now say that the lesser offences are also capable of commission in public or in private. See further below, 6–15 and 7–08—the domestic dwelling exception.

3. VIOLENCE

Violence defined

The element of violence is common to the offences of riot,[24] affray,[25]   **3–06**
and the section 4 offence,[26] and its meaning is therefore critical to a proper
understanding of the scope of the law. Violence replaces the old concept of
breach of the peace, whose precise content was (and still is) somewhat
vague[27] but which was recently interpreted by the Court of Appeal to have
violence as its principal component.[28] It is possible that the precise meaning might diverge from one context to another,[29] although there is a strong
case for saying that the same word should not bear a different meaning in
different sections of the same Act. Its general features can conveniently be
considered at this point. Violence is not further defined in the Act itself,
although section 8 extends the ordinary meaning of the term for the purposes of the Act. The extended definition will be discussed in the next section.

According to the Oxford English Dictionary, violence means "the exercise of physical force so as to inflict injury on or damage to persons or property," and the Law Commission accepted that this is its primary meaning.[30]
To that one might add conduct that is intended to have such results. There
is a difference between force and violence, and the Act has chosen the
more restricted of the two terms. It has been said that a person uses force if
he "applies any energy to [an] obstacle with a view to removing it."[31] Violence has connotations of vigorous hostility and aggression that are not
necessarily a feature of force. Violence involves a display or threat of force
that would be likely in itself to dissuade a person of reasonable fortitude
from offering lawful resistance.

In a slightly different context, the Law Commission has expressed the
view that the application of any force to the person of another will almost
automatically amount to violence.[32] In relation to the public order
offences, it may be doubted whether this is sufficient, quite apart from the
objective considerations by which the notion of violence is to be measured
in the Act. The ritual trials of strength involved in pushing and shoving on
a picket line or at a demonstration may be force, but it may be doubted
whether they really constitute violence.

Another difficulty in the interpretation of the concept of violence is
whether mere presence in large numbers can amount to violence. This was

[24] Chap. 4.
[25] Chap. 5.
[26] Chap. 6.
[27] Chap. 10.
[28] *Howell* [1982] Q.B. 416. See Chap. 10.
[29] Violence towards property is expressly excluded from the ambit of affray, which is essentially the act of fighting in public; s.8(*a*).
[30] Report, para. 5.31.
[31] *Swales* v. *Cox* [1981] Q.B. 849.
[32] Law Commission No. 76, *Report on Conspiracy and Criminal Law Reform* (1976) H.C.
176, para. 2.61. The Commission must be taken to have meant that if a person applied
force to another with the intention of securing entry, his conduct would amount to violence.

a question that had puzzled Parliament on a previous occasion, when the Law Officers expressed the opinion that such conduct did not in itself amount to violence,[33] although it may well amount to intimidation.[34]

The extended definition of violence

3–07 The meaning of violence is spelled out further in section 8, the relevant part of which reads as follows:

> " 'violence' means any violent conduct, so that–
> (a) except in the context of affray, it includes violent conduct towards property as well as violent conduct towards persons, and
> (b) it is not restricted to conduct causing or intended to cause injury or damage but includes any other violent conduct (for example, throwing at or towards a person a missile of a kind capable of causing injury which does not hit or falls short)."

Several aspects of this definition require consideration.

That Parliament should vouchsafe that "violence means any violent conduct" is as remarkable as it is unhelpful; who would have doubted it? Violence is in its ordinary usage customarily employed to refer to violence towards persons rather than things, so the express extension clarifies what might otherwise have been a doubtful point. Property is not further defined, but is a well-recognised civil law concept, most unlikely to give rise to any difficulties of interpretation in this connection. It is, in effect, anything that is capable of being the subject of ownership, and can include virtually any tangible thing, including living things such as animals. A person who attacked a police horse on a picket line could, therefore, be found guilty of this offence.

Missile throwing is specifically included as an example of violence, by imposing what is in effect strict liability as to the consequences of what is done. The Law Commission chose to proceed in this way[35] because with such conduct it is extremely difficult to prove what (if any) damage to persons or property was actually caused, and what was intended. If a person throws a missile from the heart of a mass picket in the general direction of the police or persons crossing the picket line, it may be very difficult to prove that the missile actually hit anybody. The offences against persons and property are therefore almost impossible to employ in such circumstances, even though the missile hurler is taking considerable risks that he will hit and injure somebody or something. Nor will the law of attempts to commit the specific offences remedy this defect, since they generally require proof of intention (rather than recklessness), and that too may be difficult to establish against a person who asserts in court that he was simply engaging in an act of random violence. Since the conduct might still

---

[33] See E. J. Griew, *The Criminal Law Act 1977* (1978) 45/7. In *News Group Newspapers Ltd. v. SOGAT '82* [1986] I.R.L.R. 32, the view was taken that mere abuse, shouting and swearing by pickets at a demonstration does not amount to a threat of violence.

[34] And might, as such, be an offence under the Conspiracy and Protection of Property Act 1875, s.7. B. Prichard, *Squatting* (1981) at p. 76.

[35] Report, para. 5.31.

be regarded as violent irrespective of the consequences that can be proved to ensue, it was decided to frame a provision showing that there could be violence even though it could not be proved that the person intended to cause a particular consequence. At a football match, for example, a person might be seen to throw an object in to the crowd, and it is virtually impossible for the policeman who sees him do so to be sure that it hit somebody when it landed. But there is a very real chance that it would have done so, and ought to be regarded as violence. It is, perhaps, unfortunate that an important part of the mental element of the offence[36] should appear as part of the definition of "violence."

The Law Commission says that "the conduct must be such that it can be regarded as violence towards persons or property and the jury must be sure that it was of such a character."[37] To achieve this, the Act builds in the requirement that the conduct must at least be capable of causing injury. The Law Commission instances wielding a lethal instrument or discharging a firearm in the direction of another—throwing a paper dart or a ping pong ball would be insufficient. But nails, coins, or ordinary darts would be included. Inevitably, there will be marginal cases. Can eggs, or rotten fruit, for example, be regarded as being missiles "of a kind capable of causing injury?"

The definition of violence affords a rare use of the expression "for example" in legislation.[38] This appears to invite the courts to reason by analogy, a technique that is not generally thought to be proper in the criminal law context, since it enables the courts to engage in lawmaking rather than interpretation, which is more properly their function.[39] The example given makes no reference to throwing missiles at property, and the question then arises whether throwing fire-bombs and other dangerous weapons at property constitutes violence. Plainly, such conduct comes within the extended conception of violence, and is therefore included. A can of paint thrown at a political figure is certainly capable of damaging the target's clothes, and that is probably sufficient "injury" for the purposes of the offence. But it is suggested that "violence" requires more than the "damage" that will suffice to ground a charge of criminal damage. It has been held, for example, that grass can be damaged by trampling it down.[40] To regard such conduct as violence would be to widen the scope of the offences under consideration far beyond what Parliament might have contemplated. In relation to property, something more than force is required. To open a door by turning the handle might be regarded as force, but it should not be regarded as violence.[41]

---

[36] Considered more fully in 3–07.

[37] Report, para. 5.33.

[38] This has been used in other legislation; see *e.g.* Company Securities (Insider Dealing) Act 1985, s.6(4); Merchant Shipping (Liner Conferences) Act 1982, ss.3(2)(*c*) and 5.

[39] H. L. Packer, *The Limits of the Criminal Sanction* (1969) at p. 88–91.

[40] *Gayford* v. *Chowder* [1898] 1 Q.B. 316.

[41] See Smith and Hogan, p. 754. And see J. C. Smith, *Law of Theft*, (5th ed., 1984), p. 76. In *Re an Arbitration between Calf and the Sun Insurance Company* [1920] 1 K.B. 336, the Court of Appeal held that the words "forcible and violent" in an insurance policy included sliding back a lock catch with a sharp instrument.

Threats of violence

3–08   It will be noted that the actual use of violence is not required for the offence of violent disorder. A threat of it is sufficient. This is not what was proposed by the Law Commission, which would have distinguished between threats of violence and its actual use. But the government took the view that this would lead to an unnecessary proliferation of separate public order offences. It also felt that the proposal might have had the invidious effect of requiring different members of a single incident to be tried by different courts.[42] If the threatening offence were triable summarily only and some members of the gang could be shown to have used violence, it would have been necessary to try the latter group on indictment separately. This may not properly reflect the gravity of the group's behaviour, although the distinction between those who can be proved to have used the violence and the more peripheral participants can and should be reflected in sentence.

What sort of behaviour constitutes a threat of violence as opposed to its actual use? Although this will usually be a show of force accompanied by gestures and conduct, it seems clear that a threat can be uttered by words alone.[43] But to be guilty of the offence by threats alone, it is suggested, there must be some evidence that the person uttering them is prepared to take some action to put his threats into effect.[44] It is not always easy to distinguish between genuine threats, and ritualistic or rhetorical utterances that the speakers have no intention of carrying on to effect. Vigorous abuse on a picket line, for example, even if accompanied by fist waving, should not be regarded as a threat of violence, although it may be threatening behaviour for the purposes of one of the lesser offences.[45]

The section does not make it plain whether or not threats of future violence are within its ambit. What about the threat "we'll get you when you get home, you bastard," shouted from behind a police cordon on the picket line? This would not be an offence under the less serious offence created by section 4,[46] since the victim there must fear the use of "immediate" unlawful violence, and it would be anomalous if the speaker could nevertheless be convicted of the far more serious offence. It is suggested that it should not be an offence under the section currently under discussion either. The section is couched in the present tense, and requires that the hypothetical person present should fear for his safety. It involves no straining of the words of the section therefore to say that even if the language used by the persons threatening is such that it causes a person to fear that violence may be used against him in the future, no offence is committed under this section.

---

[42] White Paper, para. 3.4.
[43] *Cf.* s.3(3), which provides that threats alone cannot amount to an affray.
[44] But see *Logdon* v. *D.P.P.* [1976] Crim.L.R. 121.
[45] *News Group Newspapers Ltd.* v. *SOGAT '82* [1986] I.R.L.R. 32.
[46] Chap. 6.

Such as would cause a person of reasonable firmness present to fear for his safety

The public order element of each of the offences is intended to be main-   **3–09** tained by the requirement that the violence used must be such that the con- duct would have caused a person of reasonable firmness present at the scene to fear for his personal safety. In assessing this, the bystander views the three as a collective entity, rather than as individuals. It is the conduct of them taken together that must be assessed for these purposes. But the bystander is a hypothetical one; it is sufficient that he would be given *cause* to fear if he were present. This follows from the fact that, although the offences created by the Act are essentially public order offences, the Act[47] makes it plain that the actual presence of a bystander is not required in any of the offences of violent disorder, riot or affray. It reads:

"No person of reasonable firmness need actually be, or be likely to be, present at the scene."

The presence or absence of a bystander is thus not a part of the definition of the offence so much as a measure of the violence being used. If a person had been present, he would have had reason to fear for his personal safety. A number of comments may be made.

Section 2(1) (and the equivalent definitional sections for riot and affray—sections 1(1) and 3(1) respectively) appear to be ambiguous; they do not say the the bystander would be frightened "*if he were* present" at the scene of the disorder, which would be more appropriate for the hypoth- etical test that the Act seeks to establish. The common law on the question whether or not a person was required actually to be present at the scene of the disorder for riot, unlawful assembly and affray was somewhat uncer- tain.[48] It might be argued that, in the light of this, whatever the intention of the framers of the Act might have been, the draftsman has not carried their intention into effect. Against this, however, it must be pointed out that the section speaks of violence that "would cause," and not "does cause," and this points to the use of the bystander as a hypothetical measure. Section 2(3) is meant to put the point beyond argument, but it is perhaps unfortu- nate that the courts will have to read in to the earlier subsections words that are only there by implication when their inclusion would have made the meaning of the section more readily apparent.

The test involves the jury in speculation as to what a person would have felt had he been present at the scene. Generally, there will have been wit- nesses to the disorder (usually the police) who will be able to attest to their reactions to what they saw. But the test that the jury must apply is a hypothetical one of what a person of reasonable firmness would have felt, rather than what actually was felt by persons present. Evidence given by those present that they were alarmed or frightened by what they saw may

---

[47] See also ss.1(4) in relation to riot, and 3(4) in connection with affray.

[48] The Act treats the presence or absence of bystanders as being a common element to each of the new statutory offences, whereas the common law was uncertain, and may well have dif- fered as between riot, affray and unlawful assembly. It appeared that the common law of riot required the presence of at least one terrified bystander. The absence of actual terror

nevertheless assist the jury in coming to a conclusion about what degree of violence was actually employed.

The hypothetical bystander must fear for his personal safety. If he fears only that property will be damaged, the test is not satisfied. The Act also makes it clear that there must be fear for his own safety, and not that of a third person. These restrictions may not greatly limit the scope of the offence. A person of reasonable firmness might feel the need to protect property (especially if it is his own) or to go to the defence of a third party (especially if the person threatened is a friend or a member of his own family). In such a situation, fear for another or for property might readily be converted into fear for himself.

The standard to be employed requires the jury to speculate about the likelihood that the witness would himself be drawn into the mêlée. If the circumstances are such that there is no prospect of bystanders being drawn into the fracas (it might be asked), what justification is there for treating the event as a breach of public order? The phraseology adopted by section 2(1) is ambiguous. It might mean that the bystander would fear for his safety if he were the object of the violence, or if he were to intervene to seek to prevent the damage to property of persons, or if he were merely present. On the other hand, it might mean that the jury are expected to make some sort of assessment as to the likelihood that the bystander really would become embroiled if he were present. Suppose the circumstances were such that the hypothetical bystander could simply walk away from the incident, as most sensible bystanders would be likely to do?[49] For example, suppose a group of men become involved in a fight in the car park of a public house just after closing time. Other customers leaving the pub can see what is going on, but the circumstances are such that it is clear that only the rival gangs are involved. They do not in fact fear for their personal safety.

---

was probably the reason why the charges of riot were dropped in *Coney* (1882) 8 Q.B.D. 534 (see Wise, *The Law Relating to Riots and Unlawful Assemblies* (4th ed., 1907), p. 41). See also *Phillips* (1842) 2 Mood 252, 169 E.R. 100; *sub nom Langford* (1842) C. and Mar. 602, 174 E.R. 653. The formulation of the common law definition of riot in *Field* v. *Metropolitan Police Receiver* [1907] 2 K.B. 853 refers to "at least one person present," and this was followed in *Munday* v. *Metropolitan Police District Receiver* [1949] 1 All E.R. 337. In *Kamara* [1974] A.C. 104, 115–116, Lord Hailsham implies that the presence of "innocent third parties" is required. *Archbold*, para. 25–15, criticises this, offering the view that *London & Lancashire Fire Insurance Co.* v. *Bolands* [1924] A.C. 836 is authority to the contrary. And see Lord Goddard C.J. in *Sharp* [1957] 1 Q.B. 552; "if disturbances such as necessitated the passing of the Public Order Act 1936 should occur again or if there were a repetition of the Trafalgar Square riots which took place towards the end of the last century when most of the club windows in Pall Mall were smashed by an angry mob it would seem to be superfluous if someone had to go into the witness box and say that he or some passers-by felt, or appeared, afraid or apprehensive." But this may have been an observation about proof, rather than a description of the ingredients of the offence. The matter is discussed by Brownlie [1965] Crim.L.R. 484. And see on this point *Devlin* v. *Armstrong* [1971] N.I.L.R. 13 at 38. So far as the law of affray was concerned, the point was settled as recently as *Attorney-General's Refce (No. 3 of 1983)* [1985] 1 Q.B. 242, arising from the decision in *Farnill* [1982] Crim.L.R. 38, where it was held that it was not necessary that there should be an actual bystander, or even that one should be likely, where the affray took place in public.

[49] A point made by the Chief Justice in the *Attorney-General's Refce* last note.

Is this violent disorder, or affray? The answer, it is suggested, is that it would be either, depending on whether the jury decide that the other ingredients of the offence are present. It is plain that the bystander is hypothetical; no bystander need be present. If the bystander were to attempt to use that particular part of the car park, as he is entitled to do, he would certainly be in fear for his personal safety. The fact that he feels the need to depart from the scene is evidence that he is in fear for his personal safety. Furthermore, once violence has broken out, it has a tendency to spread as bystanders seek to put an end to it, or are perhaps encouraged to join in. It is therefore no defence for those engaged in the disorder to argue that the bystanders could have left the scene, and had no reason to fear for their personal safety for that reason.

Who is a person of reasonable firmness? The Act does not speak of the ubiquitous "reasonable man," but identifies the aspect of that rather odious character that is of significance for testing the degree of violence used. It remains to be seen whether judges will feel that juries will need guidance as to who is a person of reasonable firmness, but if they do decide to explain his qualities, they might consider the words of Alderson B. in *Vincent*[50] which, for all their antiquity, have the ring of common sense about them. In directing the jury as a result of disturbances arising from the Chartists demonstrations, he said:

> "the alarm must not be merely such as would frighten any foolish or timid person, but must be such as would alarm a person of reasonable firmness and courage."

Presence at a scene of disorder

The Law Commission took the view that complicity questions caused no **3–10** particular difficulties in connection with the public order offences.[51] Technically, the ordinary rules of aiding and abetting apply,[52] but their application in connection with scenes of disorder represented by riots, violent disorders and affrays may require particular care; there is a real danger that where the essence of an offence is violence in combination, a person's mere presence on the scene may implicate him in a way that presence at the scene of other offences might not do. In the case of riot, for example, to establish guilt as a principal, it must be shown that the defendant actually uses violence.[53] To convict another as an aider and abettor of the rioter, it should be necessary to prove that he encouraged the other to use violence, and intended to do so. In the case of violent disorder, by contrast, the mere utterance of threats suffices to attract liability, and it will be sufficient for the prosecutor to prove that a person not himself uttering threats was encouraging others to do so.

In truth, it may often be extraordinarily difficult for a policeman in the heat of a mêlée to identify a particular defendant as being the person who

---

[50] (1839) 9 C.& P. 91. 173 E.R. 754.
[51] Report, para. 75.
[52] Glanville Williams, *Text*, p. 350; Smith and Hogan, p.124.
[53] Section 1(1).

performed an act amounting to encouragement. What is the impact of the defendant's presence on the scene when he cannot himself be proved to have been uttering threats? In *Bonsall*,[54] it was established that the defendants were present at the scene of a large picket of some 500 to 700 people, and offences of threatening, abusive and insulting behaviour contrary to the Public Order Act 1936, section 5 and watching and besetting[55] were committed. On appeal against conviction for the watching and besetting offences, the Crown Court Judge said that "if they chose to gather in such overwhelming numbers and were either themselves party to the savage utterances that there were, or by remaining there when they could have drifted away, lent by their presence a sharpened edge to the insults that are hurled, and above all the terror that their very numbers convey" the conclusion that each was here besetting was a proper one. To what extent can this be regarded as a statement of principle capable of being generalised to the other offences of group disorder?

The principles were established in the old prize fighting case where it was held that in a prosecution for assault,[56] the defendant's presence on the scene was evidence from which an intention to encourage could be inferred. In that case, the jury had been directed that mere presence, unexplained, at the prize fight, was conclusive proof of the defendants' encouragement. By a majority, the Court for Crown Cases Reserved held that this was a misdirection. Cave J. stated the law as follows:

> "Where presence may be entirely accidental, it is not even evidence of aiding and abetting. Where presence is prima facie not accidental it is evidence, but no more than evidence for the jury."

It has been held, somewhat indulgently perhaps, that presence remains no more than evidence even when it is accompanied by a secret intention to help if necessary, one of the participants in an affray.[57] So long as the defendant does not communicate his intention, he commits no offence.

On the other hand, where there is evidence that the defendant was deliberately present at the scene of the disorder, this does without more present a prima facie case against him on a charge of threatening behaviour contrary to section 5 of the 1936 Act. In *Parrish* v. *Garfitt*[58] the defendants were six members of a group of football supporters numbering about 150 in total. The crowd was seen proceeding down the road for a distance of some 1,100 yards, gesticulating and chanting. Bottles were thrown from the crowd, and the windows of three adjoining houses were broken by a bottle, a stone and an iron bar, and a car was overturned. About 116 members of the group (including the six appellants) were arrested, but there was no evidence of "identification of the various acts which took place," meaning

---

[54] [1985] Crim.L.R. 150. And see *Gedge* [1978] Crim.L.R. 167; *Maile* v. *McDowell* [1980] Crim.L.R. 586; *Mansfield JJ. ex p. Sharkey* [1985] Q.B. 613; *Smith* v. *Reynolds and ors* [1986] Crim.L.R. 559.
[55] Considered further, Chap. 12.
[56] *Coney* (1882) 8 Q.B.D. 534. And see *Clarkson* [1971] 1 W.L.R. 402, 55 Cr.App.R. 445.
[57] *Allan* [1965] 1 Q.B. 130. And see *Allen* v. *Ireland* [1984] 1 W.L.R. 903, 79 Cr.App.R. 206.
[58] [1984] 1 W.L.R. 911.

presumably that it could not be shown that any of the defendants was individually responsible for the damage caused. The justices also found that the defendants "would have had ample opportunity of disassociating themselves from the group." On appeal by way of case stated, it was argued that the magistrates fell into the error of concluding that because the defendants were members of a disorderly and threatening group, they must necessarily be guilty of the offence of threatening behaviour contrary to the Public Order Act 1936, section 5. The Divisional Court concluded that there was ample evidence that the justices were fully conscious of the fact that they could not in this instance convict the group and then impose a penalty on each individual member, unless they were satisfied that that individual had played some part in the threatening behaviour, or, at the very least, by some means encouraged the other participants.

It is, therefore, necessary to examine the precise elements of the offence with which the particular defendant has been charged. Where the offence is one of intimidation, as in *Bonsall*, mere presence as part of an intimidatory group may be sufficient. But for the offences under this Part of the Act, it must be shown that the defendant was at least encouraging others to engage in the violent or threatening conduct.

4. Unlawful Violence

The requirement of unlawfulness

Throughout the Act, the term "violence" is qualified by the epithet 3–11 "unlawful."[59] Although the use of this all-purpose expression has been criticised as being pleonastic,[60] it may be seen in this context as a convenient reminder to the courts that the statute is to be construed against the background of statutory provisions and the common law justifying the use of force in certain circumstances; the explicit reference to illegality makes it plain that it is intended that the general defences to criminal behaviour should apply in this context. Thus, the law relating to self-defence or the prevention of crime or disorder is available to explain and justify violence in appropriate circumstances. It is proposed here to deal with each of the possible defences that may be available to indicate briefly how they should apply in the public order context.

It should be noted that, although, the requirement of unlawfulness is made a constituent part of the crime, it is not for the prosecutor to prove as part of his case in the sense that he must at the outset negate all the defences that the defendant might seek to raise. There is an evidential burden on the defendant to raise the issue, and once he has satisfied that, for the prosecutor to satisfy the jury beyond reasonable doubt that the defence was not in truth relied upon.[61]

---

[59] Section 1(1) riot; s.2(1) violent disorder; s.3(1) affray; s.4(1) fear or provocation of violence.
[60] See Glanville Williams, *C.L.G.P.* para. 13.
[61] *Spight* [1986] Crim.L.R. 817. See generally, Glanville Williams, *Text*, Chap. 2.

Prevention of crime

3–12 The official use of force to prevent or quell disorder is subject to regulation by the criminal law.[62] Whether or not the use of force (including fatal force) and the deployment of potentially lethal weapons such as plastic baton rounds is justified is subject to the provisions of (1) the Criminal Law Act 1967, section 3. This provides that:

> "a person may use such force as is reasonable in the circumstances in the prevention of crime, or in effecting or assisting in the lawful arrest of offenders or suspected offenders or of persons unlawfully at large."

If a posse of policemen is engaged in effecting an arrest or superintending a picket, it might well be that the ingredients of the one or other of the offences appear to be made out. But it could not, (or certainly should not) be thought that the offence of violent disorder is committed, since the violence that they may be forced to employ is justified by the section quoted.

Self defence

3–13 The availability of the defence of self-defence to any criminal charge is governed by the common law. Parliament has never sought to regulate the matter.[63] The principles that have been established in connection with offences of assault and homicide are therefore equally applicable to the public order offences. This is one area where the old law of riot, unlawful assembly and affray is of continuing significance.

  The limits on the law of self-defence can be stated broadly as follows: before a person can properly use force, the use or threat of force must be necessary, and the amount of force used must be proportionate to the harm threatened.[64] Since one of the purposes of the criminal law is to prevent people from taking the law into their own hands, it might be expected that it should not be a defence to the more serious offences involving a number of participants. This was indeed the common law. To the general rule that unlawful assembly or riot could not be justified on the ground that it was committed in self-defence or defence of property, the common law allowed a strictly limited exception: a man might assemble his friends in defence of

---

[62] See *Lynch* v. *Fitzgerald* [1938] I.R. 382. The issue of the use of official force is not specifically dealt with in this book, although it is a subject of considerable importance, particularly in the public order context. See H. Beynon, "The Ideal Civic Condition" [1986] Crim.L.R. 580 and 647 for a discussion of police use of force. To oversimplify, the police are in general liable for any excessive use of force, in the same way as the ordinary citizen. See also s.117 PACE, which says that where that Act confers a power on a constable, the officer may use reasonable force, if necessary, in the exercise of the power.

[63] It has been argued that the Criminal Law Act 1967, s.3, which permits the use of force in the prevention of crime, has effectively abrogated the old rules of the common law regulating the use of protective force; C. Harlow, "Self-Defence: Public Right or Private Privilege" [1974] Crim.L.R. 528; Smith and Hogan, p. 326. But this view is questionable. See Glanville Williams, *Text* (1st ed.,) p. 455. The C.L.R.C. has examined the law of self-defence, and concluded that s.3 will apply to most cases of self-defence, since self-defence is generally exercised to prevent what is incidentally a crime; 14th Report, *Offences Against the Person* Cmnd. 7844 (1980) para. 281.

[64] Glanville Williams, *Text*, Chap. 23.

his house[65] or in defence against violence threatened by persons who would break into his house, but not against violence to be committed elsewhere.[66] It is suggested that these principles are equally applicable to the new offences, and that it will be a very rare case where it could be necessary for 12 (in the case of riot) or even three (in the case of violent disorder) or three to assemble with the object of using or threatening violence, given that there are other methods of dispute resolution available.

At common law, there was a rule that before a person could avail himself of the defence of self-defence, he was under a duty to retreat, or at least he was required to show an unwillingness to fight.[67] But the law is not that it is necessary to demonstrate such an unwillingness; rather, the display of unwillingness is a factor to be taken into account in deciding whether it was necessary to use force at all, and, if so, whether the degree of force used was reasonable. "If the defendant is proved to have been attacking or retaliating or revenging himself, then he was not truly acting in self-defence. Evidence that the defendant tried to retreat or tried to call off the fight may be a cast-iron method of casting doubt on the suggestion that he was the attacker or the retaliator or the person trying to revenge himself. But it is not by any means the only method of doing that."[68]

It would seem from this that if a person finds himself attacked, or thinks that he is about to be attacked, either singly or as one of a group, he must look for ways to extricate himself from the fracas as far as is compatible with the right (and need) to protect himself. It may occasionally be the case that it is necessary for him to "get his retaliation in first" in the memorable words of the football coach,[69] although the circumstances in which a jury will conclude that it was necessary for him to use force in such circumstances are likely to be quite exceptional. He may not pass from being the person aggrieved to being the one who is retaliating under the guise of acting in self-defence. Lord Goddard C.J. said as much in the context of affray in *Sharp and Johnson*.[70] If a person defends himself, and then passes on to the attack, he forfeits the right to self-defence. He must make good his escape when he can, allowing always for the fact that it might well be dangerous for him to do so.

The availability of the defence of self-defence where the defendant labours under a mistaken belief that he is being or is about to be attacked is in a state of some doubt. It is unclear whether any mistake will suffice, or, by contrast, whether the mistake must be a reasonable one. In *Gladstone*

---

[65] But not, apparently, his close—*R.* v. *Bishop of Bangor* (1796) 26 St.Tr. 463 525–526. This is, presumably, no longer the law; the Bishop would be as free (or unfree) as any of his subjects.

[66] *Russell on Crime* (12th ed., 1964), p. 257. And see E. Wise, *The Law Relating to Riots and Unlawful Assemblies* (4th ed., 1907), at p. 47; the mere fact that the common purpose was a lawful one would not prevent a gathering intent on using force from being unlawfully riotous.

[67] *Julien* [1969] 1 W.L.R. 839, 2 All E.R. 856; *McInnes* [1971] 1 W.L.R. 1600, 3 All E.R. 295, 55 Cr.App.R. 551.

[68] *Bird* [1985] 1 W.L.R. 816, 820, 2 All E.R. 513 at 516 *per* Lord Lane C.J.

[69] And in the legal context, see *Devlin* v. *Armstrong* [1971] N.I.L.R. 13.

[70] [1957] 1 Q.B. 552.

Williams[71] Lord Lane C.J. expressed the view that the facts must be judged on the basis as the defendant himself actually believed them to be, rather than as he reasonably believed them to be. The Lord Chief Justice said:

> "The reasonableness or unreasonableness of the defendant's belief is material to the question of whether the belief was held by the defendant at all. If the belief was in fact held, its unreasonableness, so far as guilt or innocence is concerned, is neither here nor there. It is irrelevant. Were it otherwise, the defendant would be convicted because he was negligent in failing to recognise that the victim was not consenting or that a crime was not being committed and so on. In other words, the jury should be directed first of all that the prosecution have the burden or duty of proving the unlawfulness of the defendant's actions; secondly, if the defendant may have been labouring under a mistake as to the facts, he must be judged according to his mistaken view of the facts; thirdly, that is so whether the mistake was, on an objective view, a reasonable mistake or not."

These remarks have been referred to as *obiter* by prosecuting counsel (with the apparent approval of the Court of Appeal) in one case.[72] But the reasoning offered by Lord Lane is compelling,[73] and if a defendant on a charge of violent disorder or affray were to raise a claim that he thought that he was being attacked, or that he was about to be, and that he therefore believed that it was necessary for him to resort to violence, it is not obvious why he should not have the defence.

Self help

3–14   In certain circumstances, the law permits the use of force by way of self help. For example, a displaced residential occupier (and those assisting him) do not commit the offence of using violence for the purpose of securing entry, by seeking to repossess property from which the displaced residential occupier has been excluded.[74] It would seem anomalous if Parliament's clear purpose of exempting the displaced residential occupier were rendered ineffective because the use of any violence happened to be an offence under some other statutory provision, or was otherwise contrary to common law. But the extent of the privilege to use force or violence for such purposes is obscure.[75] If the persons against whom force is used are themselves committing a criminal offence, the Criminal Law Act 1967, section 3 applies.[76] But where they are not, there is difficulty. At common law, it was no defence to a charge of riot that the common purpose hap-

---

[71] (1984) 78 Cr.App.R. 276, at 281.
[72] *Asbury* [1986] Crim.L.R. 258. See also *Jackson* [1985] R.T.R. 257.
[73] It is also in line with the recommendations of the C.L.R.C. as to what the ideal law should be, as Lord Lane himself observed; 14th Report, para. 72(*a*). And see *Sears* v. *Broome* [1986] Crim.L.R. 461; *Fisher* [1987] Crim.L.R. 334.
[74] Under the Criminal Law Act 1977 s.6(3)(*a*), which affords the defence where the defendant "or any person on whose behalf he was acting" is a displaced residential occupier.
[75] See E. J. Griew, *Criminal Law Act 1977*, (1978) p. 45/6.
[76] See 3–12.

pened to be a lawful one. The underlying reason for this, as Wise puts it, is that:

> "the obvious policy of the law is to prevent any interruption to the pursuits of the community at large by violence and tumult under whatever pretence, and to restrain individuals from taking the law into their own hands to redress their private grievances to the great risk of dangerous consequences.[77] Thus, for a number of persons to abate a common nuisance e.g. to destroy an unlawful enclosure, is legal, but it must be done in a peaceable manner, so that there is no breach of the peace."[78]

The policy of which Wise speaks is as important today as it was when he wrote. But if the law were that there were no claim of right, or that entitlement to use force ceased as soon as violence was used, it would render the defence nugatory. The matter was considered by the Court of Appeal in *R v. Chief Constable of Devon and Cornwall ex p. Central Electricity Generating Board*,[79] but somewhat inconclusively so. A group of protesters were disrupting the work of the C.E.G.B., a statutory authority which was attempting to survey a site for its suitability as a nuclear power station. The farmer on whose land the work was to take place objected, but an injunction was sought to restrain him (and his neighbours) from obstructing the work. Other protesters continued with their campaign of "passive resistance," which was unlawful[80] but not arrestable. The Chief Constable took the view that no breach of the peace was likely to result from this campaign, and refused to intervene, and the Board sought an order of mandamus to compel him to assist. Had the protesters been trespassers, and had the farmer wished to get rid of them, there would have been little difficulty; the farmer would clearly have had the right to use force to eject the protesters as trespassers.[81] But they were not; they were present with the farmer's apparent connivance.[82] The Court unanimously held that the C.E.G.B. nevertheless had a right to use self-help to remove the protesters. Since the exercise of this right might well give rise to breaches of the peace, the police would have ample justification for intervening. Although the courts would not require a Chief Constable to deploy his forces in one

---

[77] Citing Hawkins P.C., Vol. II, Bk. 1, c. 65, s.7; *Vincent* (1839) 9 C.& P. 91; 173 E.R. 754; *Neale* (1839) 9 C.& P. 431; 173 E.R. 899.

[78] *The Law Relating to Riots and Unlawful Assemblies* (4th ed., 1907), at 48.

[79] [1982] Q.B. 416.

[80] Town and Country Planning Act 1971, s.28(1).

[81] *Coffin* v. *Smith* (1980) 71 Cr.App.R. 221. Which is not to say that the police would necessarily wish to assist him to do so. The existence of this right does, however, call into question the need to create the new trespass offence in s.39.

[82] The Court of Appeal does not discuss the point, and commentators (including the author, at [1982] P.L. at 214) have assumed that they were trespassers. A letter cited by the Court, and written by the C.E.G.B. to the Chief Constable claims that the farmer had requested the demonstrators to leave. The fact that they were not clearly trespassers may have been a powerful reason why the Chief Constable (who did comment that the legal position was very unclear) restrained his hand. See J. Alderson, *Law and Disorder* (1984) at p. 182 who says that "the protestors were not trespassers . . . and for that reason at least could not be forcibly removed."

way or another,[83] and would not therefore grant the mandamus asked for, they plainly encouraged the police to assist the Board. On the existence and scope of the right to use self help, Lord Denning went so far as to say:

"every person who is prevented from carrying out his lawful pursuits is entitled to use self-help, so as to prevent unlawful obstruction."

This probably "goes beyond the decisions"[84] and the other members of the Court were more circumspect, limiting the existence of the power to situations where a statutory body was being obstructed in the exercise of its statutory powers. Lawton and Templeman L.JJ. said that the Board could use as much force as was reasonably necessary to remove the protesters, which is probably as accurate (if unhelpful) a description of the law as it is possible to give.[85] That is, a person has a right to use force by way of self-help where it is necessary for him to use it (and the Board could not have carried out its statutory duties had it not used some force), and may then use only the minimum amount of force that is reasonably necessary in the circumstances.

If a person charged with violent disorder were to present himself and his assistants as being engaged in the pursuit of self-help, the jury should be asked whether it was necessary to use violence at all, and if so whether the violence used was reasonable in the circumstances having regard to such matters as the availability of police assistance, the ease of access to alternative remedies (such as civil proceedings) and other factors such as the numbers of trespassers, the time of day at which the violence was used, and matters of that sort.[86] At a public meeting held on private premises, a reasonable number of stewards, who may wear emblems or badges of identification as such, may be employed to assist in the preservation of order at the meeting.[87]

5. THE MENTAL ELEMENT

The mental element in group disorder offences: intention or awareness

3–15   Historically, the mental element in the public order offences has caused little difficulty,[88] and the hope may be expressed that this situation will continue. The Law Commission went so far as to say that the mental

---

[83] Relying on *R.* v. *Metropolitan Police Commissioner ex p. Blackburn* [1968] 2 Q.B. 118.
[84] Glanville Williams, *Text*, p. 522.
[85] For a criticism of the law where it is couched in such generalised and unhelpful terms, see A. J. Ashworth, "Self Defence and the Right to Life" [1976] 34 Camb L.J. 282.
[86] In the course of his judgment, Lord Denning M.R. expressed the view that once there is a real prospect of a breach of the peace, "the law does not go in to the rights and wrongs of the matter, or whether it is justified by self-help or not." But this, with respect, cannot be so, and is inconsistent with the terms of Lord Denning's own judgment. If the law did not go in to the rights and wrongs of the matter, it would be open to the constable to tell the C.E.G.B to desist from seeking to remove the protesters, if that were the simplest way to prevent a breach of the peace. The fact is that the Board was entitled to take the risk that a breach of the peace might ensue because they were seeking to carry out a statutory duty.
[87] Public Order Act 1936, s.2(6).
[88] Report, para. 3.41. In connection with affray, the mental element was said to be "in practice a matter of no importance."

element in the group disorder offences was of "minimal practical import-ance,"[89] which perhaps explains why the sections creating the offences do not themselves specify what mental element must be proved by the prose-cutor to constitute the offence. Instead, a general section (with the mar-ginal note "mental element: miscellaneous") is devoted to the *mens rea* of the various offences.

Section 6(2)[90] provides that:

> "A person is guilty of violent disorder or affray only if he intends to use or threaten violence or is aware that his conduct may be violent or threaten violence."

Until comparatively recently, there was general agreement that a person is said to intend the consequences of his conduct when he desires that they should come about, or when he foresees that it is virtually certain that they will occur.[91] Recently, however, the House of Lords has been critical of the second limb of this formula, saying that foresight is merely evidence from which it can be inferred that a person intends the results of his con-duct.[92] The difficulty with this is that it is not now clear precisely what it is that the jury is being invited to infer.

These recent decisions are, however, principally concerned with the question whether a person intends the consequences of his conduct, whereas the Act is referring to the defendant's attitude towards his conduct rather than its consequences. This is reinforced by the Act's definition of violence[93] which makes it plain that an intention to cause a particular consequence such as injury or damage is not required. That is, a person can be shown to be engaging in violent conduct even though it is not proved that he intended to cause injury to persons or property thereby. The point is perhaps best illustrated by a consideration of the facts of *Venna*.[94] The defendant and some others were involved in a street disturbance. The police sought to restrain the defendant, and in the ensuing scuffle, the defendant broke the hand of one of the policemen, and was convicted of assault occasioning actual bodily harm, contrary to section 47 of the O.A.P.A. His defence was that it was an accident that he had struck the police officer at all. It was held that it was sufficient that he was reckless, meaning (it was before the decision of the House of Lords in *Caldwell*[95])

---

[89] Report, para. 3.50.

[90] There is a substantially similar provision for riot in s.1(1).

[91] Glanville Williams, *Text*, p. 74 *et seq.*; Smith and Hogan, p. 47. In deciding whether or not a person intends the consequences of his conduct, the tribunal of fact should take into account all the evidence, and should not presume that a person intends the natural and probable consequences of his conduct; Criminal Justice Act 1967, s.8.

[92] *Moloney* [1985] A.C. 905; *Hancock and Shankland* [1986] A.C. 455; *Nedrick* [1986] 1 W.L.R. 1025, 3 All E.R. 1; *Pearman* (1985) 80 Cr.App.R. 259; *Purcell* (1986) 83 Cr.App.R. 45. For a discussion and attempt to reconcile these cases with the previous understanding, see R. A. Duff, "The Obscure Intentions of the House of Lords" [1986] Crim.L.R. 769.

[93] Above, 3–07.

[94] [1976] Q.B. 421.

[95] [1982] A.C. 341.

that the defendant himself realised that he was likely to strike and harm the policeman, even if he did not intend to do so. On a charge of violent disorder or affray, it would not even be necessary to prove so much. So long as it could be established that the defendant's actions were of sufficient force to amount to violence, he has no defence that he lacked *mens rea* if it can be said that he was aware that his conduct was violent. What matters is his attitude towards his own conduct, rather than its consequences.

Where a sane person actually uses violence, it is difficult to envisage a situation in which he can plausibly say that he did not in this sense intend his conduct to be violent, except, perhaps, where he is drunk, for which the Act in any event makes specific provision.[96]

Where the allegation is not that the defendant intended his conduct to be violent, but was aware that it might be, it must be shown that there was an actual awareness on the part of the defendant that the conduct might be violent. This denotes what was generally meant by recklessness before the decision of the House of Lords in *Caldwell*.[97] It is not enough that the risk that the conduct might be violent would have been obvious to persons other than the defendant if he was not himself aware. If the defendant is simultaneously charged with an offence of criminal damage, the distinction between the requisite states of mind might cause difficulty for the jury (and the judge instructing the jury), especially as there are likely to be several defendants to charges of riot and violent disorder. But the mental element selected by the Commission is consistent with the law governing assaults and the offences against the person,[98] and can be justified on that basis.

Again, it is not easy entirely to translate the theory into practical terms where the defendant actually uses violence, since a claim by such a person that he was unaware that his conduct was or might be violent is inherently implausible. The following example might illustrate some of the difficulties lurking in the application of the section. Suppose a person were apprehended at a football match for throwing a drinks can. His defence to a charge of violent disorder is that he did not bring the can with him but it was thrown at him or landed near him, and he picked it up and hurled it back in a spontaneous act of what he now sees to be one of mindless hooliganism. At the time when he did the act complained of, he later claims, he did not give his conduct any thought. Although one cannot make the point with any confidence, it would seem that this would, if not disproved, amount to a defence, since he does not have the requisite state of mind. But a jury might be expected to view such a claim with a considerable degree of scepticism.

It need not be shown that the defendant intended to cause fear to bystanders or was aware that his conduct might cause such fear, since no

---

[96] S.6(5), discussed in the next section.
[97] Above, n. 95.
[98] As explained in *Cunningham* [1957] 2 Q.B. 396; *Venna* [1976] Q.B. 421, affirmed after *Caldwell* in *W (a Minor)* v. *Dolbey* [1983] Crim.L.R. 681. And see *Grimshaw* [1984] Crim.L.R. 108.

bystanders need be present.[99] Is it any defence for him to say, "I did not realise my conduct was violent, since I did not think that what I was doing was such as would cause a person of reasonable firmness present at the scene to fear for his personal safety?" On principle, this must be classified as a mistake of law, since the question whether the conduct was sufficient to amount to violence is an objective one, to be assessed by the jury.

Where the charge is of riot or violent disorder, it must be shown (should the defendant dispute it) that the defendant was aware that there were the requisite numbers using unlawful violence. No authority can be offered for the opinion, but it would seem to be consistent with principle. The rationale of the group violence offences is that persons who seek to accomplish their objects by force of numbers should be prevented from doing so. If a person is charged with an offence of group disorder, it should accordingly be a defence that he did not even realise that he was part of a group. Furthermore, he could not be guilty of complicity unless he was aware of and intended to assist or encourage the principal, and the same principles should apply in this context.

Intoxication and the public order offences

The common law governing the question when intoxication will afford **3–16** exemption from criminal liability is in an unhappy state, both because it lacks clarity and (perhaps as a result) because it does not appear to be based upon any defensible logical principles.[1] Wisely, therefore, the Act makes specific provision for the problem, borrowing from previous work of the Criminal Law Revision Committee[2] and anticipating recommendations of the Law Commission for the enactment of a more satisfactory general law.[3] Section 6 (5) provides:

> "For the purposes of this section a person whose awareness is impaired by intoxication shall be taken to be aware of that of which he would have been aware if not intoxicated, unless he shows either that his intoxication was not self-induced or that it was caused solely by the taking or administration of a substance in the course of medical treatment."

As with the general law, the intoxication may be by drink or drugs.[4]

There is an element of the hypothetical in the test laid down by the Act, since it requires the jury to come to a conclusion about what they believe the defendant would have realised had he been sober; this is necessarily a

---

[99] Ss.1(4), 2(3) and 3(4). The Report says that this was the common law of affray, and generalises this to the other offences; para. 3.41.

[1] A. Dashwood, "Logic and the Lords in *Majewski*" [1977] Crim.L.R. 532.

[2] 14th Report, *Offences Against the Person* Cmnd. 7844 (1980), Part VI.

[3] See the Report to the Law Commission, *Codification of the Criminal Law* (1985), p. 75.

[4] This mirrors the general law; *Lipman* [1970] 1 Q.B. 156. But in any event the Act expressly provides that "intoxication" means "any intoxication, whether caused by drink, drugs or other means, or by a combination of means"; s.6(6). This would include a person who is intoxicated as a result of solvent abuse.

matter of conjecture, but it probably represents the existing law.[5] It must be stressed that the test is whether the defendant himself would have realised had he been sober, and this means that a defendant is entitled to adduce evidence of his own personal knowledge and characteristics, as for example backwardness.[6]

The Act is unusual in providing for the non self-induced form of intoxication, and it is open to the defendant to show (the burden is placed on the defence, to prove on the balance of probabilities)[7] that he was not at fault in being intoxicated. Thus, if he is able to show that another person has laced his drink, he may lay the foundation for the defence. But it would still be no defence unless the person could show that he lacked *mens rea* altogether as a result of having had his drink tampered with. As was held in *Davis*[8] a drunken intent is still an intent, and the rule is that it is no defence for a person to show that he would not have acted as he did had he not been intoxicated as a result of his acquaintance's actions. This would be a matter going to mitigation.

The expression "in the course of medical treatment" is to some extent ambiguous. It would not seem to cover the sort of person who has not had the drugs properly prescribed (*i.e.* by a doctor or a properly qualified paramedical person), as for example in *Hardie*[9] where a man took his mistress's valium with the intention of calming himself down, not knowing what the consequences of taking the drug might be. It was held that the defence of adverse automatism caused by the drugs might nevertheless be available to him. If the courts were to regard the expression as referring only to properly prescribed medical treatment the Act would change the present law. On the other hand, it is clear that the defendant in *Hardie* took the drug for a genuine medical purpose, and in so far as the Act is ambiguous on the point, it can be argued that the defence should be available to the person who prescribes his own medical treatment, not knowing what its effects might be.

It is less clear whether the section would exempt the person who did not take the drugs according to the prescription. Suppose, for example, that the person in possession of the prescribed drugs takes more than the pre-

---

[5] The law is stated somewhat tentatively, and is based on the Law Commission's summary in the Report, para. 3.55 (citing *Majewski* [1977] A.C. 443 and *Caldwell* [1982] A.C. 341). But it is suggested that where Caldwell type recklessness will suffice for the offence, it is not necessary for the jury to make an estimate of what the defendant would have realised had he not been drunk; as *Elliott* [1983] 1 W.L.R. 939, 2 All E.R. 1005 shows, the test is wholly objective. Where the requisite mental element is *Cunningham* type recklessness (as the offences under discussion clearly are), however, the jury is required to make the additional assessment; *Eatch* [1980] Crim.L.R. 650. See J. C. Smith, "Intoxication and the Mental Element in Crime" in P. Wallington and R. M. Merkin (eds.) *Essays in Honour of Professor F. H. Lawson* (1986).

[6] *Cf.* the situation in *Elliott* v. *C* (last note) where it was held that, in estimating whether a defendant has been reckless for the purposes of the Criminal Damage Act 1971, s.1(1), the fact that the defendant was a backward 14 year old girl was immaterial. Under the Act, such considerations would be relevant.

[7] *Carr-Briant* [1943] K.B. 607.

[8] [1983] Crim.L.R. 741.

[9] [1985] 1 W.L.R. 644, [1984] 3 All E.R. 848.

scribed dose, or fails to observe the conditions suggested by the doctor when giving the prescription (as for example by neglecting to eat properly).[10] He may still argue with some plausibility that he was taking the medicine in the course of medical treatment, and, in the first hypothetical at least, that his mental state was caused solely by his so doing as the Act in terms requires. It is suggested that the expression "in the course of medical treatment" does not mean that the medicine must be taken entirely in accordance with medical advice, and that once he exceeds the dose advised, he is no longer within the terms of the exemption afforded by that phrase.

The second situation is more problematic, but the answer may well be that his intoxication was not in this instance caused "solely" by his ingestion of the drug, but was a combination of that and his failure to take the proper precautions. If that is the proper interpretation, the section would not apply, and intoxication would provide no answer. But this would alter the common law. Where it can be shown that he is aware that the failure to take the necessary steps might lead to his becoming aggressive, unpredictable and uncontrolled, he should not be able to rely on his intoxication. But if he does not know that, he is in a sense the victim of an accident, and it would seem unnecessary to convict him of an offence ordinarily requiring intention or awareness.

It should be noted that the rules relating to intoxication are relevant to the intention that is required to be proved under section 6. Where the offence requires proof of a mental element in addition to that specified by section 6, therefore, as in the case of common purpose in the law of riot, it is open to the defendant to give evidence of intoxication to prove the absence of the requisite state of mind. Riot is for these purposes a specific intent offence.[11]

Sentencing

Violent disorder is a new offence, and it remains to be seen what sentencing policies the courts will adopt. The available penalty is five years, which makes the offence one of intermediate seriousness between riot and affray. To some extent, the Law Commission was guided by the sentences that were imposed for unlawful assembly, for which violent disorder is a substitute, and the courts may well take their lead from this. In *Main* v. *Gawthorpe*[12] penalties of four and five years were imposed, which were the longest in recent sentencing practice.

3–17

Adopting the sentencing principle that the maximum penalty should be reserved for the worst conceivable case[13] five years should be reserved for conduct that comes perilously close to riot. Where violence has in fact been used, but the numbers are too small to constitute a riot, or where it cannot

[10] As in *Bailey* [1983] 1 W.L.R. 760, 2 All E.R. 503.
[11] Report, para. 6.28. The defendant could, however, be convicted of violent disorder as an alternative.
[12] (1982) 4 Cr.App.R.(S) 42.
[13] For a discussion of the applicability of this principle, see A. J. Ashworth (ed.), *Cross, The English Sentencing System* (3rd ed., 1981), pp. 41–43.

be shown that members of a large crowd who cause damage have a common purpose, long sentences may be imposed.

Where violent disorder is one of a number of offences of which a particular person is convicted (including, for example, specific offences against the person or property, or explosives offences), should the lead sentence be given for the violent disorder or for the other offences? In *Wilson*[14] the Court of Appeal on a charge of affray said that it was desirable to impose the lead sentence for the public order offence, and permit the others to run concurrently. But there, the available penalty for the affray was considerable (theoretically life), and it may be suggested that where the defendant can be proved to have committed other serious offences, it is more in accordance with principle to impose the leading sentence for that.

[14] (1981) 3 Cr.App.R.(S) 30.

CHAPTER 4

RIOT

1. INTRODUCTION

Introduction

Historically, riot was regarded as the most serious of the public order **4-01**
offences, akin to treason.[1] Although technically a misdemeanour, it
changed its character and became a felony after the Riot Act was read at
the scene of a riot.[2] The significance of this was that fatal force could (if
necessary) be used to disperse persons remaining at the scene of a riot an
hour after the Act had been read, persons using fatal force were given a
specific immunity if the force were used to disperse the riot, and the sentence available to the courts for the commission of the offence of riot was
death. When the distinction between felonies and misdemeanours was
abolished in 1967, the Riot Act 1714 was repealed in consequence.[3]

In recasting the common law, the Law Commission plainly intended that
riot should remain the most serious of the public order offences, and certain of its features as redefined emphasise this; it carries the most severe
penalty of all the new offences,[4] there must be 12 persons present (as
opposed to the three who together commit violent disorder) and they must
be shown to have a common purpose. Unlike violent disorder, riot requires
proof that the individual rioter was guilty of actually using violence, and
not merely threatening it.[5] Riot is an extremely serious offence reserved
for the gravest cases of disorder, which is supposed to be signalled by the
fact that no prosecution can be brought for the substantive offence or for
the incitement to commit it without the consent of the D.P.P.[6] It may well
be that because the penalty for affray is now three years only, prosecutors
who think that this penalty is insufficient will prefer the charge of riot in

---

[1] Holdsworth's *History of English Law*, vol. 2, at 450, 453; vol. 5, at 197 99; vol. 8, at
324–331; vol. 10 at 705–8. See A. H. Bodkin and L. W. Kershaw, Wise, (eds.) *The Law
Relating to Riots and Unlawful Assemblies* (4th ed., 1907).
[2] The Riot Act 1714 read as follows: "Our Sovereign Lady the Queen chargeth and comman-
deth all persons being assembled immediately to disperse themselves and peaceably to
depart to their habitations or their lawful business, upon the pains contained in the Act
made in the first year of King George for preventing tumults and riotous assemblies. God
save the Queen."
[3] Criminal Law Act 1967, s.10(2).
[4] Section 1(6). The Bill first presented to Parliament proposed a penalty of life imprisonment. This was because, shortly before the Bill was drafted, a sentence of life imprisonment for riot was passed at the Central Criminal Court. On appeal, the sentence was
described as being wrong in principle, and reduced to three years; *Whitton* (1986) *The
Times*, May 20.
[5] Subject to the complicity point discussed further below 4-09.
[6] Section 7(1). The intention has to some extent miscarried because of the enactment of the
Prosecution of Offences Act 1985, s.1(6), the effect of which is that Crown Prosecutors
have the powers of the D.P.P. to authorise prosecutions. But the Public Order Act has the
effect of precluding private prosecutions.

cases of pitched battles and gang fights where previously they would have charged affray. A better indication of the seriousness with which the offence is regarded is that it is the only offence created by the Act that is triable on indictment only.

Even where no charges of riot are brought after an incident of civil disorder, the strict definition of the offence will remain of practical significance because of the civil consequences arising from the Riot Damages Act 1886.[7]

The need for an offence of riot

4–02 Initially, one of the justifications for the existence of the offence of riot lay in its use in crowd dispersal.[8] Although rioting was a crime punishable in its own right, it gave the authorities a generalised power to order the participants in mob disorder to disperse. Under the old law, it was not then necessary to prove individual participation in the violence; mere presence at the scene an hour after the Riot Act 1714 had been read was sufficient. That rationale has now gone, and the Law Commission considered the possibility that it may not be necessary to replace the common law of riot with any modern, serious statutory offence. The argument was that such an offence would be otiose in the light of the number of relatively less serious offences, especially violent disorder[9] and an offence penalising threats or provocation of violence.[10] Furthermore, the offences against the person and property, and ancillary offences such as the possession of unlawful weapons or explosives, were frequently committed in situations of riot, and could just as readily be used. The Law Commission rejected this line of argument, preferring the rationale offered by the Court of Appeal in *Caird*[11] that:

> "[riot] derives its great gravity from the simple fact that the persons concerned were acting in numbers and using those numbers to achieve their purpose. . . . The law of this country has always leant heavily against those who, to attain such a purpose, use the threat that lies in numbers."

Persons who deliberately foment disorder, who provoke or lead wide-scale public disturbances and who resist the efforts of the police to restore order, in particular, might not fall within the scope of any of the existing offences of sufficient gravity.[12] The Commission considered that if there is evidence of prolonged, active and direct participation in the organisation of a major

---

[7] For discussion of this see 4–12. And see s.10, which provides for the construction of the expression "riot" and cognate expressions in other legislation.

[8] For an excellent discussion see the American *Model Penal Code and Commentaries (Official Draft and Revised Comments)*, Art. 250.2 of which makes failure to disperse after a warning an offence.

[9] Chap. 3.

[10] Chap. 6.

[11] (1970) 54 Cr.App.R. 499, 114 S.J. 652.

[12] Report, paras. 6.7 to 6.10.

public disturbance, this might well justify the bringing of a charge more serious than would be available in the absence of a charge of riot.

The question whether a general dispersal power similar to the one given by the Riot Act 1714 should be restored was considered by Lord Scarman[13] and by the Government in its White Paper.[14] Both came to the conclusion that difficulties with the proposal were insuperable. The problems included (1) whether there should be a statutory limit on the geographical area to be cleared; (2) whether there should be exceptions to the dispersal requirement for persons such as journalists or first aid helpers; (3) how to ensure that only those who heard the warning but refused to disperse came within the terms of the offence. It was also felt that existing police powers were adequate to disperse unruly crowds.

Subsequent experience during the miner's strike suggests that the question, though quiescent, is not yet finally settled.[15] The third objection can surely be overcome with the assistance of modern technology, and the warning to disperse could easily enough be given at repeated intervals. Lord Scarman's recommendations were made in the context of a somewhat diffuse disturbance, in which it may well have been inappropriate to employ the power. But where the disturbance is localised (as for example outside a factory gate) the power could be exercised in such a way as to require those present to leave that particular spot. This would have the advantages, for the rioters, that they are warned of police intentions to disperse them. To some extent, a dispersal power may have been afforded by section 14 of the Act, which for the first time specifically empowers the police to impose conditions on assemblies. That will be considered later.[16]

Basic definition of riot

Section 1(1) provides as follows: 4–03

> "Where 12 or more persons who are present together use or threaten unlawful violence for a common purpose and the conduct of them (taken together) is such as would cause a person of reasonable firmness present at the scene to fear for his personal safety, each of those persons using violence for the common purpose is guilty of riot."

The offence is punishable with imprisonment for a term of ten years or a fine, or both, and unlike all the other offences created by the Act it is triable only on indictment.[17]

---

[13] The Scarman Report, *The Brixton Disorders 10–12 April 1981*, Cmnd. 8427 (1981), para. 7.31.
[14] White Paper, *Review of Public Order Law*, Cmnd. 9510 (1985), para. 6.14.
[15] See, *e.g.* the Report by the Chief Constable, P. Wright, *Policing the Coal Industry Dispute in South Yorkshire* (1985), at p. 44: "it would be conducive to the restoration of good order for the police to use loudhailers or placards advising the pickets that the situation was considered disorderly and that persons should disperse. Persons failing to leave at that point should be liable to prosecution."
[16] Chap. 8.
[17] Section 1(6).

2. ELEMENTS IN COMMON WITH VIOLENT DISORDER

In many respects, riot is simply an aggravated form of violent disorder, with which it shares many common elements. These will be considered briefly, but readers are referred to the appropriate earlier discussion for more detailed treatment.

Using or threatening unlawful violence

4–04   The requirement that a number of persons should be present using or threatening violence (in this case 12 in number) is a background requirement. Riot is a continuing offence, in which a large group are present together using or threatening unlawful violence which is capable of causing fear in the bystanders. A requirement of proof of the actual use by one of the participants that distinguishes riot from violent disorder.[18] Unless one person in the group actually uses (as opposes to merely threatens) violence, no offence of riot occurs. It must also be said that, if only one person uses violence, a prosecution for riot would be most unusual.

Absence of bystanders

4–05   Whatever may have been the position at common law,[19] the Act makes it plain that it is not necessary for the prosecutor to prove that any bystander was present, nor that he was likely to be.[20] It is possible (but not very easy) to conceive of a riot without bystanders. Suppose, for example, there was a gang attack at the house of another gang. By the time the police arrive upon the scene, the disorder is over, but there is debris littered everywhere, and large numbers of persons left injured and wounded, perhaps even dead. In those circumstances, it may be virtually impossible to employ the serious offences against the person for lack of reliable evidence as to individual participation. There were no bystanders, because all those who witnessed what happened were participants or victims. So long as it could be proved that the 12 or more were present together, the perpetrators of the attack could possibly be prosecuted with and convicted of riot. As with violent disorder, the fear instilled is in a hypothetical bystander, who acts as a measure of the violence used.

Public or private place

4–06   The case for saying that persons should not be exempt from prosecutions for riot merely because they happen to occur in a private place is very strong. Gatecrashers at a private party should not be able to escape liability for terrorising the invited guests on the grounds that their conduct was private. In such circumstances, the distinction is meaningless, and the subsec-

---

[18] 4–09.
[19] 3–09, n. 48.
[20] Section 1(4).

tion to that effect[21] avoids the need to differentiate between public and private places.

The mental element

Section 6(1) provides that: **4–07**

> "a person is guilty of riot only if he intends to use violence or is aware that his conduct may be violent."

This aspect of the *mens rea* of the offence of riot is similar to that required for violent disorder and affray, and readers are referred to the earlier discussion.[22]

Suppose that the participants in a disturbance believe that they are acting peaceably, but unbeknown to them they frighten a person in the vicinity. This happened in *Ford* v. *Metropolitan Police District Receiver*,[23] where a group of revellers had gone into a house on peace night to get firewood for a bonfire. It was found that had anybody sought to interfere with them, they would have subjected the interjector to violence, and that the neighbour who overheard what was happening was too frightened to interfere. This was held to be sufficient for riot, and would continue to be so under the new law. Technically, the actual response of the bystander would be no more than evidence that the violence was of a degree sufficient to satisfy the requirements of the Act, which refer to a hypothetical bystander only.

3. THE DISTINGUISHING FEATURES OF RIOT

Twelve·or more present together

Whereas it suffices to establish violent disorder that there were only   **4–08** three persons present together,[24] for the purposes of the law of riot there must be at least 12 persons who come within that rubric. The number selected echoes the Riot Act 1714, which also called for the presence of 12 before the measure could be read. At common law, three persons only were sufficient for offence of riot, but the Law Commission felt that the numbers should be increased to reflect the fact that the weight of numbers is an essential part of the rationale for the continued existence of the offence.[25] The requirement might sometimes be expected to give rise to difficulties of proof, not so much because there will be a difficulty of establishing that there were 12 persons present together using or threatening violence, but because of the difficulties of establishing in a mêleé of such dimensions that the particular defendant actually used violence.

It need not be proved, of course, that all 12 were guilty of riot; it is sufficient that only one uses violence when all the rest are merely threatening it. This means that if, for example, there were a group on a picket line, and

[21] Section 1(5).
[22] See 3–15.
[23] [1921] K.B. 334.
[24] 3–03.
[25] Report, paras. 6–13 to 6–16.

one of the number uses violence as by throwing a brick at a strike breaker, or by assaulting a policeman, he technically commits the offence of riot.

Section 6(7) which, as has been explained,[26] says that a person may count towards the quorum of those present using and threatening violence notwithstanding that he may not have the intention to use or threaten violence, precludes the defendant from arguing that those who were with him were not culpable because, for example, they were intoxicated and lacked the necessary mental element.

Where the disorder is such as the series of events that occurred in Brixton,[27] which lasted over several days, there was a series of skirmishes and pitched battles between members of the public and the police, and on the third day, sporadic incidents of looting and arson. If a group of fewer than 12 were apprehended engaging in one or other of these activities, could they be charged with riot in addition to any offence of criminal damage or theft that might be committed? It is suggested that they could not. Even though the disturbances in Brixton took place within a fairly constricted geographical area, the proximity of other events is insufficient to constitute "presence together." There must be at least 12 persons at that spot, then and there engaging in threats or use of violence, to constitute the background requirement for the law of riot. But most of the incidents that Lord Scarman considers to have been riots under the old law (large groups of people having the common intention of attacking the police)[28] will equally constitute the offence of riot under the new law.

Use of violence

4–09   Riot is confined in its definition to those who actually use violence, as opposed to those who merely threaten it. The victim of the violence (whether it be person or property) need not be identified, so long as the jury is satisfied that violence was in fact used. This is inherent in the extended definition of violence employed by the Act,[29] which concentrates on the defendant's conduct rather than on the consequences of it.

The existence of this requirement does not mean that only those who use violence can be convicted of riot, since the ordinary principles of aiding and abetting apply. In context, this means that before a person can be convicted of riot, it must be proved that he was aware that his companion was about to use violence or realised that he might do so, and that he encouraged and intended to encourage him to do so.[30] His mere presence at the scene of the riot will not suffice, as was established in the old prize-fighting case of *Coney*,[31] a prosecution for assault.[32]

---

[26] 3–03.
[27] *Brixton, supra*, n. 13.
[28] *Ibid.* at p. 42.
[29] 3–07.
[30] *Davies* v. *D.P.P.* [1954] A.C. 378; *Anderson and Morris* [1966] 2 Q.B. 110; *Chan Wing Siu* v. *R.* [1985] A.C. 168. See above 3–10.
[31] (1882) 8 Q.B.D. 534. And see *Clarkson* (1971) 55 Cr.App.R. 445, 1 W.L.R. 402.
[32] Charges of riot were brought in that famous case, but they were not proceeded with.

If a fight were to break out at a nightclub or a party, the presence of persons there is not even evidence of any intention to encourage others in the club to employ violence.

Common purpose

The requirement of common purpose was an element of both riot and **4–10** unlawful assembly at common law,[33] and is the feature that, apart from the numbers of participants required and the actual use rather than the threat of violence, distinguishes riot from violent disorder. It is a further mental element of group intention,[34] an elusive concept that is supposed to "reflect the idea of concerted action on the part of a number of people."[35] According to the Law Commission, "the possession of a common purpose by a number of people . . . constitutes the particular danger of riot."[36]

A question arises as to whether or not the common purpose needs to be unlawful independently of the unlawful use of violence that is the essence of riot. Before the Act, it was argued that it should be,[37] but there is at least some authority for the proposition that it need not be.[38] Clearly, if the purpose is unlawful, there are no difficulties. An unlawful common purpose exists where a group agree to ransack another's house or to participate in a gang fight, or to attack a group of policemen. But what about a purpose such as closing a factory or preventing others from demonstrating by organising a counter demonstration? The tainting element at common law was that even if the purpose itself might have been lawful, the participants intended to use violence to achieve it.[39] That is, even where the participants might have been able to put forward some lawful purpose such as the defence of self-help or a claim of right, if in the exercise of that right they unreasonably and unnecessarily caused violence, the defence would

---

[33] *Field* [1907] 2 K.B. 853; *Wong Chey and Others* (1910) 6 Cr.App.R. 59.

[34] For the purposes of the defence of intoxication, this makes riot a crime of "specific intent" to which intoxication is, on general principle, a defence under the rule in *Majewski* [1977] A.C. 443. This was certainly intended by the Law Commission; Report, para 6.28. But the intoxicated person could be convicted of violent disorder; *ibid.*

[35] Report, para. 6.11.

[36] *Ibid.* para. 6.12.

[37] Smith and Hogan, arguing that if three policemen were to pursue a dangerous criminal (three were sufficient for riot at common law, but not under the Act), they cannot be guilty of riot, since they were not using violence "needlessly and without reasonable occasion"; at p. 737. But now, the violence would not be regarded as "unlawful" as the section requires. The problem discussed in the text is intimately connected with the lawfulness or otherwise of the violence used, and is discussed in 3–10 to 3–14. The Working Paper proposed a definition of the common purpose of "engaging in an unlawful course of violent conduct," but this was not proceeded with after consultation. In Standing Committee, the Secretary of State for the Home Office (Mr Shaw) in response to a question on the point said that "the purpose is for the use of violence, and not the purpose for which they may have gathered"; H.C. Standing Committee G, January 23, 1986: Official Report, col. 28.

[38] *Wolfgramm* [1978] 2 N.Z.L.R. 184; "in itself, that purpose may have been lawful or unlawful"; *per* Woodhouse J.

[39] *Graham* (1888) 16 Cox 420. Although the fact that it must be shown that the defendants are prepared to use unlawful violence limited the scope of the offence at common law.

fail, and it did not matter that their common purpose, seen in isolation, might have been lawful.[40]

Would it be enough that a group of 12 had agreed to engage in a perfectly lawful activity such as visiting a football match or going to a party together?[41] The problem is likely to arise, not because of prosecutions for the offence, but where a person whose property is damaged seeks compensation under the Riot (Damages) Act 1886.[42] Suppose that members of a large group of football hooligans on their way to a match engage in sporadic and random acts of violence, damaging cars and gardens along the route? If in the course of that, an individual's house, shop or building, or property therein[43] is damaged, can it be said that the participants have a sufficient common purpose to constitute a riot? The answer, it is submitted is that if it becomes plain that 12 (or more) of the participants have begun to use or threaten violence so that a different or additional common purpose supervenes in the course of the proceedings, it is pure technicality to say that the initial common purpose was lawful. Support for this view may be found in section 1(3), which says that common purpose can be discerned from conduct. This serves to emphasise that riot need not be part of a pre-arranged and concerted plan, but may arise spontaneously. Similarly, where the participants purport to be exercising a defence such as claim of right or the entitlement to abate a nuisance. If their conduct exceeds the bounds of what is permissible by way of those defences, it does not avail them to say that their common purpose was "lawful."

Where there are two opposing groups of six or more, but fewer than 12 in either one of them, who join together in a fight, it is unclear whether they have a sufficient common purpose to amount to riot. Suppose, for example, that a group of eight enter a club or bar with the intention of starting a fight there, perhaps as a revenge attack on persons whom they believe to be there. If the response of those attacked far exceeds what is permissible by way of self-defence,[44] the total of those fighting is greater than 12. Can it then be said that the fighters have a common purpose as against the bystanders who witness and are put in fear by their conduct? There is no authority on the point, but there is a case for saying that their joint conduct falls within the mischief at which the offence is aimed. Their common purpose is to fight one another, and it should not matter that it was spontaneously formed.

One of the reasons for retaining the requirement of common purpose was to exclude the casual participant from liability.[45] This does not necessarily mean that a latecomer to the scene of a riot could not be guilty of participating in the common purpose.[46] A person who witnesses an attack on the police, for example, and adds his own act of violence to those of others

---

[40] *Langford* (1842) Car. & M. 602, 174 E.R. 653. Suppose a group forms to abate a nuisance and appear with crowbars, spades, etc., for that purpose; *Clemens* [1898] 1 Q.B. 556.
[41] *Wolfgramm*, above n. 38, suggests that it is.
[42] 4–12.
[43] The terminology is that used in the Riot (Damages) Act 1886; 4–12.
[44] 3–13.
[45] Report, 6.12.
[46] Wise, p. 72.

could not exculpate himself on the basis that he was not there when the disorder first broke out.

Even if the argument that it is inherent in the concept of presence together that the participant should be aware of the other 11 participants is not accepted,[47] the element of common purpose must import a requirement that the defendant is aware of the others, and of their violent purpose.

The duty to prevent a riot

Under the old law, it was the duty of magistrates (and more recently the **4–11** police) to take steps to disperse an unlawful assembly, and *a fortiori* to disperse a riot.[48] The suggestion is sometimes made that there is also a general duty to suppress riots[49], the Riot (Damages) Act 1886 historically proceeded from this base.[50] In his Report on the Red Lion Square Disorders, Sir Leslie Scarman said[51]:

> "there began a riot, which it was the duty of the police to suppress, by force if necessary. Every other person in the square was, as a matter of law, under the duty of assisting the police: but common sense suggests that discretion was for them the better part of valour. The law-abiding public is wise to leave the quelling of a riot to the police unless their assistance be directly sought."

It may be suggested that this represents not simply common sense but the law, and that there is no duty in the citizen to intervene unless specifically called upon (which, in the context of modern policing, he is most unlikely to be).[52] Otherwise, his mere presence at the scene of the riot would make him guilty of it, and this is not the law.[53]

It has also been said that "there is a clear responsibility on those who organise marches or processions to take sensible precautions to maintain order among their own supporters."[54] But, if so, the responsibility is a moral rather than a legal one, and would not necessarily make the organisers responsible for any disorder that subsequently ensued. In *Atkinson*[55] in which the defendant on a charge of riot was an employer who had declined to comply with a police request that he ask his employees to desist, Kelly C.B. said that "the mere presence of a person among the rioters, even though he possessed power and failed to exercise it of stop-

---

[47] 3–04.
[48] *O'Kelly* v. *Harvey* (1883) 14 L.R.Ir. 105.
[49] R. N. Petty, "Mob Rules" (1981) 145 J.P.N. 334, citing the Committee inquiring into the Featherstone disturbances, where it was said that "by the law of this country, everyone is bound to aid in the suppression of riotous assemblages."
[50] *Red Lion Square* para. 26.
[51] L. Radzinowicz, *A History of English Criminal Law and its Administration* (1956) Vol. 2, p. 164 *et seq.*
[52] The conditions in which a constable may seek assistance are laid down in *Brown* (1841) Car. & M., 314, 174 E.R. 522.
[53] *Coney* (1882) 8 Q.B.D. 534.
[54] White Paper, para. 1.12.
[55] (1869) 11 Cox C.C. at 332.

ping the riot did not render him liable on such a charge." That being the case, there would not seem to be much point is continuing to assert that there is a duty in every citizen to suppress riots.[56]

The Riot (Damages) Act 1886

4–12   The Riot (Damages) Act 1886 is a measure that requires the local police authority to compensate for damage to property[57] caused during a riot.[58] Liability is based on the ancient notion of the collective responsibility of the community; there is no real suggestion that the police are in any sense responsible for the damage caused. In effect, residents whose property is damaged are indemnified by the other ratepayers, generally through the police authority.[59] It is not necessary that anybody should be charged with or convicted of the offence of riot as a precondition to a claim, but the victim has the burden of showing that riot has occurred, and that the damage to his property was a result.

This Act is of continuing significance because the 1986 Act, s.10(1) provides that the old law is to be construed in accordance with the terms of the new definition.[60] This will in all probability slightly reduce the circumstances in which damages are payable. Whereas under the previous law, certain robberies were covered,[61] now it would seem they could not be unless carried out by a very large gang. But the change effected is not as great as might be supposed, since compensation is payable only where the persons assembled act both riotously and "tumultuously," and it was held in *J. W. Dwyer Ltd.* v. *Metropolitan Police District Receiver*[62] that this meant in such numbers and with such commotion that the forces of law and order should have been alerted to and acted to prevent the damage. It does

[56] The imposition of an obligation on individual citizens might have been justifiable before the development of modern policing; the magistrate or individual policeman had no ready means of summoning official assistance. A modern lack of community involvement in peacekeeping tasks may be one of the prices to be paid for increasing police professionalisation in the control of public disorder. In *Albert* v. *Lavin* [1982] A.C. 564, Lord Diplock said of the duty to preserve the peace supposedly imposed on all citizens that "except in the case of a citizen who is a constable, it is a duty of imperfect obligation."

[57] "Houses, shops or buildings, or property therein"; s.1. Damage to a farmer's land is not included. The definition also excludes vehicles parked in public, but might include a car parked in a garage, and does include a garage *Jarvis* v. *Surrey C.C.* [1925] 1 K.B. 554, a sports stadium *Gunter* v. *Metropolitan Police District Receiver* (1888) 53 J.P. 249 and a wall *Field* v. *The Receiver of Metropolitan Police* [1907] 2 K.B. 853. Where a shop is damaged, no compensation is payable in respect of damage for trading losses.

[58] For a thorough account, see Alec Samuels, "Compensation for Riot Damage. The Riot Damages Act 1886" [1970] Crim.L.R. 336. And see D. G. T. Williams, *Keeping the Peace* (1967) pp. 37–41.

[59] Additional payments were made by the Home Office to help defray the expenses of the riots in Handsworth in 1985; see Standing Committee G, Official Report, February 20, 1986, col. 397.

[60] The same subsection provides that the new definition is also to apply in the case of the Merchant Shipping Act 1894, s.515, which governs the plundering of ships stranded at any place on or near the coast or any tidal water.

[61] This was thought to be the result of Lord Goddard's observation in *Sharp* [1957] 1 Q.B. 557 that three persons entering a shop and forcibly stealing were guilty of riot. But this was greatly qualified in its application to the 1886 Act by *Dwyer* (next note).

[62] [1967] 2 Q.B. 970.

not matter whether the riot occurs in a public or a private place,[63] but in assessing the compensation to be awarded, regard must be had to the precautions taken by the claimant, and "as respects his being a party or accessory to such riotous or tumultuous assembly, or as regards any provocation offered to the persons assembled or otherwise."[64]

Miscellaneous enactments

The term riot and cognate expressions is used in a number of statutes,   **4-13** and the Act makes express provisions for dealing with the question of how the newly defined offence of riot should apply in each case.[65]

Sentence

When the Bill was first published, it made life imprisonment a possible   **4-14** sentencing option. This had been considered and rejected by the Law Commission, which provisionally favoured 14 years,[66] and then ten, which was eventually chosen by Parliament.[67] Shortly before the Bill was published, a judge sentenced an offender at the Old Bailey to life imprisonment. This was held by the Court of Appeal to be wrong in principle, and a term of three years' was substituted.[68]

It may be doubted whether the new penalty will greatly affect existing sentencing practice.[69] Certain offences now triable as affray may well in future be prosecuted as riot. The courts distinguished quite sharply between two different types of affray; the spontaneous brawl, where no great injury ensued, and the premeditated, pitched battle type of offence.[70] The latter might now be tried as riot, in which case the principles established in the affray cases can be applied.

---

[63] *Munday* v. *Metropolitan Police District Receiver* [1949] 1 All E.R. 337.
[64] Section 1; *Pitchers* v. *Surrey County Council* [1923] 2 K.B. 57.
[65] See the text of the Act in the Appendix.
[66] Working Paper, para. 5.51.
[67] Report, para. 6.32.
[68] *Whitton* (1986) *The Times*, May 20.
[69] See *Muryani* (1986) 8 Cr.App.R.(S) 176; *Pilgrim* (1983) 5 Cr.App.R.(S.) 140.
[70] *Anderson* (1985) 7 Cr.App.R.(S) 210.

CHAPTER 5

AFFRAY

1. INTRODUCTION

The History of the offence

5–01   At common law, affray consisted of fighting in public to the terror of innocent bystanders, or the display of force without actual violence but with the same effect on bystanders. By the middle of the nineteenth century, the offence had fallen into desuetude,[1] but it was resurrected[2] and found to be a handy prosecutorial weapon against gang fights, because it enabled the prosecutor to circumvent the limitations imposed by the laws of complicity.[3] Although the provenance of the offence was the subject of some doubts, its existence was affirmed by the House of Lords in *Button and Swain*,[4] and the offence was judicially extended in several ways[5] shortly before it was abolished by the Act.

Thus, it was held that there was no need for a fight—in the sense of two willing participants attacking one another—actually to take place as part of the offence; where one person was attacking another and the public fear was sufficiently aroused, it should not be a defence for the attacker to assert that his victim was acting in self defence.[6] The logic of this is defensible enough where there are members of the public to be terrified, but it was subsequently held that the offence need not take place in public, on the grounds that bystanders might become just as terrified in private as they would in public.[7] Finally, the requirement that a bystander should be terrified was qualified where the offence occurred in public, so that it was not necessary to prove either that a bystander was actually terrified, or even present, or even that a bystander was even likely to be present.[8] The reason offered for this was that, by definition, a public place was one where the public were likely to be. This overlooks the point that, since the decision of the House in *Button and Swain*[9] it was not necessary to prove

---

[1] The last reported prosecution in England before *Sharp and Johnson* [1957] 1 Q.B. 552 appears to have been *Hunt and Swanton* (1845) 1 Cox C.C. 177. In Ireland, see *O'Neill* (1871) I.R. 6 C.L. 1.

[2] In *Sharp and Johnson* last note; see I. D. Brownlie, "The Renovation of Affray" [1965] Crim.L.R. 479.

[3] The propriety of this was questioned in [1982] Crim.L.R. at 489.

[4] [1966] A.C. 591; *Taylor* [1973] A.C. 964; see J. R. Spencer, [1973] 32 C.L.J. 153.

[5] See the commentary by Professor J. C. Smith on *Attorney-General's Refce (No. 3 of 1983)* [1985] 1 Q.B. 242 at Crim.L.R. 207. And see A. T. H. Smith, "The Metamorphosis of Affray" (1986) 136 New L.Jo. 521.

[6] *Scarrow* (1968) 52 Cr.App.R. 591; *Summers* (1972) 56 Cr.App.R. 604; *Taylor* [1973] A.C. 964.

[7] *Kane* [1965] 1 All E.R. 705.

[8] *Attorney-General's Refce (No. 3 of 1983)* [1985] 1 Q.B. 242, "correcting" the holding in *Farnill* [1982] Crim.L.R. 38.

[9] [1966] A.C. 591.

that the offence took place in public. Even this attritional logic left one "gap" in the law; where the affray took place in private as opposed to public, it could be argued that there was the need for the presence of an actual (as opposed to a hypothetical) bystander. The cumulative effects of section 3(4) (which provides that no bystander need be or be likely to be present) and 3(5) (which says that affray is capable of commission in both public and private places) complete the march of logic, with the result that if a person assaults another in private (for example in a domestic assault) and uses violence (of such a degree that the other members of the household would be frightened if they were there), he is technically guilty of an affray. The public order essence of the offence has been wholly lost, and affray has become a form of aggravated assault.[10] That prosecutorial discretion will almost certainly rescue the offence from this absurdity is no proper substitute for such catch-all drafting.

Typically, the common law offence was charged in cases of pitched street battles between rival gangs and for revenge attacks on individuals, and, spontaneous pub and club brawls. Frequently, the indictment also included charges alleging one or more of the offences against the person. Even though the statutory offence that replaces it reduces the public order characteristics of the offence and raises doubts as to whether affray is properly characterised as a public order offence at all, the likelihood is that it will continue to be employed in the prosecution of spontaneous brawls that result in no great injury in circumstances where the evidence of specific offences against the person is deficient.

The justification of an offence of affray

At common law, the justification of the offence of affray rested in the public fear (terror, in the terminology of the common law) that fighting in public was apt to arouse. The offence took its title from the French "effrayer," to frighten, and its essence was that the defendant deliberately took part in fighting or other acts of violence of such a character as to cause alarm to the public. As was seen in the previous section, the legal ingredients of the offence were successively whittled away so that public alarm became of relative insignificance, although the offence was apt to be charged in cases of group disorder. 5–02

The Law Commission nevertheless recommended the retention of the offence for use against fighting, principally because of the procedural advantages that the offence possesses for the prosecutor.[11] Where there has been a gang fight, as a result of which one of the participants is injured, it is sometimes impossible to prove who was responsible for causing the injury (because of the general mêleé, and because of identification difficulties when the incident occurred at night). In such circumstances, the offence of affray is a useful alternative either to one of the offences against

---

[10] It is classified as an offence against the person by Glanville Williams, *Textbook* at p. 205; J. C. Smith and Hogan, *Criminal Law: Cases and Materials* (1986) p. 387.
[11] Working Paper, para. 4.6.

the person, or some minor public order offence.[12] The prosecutor does not have to charge named persons with assaults on other named persons. If injury has actually been caused, it is not necessary to show that a particular defendant caused them, as it is when an offence against the person is alleged. The other procedural advantage is said to be that it is open to a prosecutor to include a series of incidents in the one charge, rather than as a series of assaults.[13]

The other advantage of affray for the prosecutor is that it requires a less exacting proof of *mens rea* than is required for the offences against the person. It is sufficient for the prosecutor to prove that the defendant intended to participate in an act of fighting.

As the Law Commission observed, it is possible to justify the continued existence of the offence on such grounds only where the penalty for participating in the fight is relatively light,[14] and whereas the penalty was life imprisonment at common law, it is now three years. This corresponds to what the Court of Appeal had evolved in its sentencing practices as the spontaneous kind of affray, which did not necessarily attract particularly long sentences.[15]

Basic definition of affray

5–03   Section 3 of the Act provides as follows:

"(1) A person is guilty of affray if he uses or threatens unlawful violence towards another and his conduct is such as would cause a person of reasonable firmness present at the scene to fear for his personal safety."

The offence is for the first time triable either way, and is punishable on indictment with either three years' imprisonment or a fine and summarily with six months imprisonment and a fine not exceeding the statutory maximum.[16] It also carries a power of arrest; a constable may arrest without warrant anyone whom he reasonably suspects is committing affray.[17]

---

[12] *Oakwell* [1978] 1 W.L.R. 32, 1 All E.R. 1223 establishes the (unremarkable) proposition that the mere fact that the defendant was engaged in fighting and could have been prosecuted for an affray did not preclude a conviction for the offence of threatening behaviour under s.5 of the 1936 Act (now s.4). And see *Gedge* [1978] Crim.L.R. 167.

[13] *Woodrow* (1959) 43 Cr.App.R. 105. But see *Jones* (1974) 59 Cr.App.R. 120 below, 5–05.

[14] Report, paras. 3.55–3.59. Initially, the Commission proposed a sentence of ten years' imprisonment. For comment, see [1982] Crim.L.R. at 489. See also Glanville Williams, *Text* p. 207.

[15] *Annent and Moore* (1980) 2 Cr.App.R.(S) 318; *Anderson* (1985) 7 Cr.App.R. 210. In *Crimlis* [1976] Crim.L.R. 693, involving a fight between a small number of people outside a pub, the C.A. said that magistrates were capable of dealing with this all too prevalent offence. But so long as affray was indictable only, this could not be done on a charge of affray.

[16] Section 3(7).

[17] Section 3(6). This means, of course, that if the affray is over, there is no power of arrest under this section, but it is highly likely that the policeman will be able to arrest for a breach of the peace (2–18) or because the general arrest conditions are satisfied (2–17).

As defined, affray is no longer an offence of group disorder at all—it may be committed by a single individual attacking another. It is not wholly clear whether it is permissible for the tribunal of fact to take into account the surrounding circumstances and the conduct of any person defending himself in assessing the level of violence being used, and the frightening quality of the incident. The section refers only to "his conduct" as being the cause of the fear. But it may be argued that "conduct" includes the circumstances in which the conduct takes place, including such matters as the time of day or night in addition to the ferocity of the attack.

2. ELEMENTS IN COMMON WITH VIOLENT DISORDER

Uses or threatens

The prosecutor must prove that the person charged actually uses or **5–04** threatens some violence. Evidence that the defendant was suffering from injuries, or that his clothes were torn, would be some evidence that he had participated in the fight. The prosecutor is not required to prove who the particular victim of the defendant's violence actually was.[18] There is a fine line to be drawn here, especially since the offence of affray is subject to the ordinary principles of complicity.[19] Mere presence at the scene of the disorder is insufficient to establish liability.[20] It has even been held that presence remains no more than evidence of encouragement even when it is accompanied by a secret intention to help if necessary one of the participants in an affray.[21] So long as the defendant does not communicate his intention, he commits no offence.

Unlawful violence

The offence of affray can be committed by using or threatening unlawful **5–05** violence, which is the same concept (with two qualifications) as that required for riot and violent disorder. The exceptions are that, unlike riot and violent disorder, the offence can be committed only when the violence is directed towards the person rather than property,[22] and the threats cannot be by words alone; they must be at least accompanied by threatening gestures.[23] The first of these exceptions captures the essence of the common law offence of fighting.

The second also reproduces what was thought to be the common law.[24]

---

[18] If the antagonist is so identified, and gives evidence against the defendant, he is not to be regarded as an "accomplice" for the purposes of the law of corroboration, even though he may technically be guilty of the same offence; *Sidhu* [976] Crim.L.R. 379.

[19] *Summers* (1972) 56 Cr.App.R. 604.

[20] *Coney* (1882) 8 Q.B.D. 534.

[21] *Allan* [1965] 1 Q.B. 130.

[22] Section 8(*a*).

[23] Section 3(3).

[24] Lord Hailsham in *Taylor* [1973] A.C. 964 expressed the opinion that mere words were excluded from the ambit of the offence.

The Law Commission provisionally recommended that mere displays of force should be excluded from the offence,[25] largely, it would seem, since there were several other offences by which such behaviour could be prosecuted, and because there were no modern prosecutions for this form of the offence "save in quite exceptional circumstances."[26] On consultation, it was persuaded otherwise; to limit the offence to the actual use of violence would exempt the person who threw a punch that missed, or who brandished a razor. The Commission was also impressed by the great confusion that would be caused when there were a number of participants engaged in street fighting, since it would often be difficult to prove who actually used the violence as opposed to merely threatened it. It is difficult to resist the observation that in view of the anaemic definition of the offence, affray cannot properly be characterised as being committed by a number of people fighting in public, even if that is the most commonly charged form of it.[27] To use that characterisation as a justification for removing from the definition any requirement of actual fighting as an element in the definition is bootstrap reasoning of an advanced order.

Although liability for affray is excluded where the threats are by words alone,[28] it would be a somewhat unusual altercation in which both participants stood stock still whilst uttering their imprecations and threats. It is suggested that merely shaking one's fist at another should not be treated as amounting to threats of violence. A more marginal case is where the defendant is seen to be raising his fists in anticipation of the fight. Swinging a punch with the intention of striking the other is clearly caught, and it does not matter whether the punch lands or falls short. Although there appears to have been no prosecution for attempted affray, there is no reason in principle why the inchoate offence should not apply.

Self defence is clearly available.[29] It is submitted that the fact that the participants consent to the use of violence against one another does not make their conduct lawful. Such consent would not be an answer to a charge of assault,[30] and the policy reasons that forbid consenting adults to engage in fighting for the purposes of assault should apply equally in the case of an affray. If it were still the case that affray required that the incident should take place in public, the case would be cast-iron.

[25] Report, paras. 4.17–4.20.

[26] Report, para. 3.16.

[27] The Commission's statement that it "would expect no change in prosecution practice under any new offence replacing the common law" is at best a lame justification for emasculating the offence in the way that it recommended; why should prosecutors not properly prosecute for what Parliament has said to be criminal? It is at odds with the Commission's own statement of principle that "in a modern penal statute it is desirable to make as clear as possible precisely which conduct is to be penalised"; see paras. 3.16 and 3.17.

[28] Section 3(3).

[29] *Sharp and Johnson* [1957] 1 Q.B. 552; *Khan and Rakhman* [1963] Crim.L.R. 562.

[30] *Att-Gen's Refce (No. 6 of 1980)* [1981] Q.B. 715. But see *Jones* [1987] Crim.L.R. 123, where it was held that the defence of consent to "rough and undisciplined horseplay" in public advanced in answer to a charge of inflicting grievous bodily harm should have been left to the jury, who should acquit if they concluded that there was no intention to cause injury. Even if there was no actual consent, belief in consent would suffice.

In *Woodrow*,[31] it was held that affray is a continuing offence, so that where an indictment charged the defendants with a single offence and particularised several incidents that had occurred at different places and over a period of several hours, the indictment was not bad for duplicity. This seems to be at variance with *John Jones*[32] where a number of incidents over a period were held to be duplicitously charged as a single count of affray. The principle must be that although affray is a continuing offence, where the participants can no longer be said to be using or threatening violence towards another person, the offence is complete. If there is a clear break between one attack and another, the prosecutor would be wise to include two affray counts rather than one.

Such as would cause a person of reasonable firmness to fear for his personal safety

The degree of violence that must be proved is the same as that which **5–06** would substantiate a charge of violent disorder or even riot. The offence is clearly aimed at more than merely fighting in public. Given the gradations in penalty available, this sets the threshold for liability at a surprisingly high level, and it may be wondered whether an individual defendant on his own will often be able to perpetrate that degree of ferocity, although the Act clearly contemplates this as a possibility. However, where more than one person is involved as an attacker, section 3(2) provides that:

> "(2) Where 2 or more persons use or threaten the unlawful violence, it is the conduct of them taken together that must be considered for the purposes of subsection (1)."

At common law, it was required that the bystanders should be terrified. This is no longer necessary; fear for one's personal safety is a much lower level of alarm. Mere distress or concern is however insufficient to constitute fear for one's safety.

Absence of bystanders

Section 3(4) provides that: **5–07**

> "No person of reasonable firmness need actually be, or be likely to be, present at the scene."

This resolves the point that had to some extent been an open question before the Act. The Court of Appeal had decided that, where the offence takes place in public, there was no reason to require the presence of any bystander, actual or likely,[33] since by definition a public place was a place where the public were likely to be. No objection could be taken to this when the offence actually took place in public; now, of course, it need not.

---

[31] (1959) 43 Cr.App.R. 105.
[32] (1974) 59 Cr.App.R. 120.
[33] *Att-Gen's Refce (No. 3 of 1983)* [1985] 1 Q.B. 242. The reference clearly arose out of *Farnill* [1982] Crim.L.R. 38, decided nearly three years earlier.

The evidence of actual bystanders of what they saw and felt is some evidence of what the hypothetical bystander would have been likely to feel.

Public or private place

5–08   So far as the law of affray is concerned, the provision in section 3(5) that the offence may be committed in private as well as in public[34] states the existing law on the point, and arguably "corrects the error" that had crept in to the law a century or so earlier.[35] The section puts it beyond argument that there is no defence that the affray took place in private. This has the remarkable consequence that if a man attacks his wife (or vice versa) in the privacy of their own home, the offence of affray appears to be committed if the evidence is that there was violence of a sufficient degree. But the proper charge in such an event is, clearly, the appropriate offence against the person.

The mental element

5–09   Section 6(2) has already been dealt with in connection with violent disorder, and readers are referred to the earlier discussion.[36] To recapitulate briefly, it need not be shown that the person fighting intended to put bystanders (if there are any) in fear by what he does. It is sufficient if he is shown to be intentionally using violence or if he is aware that his conduct may be violent. Gesticulating wildly in a crowded space, so that others are frightened that they might be struck by the defendant, is not punishable unless it can be shown that the defendant was at least aware that his conduct might be having such an effect.

The extended definition of violence in section 8(b)[37] applies to affray; the words in section 8(a) "except in the context of affray" apply to that paragraph only. This means that to prove the requisite degree of *mens rea* for an affray, it will be sufficient for the prosecutor to prove that the defendant knowingly took part in a fight.

3. THE DISTINGUISHING FEATURES OF AFFRAY

Violence towards another

5–10   The origins of affray as being committed by fighting are preserved by the requirement that the violence used or threatened must be directed at another person, and not (unlike violent disorder and riot) at property. This is the effect of sections 3(1) and 8(a), the relevant part of which provides that:

---

[34] For a discussion of the policy see above 3–05.
[35] In *Hunt* (1845) 1 Cox C.C. 177, Alderson B. held that the offence must take place in public. This caused some difficulties in *Morris* (1963) 47 Cr.App.R. 202; *Clark* (1963) 47 Cr.App.R. 203; *Mapstone* [1963] 3 All E.R. 930, [1964] 1 W.L.R. 439; *Kane* [1965] 1 All E.R. 705, and was followed with some reluctance by MacKenna J. at first instance in *Button and Swain*. On appeal, the House held that the offence could take place in public or private; [1966] A.C. 591.
[36] 3–15.
[37] 3–07.

"except in the context of affray, it includes violent conduct towards property as well as violent conduct towards persons."

This means that missile throwing, although technically perhaps falling within the ambit of this offence, would place on the prosecutor the burden of proving that the missile was directed at a human being rather than at property. In those circumstances, it would be simpler for the prosecutor to charge violent disorder, providing that there are sufficient numbers present together.

Although the characteristic case of an affray involves fighting in public, there may be in cases where there is no actual violence applied to the person of another, since the offence is capable of commission by those who threaten violence. At common law, it was an affray where a person armed himself with "dangerous and unusual weapons,"[38] so that displays of force were technically affray.[39] A gang walking around in public brandishing bicycle chains could have been convicted. The requirement under consideration precludes this, since there is no threat of violence towards another person involved in such conduct.

Threats by words alone

Although displays of force such as the brandishing of an offensive   **5–11** weapon could be a common law affray, a mere altercation using threatening language could not constitute an affray at common law. The Act is intended to preserve this state of affairs in section 3(3), which provides that:

"For the purposes of this section a threat cannot be made by the use of words alone."

How real a limitation on the scope of the offence this will prove to be remains to be seen. People rarely utter threats without accompanying them by threatening gestures of some sort, and the combination of words and gestures, even without the display of a weapon, is clearly within the terms of the Act. Prosecutors may feel that in serious cases of what has hitherto been threatening conduct under the Public Order Act 1936, section 5 might be proceeded against as affrays.

Sentencing practice

The maximum penalty for the offence is now three years' imprisonment   **5–12** or a fine, or on summary conviction, imprisonment for a term not exceeding six months or a fine up to the statutory maximum.[40] Originally, the Law Commission had proposed that the offence should carry a penalty of ten

---

[38] *Taylor* [1973] A.C. 964, *per* Lord Hailsham, *obiter* at 987.
[39] "Technically," because this form of the offence did not appear to have been charged, even after the offence was resurrected in *Sharp and Johnson* [1957] 1 Q.B. 552. One reason for this is no doubt that prosecutions for going armed could be brought under the Prevention of Crimes Act 1953 (possessing offensive weapons), or under the Public Order Act 1936, s.5.
[40] Section 3(7).

years, but later accepted that this was difficult to defend in terms of principle.[41]

Before the Act the courts had, as a matter of sentencing practice, isolated two different types of affray. One was a spontaneous mêlée of the kind that tends to erupt at pub closing times or in dance halls. These were regarded as relatively minor, and the sentences reflected this; only exceptional violence justified a sentence of more than 18 months imprisonment.[42] The other type of offence involved in effect a preconceived and premeditated pitched battle, often accompanied by the use of weapons. These were occasionally visited with heavy penalties,[43] but generally only in situations where an offence against the person such as unlawful or malicious wounding could have been proved.[44] The reduction in penalty from the theoretically available life to three years will mean that prosecuting policy will have to be revised in these types of affray, and that prosecutions will have to be brought either for riot or violent disorder, or for offences contrary to the Offences Against the Persons Act 1861, sections 18, 20 and 47.

---

[41] Report, paras. 3.55–3.59. The main reason is that the ingredients of the offence are so etiolated that they do not require proof of any more than that the defendant took part in a fight of sufficient severity to put others in personal fear. It is not necessary to prove that the defendant either actually caused harm, or that he intended to do so.

[42] In *Annett and Moore* (1980) 2 Cr.App.R.(S.) 318, it was indicated that three years is the top range for this type of offence. The defendant had been convicted of both affray and assault occasioning actual bodily harm. And see *Noble* (1985) 7 Cr.App.R.(S.) 233 (three years, where the defendant had kicked his victim into unconsciousness), and *Anderson* (1985) 7 Cr.App.R.(S.) 210 (spontaneous bar fight during "stag night"—three years reduced to two). And see *Sergeant* [1975] Crim.L.R. 173.

[43] In *Andrews* [1971] Crim.L.R. 175, a sentence of three years for this sort of offence was described as "deterrent." And see *Callaway and Neale* [1971] Crim.L.R. 176. But in *Keys* [1987] Crim.App.R. 20, it was held that offenders might expect sentences of seven years and upwards in particularly bad cases.

[44] *Luttmann* [1973] Crim.L.R. 127. The defendant had shot his opponent in the stomach with a sawn-off shotgun at a range of six feet in the course of a very large pitched battle involving over 100 people. His sentence was reduced from 12 years to eight.

CHAPTER 6

CAUSING FEAR OF VIOLENCE, OR PROVOCATION OF VIOLENCE

1. BACKGROUND TO THE OFFENCE

History

The somewhat unwieldy title of this chapter, and the difficulty of finding **6–01** a brief but accurate label to designate the offence created by section 4 reflect the fact that the section is concerned with two quite separate species of wrongdoing. It is in part an offence of intimidation by threats, abuse or insults—a species of assault. The second, and quite different variety of wrongdoing involves provoking the use of unlawful violence by others, by the use of threats, abuse or insults. Only section 7(2)[1] prevents us from treating it as two separate offences.

The offence created by section 4 is intended to replace the Public Order Act 1936, section 5.[2] Since it is couched in similar terms to its predecessor in its reference to "threatening, abusive or insulting words or behaviour," at least some of the case law on the previous section is still pertinent.[3] But in several respects, it is crucially different from that familiar standby of public order law. The new offence requires that the conduct be used "towards another person" which the old offence did not, there is a different mental element, violence replaces breach of the peace, and the new offence can be committed in private as well as in public.

Section 5, enacted to deal with Fascist marches in the East End of London, had become unsatisfactory for several reasons. One defect was that it required proof of the likelihood of a breach of the peace as a result of the defendant's conduct. This had two vices; the common law concept was vague, and it seems highly likely that the offence was sometimes used to prevent nuisances of a relatively minor kind not aimed at by Parliament.[4] Several decisions of the higher courts had, shortly before the Act, injected

---

[1] See 2–05. The section abrogates *John* [1971] Crim.L.R. 283, which held that s.5 created two offences, which in truth it does. And see *Garfield* v. *Maddocks* [1974] Q.B. 7.

[2] Abolished by s.9(2)(*b*). Astonishingly, the equivalent section in the Theatres Act 1968, s.6, has been permitted to survive. It is, surely, otiose, the more so now that the offence under s.4 can be committed in private as well as in public.

[3] It seems highly likely that the distribution of functions between judge and the tribunal of fact, now usually magistrates rather than the jury, as explained by the House of Lords in *Brutus* v. *Cozens* [1973] A.C. 854 will remain as before. See 2–14. Although s.4 is triable summarily only, it may in exceptional circumstances be decided by the jury; s.7(3). Until the Criminal Law Act 1977, s.15 and sched. 1(1) the s.5 offence was triable either way, which explains the references to the jury rather than magistrates. The principles should be the same.

[4] See the remarks of Hodgson J. in *Nicholson* v. *Gage* (1984) 80 Cr.App.R. 80 and Lawton L.J. in *Ambrose* (1973) 57 Cr.App.R. 538, 540; *Venna* [1976] Q.B. 421. See D. G. T. Williams, "Threats, Abuse, Insults" [1967] Crim.L.R. 385; A. Dickey, "Some Problems Concerned With the Offence of Conduct Likely to Cause a Breach of the Peace" [1971] Crim.L.R. 265.

greater clarity into the law and linked breach of the peace more firmly to the notion of violence to persons or property.[5] But there were still uncertainties surrounding the notion, and rather than try to define it further, the new offence dispenses with the requirement of breach of the peace altogether, and replaces it with "unlawful violence."[6] Another serious defect in the previous law, pinpointed by the Law Commission, was that when the section was read literally, liability was seen to turn on the question whether the victim was likely to respond in a way that constituted a breach of the peace in the face of threats, abuses and insults.[7] When the victim was an inoffensive law abiding citizen, therefore, or a constable[8] who, by virtue of his training, is unlikely to respond to what the defendant was doing by committing a breach of the peace, there was little real likelihood of a breach of the peace, and no offence was committed, in spite of the defendant's intolerably bullying behaviour.

The reformulated law makes it plain that an offence is committed if the defendant conducts himself in a way that causes his victim to anticipate that the defendant is about to use unlawful violence. In addition, the new section captures the essence of the old law, that the conduct is caught if it is intended or likely to provoke others to cause unlawful violence.[9] As will be considered further, it is not at all clear, however, that the newly formulated offence entirely cures what might be called the policeman defect.

Because it imposes constraints by reference to what a person says, the section clearly sets limits to freedom of speech, and if too stringently enforced, is a potential threat to the civil liberties of the individual. In *Jordan* v. *Burgoyne*[10] Lord Parker C.J. made the point that the expressions "threatening, abusive or insulting" are all "very strong words," and Lord Reid in *Brutus* v. *Cozens*[11] repeated the warning against too expansive a reading of the section, observing that "vigorous and it may be distasteful or unmannerly speech or behaviour is permitted so long as it does not go

---

[5] Principally *Howell* [1982] Q.B. 416; *cf. Chief Constable for Devon and Cornwall, ex p. C.E.G.B.* [1982] Q.B. 459. See Glanville Williams, (1982) 146 J.P.N. 217, who points out that even after the attention of the courts, some uncertainties persist. See Chap. 10.

[6] Breach of the peace remains a central feature of public order law, particularly in connection with obstruction of a constable in the execution of his duty, and it is considered in 10–06.

[7] Report, paras. 5.15, 5.16.

[8] *Parkin* v. *Norman* [1983] Q.B. 92; *Marsh* v. *Arscott* (1982) 75 Cr.App.R. 211; *Read* v. *Jones* (1983) 77 Cr.App.R. 246; *Nicholson* v. *Gage* (1984) 80 Cr.App.R. 40.

[9] In the Law Commission's proposals, this was to be a group violence offence, requiring the presence of three or more, and was to be a replacement for unlawful assembly as well as for s.5. See the draft bill, cl. 4. But the Public Order Act 1936, s.5 was not within the Commission's remit, and when the Government considered the matter, it came to the conclusion that its own reformulated s.5 offence and that proposed by the Commission were "virtually identical," and "concluded that it would be sensible to fuse the two"; White Paper, para. 3.6. But in the fusion, certain features that are arguably more appropriate for a serious offence have crept in to what was a relatively well settled offence under s.5. In Para 3.11, for example, the government says that the requisite mental element will be "the same objective test that currently exists in relation to s.5"; this completely overlooks s.6 (3).

[10] [1963] 2 Q.B. 774.

[11] [1973] A.C. 854.

beyond any of these limits." Speech that might be regarded as insulting because it attacks the cherished views and beliefs of the audience at which it is directed is in particular jeopardy from this section.[12] The offence is not designed to penalise the expressions of opinion that happen to be disagreeable, distasteful, or even offensive, annoying or distressing. The language (or conduct) must be threatening, abusive or insulting.[13] So long as these considerations are borne in mind by those whose task it is to apply the section, and the public order requirements of the offence are rigidly insisted upon by the courts,[14] only such speech as is likely to give rise to immediate unlawful violence is in jeopardy, and that should be outside the protection afforded freedom of speech in a democracy.[15]

Definition of the offence

Section 4 of the Act provides: 6–02

"(1) A person is guilty of an offence if he—
    (a) uses towards another person threatening, abusive or insulting words or behaviour, or
    (b) distributes or displays to another person any writing, sign or other visible representation which is threatening, abusive or insulting,

with intent to cause that person to believe that immediate unlawful violence will be used against him or another by any person, or to provoke the immediate use of unlawful violence by that person or another, or whereby that person is likely to believe that such violence will be used or it is likely that such violence will be provoked."

The offence carries a power of arrest where a constable reasonably suspects that a person is committing an offence under the section,[16] is triable summarily only,[17] and punishable with six months or a fine to level 5.[18]

Subsections 1(a) and (b) broadly replicate the earlier law, and are readily enough comprehensible. But the second part of the subsection, which seeks to reproduce the essence of the previous law—allowing for the substitution of "violence" in place of "breach of the peace"—is potentially

---

[12] D. G. T. Williams, "Insulting Words and Public Order" (1963) 26 M.L.R. 425.

[13] The same expressions are used as the basis of the law of incitement to racial hatred, which is considered in Chap. 9.

[14] The evidence that the language of the statute is sometimes stretched beyond that which it can properly bear is frequently culled from newspaper reports, which are apt to be unreliable; see, e.g. Supperstone, p. 7, notes 19, 20, 1 and 2. And see Dickey, loc. cit. It seems highly probable that guilty pleas are often entered for fear of prosecution for even more serious offences.

[15] See G. Marshall, "Freedom of Speech and Assembly" in Constitutional Theory (1971) at p. 166 for an extended discussion of the previous law.

[16] Section 4(3). This means that there is no power of arrest after the offence has been committed, although the general arrest powers under s.25 of PACE would then come into play; 2–17.

[17] Section 4(4), subject to the fact that a conviction of this offence is available in certain circumstances as an alternative offence in trials on indictment; s.7(3).

[18] Section 4(4).

confusing, because it contains both subjective and objective requirements as alternatives. The whole clause is not qualified, as it appears to be on first reading, by the opening words "with intent." If a person acts with the intention of frightening or provoking, there is no difficulty. But if his defence is that it was not his intention to cause fear of violence or to provoke its use, his conduct might still come within the ambit of the subsection by virtue of its latter part. This objective aspect of the subsection is in fact the most practically important. The whole is complicated by the fact that, by virtue of section 6(3), the prosecutor has to prove a degree of *mens rea* that was probably not a requirement of the previous law.[19]

2. THE PHYSICAL ELEMENT

Uses towards another

6–03   The conduct in question must be used towards another person (which will include a group of persons). This was not an express requirement in the previous legislation, and it is not obvious why it should have been introduced into the new law. It harmonises the section with the other offences in this Part of the Act (apart from section 5), and sharpens the public order element of the offence. Violence is altogether more likely to arise where the conduct is actually directed towards another person. The expression emphasises that the offence is not a "victimless" one, but requires the actual presence of persons who are or are likely to be threatened, abused or insulted.

One difficulty that the new phrase might cause to the prosecutor arises where a person has been apprehended as part of a large and threatening group. Under the previous law, the conduct of the members of the group taken together could be assessed in deciding whether or not the behaviour was threatening.[20] Under the new law, liability is further particularised by the expression in question, so that it must be shown that the conduct was used towards another. Even though the prosecutor is able to rely upon the principles of complicity to establish that the particular defendant was guilty,[21] he still has to show that the defendant was encouraging others to use the conduct in question.

Another effect of the phrase would seem to be that it enables the person uttering the remarks or engaging in the behaviour to assert that he was unaware of the presence of his audience, which duplicates the requirements of intention now built into the section.[22] Our ordinary sense of language suggests that it is not possible for a person to use words or conduct "towards another person" if he is unaware of that person's existence. Some support for this interpretation may be found in the fact that section 5 affords a speaker or actor the specific defence that he was unaware and had

---

[19] *Parkin* v. *Norman* [1983] Q.B. 92.
[20] *McMahon* v. *Dollard* [1965] Crim.L.R. 238.
[21] *Smith* v. *Reynolds and Others* [1986] Crim.L.R. 559. And see the cases cited in 3–10.
[22] The mental element is considered further in 6–17 and 6–18.

no reason to suspect that his conduct may have been witnessed,[23] and it would be anomalous if there were no similar defence for the more serious offence. There would still be the difference between the two sections that, whereas section 5 plainly places the probative burden on the defendant, under section 4, the defendant would have no more than an evidentiary burden to raise the issue, in which case it would be for the prosecutor to establish that he knew that witnesses were present.

If this is the correct interpretation, it would mean that a case like *Masterson* v. *Holden*[24] would probably be differently decided on this point. There, two homosexuals were seen engaging in acts of intimacy early one morning in Oxford Street. There was evidence that passers-by were annoyed, and were on the verge of resorting to violence when the police intervened. The magistrates concluded that such conduct was "insulting,"[25] and the Divisional Court declined to reverse this holding of fact There was no evidence that the defendants were aware of the existence of those whom their conduct offended, although the court said that there was evidence from which the magistrates were entitled to infer that the appellants "must have known that other people would be likely to be present." The magistrates had found that "the appellants appeared wholly unaware of other persons in the vicinity," and even if there was evidence that they ought to have known, that is not necessarily the same as actual awareness. It is difficult to see how conduct could be said to be "used towards" another person of whose existence one was oblivious.[26]

Where the conduct consists of a distribution or display, that distribution must be "to another person." This also amends the previous law, and presents some potential difficulties. Does a person who exhibits his display to the whole world display to another person? Even granted that the singular can include the plural, so that "another" can include "others," a standing display is not necessarily displayed towards others. Suppose, for example, that a person has in his front window, a large and objectionable rascist poster, clearly visible from the street. His argument that he was not displaying it towards another gains strength from the fact that, under section 18 (which is explicitly concerned with the offence of stirring racial hatred) the word "display" is not similarly qualified. It may therefore be necessary to proceed against him under the latter section, supposing that the requisite intention can be established, or under section 5. Certainly, the exhibitor could be required to remove the offending poster by virtue of section 5. The same problem arises where a person is wearing an insulting emblem on his clothing. If there is an offence at all in such circumstances, it is probably under section 5 rather than section 4.

[23] 7–101.

[24] *Masterson* v. *Holden* [1986] 1 W.L.R. 1017, 3 All E.R. 39, a prosecution under the Metropolitan Police Act 1839, s.54(13), now repealed.

[25] 6–09.

[26] Which is not to say that such conduct should not be criminal; in 1976, the Law Commission recommended that there should be created a minor offence of engaging in sexual behaviour in such circumstances where the person knows "or ought to know" that the conduct was likely to be seen by and give offence to others. Report No. 76, *Report on Conspiracy and Criminal Law Reform*. The suggestion was not proceeded with.

Words or behaviour

6–04   Although the Act uses the expressions "words or behaviour" disjunctively, it is plain not only that either on its own will do, but also that words and behaviour may be considered cumulatively. The section means words and/or behaviour. Goose-stepping, giving a nazi salute and shouting "Seig Heil" have a significance when taken together which is not present when each element is considered separately. Certain kinds of behaviour, even when considered on its own, may have a symbolic significance that its witnesses find insulting. That symbolism can be taken into account in assessing the "threatening, abusive or insulting" quality of what is being done.

Distributes or displays

6–05   Where the offending message is in written form, the offence is committed where the defendant "distributes or displays" it. The offence would be committed by a single act of distribution, and the recipient may be a single person. This contrasts with the racial hatred offence, where the distribution must be to the public or a section of the public.[27] A contrast might also be made with section 5, which penalises "display" only. Persons who hand out leaflets clearly distribute them, and so might be guilty under section 4.

Writing, sign or visible representation

6–06   This phrase, which appears sufficiently comprehensive to apply to any visible image, was not included in the original Public Order Act 1936, but was introduced only when incitement to racial hatred was first made a criminal offence.[28] It will clearly include such relatively ephemeral representations as placards and banners, as well as slogans daubed on walls. It need not be confined to the written word[29]—symbols such as the swastika, and other offensive images will suffice. It would also include slogans on clothes, but not the adoption of an offensive uniform.[30]

Threatening

6–07   In view of the frequency with which section 5 was prosecuted, there is surprisingly little authority as to what constitutes threatening behaviour. According to Lush J., "it is the very essence of a threat that it should be made for the purpose of intimidating or overcoming the will of the person to whom it is addressed."[31] The threat need not be one offering physical violence, since it may be such as to provoke another to engage in violence, although it usually will be an offer of force of some kind leading the victim

---

[27] 9–14. The conduct of the defendant in *Britton* [1967] 2 Q.B. 51 might, therefore, be brought within the ambit of this section, so long as there is a real risk that violence will be provoked.

[28] By the Race Relations Act 1965.

[29] Writing is defined by the Interpretation Act 1978, s.5, Sched. 1 to include "typing, printing, photography and other modes of reproducing words in a visible form."

[30] The symbolism represented by the adoption of a uniform is prohibited under the Public Order Act 1936, s.1; 14–05.

[31] *Wood* v. *Bowron* (1866) L.R. 2 Q.B. 21 at 30.

to believe that violence against him or another person is about to be used or provoked. Indeed, as the new offence is defined, it creates what is essentially a statutory form of assault.[32] It seems tolerably clear that, in principle, the offence is capable of commission by words alone,[33] although conduct will give additional force to any words that are uttered.

Not every act of rowdyism is necessarily a threat. In *Hudson* v. *Chief Constable, Avon and Somerset Constabulary*,[34] the defendant was one of a group of football supporters who "became excited, jumping up and down and clapping his hands above his head." He fell forward, as a result of which there was a crowd surge and the people in front of him stumbled down the terraces. The Divisional Court concluded that nothing in that statement of facts constituted a threat, and the conviction was quashed.

It would appear from the report of *Hudson* that the defendant had simply overbalanced in his excitement. But suppose he had deliberately pushed those in front of him. Can the actual use of deliberate force constitute a threat, or more accurately "threatening behaviour?" The question will assume practical significance because of the potential overlap with the offence of violent disorder, to which section 4 constitutes an alternative offence. The point arose in *Oakwell*[35] where the evidence against the defendant on a charge of threatening behaviour was that he was seen fighting with another. This clearly might have been proceeded against as an affray, and counsel's argument before the Court of Appeal appears to have been that once violence had actually been used, the proper course would have been to charge that offence. The Court concluded, rightly it is submitted, that the mere fact that the defendant happens to have committed another offence in addition to the one with which he has been charged should not preclude a conviction. Counsel's second argument was that all the evidence presented to the court was that the defendant had been seen engaging in actual violence, but not threatening it, as the section requires. On this submission the Court concluded that there was sufficient evidence in the narrative presented to the jury from which they were entitled to conclude that there was threatening behaviour. It is not clear what the Court meant by this. One possibility is that the fight was in all probability preceded by an exchange of threats, however brief, and the jury would be entitled to infer this even if there was no direct evidence of it. A second possibility is that the use of violence itself amounts to threatening behaviour. This is more problematic, since threats generally refer to some future contingency rather than the present, and the section requires belief that violence "will be used"[36] The Court of Appeal certified that a point of law

---

[32] The question whether there should be an assault by words only is considered by the C.L.R.C. in its 14th Report, *Offences Against the Person*, Cmnd. 7844 (1980), para. 159. Wittingly or otherwise, the Act pre-empts the discussion by making threats an offence.

[33] Contrast affray, where it is explicitly stated that words alone do not constitute sufficient threat; s.3(3).

[34] [1976] Crim.L.R. 451. But see *Maile* v. *McDowell* [1980] Crim.L.R. 586.

[35] [1978] 1 W.L.R. 32, 1 All E.R. 1223.

[36] This was the point taken by the Court in *Marsh* v. *Arscott* (1982) 75 Cr.App.R. 211, that what Parliament envisaged was that the breach of the peace should be caused by what the defendant did.

of general public importance was involved in the question whether an offence under section 5 can be committed by a person who is already breaching the peace by the acts complained of. The House of Lords did not grant leave to appeal, the point remains a difficult and important one but the Act may have clarified the point, at least where the scuffle is an ongoing one. Whereas the essence of the previous law was that the threat was required to *cause* the breach of the peace,[37] now it is enough if the conduct causes a person to believe that there will be violence, which might include continued violence if the scuffle is already in progress when the witness appears on the scene. In those circumstances, he believes that violence will be used, and that is sufficient.

Another possible way of resolving the difficulty where the sole evidence is that the defendant was actually fighting is to say that, in the course of the fight, there is a series of threatening gestures, each one of which constitutes a fresh offence.[38] This reasoning seems slightly artificial where the essence of what is alleged is fighting, and the better course may be to charge the person fighting with assault, or affray, or both.

Where there is a single act of violence rather than an ongoing event, the law is slightly more problematic; its application to a case of missile throwing, for example, is not certain. A person who throws a missile at a football match can clearly be guilty of violent disorder (provided always that there are three or more present using or threatening violence), since his conduct can be regarded as violence by virtue of the extended definition of "violence" in the Act.[39] But such behaviour is not obviously threatening (although it is almost certainly disorderly),[40] and it may be doubted whether a conviction of the section 4 offence is proper unless the conduct complained of is such that it is likely to lead to further violence.

Where a group of persons is acting in a threatening manner, the pre-Act cases established that conduct of the defendants taken together should be considered. In *McMahon* v. *Dollard*[41] the two defendants were part of a group of "rockers" dressed in the appropriate "uniform" of black leather jackets, and chanting anti "mod" slogans. In their progress they took up the whole width of the footpath. The Divisional Court treated their conduct as an act of group violence, so that each member of the joint group was guilty of threatening behaviour. One obstacle to adopting the same course under the new Act is that, in the cases of riot, violent disorder and affray, where the conduct of joint defendants is to be assessed together, the Act actually says so.[42] By implication, therefore, the opposite is the case when the Act does not say so, as is the case in the section under consideration, *Expressio unius, exclusio est alterius* is the Latin maxim governing the

---

[37] *March* v. *Arscott* last note.
[38] See *Gedge* [1978] Crim.L.R. 167.
[39] See 3–07.
[40] See *Wilde* v. *Police* [1984] 2 N.Z.L.R. 673.
[41] [1965] Crim.L.R. 238. And see *Simcock* v. *Rhodes* (1977) 66 Cr.App.R. 192; *R.* v. *Mansfield JJ. ex p. Sharkey and Others* [1985] Q.B. 613.
[42] Sections 1(1), 2(1) and 3(2). The last of these is the most explicit, and the most difficult for the prosecutor to circumvent, since like s.4, affray is an offence that can be committed by one person acting on his own.

point. That is, where one has been explicitly mentioned, the other is impliedly excluded. The difference is to be explained by the historical origins of the various sections. If the pre-existing law is permitted to prevail, it will serve to emphasise how little like a code the Act really is.

Can one "threaten" for the purposes of the section by offering to do that which is lawful? For example, would the section apply where, in the course of a heated dispute between neighbours, one of the participants were to "threaten" to call in the police, or to refer the matter to his solicitors, with the result that the other protagonist resorted to violence. Two possible solutions to this potential difficulty may be suggested. One may be to say that, although the use of the word "threatening" is primarily a matter for the tribunal of fact, as a matter of law a person cannot be held to threaten when his threatened conduct is "lawful." Alternatively, it might be said that since it is unreasonable of a person to respond to such a threat by unlawful violence, it can be said that the conduct is not "likely" to have such a result.[43]

Conditional threats are covered by the section, unless the condition expressed is such as to make it abundantly plain that the person uttering it had no intention of carrying out his threat. The person to whom it is addressed cannot be expected to conduct a minute linguistic analysis of what is said to him where this is accompanied by aggressive gestures. A threat expressed in the form "if I catch you when there are no police about" addressed to an adversary is not caught by the section, since it is not a threat of such as to cause the victim of it to believe that he will be the object of "immediate" violence. But it may be likely to provoke the victim into the use of violence, in which case it would be caught by the section.

Abusive

The point has been made that "abusive" and "insulting" are semanti-   **6–08**
cally very similar,[44] and can be used more or less interchangeably (the information or indictment can use the blunderbuss language of threatening, abusive or insulting without offending the rule against duplicity).[45] In a sense, then, it is unnecessary from a practical point to distinguish between the various forms of offensive words or behaviour. But it is necessary to establish that the words or behaviour in question fall within the terms of one or other (or perhaps both) of these epithets.

Can a true statement be abusive or insulting? Yes, must be the answer. A person who is illegitimate may very well resent being called a bastard,

---

[43] See the discussion of the objective requirement, 6–10 to 6–12.
[44] A. Dickey, [1971] Crim.L.R. at 268.
[45] *Vernon* v. *Paddon* [1973] 1 W.L.R. 663, 3 All E.R. 302; Melford Stevenson J.'s dictum in that case that the section covered "any form of human conduct which is intended to provoke a breach of the peace, or whereby such a breach is likely to be occasioned" is, it is submitted, quite wrong. It is at variance with the remarks of Lord Reid in *Brutus* v. *Cozens* [1973] A.C. 854, cited in 6–01. One of the criticisms levelled at the offence of incitement to racial hatred is precisely that seditious language can be couched in moderate terms, and is not then within the ambit of the law, even though it is likely to cause racial hatred; see Supperstone, p. 18. Of course, if the language is likely to provoke another to violence, it will more readily be adjudged threatening, abusive or insulting in its own right.

although it happens literally to be true. Of course, if the person making the observation is unaware of the illegitimate status of the person to whom he is addressing his remarks, he would not be guilty of the offence since he would lack *mens rea*.[46]

Insulting

6–09   Of the three epithets employed by the section, "insulting" has received most attention from the courts.[47] It was in respect of this word that the House of Lords in *Brutus* v. *Cozens*[48] developed its doctrine that "ordinary words" are the province of the tribunal of fact. The potential mischief of uneven application that such a doctrine opens up was examined earlier.[49]

In *Brutus* v. *Cozens*, the House declined to attempt to define what is meant by insulting, and later courts have not sought to do what the House would not, although they have sought to give guidance as to what the term might mean. In *Parkin* v. *Norman*[50] where the defendant had engaged in masturbation within sight of a plain clothes policeman in a public lavatory, McCullough J. put the matter as follows:

> "The Act does not make it criminal to use offensive or disgusting behaviour whereby a breach of the peace is likely to be occasioned. It requires . . . 'insulting behaviour.' What then is an insult? We do not propose to attempt any sort of definition, particularly after the speeches in *Brutus* v.*Cozens*, but some consideration of its characteristics are necessary in the light of counsel's submissions that behaviour of the type here is not insulting. One cannot insult nothing. The word presupposes a subject and an object and, in this day and age, a human object.[51] An insult is perceived by someone who feels insulted. It is given by someone who is directing his words or behaviour to another person or persons. When A is insulting B, and is clearly directing his words and behaviour to B alone, if C hears and sees is he insulted? He may be disgusted, offended, annoyed, angered and no doubt a number of other things as well; and he may be provoked by what he sees and hears into breaking the peace. But will he be insulted? The appellant's conduct was aimed at one person and only one person. He obviously hoped, and after a little while would presumably have believed, that the person to whom it was directed was another homosexual. Whatever he was trying to do, he was not trying to insult him. Whatever another homosexual would have felt, he would not, pre-

---

[46] See 6–18.

[47] A number of cases on the point are decisions under s.54(13) of the Metropolitan Police Act 1839, now repealed; the section was in all material respects identical.

[48] [1973] A.C. 854.

[49] 2–14.

[50] [1983] Q.B. 92.

[51] In *O'Dowd*, [1985] April 4, *The Times*, (news item), it was reported that magistrates were persuaded to hold that miaowing at a police dog was, in the words of the arresting sergeant, "abusive in the situation." The Divisional Court quashed the conviction. In *Kinney* v. *The Police* [1971] N.Z.L.R. 924 (a prosecution for disorderly behaviour for paddling in a public fish pond) the remarks of Woodhouse J. that "the ducks seemed unperturbed . . . the attitude of the goldfish was unknown" were only partly facetious.

sumably, have felt insulted. In fact, the second person was a police officer. Was he insulted? He had gone in there in plain clothes to catch anyone he saw doing this sort of thing, and he caught one. It seems to us quite unrealistic to say that he would have felt insulted. Suppose, as was possible, that the person to whom the behaviour was directed had been a heterosexual using the lavatory for its proper purpose. He would almost certainly have felt disgusted and perhaps angry, but would he have felt insulted? The argument that he would is that the behaviour was tantamount to a statement 'I believe you are another homosexual,' which the average heterosexual would surely regard as insulting. We regard this as the only basis on which the behaviour could fairly be characterised as 'insulting.' ''

It will be seen from this passage that the question whether or not conduct can be insulting may depend upon a complex mixture of objective fact and the maker's intention which the new Act does not entirely manage to disentangle. A person is not now guilty of the offence unless he is at least aware that his conduct may be insulting.[52] Even though he does not intend to insult, or is not seeking to insult, he can be guilty of the offence if he is aware that his conduct is or might be insulting. Equally, it would be no defence to the charge of insulting behaviour founded upon, for example, handing out leaflets seeking to persuade soldiers to desert that it was not the leafleter's intention to insult, so long as the leaflet was in fact insulting, and the person distributing it was at least aware that it might be regarded as insulting by the person to whom it was addressed.[53]

What then does insulting mean? Glanville Williams offers the following elaboration:

"language or conduct is not said to be insulting unless it is intended to show contempt or disesteem, or is understood by the hearer or observer to show this attitude."[54]

It is suggested that this captures the core of what it is for conduct to be insulting. The witness of an insult, or the victim of it, will feel that his dignity is impugned and regarded as a matter for contempt by the person whose conduct he witnesses. A definition of that sort might allow the person addressed to take into account the fact that the person making the utterance was seeking to make a serious point, or engage him in reasoned discussion, or was acting unintentionally.[55] Even making allowances for these factors, a person might be insulted if the actor makes it plain by his words or conduct that he holds in contempt those (including the victim) who do not share his point of view.

[52] 6–03 (uses towards another), and s.6(4) below, 7–09.
[53] *Williams* [1968] Crim.L.R. 563 and *Arrowsmith* [1975] Q.B. 678.
[54] *Textbook*, at p. 64.
[55] According to Supperstone, p. 11, n. 12, counsel argued in the course of *Williams* [1968] Crim.L.R. 563 that no appeal to reason could be regarded as insulting. The report does not disclose either this fact, or the response of the court. The submission surely goes too far, and it would depend upon the precise circumstances in which the appeal to reason was made.

In *Masterson* v. *Holden*[56] it was held that the conduct was insulting because the magistrates might properly have taken the view that such objectionable conduct in a public street may well be regarded as insulting in that it suggests to a witness that he or she is somebody who would find such conduct in public acceptable himself or herself. If that is so, then it may be doubted whether the earlier decision of *Bryan* v. *Robinson*[57] was correctly decided. In that case, the hostess of a club selling non-alcoholic beverages importuned three passers by. The persons solicited in this way reacted with annoyance, perhaps indicating that they supposed that they were being solicited for the purposes of prostitution (the magistrates having found as a fact that "it would be impossible for anyone so touted or solicited without enquiry to appreciate the purpose of the solicitation, and that a solicitation for this purpose in the circumstances of time and place was such an affront that it might provoke a breach of the peace.") These findings of fact were given remarkably short shrift by Lord Parker C.J. who held that the conduct could not amount to insulting behaviour. If it is insulting to suggest to a person that he is a homosexual, is it not equally insulting to suggest to a man that he is the sort of person who might be susceptible to solicitation in the streets by women? Lord Parker's response to that suggestion was that no offence had been committed in any event because, even if it could be said that such conduct was insulting (which he doubted) most men approached in such a way are not likely to resort to violence.[58]

The objective conditions

6–10   If it cannot be shown that the person uttering the remarks intended to induce his victim to believe that he was about to engage in violence himself, or intended to provoke the object of his remarks into using unlawful violence,[59] what will be termed here the objective conditions come into operation. These focus on the propensities of the defendant's conduct to instil fear of violence, or alternatively to provoke it, whatever the defendant's intention may have been.

Abstracting the references to intention from the section, it can be reconstructed to read that a person is guilty if he uses language or conduct towards another person that is threatening, abusive or insulting in circumstances:

> "whereby that person is likely to believe that such violence (*i.e.* immediate unlawful violence against him or another) will be used or it is likely that such violence will be provoked."

This establishes two grounds of liability; for the first, it must be likely that

---

[56] [1986] 1 W.L.R. 1017, 3 All E.R. 39.
[57] [1960] 1 W.L.R. 506. The decision precedes *Brutus* v. *Cozens* and shows a greater readiness to disturb the finding of the magistrates than the decision of the House of Lords would appear to permit.
[58] This consideration will exculpate where the charge is brought under s.4, but not necessarily under s.5; Chap. 7.
[59] Intention is considered further in 6–17.

the person at whom the conduct is directed believes that the use of violence is imminent. For the second, it must be shown that it is likely that violence will be provoked. Each will be considered in turn.

Whereby that person is likely to believe

The expression "towards another person" which has already been con- **6–11**
sidered[60] narrows the scope of the offence by comparison with the previous law. It is the person towards whom the words or conduct are directed—an actual rather than a hypothetical person—who must be likely to believe that the violence will be used, either against himself or another. If a policeman encounters a person using threatening language against another, he must make a judgment as to whether or not the addressee of the threats is likely to believe that the threats will be implemented.

It is insufficient that the person addressed should fear or be likely to fear violence against property. This means that the section is in this respect more restricted than was section 5. A breach of the peace included a threat made to a person's property in his presence.[61] A threat to a person's property in his presence might very well provoke the use of force by way of self-protection, which would seem to qualify. The difficulty is that the violence referred to by the subsection must be immediate "unlawful" violence, and a person is entitled to employ a certain amount of force in the protection of his property. This means that if a person is threatening another's property in such a way that he is likely to cause another to act in self defence, he commits no offence. The logic of this is not easily discerned.

The best evidence that the victim—the person towards whom the threats, abuses or insults were directed—did believe that he was about to be subjected to immediate violence would come from the mouth of the victim himself, but it is not necessary to produce a bystander as a witness in court to prove the point; it can be a matter for inference from the narrative of events presented to the court. Where the allegation is that the person to whom the remarks were addressed was likely to form a given belief, it means "likely to form" and not "did form."[62] If the particular addressee of the remark happens to be unusually unimaginative or drunk, the conduct may still fall within the terms of the section. It is the risk to public order inherent in the defendant's words or conduct that represents the harm struck at by the section.

A constable may be a victim for the purposes of this offence, in certain circumstances, under this limb of the objective condition. This alters the previous law, where it was held in effect that where a policeman was the only witness to what had occurred, no offence was committed. In the case in which the defect in the law was first exposed, *Marsh* v. *Arscott*[63] the defendant who was drunk began using a stream of abusive language

---

[60] 6–03.
[61] *Howell* [1982] Q.B. 416.
[62] *Marsh* v. *Arscott* (1982) 75 Cr.App.R. 211. In *Parkin* v. *Norman* [1983] Q.B. 92 at 99, the Court said that "insulting behaviour does not lose its insulting character simply because no-one who witnessed it was insulted."
[63] Last note; followed in *Read* v. *Jones* (1983) 77 Cr.App.R. 246.

directed at the policemen who were investigating his suspicious presence in a car park. It was held that no offence was committed; Parliament was concerned in section 5 with cause and effect, and the causal sequence was not present in the situation confronting the court because, even if the defendant himself was engaging in a breach of the peace, he was not likely to cause or occasion a further breach. Where policemen were the only witnesses to what had occurred, there was most unlikely to be a breach of the peace, since the policemen were unlikely to engage in the use of unlawful violence. The new law remedies this defect, to a certain extent. It will be argued that if a policeman is confronted by a situation in which he fears that violence will be directed towards him if he intervenes, or it is likely that there will be such violence, the offence is committed.

In *G. v. Chief Constable for Stroud*[64] for example, the defendant (a youth of 15) was using public recreational facilities designed for younger children. He was asked to leave, but declined to do so, and the police were called. After some prompting, the defendant gave the police his name and address, and then at his mother's prompting began to leave the scene, using foul language as he went. He was told by the police to desist, but did not do so, and when arrested, used considerable force to resist. The justices found that there had been a breach of the peace before the police arrived, because the mother-in-law of the person who had asked the defendant to leave the swings had been "alarmed" by the defendant's conduct. This was held to be incorrect, but irrelevant; incorrect, because a mere sense of alarm was insufficient to give rise to a fear of a breach of the peace, and irrelevant because the justices had found (or there was evidence from which they could have found) that the constables reasonably believed that the defendant's own behaviour was likely to constitute a breach of the peace. If the justices had applied the wrong criteria as to what constituted a breach of the peace in the case of the mother-in-law, it is difficult to see how the court could have been so sure that the justices had applied the right criteria to the decision of the policeman. The plain truth is that in such a situation, when the defendant was actually walking away from the scene, no further breaches of the peace were likely to be occasioned by him.

Should the same scenario arise under the new law, it is suggested that the following analysis applies. The police are entitled to tell the person walking away from the scene to discontinue using his filthy language, which would in all likelihood constitute an offence under section 5 of the new Act. If they fear that in calling for quiet, and seeking to ensure it where the subject declines to desist, they might themselves be the objects of violence, the offence is made out. Indeed, it is sufficient that it is likely that they will fear the use of violence.

Another but more legally complicated way of arriving at the same result under the subsection is to say that, when the police seek to intervene, it is likely that a belief is likely to arise in the mind of the first victims, that violence towards the police is a likely outcome of the defendant's conduct.

---

[64] [1987] Crim L.R. 269.

Where a policeman is surrounded by a group of youths, one of whom he is attempting to pacify or arrest, and the youth uses language such that the policeman is or feels threatened, it is submitted that an offence is committed.[65] Even if the defendant himself can plausibly say that he did not intend to use violence, it is sufficient if he uses the language or behaviour in a situation where the addressee is likely to believe that violence will be used against him either by the speaker or by other persons. Only where the person using the foul language makes it plain that he has no intention of resorting to violence, and there is no bystander who is likely to be provoked by what the defendant is doing, is no offence committed under this section.[66]

Where the victim of the threats, abuses or insults is a law abiding citizen who is unlikely to be provoked into using violence,[67] an offence may nevertheless be committed under this limb of the subsection. This was perceived to be a "loophole" in the previous law, and according to the White Paper, the new formulation under consideration is designed to resolve this problem.[68] But it is not wholly clear that the problem has disappeared. If, for example, two people watch young tearaways behaving in an abusive manner towards them from a safe distance across the street, a conviction would be proper only if they were really likely to fear that violence would be likely to be used against them (or another).

It is likely that violence will be provoked

The expression to be considered in this section stands in splendid isola- **6–12** tion at the end of the subsection. Although it appears to be grammatically linked to the remainder of the subsection, it is not qualified by much of what appears before it. It does not mean that the person at whom the conduct is directed must believe that it is likely that violence will be provoked. It is enough if the defendant has used threatening, abusive or insulting language or conduct such that it is likely that violence will be provoked. This is an altogether more simple reading of the section, and would apply where the policeman comes across a person who is using abusive language, and comes to the conclusion that it is likely that somebody in the audience will intervene to put a stop to it, using unlawful violence (citizens may have the power to prevent a breach of the peace, but not to preserve the public quiet). If the person seems likely to overreact to the abuse or insults, and to use more force than he is entitled to employ, then it is likely that unlawful violence will be used, and the offence is committed.

One of the defects under the previous law was that where the person being addressed was a police constable no offence was committed, since a constable would be unlikely, because of his training, to react by being pro-

---

[65] As in *Simcock* v. *Rhodes* (1976) 66 Cr.App.R. 192. See also *Read* v. *Jones* (1983) 77 Cr.App.R. 246; *Grant* v. *Taylor* [1986] Crim.L.R. 252.
[66] Although the policeman may very well be entitled to ask the person to desist from the offensive conduct under s.5, and to arrest should the defendant fail to do so.
[67] 6–12.
[68] Para. 3.9.

voked into breaking the peace.[69] He is no more likely to be provoked into acts of violence, even though he is made the subject of abusive and insulting remarks and conduct, and it is suggested that in this respect the law remains precisely the same. Unless the circumstances are such that he fears that violence is likely, no offence is committed.

The difficulty is well illustrated by the facts of *Nicholson* v. *Gage*,[70] in which a Peeping Tom was caught in a public lavatory looking through a hole in the wall into the women's lavatory. He was seen doing so by a policeman and arrested, but it was held by the Divisional Court that he should not have been convicted, since on those facts (even accepting that the conduct was insulting) no breach of the peace was likely. For the same reason, no offence is committed under the new law either. The Peeping Tom was not himself likely in the circumstances to resort to violence, and the constable was certainly not. It is possible that a third person might have entered the lavatory and been provoked into violence by what the defendant was doing—the woman's partner, for example. But it really stretches the bounds of possibility too far to say that it is likely that this will happen. In *Parkin* v. *Norman*,[71] McCullogh J. said that "it is to be noted that the words of the statute are 'whereby a breach of the peace is likely to be occasioned' and not 'whereby a breach of the peace is liable to be occasioned.' This is a penal measure and the courts must take care to see that this former expression is not treated as if it were the latter."

Where the "victim" of the threats, abuse or insults is a well-behaved, law abiding member of the public, he or she is unlikely to be provoked to use unlawful violence by the speaker's comments, and no offence is committed under this limb of the section. But if the prosecutor can show an intention to provoke unlawful violence, as by causing a policeman to over-react, a prosecution will succeed because of the defendant's intention to be considered presently.

Under the previous law, the offence was committed where the onlooker believed that violence was intended to be provoked or "whereby a breach of the peace is likely to be occasioned." Section 4 is worded somewhat differently, and uses the term "provoked" where hitherto "occasioned" was used. It is arguable that this change in terminology might be an occasion for the rethinking of the doctrine enunciated by Lord Parker C.J. in *Jordan* v. *Burgoyne*[72] that the speaker must take his audience as he finds it. There can be little doubt that the speaker in that case intended to provoke the immediate use of unlawful violence by those whom he was addressing. It would have suited his purposes admirably well to have had the police arrest them for responding to his antagonism. There can be little doubt that, however understandable their response would have been, a violent response would have been an unlawful one. A person may be the occasion of violence without necessarily provoking it. If counter-demonstrators determined to thwart the right of a person to speak unpopular opinions resort to

---

[69] *Parkin* v. *Norman* [1983] Q.B. 92.
[70] (1984) 80 Cr.App.R. 40.
[71] Above n. 69.
[72] [1963] 2 Q.B. 744; 1–08.

force as a result of what he is saying, the speaker is not for that reason alone to be regarded as using threatening, abusive or insulting words or behaviour "whereby it is likely that such violence will be provoked." It may be likely that the audience will respond adversely, entitling the police to request the speaker to desist. But it may be doubted whether he necessarily commits an offence under section 4 should he fail to do so.[73]

Imminence of fear or provoked violence

The victim of the threatening, abusive or insulting behaviour must **6–13** believe that violence is imminent, since the section refers to "immediate" unlawful violence. This clarifies the pre-existing law. This requirement is appropriate in a Public Order Act, and resolves the point left open by the court in *Ambrose*.[74] That case well illustrates the dangers of conceptions such as "likelihood" that an event will or will not occur. The appellant had used offensive language to a 12 year old girl who had run home and complained to her father. The father said in evidence that he had felt very angry and felt like assaulting the appellant, who was convicted under section 5. It was held that the words used were incapable of being insulting (even though they were rude and offensive), and the Court left open the question currently under discussion. The section resolves the point, although the question of what is or is not immediate is, of course, still a matter of degree.

Unlawful violence

A person who threatens lawful violence cannot be convicted under this **6–14** section. If he disturbs a trespasser, for example, and tells him that he is about to use force to expel the intruder, there is no doubt that the intruder realises that he is being threatened, and that violence is about to be used against him. But it is not unlawful force, and the intruder is aware that it is not, and no offence is committed.

Public or private—the dwelling exception

Under the previous law, the offence could be committed in public only. **6–15** Distinguishing between public and private places caused the courts a great deal of difficulty.[75] The Government took the view that the distinction between public and private was meritless, partly because in the course of the miners' dispute, summonses brought under the 1936 Act, section 5 were dismissed because the persons charged were able to show that they were on National Coal Board or other private property, and no offence

---

[73] Although he may still be guilty of obstructing a constable in the execution of his duty; Chap. 10.
[74] (1973) 57 Cr.App.R. 538. In the White Paper, para. 3. 10, the government indicated that it did not intend to change the law in this respect, and proposed to delete the requirement of immediacy as advocated by the Law Commission; see Report, para. 5.46. Why this should have been reinstated is unclear, but it is certainly in keeping with the public order character of the offence.
[75] *Wilson* v. *Skeock* (1949) 113 J.P. 294; *Ward* v. *Holman* [1964] 2 Q.B. 580; *Cawley* v. *Frost* [1976] 1 W.L.R. 1207, 3 All E.R. 743; *Edwards* v. *Roberts* (1978) 67 Cr.App.R. 228.

was committed even though the victims of the threats were on the public highway.[76] Other instances offered as giving rise to meritless acquittals were where protestors invaded military bases or private farmlands. In order to exclude domestic disputes, there is a proviso that the offence cannot be committed inside a private dwelling.

Section 4(2) reads:

> "(2) An offence under this section may be committed in a public or a private place, except that no offence is committed where the words or behaviour are used, or the writing, sign or other visible representation is distributed or displayed, by a person inside a dwelling and the other person is also inside that or another dwelling."

What constitutes a dwelling for the purposes of the section is further spelled out in section 8, which provides:

> " 'Dwelling' means any structure or part of a structure occupied as a person's home or as other living accommodation (whether the occupation is separate or shared with others) and does not include any part not so occupied, and for this purpose 'structure' includes a tent, caravan, vehicle, vessel or other temporary or movable structure."

The effect of the section is now plainly that neighbours in the garden or yard who threaten, abuse or insult one another may be convicted of the offence under this section. Indeed, it would seem that members of the same family who quarrel in the garden may be guilty of the offence. For the purposes of this legislation, the principle that an Englishman's home is his castle bears a very restricted scope; a person is safe from conviction only inside his own front door, and then, only when his victim is also inside the house. He commits the offence if the "victim" of his conduct is outside the door. A person who stood at his window shouting threats, abuse or insults would commit the offence so long as the victim was in the garden or elsewhere outside the structure of the dwelling. There is also a somewhat curious exemption from liability where the victim is in "another dwelling." If the victim is in an adjoining house, or in one across the street, no offence is committed. If the victim emerges from his own dwelling, and his protagonist repeats his threats or insults, the offence is committed. Similarly, the case of displays or visible representations, the offence is committed if the material is visible to the public generally, but not, apparently, if it can be seen only by persons inside another dwelling. But in this instance, the exception is more apparent than real, since if the person insulted or abused can read the display from his garden, the offence is committed (assuming, of course, that it satisfies the other requirements of the section). Only

---

[76] White Paper, para. 3. 8. Whether the summonses were properly dismissed on this ground is, in the light of the decisions in the last note, highly questionable. In *Edwards* v. *Roberts*, Bridge L.J. says (approving remarks of Lord Goddard in *Wilson* v. *Skeock*) that "the offence may be committed if the person to whom the words or behaviour are directed is in a public place." And see *Smith* v. *Hughes* [1960] 2 All E.R. 859 at 861.

those displaying offensive materials in the windows of multi-storey apartment buildings would seem to be safe from conviction.

3. THE MENTAL ELEMENT

Background

The mental element of this offence has already been touched upon in the **6–16**
discussion of the requirement of "towards another,"[77] which, it was suggested, entailed an awareness on the defendant's part of the existence of the person threatened, abused or insulted. In addition, the section contains two further references to intention, which will be dealt with in this Part. Section 4(1) provides that the offence is committed if the defendants act with intent to cause a person to believe that immediate unlawful violence is about to be used, or with intent to provoke such unlawful violence. This probably repeats the existing law. In addition there is specific provision in section 6(3), which provides that the defendant must as a minimum be aware that his conduct is or might be threatening, abusive or insulting. This probably changes the existing law, making the offence more difficult to prove.

With intent

The current meaning of the word "intent" has been discussed in connec- **6–17**
tion with violent disorder.[78] Applying what was explained there, it may be said that a person intends to cause a person to believe that immediate unlawful violence will be used against him when he (the person uttering the threats, etc.,) either desires to cause such an effect, or when he realises what impact his conduct is almost certain to have and nevertheless persists with it. Similarly where the charge is that he intends to provoke another to use such violence. It may be noted that a person may intend to cause a particular outcome, even though its occurrence is unlikely. This means that if a person intends to cause a policeman to react unlawfully, and uses threats, abuse or insults in an attempt to cause the policeman to overreact, he commits the offence if the other ingredients are proved to have occurred.[79] It would not be enough that the actor merely intends to have himself arrested, for example by way of protest. There, his intention is that the policeman should act lawfully, and that is not sufficient. But sometimes, protesters may act with the intention of causing unlawful conduct on the part of the police, with a view to making complaints at a later stage. They have the requisite intention under the section if that is what they intend to do. In the situations where the actor does not desire the result, but merely sees it as a foreseeable outcome of his conduct, the House of Lords has said that there is merely evidence from which the tribunal of fact can infer that he intends.[80]

This intent requirement is, of course, an alternative to the objective con-

[77] 6–03.
[78] 3–15.
[79] *Grant* v. *Taylor* [1986] Crim.L.R. 252.
[80] *Moloney* [1985] A.C. 905.

ditions,[81] on which the prosecutor is far more likely to place reliance. Although it may be important for sentencing purposes to know whether the conduct was deliberate or otherwise, it does not affect liability, so long as one or other of the conditions is satisfied.

Section 6(3)

6–18   Before the Act, there was some doubt as to whether or not a person had to be aware that his conduct or language was or might be regarded as being threatening, abusive or insulting.[82] The matter has been resolved in principle by section 6(3) which provides:

> "A person is guilty of an offence under section 4 only if he intends his words or behaviour, or the writing, sign or other visible representation, to be threatening, abusive or insulting, or is aware that it may be threatening, abusive or insulting."

As a result of this section, it is now open to a person to claim that he was unaware of the effect that his words or conduct might be having, in which case it is then for the prosecutor to prove beyond reasonable doubt that he was so aware. Where the prosecutor relies on a continuing course of conduct, as will often be the case with offences under this section, a claim that the actor had failed to advert to the consequences that his conduct was having will lack plausibility. The fact that the defendant was intoxicated, and his awareness was impaired for this reason will not avail, since the Act expressly provides that it should not do so.[83] Where the defendant claims that as a result of intoxication, he did not realise that his conduct was or might be regarded as threatening, abusive or insulting, the magistrates must make a determination as to what they considered that the defendant would have realised had he been sober, and the conclusion that he would have realised will be virtually inevitable. If the defendant can plausibly assert that he is sufficiently without perception even when he is sober, he must be acquitted.

The awareness provision would not necessarily mean that the defendant in *Parkin* v. *Norman*[84] lacked sufficient *mens rea*. There was no intention to be insulting—quite the reverse—but it might readily be inferred that the defendant must have realised and did realise that his homosexual overtures might not be welcomed by the person at whom he was directing them. The

---

[81] 6–10.

[82] In *Parkin* v. *Norman* [1983] Q.B. 492, the Divisional Court held that there need be no intention to insult. Smith and Hogan argued that there was, in principle, a requirement of at least awareness (at p. 744), whereas *Archbold* expressed the view that this was unlikely to commend itself to the Appellate courts; para. 25–8. In the summary of the changes that it proposed to s.5 in the White Paper, the Government makes no reference to this aspect of the law, and it may be that the change was in that sense accidental. The Law Commission had recommended such a change in its reformulation, but it was advocating the change in connection with a proposed offence that was to be triable either way, and carry a penalty of two years; Report, para. 5.47–5.49. But the decision is defensible in principle, for the reasons given in Smith and Hogan.

[83] Section 6(5), considered more fully in 3–16.

[84] Above, n. 82.

court held that no offence was committed in that case, since the person at whom the conduct was directed was an undercover policeman who was unlikely to be provoked to violence, and no offence would be committed under the Act either, for the same reasons. Had the victim been someone other than a policeman, however, who might more readily have been provoked by the defendant's conduct, the defendant would have had sufficient *mens rea* under the section, since he would have been aware that his conduct might be insulting.

Whether any particular conduct is or is not threatening, abusive or insulting is, of course, a matter of objective judgment for the tribunal of fact. So far as *mens rea* is concerned, the issue is not whether the defendant himself considered that the words or conduct in question was insulting, but whether he realised that the persons whom he was addressing might do so. This may cause difficulty where the audience were annoyed or distressed by what the defendant was doing. In *Williams*[85] where the defendant was convicted of handing out leaflets advising American servicemen to consider deserting, several people responded angrily. It is suggested that the reaction would be sufficient to alert the defendant to the fact that others may regard his conduct as insulting; that is, he was aware of all the facts by virtue of which the tribunal of fact comes to the conclusion that his conduct was insulting, and that is sufficient. His claim that he did not consider it insulting is, technically, a mistake of law, and as such no excuse.

[85] [1968] Crim.L.R. 678.

CHAPTER 7

OFFENSIVE CONDUCT

1. BACKGROUND TO THE OFFENCE

The title of the offence

Section 5 of the Act creates a relatively minor offence[1] which is likely to be of considerable practical significance. In this book, it will be called "offensive conduct," because although the marginal note speaks of "harassment, alarm and distress," and although it was commonly referred to in the Parliamentary debates as the "disorderly conduct" clause, this is not the most accurate description. Section 5(4) gives the police a power of arrest in certain circumstances for "offensive conduct."[2] The Act then defines "offensive conduct" to mean "conduct the constable reasonably suspects to constitute an offence under this section."[3] It would therefore seem sensible to refer to the offence by the descriptive label that Parliament itself has provided. This provides a neat solution to the brief description of what is otherwise a somewhat amorphous offence in its definition and contours.

The origins of the offence

The definition in terms of "threatening, abusive or insulting behaviour," is modelled upon the Public Order Act 1936, section 5, but its scope is much wider than the old offence, and is meant to be. This is signalled in part by the introduction of "disorderly behaviour" as a constituent of the new offence, and by the abandonment of the requirement of a breach of the peace, and its replacement with the requirement that the conduct should take place "within the hearing or sight of a person likely to be caused harassment, alarm or distress thereby." This is a much lower threshold of liability than the notion of violence that underlay the common law concept.

Before the Act, section 5 of the 1936 Act was supplemented by a miscellany of powers to be found in local legislation, which empowered the police to deal with minor nuisances and acts of hooliganism. However, as a result of the reorganisation of local government effected by the Local Government Act 1972, section 262, most of this legislation had lapsed or been repealed, and it was felt necessary to enact something to replace it. Section

---

[1] The offence is punishable summarily with a fine not exceeding level three; s.5(6). Since there is an associated power of arrest, the deprivation of liberty that might be entailed makes the offence a more serious one than the sentence would perhaps otherwise indicate. Where a power of arrest is used to stop an essentially peaceful demonstrator from expressing a point of view, the opportunity for effective protest may be aborted. Wrongful arrest can be visited with the award of exemplary damages, which is a measure of the seriousness with which the law regards this deprivation of liberty.

[2] Considered below, 7–11.

[3] Section 5(5).

5 is the result. This was a Government proposal, first made in the White Paper, which gave as instances of misbehaviour that might not be the subject of control without some such provision[4]:

> "hooligans on housing estates causing disturbances in the common parts of blocks of flats, blockading entrances, throwing things down stairs, banging on doors, peering in at windows,[5] and knocking over dustbins;
> groups of youths persistently shouting abuse and obscenities or pestering people waiting to catch public transport or to enter a hall or cinema;
> someone turning out the light in a crowded dance hall, in a way likely to cause panic;
> rowdy behaviour in the streets late at night which alarms local residents."

It must be emphasised that the question whether or not such conduct is now covered by section 5 cannot be determined by this statement of governmental intentions. The proposal was not even expressed in Bill form in the White Paper, and the proper interpretation of the legislation once enacted is a matter for the courts.[6] At most, the White Paper can be used to identify the mischief at which the legislature was aiming. It should perhaps be added that the amended section 4 would not necessarily have caught the conduct in question, because of its definition in terms of violence which might follow from the defendant's conduct. The point of the new section is that acts of hooliganism may cause harassment, alarm or distress to those who witness it. The victims being weak, vulnerable, or simply law abiding are not likely as a result to resort to violence, however great the provocation by threats, abuse or insults. Yet the experience to which they have been subjected is one of which it is proper for the criminal law to take notice.

Because of the potential breadth of the language in which the section is drafted, it affords scope for injudicious policing; considerable common sense and restraint on the part of the police will be called for in the application of the section. In advocating the creation of the new offence, the Government made it plain that it did not wish to promote legislation too similar in this respect to the discredited "sus" laws.[7] However, the Bill did not incorporate all of the safeguards against this possibility that were adumbrated in the White Paper, and it was substantially redrafted in the light of opposition objections in the course of its Parliamentary passage. In addition to the requirement that the conduct be "disorderly," it is subject

---

[4] Para. 3.22.

[5] In *Smith* v. *Chief Superintendent of Woking Police Station* (1983) 76 Cr.App.R. 234, it was held that such conduct might amount to an assault where the person spied upon saw the Peeping Tom, and was frightened by him, so long as the defendant intended to frighten.

[6] See 2–13.

[7] The "sus" laws, so-called because of the abbreviation of their origins in the "suspected persons" section of the Vagrancy Act 1824, were abolished by the Criminal Attempts Act 1981, s.8 in the wake of the Third Report of the Select Committee on Home Affairs, H.C. 271 of 1980–1981.

to the objective requirement that the conduct must be such that it is, independently, "within the hearing or sight of a person likely to be caused harassment, alarm or distress thereby." This is more than a mere measure of the offensive character in question. It requires the presence of an actual victim.

Definition of the offence

7–03   Section 5 of the Act provides as follows:

> "(1) A person is guilty of an offence if he—
>   (a) uses threatening, abusive or insulting words or behaviour, or disorderly behaviour, or
>   (b) displays any writing, sign or other visible representation which is threatening, abusive or insulting,
>
> within the hearing or sight of a person likely to be caused harassment, alarm or distress thereby."

Although the section is similar to section 4, several important distinctions between the two offences may be noted. There is the difference that the conduct in question need not be directed "towards another person" as is required for section 4. The conduct struck at by the section may cause misery without being aimed at any particular victim. Nor is the offence under section 5 expressed to be committed by the distribution of offensive matter, as opposed to its display.[8] Presumably, it will be committed if the distribution of offensive literature were itself sufficiently ostentatious to constitute a display. A court should be slow to draw any such inference, however, since Parliament has in section 4 indicated its intention that an offence should be committed only where the distribution of literature is likely to lead to the use of violence. Pickets handing out leaflets to passers by may thereby cause harassment, alarm or distress, but they should not be held to be guilty of an offence on that account alone. If, however, their conduct is itself disorderly, they may commit the less serious offence. But the principal difference between the two is that the section 5 offence is not designed to prevent violence; its aim is to prevent harassment, alarm or distress.

2. THE ELEMENTS OF THE OFFENCE

Threatening, abusive or insulting words or behaviour

7–04   The meanings of these expressions was considered in the previous chapter,[9] and it may be expected that they will be interpreted in essentially the same way in this context. Even though the offence is a relatively minor one, the words remain "strong" ones, and the criminal sanction should not be invoked unless its use is really called for.

---

[8] In *Alexander* v. *Smith* (1984) S.L.T. 176, it was held by the High Court of Justiciary that distributing by selling a rascist magazine constituted disorderly conduct.
[9] Chap. 6.

Disorderly behaviour

Whereas the other forms of offensive conduct may be by words or conduct, "disorderly behaviour" is specified to be capable of commission by behaviour only. In truth, language cannot be disorderly, at least on its own. Where the misconduct complained of consists of both words and conduct, it seems likely that both will be considered by the magistrates in deciding whether or not what the defendant did amounted to disorderly conduct. It would be artificial in the extreme were the courts to seek to separate words from conduct, as the section seems to envisage. 7–05

It is extremely difficult to say in advance whether or not any particular action or series of actions will be regarded as disorderly conduct.[10] The word "disorderly" appears to fall into that category of "ordinary" words of which Lord Reid spoke in *Brutus* v. *Cozens*[11] which may well mean that the higher courts will be reluctant to spell out for magistrates and the police exactly what conduct does or does not fall within the ambit of the section. Such a state of affairs would be highly unsatisfactory, given the civil liberties implications for both the police and the individuals who are subject to the Act. There is a great deal of potential here for criminalising conduct that amounts to little more than arguing with a policeman, which it should be one of the aims of public order law to prevent.[12]

There may be a strong temptation for those responsible for the implementation of the Act[13] to reason that if conduct is not "orderly," then it must be "disorderly." But these are not precise antonyms, and it must be borne in mind that the purpose of the use of the word is to stigmatise certain types of behaviour as criminal. That the Oxford English Dictionary should define disorderliness in terms of "violating moral order, constituted authority, or recognised rule" simply serves to reinforce concern that the section may be seen to create an offence whose commission is in the eye of the beholder. The Government adverted to this problem in its White Paper, recognising that "it is not easy to define in a manner which conforms with the normally precise definitions of the criminal law, but which at the same time is sufficiently general to catch the variety of conduct aimed at. The Government recognises that there would be justifiable

---

[10] Some guidance as to what might constitute disorderly conduct may perhaps be had from the decisions of other jurisdictions, especially Commonwealth ones. For a survey of the New Zealand law, see G. G. Hall, "Identifying Disorderly or Offensive Conduct: The Scope of Judicial Discretion under Section 3D of the Police Offences Act 1927" (1979) 4 Otago U.L.R. 217. But it should be noted that the New Zealand statute (now the Summary Offences Act 1981) does not contain any independently objective standards for the offensiveness of the conduct in question (such as its tendency to harass, alarm or distress), and the New Zealand judges have therefore tended to read these in to the element of disorder. The disorderly conduct article of the American Model Penal Code s.250(2) defines with some specificity what sort of conduct is included within the concept of disorderliness.
[11] 2–14.
[12] 1–03.
[13] An assurance was given by a Home Office spokesman in Parliament that a circular on the implementation of the section would be issued by the Home Office, reminding the police "of the importance of the traditional rights of free assembly and the European Convention on Human Rights"; Lord Glenarthur, H.L. vol. 479, col. 584, June 13, 1986. See the Home Office circular No. 11/1987, especially para. 11.

objections to a wide extension of the criminal law which might catch conduct not deserving of criminal sanctions.'' The spirit of these comments, which reflect the traditional attitude of the courts towards the imposition of criminal liability, might properly be borne in mind by the courts in giving content and scope to the new legislation.

In deciding whether or not conduct is disorderly, the magistrates may take into account factors such as the place where the incident occurs, and the time of day. Behaviour that might be tolerated at New Year's Eve celebrations or at a football match could be regarded as disorderly at a solemn thanksgiving ceremony. Mere drunkenness will not of itself amount to disorderliness,[14] although it might readily give rise to disorderly conduct.

Within sight or hearing of a person likely to be caused

7–06 The evidence must show that there was a bystander within sight or hear- **7–06**
ing of the defendant who might be caused harassment, alarm or distress as a result of what the defendant was doing. The bystander requirement in section 5 is not simply an objective hypothetical measure of the quality of the defendant's conduct, as in the first three sections of the Act; rather, the policeman or other witness who gives evidence of the defendant's misconduct must satisfy the magistrates that there was a person present who was likely to be harassed, alarmed or distressed. If the person who was the victim is prepared to give evidence that he experienced harassment, alarm or distress, so much the better. The victim's evidence is not conclusive on the point, since the question is whether the conduct was likely to have one of the requisite effects. Nor is it necessary that the "victim" should give evidence. This was a matter of some controversy during the passage of the Bill. Because of the vague character of "disorderly conduct," the White Paper proposed that actual feelings of harassment or alarm must be experienced by the bystander, and the best evidence of that would be direct testimony from the victim.[15] The difficulty with such a proposal, however, is the question of proof. The vulnerable persons whom it is the aim of the section to protect are precisely those least likely to be prepared to attend court to give evidence, if only for fear of later reprisals. Experience with previous legislation framed in similar terms showed that the courts in practice were often prepared to dispense with the evidence of a "victim," and accepted instead the word of a complainant (usually a policeman) that the victim appeared to have been harassed or annoyed. This was a disreputable subterfuge,[16] yet it appears that the same sort of procedure is enjoined by the new Act. At most, the prosecution witness is obliged to testify that there was a person present or in the vicinity who was likely to have been subjected to the sensations described.

The section is unclear on a related point. The conduct must take place within the hearing or sight of a person likely to be caused the sensations in

---

[14] Para. 3.26.
[15] Para. 3.26.
[16] See the 16th Report of the Criminal Law Revision Committee, *Prostitution in the Street* Cmnd. 9329 (1984), para. 6.

question; does this mean that the conduct must actually be seen or heard by the person whom it is intended to offend? Suppose, for example, that a person were to walk behind another person who suffered from a physical deformity (such as a limp) imitating it, for the amusement of his friends. Had the target turned round, he would have seen the conduct and been distressed by it. It is submitted that the offence is made out in such circumstances, and that a policeman would be justified in calling upon the "joker" to desist (under subsection 4). That is, conduct may be within the sight or hearing of another, even though the other may not actually have heard it. The section might otherwise be very difficult to work in cases where, for example, the defendant(s) were engaged in kicking over dustbins on an estate. Although the police do not need to be certain that a person has heard or seen what is going on before they can call for quiet under the Act (since it is sufficient that they have reasonable cause to believe that an offence is being committed), they would afterwards have to conduct house to house enquiries before they could truthfully say that the conduct was actually heard or seen by a bystander.

Harassment, alarm or distress

7–07   The requirement that the victim might suffer harassment, alarm or distress is a much lower threshold than the violence or possibility of violence that is the touchstone of the other offences under Part I of the Act. Each of the terms has a significance that should not be overlooked in the application of the Act. Mere annoyance or irritation caused by inconvenience is not sufficient. Although in this connection too the higher courts are likely to say that the terms used are matters of fact for the magistrates,[17] it will be open to those courts to say that in certain circumstances, the reactions of the victim were not likely to be those of harassment, alarm or distress. It may be doubted, for example, that a single act could give rise to a sensation of harassment; it would be an unusual use of language to say that a person was harassing another by a single act (such as a wolf whistle), since that term generally connotes an element of persistence.[18] As a corollary the object of the conduct may feel upset or annoyed, but not harassed. Upset and annoyance seem rather less strong emotions than "distress," which connotes some degree of perturbation and emotional upset. Although alarm is not expressed to relate to any particular source of concern, we do not usually speak of alarm in a vacuum. A person who is alarmed experiences a sudden fear or apprehension of danger—some sort of anxiety.

There is no reason why a policeman should not be regarded as the victim of this conduct. It may perhaps be more difficult to alarm him than it would be to alarm the vulnerable persons whom the offence is principally designed to protect. But unlike the Public Order Act 1936, section 5, the

7–07

---

[17] See the discussion of *Brutus* v. *Cozens* [1973] A.C. 854 at 2–14.

[18] "Harassment" is the basis of criminal liability in two other situations in English law; it is an offence to harass debtors under the Administration of Justice Act 1970, s.42. It is also an offence to harass a residential occupier with the intention of causing him to quit under the Prevention from Eviction Act 1977; Chap. 14.

test here is not whether or not the victim is likely to be provoked into responding violently, but whether he is likely to experience alarm, distress or
harassment as a result of what is being done and said. Even if it can be said
that, in the course of his duty, a policeman will become hardened to certain
sorts of ritual taunts and insults, there is no reason to doubt that he can also
experience harassment and distress.

Public or private place

7–08   As with the offence under section 4, domestic disputes are excluded   **7–08**
from the operation of the section and the private dwelling exemption also
applies in this context. Readers are referred to the earlier discussion.[19]

3. THE MENTAL ELEMENT

The mental element

7–09   For an offence of such relative insignificance, the mental element is one   **7–09**
of considerable complexity, and possibly places a greater onus on the prosecutor than is warranted. To begin with, section 6(4) provides:

> "A person is guilty of an offence under section 5 only if he intends his
> words or behaviour, or the writing, sign or other visible represen-
> tation, to be threatening, abusive or insulting, or is aware that it may
> be threatening, abusive or insulting or (as the case may be) he intends
> his behaviour to be or is aware that it may be disorderly."

With the change in wording necessitated by the inclusion of "disorderly,"
this is in virtually identical terms to the provision in relation to section 4,
and would therefore seem to open up the same possibilities for argument
that that section does through section 6(3).[20] A person is permitted under
the section to argue that he was unaware that his conduct was likely to be
regarded as disorderly by those who witness what he is doing. Where there
is a protracted course of conduct, and those who witness it respond angrily
to what is occurring, there will perhaps be no difficulty. But where there
has been a single incident, the claim to ignorance may carry some plausibility, and be difficult for a prosecutor to overcome.

There is a difference between sections 4 and 5 that the conduct
impugned does not need to be used "towards another" under section 5.
One consequence of this distinction is that the prosecutor bears no burden
of showing that the defendant was aware of the existence or presence of
another who was likely to be harassed, alarmed or distressed. This reading
of the section is reinforced by the existence of the defence in section
5(3)(a) that the actor had no reason to believe that there was any person
within sight or hearing likely to suffer harassment, alarm or distress.

When the two subsections are juxtaposed, however, they seem to create
a difficulty. It might be asked how a person could be proved to be "aware
that his conduct may be disorderly" when he genuinely but thoughtlessly is

---

[19] 6–15.
[20] 6–18.

unaware of the existence of a bystander. In *Masterson* v. *Holden*[21] for example, it was not shown against the homosexual couple in Oxford Street that they were actually aware of the presence of bystanders who were incensed at what the defendants were doing, even though they had every reason to be so aware. In such circumstances, the prosecutor would appear to have two arguments open to him. He could ask the magistrates to infer that the defendants were actually aware of the presence of bystanders, and that they were as a corollary aware that their conduct was disorderly. Alternatively, he could argue that a defendant has sufficient awareness for the purposes of section 6(4) if he knows of the circumstances by which it is said that his conduct is disorderly. Even though the defendant does not regard the nature of his own conduct as being disorderly, he has a sufficient *mens rea* to satisfy the section by being aware that he is using offensive language, or kicking over dustbins or turning out the lights in the cinema, or whatever else may be alleged to constitute the disorderly behaviour. He then has the defence under section 5(3) that he was unaware of the bystander's presence, but carries the burden of establishing his defence.

4. THE DEFENCES

The defences outlined

7–10   Section 5(3) affords to the defendant a number of defences relating to   **7–10**
lack of fault that are not available on a charge under section 4. The section provides:

> "It is a defence for the accused to prove—
>
> (a) that he had no reason to believe that there was any person within hearing or sight who was likely to be caused harassment, alarm or distress, or
> (b) that he was inside a dwelling and had no reason to believe that the words or behaviour used, or the writing, sign or other visible representation displayed, would be heard or seen by a person outside that or any other dwelling, or
> (c) that his conduct was reasonable."

These are defences in the strict sense that they place on the defendant a burden of proving his innocence, on the balance of probabilities.[22] Paragraph (a) has already been examined in the context of the mental element in the offence, and will not be considered further. Paragraph (b) supplements the domestic dwelling exemption in section 5(2). Presumably, it is necessary because the offence does not require proof that the conduct in question was used "towards another person." The defendant who accidentally offends a passer-by or the neighbour has quite a heavy burden to discharge, having to show that he was not negligent in acting as he did.

Paragraph (c) is a quite extraordinary delegation (if not abdication) of

---

[21] [1986] 1 W.L.R. 1017, 3 All E.R. 39.
[22] *Hunt* [1986] 3 W.L.R. 1115. See Patrick Healy, "Proof and Policy: No Golden Threads" [1987] Crim. L.R. 355.

legislative responsibility, of which the courts may have some difficulty in making sense. It prompts in the lawyer the question, "reasonable, having regard to what"? If circumstances such as time and place are relevant to the question whether the conduct is disorderly in the first place, what sorts of factors should the court (or the policeman on the spot) take into account in deciding whether or not the conduct was "reasonable"? The test is clearly an objective one, in the sense that it is for the magistrates to say after the event whether or not what the defendant did was reasonable. One factor that might be taken into account, it is suggested, is the actor's purpose in behaving as he did. This means that it is open to a defendant to argue that his conduct was reasonable because he was attempting to obtain or communicate information. Ultimately the test to be applied is that of the magistrates, and they may also take into account such factors as the likelihood that disorder might ensue as a result of what the defendants were doing, and the reasons prompting the constable to intervene in the first place.

5. THE POWER OF ARREST

The power of arrest defined

7–11   Sections 5(4) and (5) contain somewhat unusual powers of arrest. They **7–11** provide:

> "A constable may arrest a person without warrant if—
> (a) he engages in offensive conduct which the constable warns him to stop, and
> (b) he engages in further offensive conduct immediately or shortly after the warning
>
> (5) In subsection (4), 'offensive conduct' means conduct the constable reasonably suspects to constitute an offence under this section, and the conduct mentioned in paragraph (a) and the further conduct need not be of the same nature."

A number of features of this power require comment. At the time when he calls for the actor to desist, the constable must already have reasonable grounds to believe that an offence has occurred. In the circumstances, he must already have sufficient evidence to enable him to proceed by way of summons, and could also arrest if the general arrest conditions of PACE are satisfied.[23] There may also have been a breach of the peace and the prospect of its repetition, so that the common law powers will also continue to apply.[24] In circumstances of group disorder, in particular, it may be quite impractical to expect the constable to issue a request for the actor to desist before making his arrest. But there is nothing to preclude a charge being brought under section 5 even though the arrest was not effected under the section.

The Act does not appear to require the constable to warn the offender

[23] 2–17.
[24] 2–18.

that he may be arrested if he fails to desist as required. "Warn" is therefore used in a slightly unusual sense if that is the correct interpretation, since it usually connotes reference to a consequence that will arise in the event of non-compliance. Even if it is not technically required, it would no doubt be sensible police practice to spell out the fact that an arrest is imminent in the event of non-compliance.

A constable need not be in uniform when he effects the arrest (and calls for the defendant to desist as a preliminary), although if an off-duty police-man does attempt to implement the Act, strict conditions should be observed as to what he must do and say to make it plain that he is a con-stable. There is otherwise a grave danger that the people whom he addresses might well regard the policeman as a rival lout.

A difficulty of interpretation arises over the question whether it must be the constable who warns who effects the arrest. Where two constables are present seeking to restore order, and one warns the offender to desist, it must be quite common for a colleague to effect the arrest. Unhappily, the section does not appear to authorise him to do so, since it refers in para graph (a) to "the constable," a reference back to the constable who has issued the warning in the first place. Had paragraph (a) repeated the indefi-nite article, and said that "a" constable warns him to stop, the point would have been plain. If the courts are to make the section wholly efficacious, therefore, they may have to interpret "the" to mean "a." Alternatively, they may regard the single warning given by one policeman in the presence of a colleague as issuing from both. There is in truth an element of fiction in both of these courses, and it may be sensible for policemen acting in con-cert to adopt the stratagem of issuing a joint warning, as for example by telling the actor that "we are warning you to stop what you are doing."

The constable need not have witnessed the conduct in question before he utters his warning; he could act on the basis of a report that he received from a person who has been caused harassment, alarm or distress, or on the report of somebody who has witnessed it. He would then have reason-able cause to believe that an offence had been committed. Furthermore, even if the person warned did not repeat the conduct about which he had been warned, he could be arrested if he engaged in a different act or course of offensive conduct. The section does not specifically empower the police-man to give directions as to how the actor should conduct himself in the future (as by leaving the spot). This must be found in his powers to prevent a breach of the peace, or in his powers to prevent an obstruction to the highway.

6. MISCELLANEOUS DISORDERLY CONDUCT OFFENCES

Misconduct at public meetings

7–12   Police powers to control public meetings and the offences that might be committed at such meetings are the principal subject of this book. In addition to the general law, there are two specific statutory provisions, one dealing with public meetings of any description, and the other with election meetings only.   **7–12**

Section 1 of the Public Meeting Act 1908 provides:

"(1)　Any person who at a lawful public meeting acts in a disorderly manner for the purpose of preventing the transaction of the business for which the meeting was called together shall be guilty of an offence . . .

(2)　Any person who incites others to commit an offence under this section shall be guilty of a like offence.

(3)　If any constable reasonably suspects any person of committing an offence under the foregoing provisions of this section, he may if requested to do so by the chairman of the meeting require that person to declare to him immediately his name and address and, if that person refuses or fails to so declare his name and address or gives a false name and address he shall be guilty of an offence under this subsection."

The offences under subsections (1) and (2) are punishable with imprisonment for a term of six months,[25] or a £1,000 fine,[26] and are therefore triable summarily only. Section 1(3) carries a level one fine only. There is no power of arrest under the section, so that arrest is available only where the general arrest conditions of PACE are satisfied,[27] or the disrupters are committing some other arrestable offence.

The offence could be used against counter-demonstrators who set out to "smash" their opponents or to stop them from expressing the point of view that they set out to express. There has been an historical reluctance on the part of the police to enforce the section,[28] which is perhaps to be regretted. Where persons set out deliberately to prevent others from conducting perfectly lawful business, they do the cause of freedom of speech a disservice. Heckling, or seeking temporarily to disrupt the speaker are insufficient to amount to such an offence. There must be an intention to prevent the transaction of the business, so that the speakers are forced to stop. The use of the word "lawful" to qualify the public meeting in question does not add a great deal. In *Burden* v. *Rigler*[29] justices acceded to a submission that a meeting on the highway was *ipso facto* unlawful, and dismissed the proceedings. It was held by the Divisional Court that they should not have done so, and the case was remitted with directions to the magistrates to ascertain whether or not the ingredients of the offence were made out.

The offence under the Public Meeting Act does not apply to election meetings.[30] Specific provision is made by the Representation of the People Act 1983,[31] which makes it an "illegal practice" under electoral law.

---

[25] 2–08.
[26] Criminal Law Act 1977, Sched. 1.
[27] 2–17.
[28] *Supperstone*, p. 21.
[29] [1911] 1 K.B. 337.
[30] Public Meeting Act 1908, s.1(4).
[31] Sections 97 and 169.

What constitutes a "public meeting" as opposed to a private one for the purposes of these sections is not spelt out any further in the legislation.[32]

Public drunkenness

7–13   Public drunkenness is an offence under the Licensing Act 1872, section **7–13**
12[33] which reads:

> "Any person who in any public place is guilty, while drunk, of disorderly behaviour may be arrested without warrant by any person and shall be liable on summary conviction to a fine not exceeding level three."

The offence is commonly associated with the persistent drinker and alcoholic,[34] but is by no means limited to such persons in its application.

Whether or not a person is "drunk" is a question of fact and degree.[35] Although the Shorter Oxford Dictionary says that it means that the person has drunk "intoxicating liquor to an extent which affects steady self-control," it is arguable that the person must have taken intoxicating liquor to excess so that he has lost the power of self control. It has been held that the term relates to being under the influence of intoxicating liquor, and the offence is not capable of commission where the intoxication is induced by a substance other than alcohol, such as a solvent.[36]

Disorderly conduct bears the same significance as it does in the section 5 offence, and is likely to involve conduct such as shouting or singing in such a way as to alarm persons near by, uncertainty of gait, staggering, lurching

---

[32] *Cf.* Public Order Act 1936, s.9, which defines a public meeting for the purposes of the uniforms offence in s.1, by providing that " 'meeting' means a meeting held for the purpose of the discussion of matters of public interest or for the purpose of the expression of views on such matters"; and " 'Public meeting' includes any meeting in a public place and any meeting which the public or any section thereof are permitted to attend, whether on pay ment or otherwise"; and " 'public place' includes any highway and any other premises or place to which at the material time the public have or are permitted to have access, whether on payment or otherwise."

[33] As amended by the Criminal Justice Act 1967, s.91(2), and PACE, Sched. 6, para. 21. There is also a lesser level one offence of being found drunk in a public place; Licensing Act 1872, s.12. It is an offence under the same provision to be drunk in possession of a loaded firearm, which includes a loaded air rifle.; *Seamark v. Prouse* [1980] 1 W.L.R. 698, 3 All E.R. 26, (1980) 70 Cr.App.R. 236.

[34] See R. Light, "The Decriminalisation of Public Drunkenness" (1985) 135 New L.J. 66. And see D. Farrier, *Drugs and Intoxication* (1980), Chap. 3.

[35] In *Presdee* (1927) 20 Cr.App.R. 95, the Chairman told the jury on a drink driving charge that "drunk" meant "unfit to drive." The conviction was quashed on appeal, on the basis that drunk means intoxicated, and not merely unfit to drive.

[36] *Neale v. RJME (A Minor)* (1984) 80 Cr.App.R. 20. See also *Lanham v. Tickwood* (1984) 148 J.P. 737, to the effect that where the defendant has been taking a mixture of drink and drugs, the tribunal of fact must be sure that the defendant's intake of alcohol alone is such as to make him drunk. Where the solvent abuser is on school grounds, he commits an offence of nuisance under the Local Government (Miscellaneous Provisions) Act 1982; *Sykes v. Holmes and Maw* [1985] Crim.L.R. 791.

or swaying, and behaviour that causes people to take evasive action. For the constable, the advantage of this section is that it confers an immediate power of arrest. A disadvantage, from the policeman's perspective, is that the offence must take place in a public as opposed to a private place.[37]

By virtue of Sports Events (Control of Alcohol) Act 1985, section 2(2), it is an offence to be drunk in or while trying to enter a designated sports ground during the period of a designated sporting event.[38] These include virtually all English and Welsh football grounds at which professional football is played, and all professional football matches in England and Wales, or matches abroad in which English and Welsh clubs are taking part.

Disrupting religious ceremonies

7–14   The Ecclesiastical Courts Jurisdiction Act 1860, section 2 makes it an   **7–14**
offence to engage in "riotous, violent or indecent[39] behaviour" in places of worship belonging to the Church of England and places of worship certified under the Religious Worship Registration Act 1855. The Burial Laws Amendment Act 1880, section 7 penalises the same sorts of behaviour at any burial under the Act (burials without Church of England rites). Both of these offences are currently under review by the Law Commission,[40] which canvassed suggestions that the existing law should be modernised to prevent the disruption of religious services or offensive conduct in places of public worship. Whether any further legislation is necessary in view of the enactment of the Public Order Act 1986 is a matter that needs to be considered afresh.

Misconduct on public transport

7–15   Statutory authority is given to the various public transport authorities to   **7–15**
regulate the conduct of those who use their services. It is an offence under bylaw 17(4) of bylaw 2 of the British Railway Board Bye Laws[41] to molest or wilfully to interfere with the comfort or convenience of other passengers. The Public Service Vehicles (Conduct of Drivers, Conductors and Passengers) Regulations[42] makes it an offence for a person to "use obscene and offensive language, or to conduct himself in a riotous or disorderly manner."

---

[37] As defined in the Licensing Act 1872, s.8, to include "any place to which the public have access, whether on payment or otherwise." *Martin* v. *McIntyre* (1910) 74 J.P.N. 842; *Lester* v. *Torrens* (1877) 2 Q.B.D. 403; *Young* v. *Gentle* [1915] 2 K.B. 661; *Pelly* [1897] 2 Q.B. 33.
[38] S.I. No. 1151, 1985.
[39] In *Abrahams* v. *Cavey* [1968] 1 Q.B. 479, it was held that interrupting a church service attended by members of the Government for the purpose of protesting against support for the Government's policies in relation to the Vietnam War was indecent. And see *Farrant* [1973] Crim.L.R. 240.
[40] *Criminal Law: Offences Against Religion and Public Worship* (1985) Law Com. No. 145.
[41] Made under the Transport Act 1962, s.67.
[42] S.R. and O. 1936 No. 619, as amended 1946 No. 457, continued in force by the Public Passenger Vehicles Act 1981, ss.24(1) and 25(1).

Town Police Clauses Act 1847

7–16   The Town Police Clauses Act 1847, section 28,[43] remains law, penalising   **7–16**
the most extraordinary agglomoration of obstructions and street nuisances.
Since many of the acts penalised are likely to amount to offensive conduct
within the terms of section 5, it is to be regretted that the opportunity was
not taken to examine this jurisprudential anachronism which, although it
no longer carries a power of arrest,[44] should perhaps be either modernised
or repealed in its entirety.

---

[43] And in London, see the Metropolitan Police Act 1839, s.54. Section 54(13) is repealed by
the Public Order Act 1986, s.40(3), Sched. 3. For the text of the 1847 Act, see Stones Justices Manual, para. 4–9985.
[44] PACE, Sched. 7. See *Wills* v. *Bowley* [1983] A.C. 57.

CHAPTER 8

PROCESSIONS AND ASSEMBLIES

1. INTRODUCTION

Background to Part II

8–01   The use of the streets and other public places as venues in which to air   **8–01**
grievances and complaints (and to celebrate achievements) has a long and
hallowed history. Media coverage in the television age ensures that public
attention is captured whilst slogans are shouted and wrongs exposed. The
policing of processions, marches, demonstrations and meetings of various
sorts represents a considerable call on modern police resources,[1] especially
in the Metropolitan Police area of London,[2] whose central location makes it
particularly attractive to groups wishing to express a point of view in public.
Under our system, it falls to the police to ensure that such events are organised in such a way that disorder does not ensue, and that so far as is possible,
the event can take place with as little dislocation to the ordinary life of the
community as is compatible with the proper exercise of freedom of speech in
public.[3]

For the most part, a balance between these potentially conflicting aims is
achieved through cooperation between the police and march organisers
rather than through the use of the law. With the exception of the Public
Order Act 1936, section 3, there was no national legislation to deal explicitly,
let alone comprehensively with this sensitive and potentially controversial
area of social existence.[4] Instead, reliance was placed on the use of general
police powers to prevent disorder; the common law duty to preserve the
peace (and the correlative offence of obstructing a constable in the execution
of his duty where the demonstrator declined to comply with the constable's
reasonable instructions issued pursuant to his mandate),[5] and the offence of
obstructing the highway.[6]

---

[1] See the Fifth Report of the Home Affairs Committee, *The Law Relating to Public Order*
(1979–80), H.C. 756–I, and successive Annual Reports of the Commissioner of Metropolitan Police.

[2] Even after the Act, the Metropolitan and City of London Police forces retain special statutory powers; City of London Police Act 1839, s.22 and Metropolitan Police Act 1839, ss.52
and 54(9) empower the Commissioners to make regulations for the route to be taken by
carriages, horses and persons to prevent obstruction of streets and thoroughfares within the
metropolitan police district "in all times of public processions, public rejoicings or illuminations." See *Papworth* v. *Coventry* [1967] 1 W.L.R. 663, 2 All E.R. 41. See G. Zellick on
the irregular use of the section in [1984] P.L. 343.

[3] For a survey of the legal issues, see A. Grunis, "Police Control of Demonstrations" (1978)
56 Can.Bar.Rev. 392.

[4] By virtue of the Town Police Clauses Act 1847, s.21, it is open to the local authority from
time to time to make "orders" "for the route to be observed by all carts, carriages, horses
and persons for preventing obstruction of the streets in all times of public processions,
rejoicings or illuminations, and in any case when the streets are liable to be obstructed."
This does not confer a power to make general orders; *Brownsea Haven Properties Ltd.* v.
Poole Corpn. [1958] Ch. 574. A criminal breach of the order must be proved to have been
"wilful" *Waring* v. *Wheatley* (1951) 115 J.P. 680.

[5] Chap. 10.

[6] Chap. 11.

The existing law

8–02   At common law, a distinction was drawn between processions and static   **8–02**
meetings and assemblies, more particularly where these took place on the
highway. Since those engaging in a procession were using the highway for its
primary purpose of passing and repassing,[7] their use of it was prima facie a
protected one. But a static gathering was likely to amount to an obstruction,
which could be cleared by the police exercising common law powers. Partly
because of this distinction in favour of processions at common law, it was
seen to be necessary for the police to be given statutory powers to control
potentially disruptive processions (but not meetings) in the Public Order Act
1936. Power was conferred upon the chief officer of police to impose conditions on the holding of public processions where he had reasonable
grounds to believe that serious public disorder was likely to ensue from the
holding of a procession. If the chief officer was of the opinion that the
resources available to him were inadequate to prevent the feared disorder,
he could take certain steps to have the procession banned altogether.[8]

     There was no nationwide obligation imposed on organisers to warn the
police in advance that such a march was to take place. Instead, local legislation in various local authority areas[9] imposed such obligations, and there
were varying time limits as to how soon before the date of the proposed procession notice was required. As a result of the Local Government Act 1972,
section 262, much of this legislation was repealed (and in some localities
replaced)[10] successively in the years leading up to 1986.

     There were no corresponding statutory powers of control in relation to
static meetings and assemblies. Police controls over such gatherings had to
be exercised on the spot, rather than in advance. But local authorities are
generally empowered to make regulations and by-laws for the use of public
places where meetings might be held (such as parks and squares),[11] and the
assertion of quasi-private property rights are generally sufficient to exclude
the claims of those seeking to exercise rights of freedom of speech in public.[12]

---

[7] Chap. 11.

[8] Since these are virtually identical to the new law, their full description is left to 8–06.

[9] According to the White Paper, there were 92 local authority areas which operated some
such advance notice requirement; para. 4.3.

[10] For example in the County of Merseyside Act 1980, the West Midlands County Act 1980,
Cheshire County Council Act 1980, Greater Manchester Act 1981, the relevant parts of
which are repealed by the Act, s.40(3) and Sched. 3.

[11] One suspects that many of these are in practice overlooked or ignored by both participants
and the police. But some, such as the regulations made under the Trafalgar Square Act
1844 (S.I. 1952, No. 776), which require written permission before an public address can
be given in Trafalgar Square are rigidly policed. The Public Order Act 1936, s.1 forbids
trespass on or approaches near certain prohibited places; *Chandler* v. *D.P.P.* [1964] A.C.
763. And see the Military Lands Act 1892, s.14(1).See also the Parks Regulations Act 1872
and the Royal and other Parks and Gardens Regs., (S.I. 1977 No. 217).

[12] In *British Airports Authority* v. *Ashton* [1983] 3 All E.R. 6, for example, it was held that the
Byelaw 5(34) of the Heathrow Airport London Byelaws 1972, which provides that "no person shall organise or take part in any public assembly, demonstration or procession likely
to obstruct or interfere with the proper use of the aerodrome or cause serious public disorder or obstruct or interfere with the comfort and convenience or safety of passengers or
persons using the aerodrome" took precedence over the terms of the Trade Union and
Labour Relations Act 1974, s.15 as amended by the Employment Act 1980, which provides
that "it shall be lawful for a person to attend at or near his own place of work," so that
picketing employees committed an offence under the byelaw.

A summary of changes effected by the 1986 Act

8–03   Part II of the Act extends and modernises the system of controls on pro- **8–03** cessions and meetings hitherto found in the Public Order Act 1936 and miscellaneous pieces of local legislation. For the first time, there is a national requirement that the police must be told by the organisers of a procession what they propose to do. The principal justification offered for this is that it triggers discussion between the police and organisers, and prevents demonstrators from springing surprises on the police. The legislation gives the police statutory powers for the first time to impose conditions on public meetings (although not to ban them outright). Nor does the Act impose a requirement of advance notice of meetings and assemblies. Much of this Part of the Act is administrative in character, but it clearly has a considerable bearing on the scope of the rights to public meeting and assembly in Britain,[13] and accords statutory recognition to the central position of the police in the determination of the proper exercise of freedom of speech in public. The ultimate sanction for failure to comply with the various controls are criminal in character, even if the penalties available are relatively slight. The elements of the administrative structure will be sketched as a preliminary to discussion of the offences created by this Part of the Act.

2. THE ADMINISTRATIVE STRUCTURE

Advance notice of public processions

8–04   Section 11(1) of the Act[14] requires advance written notice to be given to **8–04** the police[15] of any public[16] procession "intended"[17] to demonstrate support for or opposition to the views or actions of a person or body, which is being held to publicise a cause or to mark or commemorate an event "unless it is not reasonably practicable to give any advance notice of the procession."[18] This restriction to certain defined events would appear to

---

[13] See generally D. G. T. Williams, "Processions, Assemblies and Freedom of the Individual" [1987] Crim.L.R. 167.

[14] The full text of which is to be found in the Appendix below. The section came into force on January 1, 1987. It is modelled on the local legislation which it replaces, and on the Civic Government (Scotland) Act 1982, which had created a similar advance notice stipulation north of the border.

[15] Section 11(4)(a) and (b)—rather than, as in Scotland, to a local authority.

[16] Public procession is defined in s.16 to mean "a procession in a public place," and a public place is defined in the same section to mean "(a) any highway, or in Scotland any road within the meaning of the Roads (Scotland) Act 1984, and (b) any place to which at the material time the public or any section of the public has access, on payment or otherwise, as of right or by virtue of express or implied permission." The definition is similar to that found in the Prevention of Crime Act 1953 (Chap. 13), but with the addition of the words relating to "express or implied permission." This would seem to include private land which the procession will enter when persons entering are not to be regarded as trespassers, but visitors or licensees. A university campus might, in appropriate circumstances, fall within this definition.

[17] Presumably, the intention referred to must be that of the organisers, since a corporate grouping can scarcely be said to have a single "intention." It is as fictional as the "intention" of Parliament.

[18] The meaning of this is considered in 8–11.

exclude commercial gatherings, and aimless events (once depicted as "happenings"). It may perhaps be questioned whether such restrictions were necessary, since a procession is capable of causing disruption whatever the purpose of those organising it may happen to be. But without some such provision, school crocodiles would fall within the terms of the Act, and this would be unnecessarily time consuming for all concerned.

Processions commonly or customarily held, and funeral processions are exempt from the notice requirement,[19] presumably because the police will already be fully aware that they are to be held, and do not therefore fall within the "triggering" rationale of the requirement. That is, the justification for the enactment of an advance notice requirement is that it forces the organisers to discuss with the police arrangements for the conduct of the procession which enable the event to be held in such a way as to minimise the risks of disorder. What constitutes a procession that is commonly or customarily held? Plainly, events such as the Durham Miners' Gala, which has been held for decades fall within the rubric. An event that has been occurring for only five years before the enactment of the 1986 Act is of a more dubious standing. But it might well be thought that if a procession has been regularly held even for such a comparatively short period of time, the police are aware that it is likely to take place, and it is therefore outside the rationale behind the advance notification requirement. Even without notification, the police would be entitled to impose conditions on the holding of the procession.

There are detailed requirements as to what the notice must contain, including the date when it is intended to hold the procession, the time when it is due to start (but not finish), the proposed route and the name and address of the organiser.[20] These details facilitate planning, and give the police greater opportunity to protect those who wish to engage in free speech; the police are enabled to warn those who might be significantly inconvenienced by a proposed march to take avoiding action. No estimate of numbers need be given, although this is clearly of considerable importance in making tactical decisions about how the procession is to be policed. The notice must reach a police station in the area where the procession is to be commenced not less than six clear days before the intended date of the procession.

The section does not create what might be referred to as a permit requirement, since subject to what is said below, it does not empower the police to refuse permission to hold the procession, as is the law in certain other jurisdictions.[21] Nor does the fact that notice has been given confer any immunity on the participants from the operation of the general criminal law.[22]

---

[19] Section 11(2).
[20] Section 11(3).
[21] See V. Blasi, "Prior Restraint on Demonstrations" (1970) 68 Mich.L.R. 1481 for a discussion of the constitutional issues involved in imposing such conditions.
[22] As in some Australian jurisdictions. See for example the South Australian Public Assemblies Act 1972, as interpreted in *Samuels* v. *Stokes* (1973) 130 Cth L.R. 490. See generally A. Hiller, *Public Order Law* (1983).

Imposing conditions on processions

8–05   By section 12, the senior police officer[23] is empowered to impose con-   **8–05**
ditions on the proposed march if he reasonably believes that it may result
in serious public disorder, serious damage to property or serious disruption
to the life of the community, or alternatively that the purpose of persons
organising the march is to intimidate others "with a view to compelling
them not to do an act they have a right to do, or to do an act they have a
right not to do."[24] This may be done either in advance, or by the senior
police officer on the spot where the procession is in progress.

By comparison with the previous law, which confined the ground to that
of serious public disorder, this greatly extends the matters that the chief of
police may take into account in deciding whether or not to impose conditions. There is a danger that, if the powers are used too freely, the symbolic significance of a demonstration may be lost. For example, if the
proposed route of the march takes the participants past an embassy[25] or a
particular factory against whose occupants the organisers wish to protest,
the prescription of a different route or terminus may obviate the whole
point of the demonstration, and amount to in effect a disguised ban. There
might then be a further danger that the instructions will be ignored, leading
to even greater disorder. Such conditions might well be, as the police are in
practice aware, counter-productive.

What constitutes "serious damage to property" is obviously a matter of
degree, but it probably means something rather more serious than a few
broken windows. Serious disruption to the life of the community is a much
more difficult question of judgment. Taken literally, it involves nothing
less than a judgment about the competition for alternative uses of public
resources, and involves the individual police officer making a judgment
about what the ordinary "life of the community" entails. It means more
than serious inconvenience, or even widespread inconvenience (so that
people might not be able to park where they usually do, or drive down a
particular street or perhaps miss a train as a result of the demonstration).
None of these are in themselves "serious disruptions" to the life of the
community. But if access to the ordinary commercial activity of a shopping
precinct were to be blocked for a considerable period at a particularly busy
time of day, so that people were prevented from conducting their ordinary
business and social affairs, there is a disruption of sufficient significance to

---

[23] Defined in ss.12(2) (processions) and 14(2) (meetings) as follows: "(a) in relation to a procession being held, or to a procession intended to be held in a case where persons are
assembling with a view to taking part in it, the most senior in rank of the police officers
present at the scene, and (b) in relation to a procession intended to be held in a case where
para. (a) does not apply, the chief officer of police." Powers of delegation are afforded by
s.15; the chief officer of police may delegate his functions to a deputy or assistant chief constable, and in London to an assistant commissioner of police.

[24] Section 12(1)(*b*). The terminology is taken from the Conspiracy and Protection of Property
Act 1875, s.7.

[25] The Vienna Convention on Diplomatic Relations signed in 1961 (Diplomatic Privileges Act
1964) requires the receiving State to take all appropriate steps to protect the premises of a
mission against any intrusion or damage, and to prevent disturbances of the peace of a
mission or impairment of its dignity.

warrant the imposition of conditions.[26] One of the difficulties that the senior police officer must consider when deciding whether or not disruption is serious is that, if it seems likely that very large numbers of marchers will be involved, the strength of public support in favour of the particular cause must be weighed against the degree of disruption caused. He may not take into account the disproportionate cost of policing the demonstration nor the content of the processor's message.

The law requires the chief of police to make educated guesses about the likelihood that disorder, damage or disruption will occur. Quite apart from what the organisers tell him of their intentions, he may have sources of information that have a bearing on how he comes to a conclusion about predicted outcomes. In deciding whether or not the conditions exist for the issuing of conditions, the chief of police may take into account such factors as disturbances that have arisen in the past when the same organisation processed on a previous occasion. He may presumably take into account his previous experience of the particular applicants, if they have organised marches in the past. If they have provided inadequate stewarding on previous occasions, for example, he might make it a condition that more stewards and better prepared ones are provided on the occasion in question. Presumably, he is entitled to take into account the likelihood of opposition to the march in question, although this is problematic. If it seems likely that a particular march will encounter a large and aggressively hostile opposition, the proper course is for the police to organise in such a way as to protect the marchers against the opposition. If the route chosen by the marchers is such that there are places where the policing could not be adequate to prevent serious disorder, then conditions could be imposed.

Where the grounds upon which it is intended to impose conditions are the intimidatory purposes of the persons organising,[27] the chief constable is entitled to take into account the previous conduct of the organisers, including relevant criminal convictions if the organisers have any. The wording of section 12(1)(*b*) is, however, slightly unfortunate in requiring the intimidation of others "with a view to compelling them not to do an act they have a right to do, or to do an act they have a right not to do." The section is intended to give the police power to impose conditions on "coercive" marches which will not necessarily give rise to disorder; a National Front march through a predominantly Asian district may well prompt many of the citizens simply to board up their properties and remain indoors.[28] The difficulty is that although sometimes it is possible to point to an intention to compel action on the part of the target, as when the aim is to prevent employees from working, or to force a local councillor to vote differently, or to stop another organisation from marching that intention is not invariably present. Sometimes the purpose is simply intimidatory, as with the

---

[26] Under the previous law, it was very rarely necessary for the police formally to impose conditions, since agreements were generally arrived at whereby the ordinary life of the community could be permitted to proceed. Only half of the carriageway of a street might be given to a procession, for example. It seems probable that the new law will not greatly affect this situation.

[27] It has been said that intimidation is not a term of art, but must be given a "reasonable and sensible interpretation"; *Gibson* v. *Lawson* [1891] 2 Q.B. 545.

[28] This was the example given in the White Paper, para. 4.24.

rascist march, rather than an attempt to coerce persons into taking or not pursuing any particular course of action, and it is difficult to see that conditions could be imposed on a "rascist" march on this ground alone. In those circumstances, a chief constable who wishes to impose conditions would be justified in taking into account the risk of serious disorder and serious disruption to the life of the community, and impose conditions as to route on those alternative grounds. It would have been preferable, it is suggested, had the power been given to control intimidatory marches without more.

The directions that he may give must appear to him necessary (but not reasonably necessary) to prevent such disorder, damage, disruption or intimidation, and may specifically include instructions not to enter a particular area. The conditions are not limited to such matters and the timing of the procession or the numbers who may participate,[29] so long as they are referable to the purposes mentioned. They might very well, for example, relate to the sorts of implements that may be carried on the procession which, even if they are not offensive weapons at the beginning of the procession[30] may become so during its course.

It is open to the senior police officer present to impose conditions under this section whilst the march is in process, and on the same grounds as those on which he may act in advance. This was a power suggested by Lord Scarman, but only on the grounds of threats to public order.[31] It remains to be seen whether this new power will be used in such a way as to augment the existing powers that the police enjoy to give directions to prevent the occurrence of a breach of the peace.

Prohibiting processions

8–06   Section 13 of the Act, which permits the senior police officer to seek to have processions banned, is in essence very similar to section 3(3) of the Public Order Act 1936.[32] If the chief of police reasonably believes that any conditions that he may impose will not prevent "serious public disorder," he shall apply to the district council for an order prohibiting for a specified period (not exceeding three months) the holding of all public processions or a specified class of processions. The council may, with the consent of the Home Secretary make an order in the terms applied for or as modified by the Secretary of State. In the City of London or the Metropolitan Police District, the Commissioner for London or the Metropolitan Police Commissioner (respectively) applies directly to the Home Secretary. As was the case under the previous law, there is no power to ban specific as opposed to classes of marches, or all marches, and a proposal to the effect that there should be such a specific power[33] was rejected,[34] on the grounds that it would place the police in a situation where they would be subject to alle-

8–06

---

[29] *Cf.* s.14(1) relating to meetings.
[30] Chap. 13.
[31] *Red Lion Square*, para. 131.
[32] For details of the use to which this section was put, see D. G. T. Williams, [1987] Crim.L.R. 167.
[33] By Lord Scarman in *Brixton*, paras. 7.41–7.49.
[34] This was the explanation offered by the Minister of State for the Home Office (Mr Giles Shaw), H.C.Deb. vol. 89, col. 861, January 13, 1986.

gations of political motivation and partiality whenever they exercised the power to seek a ban on a particular march.

In practice, rather than seek bans, the police operate on a "first come, first served" basis. That is, if a group announces that it will organise a counter demonstration in opposition to one of which the police have been notified under section 11, the police can if necessary subject the late comers to conditions imposed under sections 12 or 14 that effectively prevent the two groups from clashing, or permitting them to meet only in carefully controlled conditions.

Unlike the power to impose conditions on processions, the grounds upon which a ban may be sought are still restricted to those of serious public disorder which the senior police officer believes that he will be unable to prevent, even taking into account the imposition of conditions under section 12. This refers to disorder on a widespread scale, and the officer should take into account not merely his own resources, but those that can be made available to him through the use of the mutual aid provisions of the Police Act 1964.[35]

The new provision differs from the old in one significant way, by altering the terminology in which the Act is couched from the senior police officer's "opinion" that he is unable to prevent the serious public disorder to "reasonably believes" that the imposition of conditions will not enable him to preserve order. Because of the more objective terminology in which this is couched, it invites the readier use of the powers of judicial review. Whether this will in practice make a great difference may be doubted, since it seems unlikely that a court will come to the conclusion that a chief constable of police has come to a decision that he could not reasonably arrive at, which is the critical test for the exercise of the powers of judicial review.[36] The risk that, if the marches goes ahead and results in serious disorder is not one that the courts could be expected to undertake. Only if the chief constable expressed his order in terms such as that he considered any injury to his men to constitute serious public disorder might the courts be prepared to intervene.

Imposing conditions on public assemblies

8–07 For the first time in English law, the police are empowered by the Act to impose conditions upon public assemblies, both in advance of the assembly, and during the course of the gathering. The grounds upon which the powers to impose conditions may be exercised are very similar to those which are available in relation to processions; section 14 provides that if the senior police officer believes that a public assembly may result in serious public disorder, serious damage to property or serious disruption to the life of the community, or that the purposes of the persons organising it is to intimidate others with a view to compelling them not to do an act they

---

[35] Section 14.
[36] *Associated Picture Houses Ltd.* v. *Wednesbury Corporation* [1948] 1 K.B. 223. The subject of judicial review is further considered in 8–08.

have a right to do, or to do an act they have a right not to do, he may impose conditions as to the place of the assembly, its maximum duration or the maximum number of persons who may constitute it as may appear to him necessary to prevent the disorder, damage, disruption or intimidation. There is no power under the section to impose any other sorts of conditions, such as those relating to the sorts of implements that may be carried at the assembly, or as to the apparel that may be worn, although these may fall within the general law relating to the possession of offensive weapons[37] or the wearing of uniforms.[38]

The powers conferred by section 14 are new, at least in their statutory form. It is a difficult question to know how far they merely duplicate the existing common law powers that arise from the obligation imposed upon the police to preserve the peace, which plainly permit the police to give instructions to limit the numbers at a gathering if that should be necessary to prevent an imminent breach of the peace.[39] Insofar as the section enables instructions to be given well in advance of the public assembly, it might be thought to augment the existing powers, since the breach of the peace (or other disorder) may be some days distant when the conditions (which must be in writing when they are given in advance)[40] are issued. Where the gathering is already under way when the decision to impose conditions is taken, the section permits the "most senior in rank of the police officers present at the scene"[41] to impose the conditions. It remains to be seen whether this becomes a modified form of dispersal power. For example, it would appear to be open to the senior officer to inform the organisers of the meeting in question that the numbers of the meeting are too great, and require the organisers of the meeting to assist the police in dispersing the mob. Failure to comply with that request would amount to an offence under section 14(4). There is no obligation imposed on the organisers of an assembly to notify the police in advance that they intend to hold such a gathering.

An assembly is defined as being a gathering of "20 or more persons in a public place which is wholly or partly open to the air."[42] They need not have a common purpose, although they will frequently do so. A football crowd of sufficient dimensions is within the ambit of the section. The definitions does not cover gatherings that are wholly indoors, since these can usually be controlled readily enough by the monitoring of exits and entrances. In *Roffey*[43] it was held that a procession was an "assembly" for the purposes of the Air Navigation Order 1954, and the commentary on

---

[37] Chap. 13.

[38] Chap. 14.

[39] As exemplified most particularly in *Piddington* v. *Bates* [1961] 1 W.L.R. 162, 3 All E.R. 660. These are considered further in Chap. 10.

[40] Section 14(3).

[41] Section 14(2)(*a*).

[42] Section 16. "Public place" is further defined by the same section to mean "—(a) any highway, or in Scotland any road within the meaning of the Roads (Scotland) Act 1984, and (b) any place to which the public has access, on payment or otherwise, as of right or by virtue of express or implied permission."

[43] [1959] Crim.L.R. 283.

that case points out that a procession was regarded as an assembly for the purposes of the old offence of unlawful assembly.

It is unclear whether the section gives the chief officer of police the power to limit the numbers present at the assembly below the 20 who must be present to constitute the assembly. It would appear that he can do so, since section 14(1) provides that he may impose without apparent qualification limits on "the maximum number of persons who may constitute it." Against that, however, the view may be taken that the word "it" refers to a public assembly, and since the gathering will no longer constitute such an assembly if the numbers fall below 20, it would be *ultra vires* the powers of the police to attempt to limit the numbers below the requisite numbers. A person who was prosecuted for organising a public assembly contrary to section 14(4) or for taking part in such a gathering or inciting another to do so,[44] would be able to argue that what he was involved in was not an unlawful assembly within the definition. If the police wish to limit an assembly to below the number 20, they will be forced to use their common law powers to prevent a breach of the peace, which survive the Act intact.[45]

As with the conditions imposed under section 12, there is a danger that if they are too readily imposed, the powers could be used to implement disguised bans. The point of a demonstration may be nullified if the target of the protest is not within the sight or hearing of the demonstrators, and it may be expected that it would only be in exceptional circumstances that conditions would be imposed preventing such a gathering.

Challenging the conditions

8–08 No right of appeal is afforded by the Act against the imposition of conditions on either processions or assemblies nor on the power to impose bans. But the exercise of the powers conferred by the Act is subject to judicial review[46] by the higher courts. Lord Diplock has characterised the essential nature of this power as follows: **8–08**

> "one can conveniently classify under three heads the grounds on which administrative action is subject to control by judicial review. The first ground I would call 'illegality,' the second 'irrationality' and the third 'procedural impropriety.' That is not to say that further development on a case by case basis may not in the course of time add further grounds."[47]

Spelt out slightly more fully (and at the risk of oversimplification), this means that a decision is open to review where it has been arrived at as a result of a mistaken view of the law, or where the decision is one that could not reasonably have been arrived at, in the sense that the person deciding must have taken into account irrelevant considerations, or failed to take

---

[44] Contrary to s.14(5) and (6) respectively.

[45] Section 40(4).

[46] For an up-to-date and comprehensive account of the principles according to which the courts will decide whether or not to exercise their powers of judicial review, see C. T. Emery and B. Smythe, *Judicial Review* (1986).

[47] *Council for Civil Service Unions* v. *Minister for the Civil Service* [1985] A.C. 374, at 410.

into account relevant ones,[48] or where he has failed to observe the dictates of natural justice which require him to give the parties a hearing before arriving at his decision.[49]

Both sections 12 and 14 allow the senior police officer to impose conditions only if he "reasonably believes" that the stipulated events will occur, and the Government White Paper expressed the view that the new law would "ensure that demonstrators have an effective means of challenging any decision by the police to impose conditions which is not justified by a real risk of serious disorder, disruption or coercion."[50] In addition, a challenge may be issued by a person who is prosecuted with one of the offences to be considered that the conditions were improperly imposed in the first place.

In connection with the powers of review, a number of points should be made. Even though the process of applying to the High Court may be a somewhat slow one (in a context where speed of response may be all important),[51] the application for review may enable the court to give useful guidance for the future relating to, for example, the meaning of a term like "serious disruption to the life of the community." A distinction should be drawn between the imposition of conditions under sections 12 and 14, and a ban imposed under section 13. The grounds upon which a ban is imposed relate to public disorder only, and if the banning authorities can be shown to have taken irrelevant considerations into account in deciding whether to exercise the power to ban, they have acted *ultra vires*. The banning procedure has a considerable political input, in the sense that both the district council and the Home Secretary act as controllers of the decision taken by the senior police officer. By contrast, the decision to impose conditions is taken by the policeman, and it may be that the courts will not defer so readily to the judgment of a single person as to what the scope of his powers actually is.[52] Technically, the Act does not oblige the person imposing the conditions to specify which of the alternative grounds he relies upon for his authority to do so, although where the event is to be held in the future, the directions given by the chief of police must be in writing. But it may perhaps be expected that where the true grounds are that the police officer fears "serious disruption to the life of the community" his order will say so. It is expecting a great deal of the courts to ask them to review the operational judgment of a chief of police who indicates

---

[48] It was confirmed in *Mohammed-Holgate* v. *Duke* [1984] A.C. 437, that police decisions are subject to this rule of review.

[49] There is no statutory obligation on the chief of police to indicate to the proposing marchers that he proposes to impose conditions or to seek a ban. One might suppose that the need formally to impose conditions will become apparent in the course of negotiations that it is the object of s.12 to ensure. The requirements of natural justice are imprecise, but they are now frequently summarised as involving a "duty to act fairly." See De Smith, *Judicial Review of Administrative Action* (4th ed., 1980), Chaps. 4 and 5; H. W. R. Wade, *Administrative Law* (5th ed., 1982), Part V.

[50] White Paper, para. 4.25.

[51] The application for judicial review is governed by Order 53 of the Rules of the Supreme Court, made under the Supreme Court Act 1981, s.31.

[52] Although it would be open to the senior police officer to consult the local authority, when he is minded to impose conditions.

that he reasonably believes that his forces are insufficient to prevent serious public disorder or serious damage to property.[53] In *Kent* v. *Metropolitan Police Commissioner*,[54] a blanket ban had been imposed for 28 days in the light of the Brixton disorders of 10–13 April,[55] and disorder at several Bank Holiday fairs. In holding that the ban was not *ultra vires*, Sir Denys Buckley J. made the points that the order-making authority should put clearly before the courts the considerations which led to the making of the order. But even where, as here, the reasons offered "seemed meagre," the court unanimously declined to interfere. The burden of proving that the authority had misused its powers rested with the applicant for judicial review.

If the courts are understandably reluctant to interfere where "serious disorder" is concerned, what constitutes "serious disruption to the life of the community" is much more a matter of judgment, and not one in which the police are necessarily more expert than the courts. Against the need for a society in which persons are free to go about their business unmolested might be weighed other considerations such as the importance to be placed on freedoms of speech and assembly. If the reasons given by the chief officer of police are such that a court concludes that no reasonable officer could form the judgment that serious disruption would ensue, it is possible that the courts will prove readier to intervene than they ever were under the previous legislation, which referred to "serious public disorder" only. In practice, however, the scope of the Act is more likely to be tested by the blunderbuss of prosecution and conviction.

3. THE OFFENCES

The offences outlined

8–09   The Act creates several offences, all of which are committed by organisation, participation or incitement in a controlled or banned procession, or controlled meeting in breach of the conditions imposed. The offences are subject to defences that may be summarised as being "no-negligence" defences, that is, that the organiser was not responsible for any default that may have occurred in the conduct of the meeting or procession. In summary, the offences are:

1. Organising a public procession when the requirements as to notice have not been complied with, or organising a procession that differs from that for which the notice has been given.[56]

2. Organising a procession, and knowingly failing to comply with the conditions imposed.[57]

---

[53] D. G. T. Williams *Keeping the Peace* (1967) Chap. 2 and M. Supperstone, p. 57 for fuller discussion.
[54] *The Times*, May 15, 1981.
[55] These were the subject of the Brixton Report.
[56] Section 11(7).
[57] Section 12(4).

3. Participating in a procession and knowingly failing to comply with a condition imposed,[58] or inciting another to do so.[59]

4. Organising,[60] participating in[61] or inciting another to participate in a banned procession.[62]

5. Organising a public assembly and knowingly failing to comply with a condition imposed,[63] taking part in a public assembly and knowingly failing to observe a condition imposed,[64] or inciting another to participate in such a procession.[65]

Penalties, procedure and powers of arrest

8–10   All of the offences created in Part II of the Act are triable summarily   **8–10**
only.

The penalties imposed upon organisers and inciters are far heavier than those imposed upon mere participants. A person who organises a procession without complying with the notice requirements is guilty of a level three offence only.[66] By contrast, a person who organises a procession or a meeting and knowingly fails to comply with the conditions imposed commits an offence punishable with three months' imprisonment or a level three fine.[67] Inciting another to take part in such a procession or meeting is punishable with the same level of penalty.[68] Where the procession has been banned, the penalty for the inciter is slightly higher, a level four fine in addition to the three months' imprisonment.[69] Merely taking part in a procession or assembly and knowingly failing to observe the conditions, and knowingly taking part in a banned procession are all punishable with level three fine only.[70]

There is no power of arrest for the offence under section 11 (organising without notice). But a constable in uniform may arrest anybody found committing any of the offences under section 12,[71] 13[72] and 14.[73]

When is it not "reasonably practicable" to give notice for the purposes of section 11(1), and 11(6)?

8–11   Where a procession is organised without notice, no offence is committed   **8–11**
if it was not "reasonably practicable" to give such notice, either at all, or within the specified six clear days. The burden of proving that it was not

---

[58] Section 12(5).
[59] Section 12(6).
[60] Section 13(7).
[61] Section 13(8).
[62] Section 13(9).
[63] Section 14(4).
[64] Section 14(5).
[65] Section 14(6).
[66] Section 11(10).
[67] Sections 12(8) and 14(8) respectively.
[68] Sections 12(10) and 14(10) respectively.
[69] Section 13(13).
[70] Sections 12(9), 13(12) and 14(9).
[71] Section 12(7).
[72] Section 13(10).
[73] Section 14(7).

reasonably practicable would appear to fall on the defendant.[74] This saddles the defendant with the task of proving that it was not practicable that the procession should have been postponed. The exemption is a recognition of the desirability of spontaneity in certain circumstances; where there are sudden events such as the "release of pollutants, a traffic accident, a shipment of nuclear waste or a visit by a political leader,"[75] the response to such events must be immediate if it is to be effective, and the giving of notice is in such circumstances not reasonably practicable.

A particular point of contention is likely to arise where a group claims that it was unaware of an intention to hold a march by a group to which it holds opposing views until some time within the notification period. In such circumstances, it would still be under an obligation to give notification of its intention to march, and the courts should perhaps hold that no offence is committed under section 11(7) if notice has been given, however shortly before the proposed "counter march," where this would still permit the imposition of conditions by the police, if necessary, under section 12. This would mean that the courts could take into account, as in other contexts where the expression is encountered, the purposes for which the notification is required.[76]

"Commonly or customarily held"

8–12   There is likely to be some uncertainty in the initial months of the operation of the Act as to whether or not any particular procession is commonly or customarily held. No figure can be put on the number of years for which such a procession must have been held to qualify for the exemption; any figure that is imposed is likely to be arbitrary. It might be said that if the police are aware that the procession is likely to take place because it has occurred in the past, the "triggering" justification for requiring advance notice is satisfied, and the chief of police could require compliance by indicating to those who have organised such marches on previous occasions that he is prepared to use his powers under section 12 to ensure co-operation if necessary.   **8–12**

"Procession"

8–13   What constitutes a "procession" for the purposes of the various offences is not further defined in the Act. Unlike the law relating to "public assemblies,"[77] no minimum number of participants is required. One person on his   **8–13**

---

[74] By virtue of the Magistrates' Courts Act 1980; *Ewens* [1967] 1 Q.B. 322. See now *Grant* [1986] 3 W.L.R. 1115.

[75] See the Report of the Home Affairs Committee, *The Law Relating to Public Order*, Evidence and Appendices, H.C. 756–II of 179–80, p. 302, and Lord Scarman, *Brixton* para. 7.45.

[76] *Nu-Swift International* v. *Mallinson* [1979] I.C.R. 157; *Dedman* v. *British Building and Engineering Appliances* [1974] I.C.R. 53; *Walls Meat Co.* v. *Khan* [1979] I.C.R. 52; *R.* v. *Chief Constable of the Merseyside Police, ex p. Calvely* [1986] 1 Q.B. 424. These were decisions in employment law, with different consequences for the individuals affected. Since the failure to notify results in the imposition of a criminal sanction, and since freedom of speech is in issue, the courts might be all the readier to construe the section strictly in favour of a defendant.

[77] Section 16.

own could not constitute a procession, but if a person were to march on his own, having publicised the fact widely in advance, it would seem that he might be said to be organising a procession if, Pied Piper like, he were to draw a crowd of supporters and followers. Paradoxically, if such a person were to fail to give notice, he might then be said to be committing an offence even though, because of the hypothesised publicity, it is most unlikely that the police will not already know about his proposed march. In *Flockhart* v. *Robinson*[78] Lord Goddard C.J. said that it is "not a mere body of persons; it is a body of persons who are moving along a route." Whether or not they must have a common purpose to constitute a procession is perhaps a moot point,[79] but it will be remembered that unless the procession is to be held which is "intended" to fulfil one of the purposes mentioned in section 11(1),[80] no notice is required. A procession of "hippies" proceeding from one town to the next would not constitute a "procession" for these purposes. It may be doubted whether a picket in which the members move around in a circle amounts to a procession[81]; the term denotes the intention on the part of the participants to move from one location to another. Clearly this is a matter of degree. If the participants intend to circle a block, arriving eventually back at the starting point, they probably would be processing.

Organises

8–14 It is notoriously simple for those who initiate gatherings to disclaim any organisational purpose or activities. The advance notice requirement circumvents this by obliging the processors to nominate one or more of their number as an organiser. Such nomination is not decisive. Generally, a person organises a procession or an assembly when he makes the necessary arrangements for the conduct of the event by initiating it, planning the route or location, or assists in doing so. Although the term might seem naturally to denote prior arrangement, it was held under the previous law that the word is "not a term of art"[82] and that a person can organise spontaneously by giving directions on the spot as to such matters as the route to be taken, when to stop and when to advance and so forth. This being so, liability would not be restricted to those persons named in the advance notice of the procession given in accordance with section 11, but would also be imposed on marshalls or stewards who, for example, knowingly incited participants to ignore the conditions imposed.

Incites

8–15 The concept of incitement is a familiar one in the criminal law. It denotes the encouragement of an individual to do or to omit to do an act. This may be by way of "proposal, request exhortation, gesture, argument, persua-

---

[78] [1950] 2 K.B. 498.
[79] See Isaacs C.J. in *Melbourne Corpn* v. *Barry* (1922) 31 C.L.R. 174 at 176. And see *McGill* v. *Garbutt* (1886) 5 N.Z.L.R. 73 at 75.
[80] 8–04.
[81] As in *Tynan* v. *Balmer* [1967] Q.B. 91. This was described as a "colourable pretence" at disguising a picket as a procession in *Hubbard* v. *Pitt* [1976] 1 Q.B. 142 at 157.
[82] *Flockhart* v. *Robinson* [1950] 2 K.B. 498. See however the dissenting judgment of Finnemore J., who took the view that the procession formed itself spontaneously in that case.

sion, inducement, goading or the arousal of cupidity."[83] The offence is committed whether or not the incitement is effective, but it must be at least communicated to the person incited. The incitement provisions in the Act do not really extend the law greatly, since it is in any event a common law offence to incite another to commit an offence, even a summary offence. The general rule is that the penalty available in such circumstances is the same as that for the substantive offence incited,[84] in this case level three, and since the legislature, thought that greater punishment than that was appropriate, specific provision is made for three months' imprisonment, or a level 4 fine.

Takes part in

8–16   A person takes part in an event when he is a willing participant in it. A   **8–16** question might arise as to whether spectators can be given directions under sections 12 or 14, or be guilty of offences of failing to comply with such conditions. A journalist, for example, or a first aid attendant, or a person acting as an "observer" for an organisation such as the N.C.C.L. does not really take part in the event itself, although he may occasionally make the police task of keeping order more difficult. A more certain course, in such a case, would be for instructions to be given pursuant to the breach of the peace powers, and a prosecution for obstruction of the constable in the execution of his duty in the event of non-compliance.[85]

Knowingly

8–17   There is no requirement in the Act for the police to tell the individual   **8–17** that the procession or assembly is being held in breach of the conditions imposed.[86] Since the mental element required for the commission of the the offences of organisation and participation is knowledge[87] which the courts increasingly interpret to require an awareness of all the circumstances by virtue of which it is said that an offence is committed,[88] it may well be sensible police practice to issue a warning before arresting and prosecuting with an offence under this Part of the Act.

The defences

8–18   The offences of organisation and participation are made subject to what   **8–18** might be seen as a kind of impossibility defence. The relevant sections state that "it is a defence for him to prove that the failure arose from circumstances beyond his control."[89] This clearly places the burden of proof upon

---

[83] *Nkosiyana* 1966, (4) S.A. 655 at 658, *per* Holmes J.A.
[84] Criminal Law Act 1977, s.30(4).
[85] Chap. 10.
[86] Compare the Metropolitan Police Act 1839, s.54(9).
[87] Sections 11(8), 12(4)(5), 13(7)(8), 14(4)(5).
[88] *Westminster C.C.* v. *Croyalgrange Ltd.* [1986] Crim.L.R. 693. (H.L.).
[89] Sections 12(4), (5) and 14(4), (5).

the defendant, to establish his innocence on a balance of probabilities.[90] A person who was swept along by the crowd (in a literal bodily sense), or who encountered unexpected barriers when attempting to comply with police conditions, would be able to avail himself of this defence.

---

[90] Magistrates Courts' Act 1980, s.101. For critical comment, see A. J. Ashworth, editorial, [1987] Crim. L.R. 154–5.

CHAPTER 9

RACIAL HATRED OFFENCES

1. INTRODUCTION

Background

9–01	Legislation making the making of racialist sentiments a criminal offence	**9–01**
was first introduced in Britain[1] in 1965 by the Race Relations Act.[2] The
common law offence of sedition, which consists of stirring hatred amongst
different classes of Her Majesty's subjects had fallen into disuse, and an
unsuccessful attempt to use it[3] to prosecute for the making of anti-semitic
remarks appears to have discouraged prosecuting authorities from seeking
to persuade the courts to mould the common law to deal with new problems posed by those who promote ill-will in an increasingly multi-racial
society. For reasons to be explained,[4] the original legislation was found to
be defective, and was amended in 1976 (and placed into the legislative context of the Public Order Act 1936), but even after amendment it still gave
rise to complaints that it fell short of the aspirations of its promoters in its
effects.[5]
When the Bill was introduced into Parliament in December 1985, it
made some important but relatively minor adjustments in the pre-existing
law relating to racial hatred offences. During proceedings in Committee in
the House of Commons, it became apparent that there was all-party support for extending the law rather further than was initially proposed, and
this Part of the Bill was substantially redrafted. The various laws relating to
incitement to racial hatred hitherto scattered in such diverse places as the
Public Order Act 1936 (as amended) the Theatres Act 1968 and the Cable
and Broadcasting Act 1984 were drawn together in a single Act. For fear
that those who disseminate rascist propaganda would turn to newer
mediums of communication, it was decided to deal explicitly and compre-

---

[1] The earlier legislation extended to Scotland, as does Part III; s.42(2). For Northern Ireland, see the Public Order (Northern Ireland) Order (1981) No. 609, N.I. 17.
[2] Section 6. See D. G. T. Williams, "Racial Incitement and Public Order" [1966] Crim.L.R.
320; P. Leopold, "Incitement to Racial Hatred The History of a Controversial Offence"
[1977] P.L. 389. The offence took its title from the cross-heading to the Race Relations Act
1965, s.6, although technically, "incitement" is not an ingredient of it.
[3] In *Caunt* (1947), discussed in 64 (1948) L.Q.R. 203. In *Edwards* (1983) 5 Cr.App.R.(S)
145, Lawton L.J. describes the offence as the modern form of sedition.
[4] Below, 9–10.
[5] Recently, the Attorney-General informed Parliament that between January 1, 1979 and
March 19, 1986, 59 people were prosecuted for the offence under the previous law; H.C.,
March 19, 1986, vol. 94, c. 188. For a discussion of some of the shortcomings of the law
shortly before the Act, see G. Bindman, (1982) 132 New L.J. 299. Some of these points
were also addressed in the Government's Green Paper, *Review of the Public Order Act
1936 and Related Legislation* Cmnd. 7891 (1980) and the White Paper, (1985). On the uses
to which the previous legislation was put, see P. Gordon, *Incitement to Racial Hatred*
(1982) Runnymede Trust, discussed by R. Cotterell, "Prosecuting Incitement to Racial
Hatred" [1982] P.L. 378.

hensively with all forms of communication such as films, tapes, records and video recordings,[6] not all of which would unambiguously have fallen within the proposed law. In effect, Part III became a self contained code of the offences relating to racial hatred. A rapidly re-drafted Part III was introduced into the House of Lords at the Committee stage, after the summer recess, and was therefore deliberated upon with some speed.

The Act effects several important changes to the pre-existing law. For the first time, it makes it an offence to possess racially inflammatory material, and films, videos and records are brought explicitly within the ambit of the Act. The Act confers powers of entry, search and seizure on the police, and places the burden of proving lack of intent to incite racial hatred on the defendant in several of the offences. It also alters the definition of what amounts to distribution, so that members of rascist organisations can no longer shelter behind the plea that they intended to circulate their seditious material amongst their own number. This is controversial, since it inhibits an escape valve for those who wish to discuss their views with those of a like mind. It was considered that there was too great a danger that the material would, once created, reach and affect a wider audience.

Civil liberties implications

9–02   Underlying the offences now found in Part III is the assumption that a
serious threat to public order is inherent in certain forms of expression. The assumption is controversial,[7] and there are obvious dangers that freedom of expression will be unnecessarily curtailed. Where speech is made criminal by direct reference to its contents, the way is opened for those in authority to censor minority or officially deprecated opinions. The legislature has sought to steer a course between these conflicting considerations by building public order elements into the definitions of the offences in the requirement that the conduct be threatening, abusive or insulting, and in the requirement that "hatred" should be an intended or likely outcome of the expression impugned. The difficulty then is perceived by some to be that the law does not reach those persons who couch their racialist sentiments in moderate terms rather than virulently abusive ones, whereas—so the argument runs—this propaganda is equally insidious. The fear is that, as Lawton L.J. put it in *Relf*[8] "in this class of case, constant repetition of

---

[6] The Video Recordings Act 1984 sets up a scheme whereby videos require a licence without which it is in certain circumstances an offence to supply such an article; s.9. But there is nothing explicit about racial hatred in the Act. For a scathing attack, see N. M. Hunnings, "Video Censorship" [1985] P.L. 215.
[7] Discussed in greater detail in E. Barendt, *Freedom of Speech* (1985), pp. 161–167. And see G. Hughes, "Prohibiting Incitement to Racial Hatred" (1966) 16 U. of Toronto L.R. 361. In *Glimmerveen and Hagenbeck* v. *The Netherlands* (1979) 4 E.H.H.R. 260, it was held that comparable Dutch legislation was not in breach of Article 10 of the European Convention on Human Rights and Freedoms, which guarantees freedom of speech. For a balance discussion of the issues, see the Australian Human Rights Commission Report No. 7, *Proposals for Amendments to the Racial Discrimination Act to Cover Incitement to Racial Hatred and Recial Defamation* (1984).
[8] (1979) 1 Cr.App.R.(S) 111.

lies might in the end lead some people into thinking that the lies are true. It is a matter of recent history that the constant repetition of lies in Central Europe led to the tragedy which came about in the years 1939 to 1945."

The stance adopted by the Act does not concede the full force of the argument that "there may be a need for a clear legislative recognition that expression of unashamedly rascist sentiments, as such, is an aspect of freedom of speech too costly in terms of long-term social disharmony to be tolerated in a pluralistic society where ultimately the possibility of democracy and civil liberty may depend on wholehearted public commitment to the fostering of social solidarity."[9] Instead, it compromises; expressions of opinion, however distasteful or offensive they may be, are not within the ambit of the legislation without the additional public order elements.

The Attorney-General's consent

The political sensitivity of prosecutions in this area is reflected in the fact that no prosecutions can be brought under this Part of the Act (in England and Wales)[10] without the consent of the Attorney-General,[11] who will no doubt bear in mind that proceedings should not be brought when this is likely to penalise or inhibit legitimate controversy. In 1965, an undertaking was given that only serious breaches of the Act should be proceeded against.[12] No similar undertaking has been expressed in 1986, and it remains to be seen what prosecution policies will be adopted in the light of the new law. Government spokesmen in both Houses were at pains to stress that the Government was concerned with the public order aspects of the law. The argument that, since the Crown Prosecution Service was established,[13] the Attorney-General's fiat was unnecessary was rejected by the Government on the grounds that, since the Act was being considerably strengthened, prospects of increased use of the law must be considered.[14] It was argued that it would be undesirable to open up the possibility of private prosecution, and that the sensitivity of the area was such that it was imperative that prosecution policy be consistent. These arguments do not carry complete conviction, since the requirement of the D.P.P.'s consent would preclude private prosecution, and consistency was one of the aims behind the establishment of the Crown Prosecution Service in the first place. But the Service was in its infancy when the matter was under consideration, and the there is something to be said for the status quo in those circumstances.

[9] R. Cotterrell, [1982] P.L. at 379.
[10] In Scotland, prosecutions are subject to the control of the Advocate General.
[11] Section 27(1); see *Pearce* (1980) 72 Cr.App.R. 295.
[12] See P. Leopold, *op. cit.* who points out that, ironically enough, one of the first (unsuccessful) prosecutions under the Act was of a single 17 year-old youth in *Britton* [1967] 2 Q.B. 51. The requirement of the Attorney-General's consent was described as by the Commission for Racial Equality as "a possible constraint on the effective use" of the previous law in evidence to the House of Commons Home Affairs Committee's 5th Report, Session 1979–80 *The Law Relating to Public Order*; para. 97. It seems likely, in particular, to inhibit a constable contemplating the exercise of a power of arrest under s.18(3).
[13] Prosecution of Offences Act 1985.
[14] See Standing Committee G, col. 885–892.

The offences outlined

9–04   The Act creates six offences,[15] all of which involve the use of language or material that is "threatening, abusive or insulting," each of which will be considered in turn. These are the use of words or behaviour, or the display of inflammatory written material,[16] the publication or distribution of racially inflammatory written material[17] publicly performing a play containing inflammatory material,[18] distributing, playing or showing a recording containing such material,[19] broadcasting or including inflammatory material in a cable programme service[20] and possessing it with a view to publishing or distributing it.[21]

Procedure, sentence and powers of arrest

9–05   Each of the offences is triable either way and punishable with imprisonment for two years on conviction on indictment, and summarily with six months and a fine to the statutory maximum.[22] Section 27(2) provides that for the purposes of the rule against duplicity, each of the offences created by sections 18 to 23 create one offence.[23] Proceedings under this Part of the Act will usually be initiated by way of summons; only section 18 carries a power of arrest.[24] Unlike the previous law, companies may be convicted of offences under this Part of the Act,[25] so that the perpetrators of racial hatred are unable to hide behind their organisation's corporate nature to avoid personal liability.

Where a person is convicted of an offence relating to the display of material under section 18, or of one of the offences contrary to sections 19, 21 or 23, forfeiture of the material is mandatory.[26] The material is impounded until the expiry of the ordinary time within which an appeal may be instituted,[27] after which it may be destroyed or otherwise disposed of.

Where a prosecution is brought under section 20 (theatres) or section 22 (cable broadcasting), the provisions of the earlier legislation[28] as to such

---

[15] Although there may be alternative modes of committing the one offence. S.27(2) provides that for the purposes of the rule against duplicity, each of ss.18 to 23 creates one offence. If the prosecutor wishes to have the material that is the subject of a charge under s.18 forfeited, he must particularise the offence as being one of display; see s.25(1)(a).

[16] Section 18.

[17] Section 19.

[18] Section 20.

[19] Section 21.

[20] Section 22.

[21] Section 23.

[22] Section 27(3).

[23] *Cf.* s.7(2) 2–05.

[24] Section 18(3) provides, "a constable may arrest without warrant anyone he reasonably suspects is committing an offence under this section."

[25] Section 28.

[26] Section 25(1).

[27] Section 25(2)(*a*). Where the order is made in Scotland, the time limit for the appeal is that set by statute; s.25(2)(*b*).

[28] The Theatres Act 1968, ss.9, 10 and 15, and the Cable and Broadcasting Act 1984, ss.33, 34, and 35.

matters as using scripts as evidence, making copies of scripts and records and powers of entry and inspection remain applicable.[29]

The meaning of racial hatred

To give guidance on the meaning of "racial hatred," section 17 provides:

> "In this Part 'racial hatred' means hatred against a group of persons in Great Britain defined by reference to colour, race, nationality (including citizenship) or ethnic or national origins."

The word "hatred" which is not further defined[30] is a word of some strength. It means rather more than disharmony, ridicule or derision; the Act is not meant to penalise those who tell tasteless rascist jokes. The *Shorter Oxford Dictionary* defines it to include "active dislike, detestation; enmity, ill will, malevolence." As one study puts it, "in effect, hatred is enmity."[31]

The formulation of the categories of person who must not be vilified, which is similar to the formulation adopted by the Race Relations Act 1976, section 3(1), does not include religious groupings, so that incitement to religious hatred is therefore outside the ambit of the British law[32]; attacks on Roman Catholicism or Anglicanism[33] are not covered. The distinction between a racial group as opposed to a religious one is by no means clear cut. Shortly after incitement to racial hatred became criminal for the first time in 1965, for example, some commentators questioned whether Jewish persons were covered by the Act, pointing to the argument that the Jewish community has a religious rather than a racial identity.[34] In a New Zealand case,[35] it was held that Jewish persons are protected by the phrase "ethnic origins," and there is no real reason to suppose that the law

---

[29] Sections 20(6), 22(8).

[30] It seems probable that the word is an "ordinary" one within the meaning of the principle in *Brutus* v. *Cozens* [1973] A.C. 854; above, 2–14. But the phraseology of s.17 is taken from the Race Relations Act 1976 (which prohibits but does not make criminal other forms of racial discrimination), and it would be unfortunate if there were to be a variance between the civil and the criminal laws in this respect. For this reason, it is suggested, what constitutes "ethnic or national origins" should be treated as a matter for the judge.

[31] The Canadian Law Commission Working Paper No. 50, *Hate Propaganda* (1986), p. 30. The Paper contains a useful bibliography of the law of hate propaganda; p. 49.

[32] *Cf.* the law in Northern Ireland which is different by virtue of the Public Order (Northern Ireland) Order 1981, title 13. As was pointed out by Kerr L.J. in *Mandla* v. *Dowell Lee* [1983] Q.B. 1 at 20, the decision to exclude religious hatred from British law was taken as a matter of deliberate legislative policy; Law Commission W.P. No. 79, *Offences Against Religion and Public Worship* (1981), paras. 5.9–5.11 and 8.5. An Opposition amendment seeking to include religious beliefs was withdrawn in Committee G, col. 839.

[33] Sufficiently scurrilous attacks might amount to blasphemy; *Lemon* [1979] A.C. 617. This has recently been the subject of a Report by the Law Commission, which has recommended the abolition without replacement of the offence of blasphemy; *Offences Against Religion and Public Worship* (1985), H.C. 442.

[34] B. A. Hepple, "Race Relations Act 1965" (1966) 29 M.L.R. 306.

[35] *King-Ansell* v. *Police* [1979] 2 N.Z.L.R. 531 and comment by W. Hodge, (1981) 30 I.C.L.Q. 918.

is not the same in Great Britain. A common religion and a common cultural tradition are two of the factors identified by the House of Lords in the leading case of *Mandla* v. *Dowell Lee*[36] as characteristic of the existence of a racial group, in that case Sikhs. There is some difficulty over whether or not gypsies fall within the definition. That term is sometimes used loosely to refer to travellers and persons of nomadic habits, and in *Mills* v. *Cooper*[37] a Divisional Court accorded the term such a meaning for the purposes of the Highways Act, which made it an offence for a gypsy to encamp on a highway. The Court declined to confine the term to persons of Romany origin. It seems reasonably clear, however, that persons who are of Romany origin constitute an ethnic grouping and are within the protection afforded by the Act for that reason.

The group of persons against whom the hatred is stirred must be in Great Britain. This would not exempt a person who, for example, launched his crusade against Sikhs in India if the effects of his conduct were felt by Sikhs in this country.

2. INFLAMMATORY WORDS, BEHAVIOUR OR WRITTEN MATERIAL

The offence defined

9–07　　　Section 18 reads as follows:　　　　　　　　　　　　　　　　　　　**9–07**

> "(1) A person who uses threatening, abusive or insulting words or behaviour, or displays any written material which is threatening, abusive or insulting, is guilty of an offence if
>   (a) he intends thereby to stir up racial hatred, or
>   (b) having regard to all the circumstances racial hatred is likely to be stirred up thereby."

The offence is in outline very similar to the pre-existing offence under the Public Order Act 1936, section 5A,[38] although it adds "behaviour" to the list of proscribed activities for the first time. It shares many of the features of the offence under section 4,[39] although the penalty at two years' imprisonment is greater. There are other differences. Whereas the earlier section requires that the language or conduct be used "towards another person," the section currently under consideration does not do so; it is enough that the language be broadcast generally. A person who is displaying an offensive banner in his front window so that it is visible to all the world clearly "displays" within section 18 even if not under section 4. The meaning of "threatening, abusive or insulting" should be the same in both contexts, and is in both cases a matter for the tribunal of fact.[40] The com-

---

[36] [1983] A.C. 548. See H. Beynon and N. Love, "*Mandla* and the Meaning of 'Racial Group' " (1984) 100 L.Q.R. 120. In *Gwynedd C.C.* v. *Jones* [1986] I.C.R. 833, it was held that Welsh language speakers were not a racial group on that ground alone.
[37] [1967] 2 Q.B. 459.
[38] As amended by the Race Relations Act 1976, s.70.
[39] Chap. 6.
[40] Discussed more fully in Chap. 6.

bative quality of these expressions has the effect, it might be argued, that those who couch their racialist observations in moderate language commit no offence, even though it might be likely to result in stirring up racial hatred. It might be thought that, in such an event, a jury (or magistrate, should the defendant elect summary trial), will find that the language is, at least, insulting to those likely to read and be offended by it, and could enter a convention on these grounds.

"Written material"

9–08   Written material "includes any sign or representation"[41] so that illus-   **9–08**
trations, symbols or signs (such as swastikas) are within the ambit of the section. The conduct of persons who daub walls with rascist graffiti is also nominally caught, although for practical reasons it may be simpler for the police to arrest and a prosecution brought for criminal damage, which carries a higher penalty if the damage done is sufficiently great,[42] always supposing that the culprit can be apprehended. The requirement of the Attorney-General's consent is likely to be, in reality, a significant inhibition. Similarly with banners and lapel badges; the amount of work that is involved in preparing a case for the consent of the the Law Officer make arrest and charge under section 4 or 5, in practice seem an altogether more attractive alternative for the policeman on the spot.

Public or private

9–09   Like its counterpart in section 4, the offence can be committed either in   **9–09**
public or in private, subject to the private dwelling exemption.[43] Private conversations are therefore excluded from the scope of the Act. It is difficult to see, in any event, how such private conversations could really be intended to stir hatred, or be likely to do so. A person who harassed a neighbour with rascist abuse would nevertheless have no defence that he was not acting in public if his words were, (as he knew)[44] audible to the person next door. Although there is a power of arrest, it would appear that when there is a private meeting, there is no power of entry to effect an arrest under the section.[45] This is perhaps surprising in view of the fact that the penalty carried by the section is more severe than the equivalent under section 4 for which there is a power of entry.[46]

---

[41] Section 29 provides that " 'written material' includes a sign or other visible representation." The section does not apply to the broadcast word, published on either radio or television. These are covered by ss.21 and 22. And see s.18(6), which specifically exempts cable programmes.

[42] Under the Criminal Damage Act 1971, the penalty is ten years; s.4(2). But where the value of the property does not exceed £200, the offence is triable summarily only. See *R. v. Canterbury JJ. ex p. Klisiak* [1982] Q.B. 398.

[43] Section 18(2). See the discussion in 6–15.

[44] There is a restricted defence of lack of knowledge in s.18(4).

[45] A power of arrest was not included in the Bill, but was added subsequently as a result of opposition pressure.

[46] PACE, s.17(1)(c)(i) as amended.

3. THE MENTAL ELEMENT

Background

9–10   The requisite mental element in the offences created in this Part has   **9–10**
proved troublesome from the outset, and a brief historical excursus is
essential to a full explanation of this aspect of the Act. When incitement to
racial hatred was first criminalised in 1965, the legislation made it a
requirement that an intention to incite racial hatred be proved. The Act
had the effect of penalising extremely crude forms of racial abuse where
such an intention could reasonably easily be inferred because of the overt-
ness of the language or conduct in question. An incidental effect was that
more subtle forms of propaganda began to appear, from which it was difficult for a jury to infer that the defendant intended to stir up racial hatred.
Since material was couched in more moderate tones than hitherto, it was
difficult to disprove claims that the speaker was intending to engage in
reasoned debate.[47] The law became, in the words of Lord Scarman,
"merely an embarrassment to the police,"[48] and a change in this aspect of
the law was advocated. Largely as a result of these influential criticisms,
the law was altered so that the requirement of intent was abrogated.
Instead a person could be held to commit an offence if he used words or
published written matter which were threatening abusive or insulting in
situations where, "having regard to all the circumstances, hatred is likely to
be stirred up against any racial group in Britain."[49] This made the task of
the prosecutor somewhat easier, but it had the paradoxical effect that a
person who distributed such material with a mischievous intention could
argue that the recipients of his material were unlikely to be influenced by
it, and he was therefore not guilty if his audience were already corrupt, or
were members of an anti-rascist organisation,[50] or if the publication or
spoken words were so contrary to human decency that they would be likely
to provoke sympathy for the intended victim rather than hatred of him. In
an attempt to counter defences such as this, the Act reintroduces the
requirement of an intent to stir up racial hatred as an alternative to the
objective formula.

Throughout this Part of the Act, a sharp differentiation is made between
the person who intends to stir up racial hatred, and a person who behaves
in such a way that racial hatred is likely to be stirred up by his behaviour. If
it can be shown to the satisfaction of the jury that the defendant had the
intention, he has very little opportunity to exculpate himself on the

---

[47] White Paper, *Racial Discrimination* (1975), p. 30.
[48] *Red Lion Square*, para. 125.
[49] Public Order Act 1936, s.5A(1)(*a*) and (*b*).
[50] R. Cotterell, [1982] P.L. at 379. The authorities cited for this view appear to be at Crown
Court level (and in one case a refusal by the Attorney-General to prosecute), and their
conclusions are surely questionable. The courts have certainly not been persuaded by similar arguments in connection with pornography; *Whyte* [1972] A.C. 849, where it was held
that the already corrupt were not immune from further corruption; *cf.* however *Clayton* v.
Halsey [1963] 1 Q.B. 163.

grounds that he lacked *mens rea*, as will be explained further presently. By contrast, certain defences are provided for the person who is not proved to have formed the intent, but whose language or conduct is likely to give rise to racial hatred.

A general issue concerning the mental element for the offence is whether the defendant must intend that his conduct should be threatening, abusive or insulting, or be aware that it might be. In the case of a defendant who uses words, a person can hardly fail to be aware of what he is saying, although he may possibly not know that what he is displaying (if it be a book) contains offensive material of which others are aware but he is not. Before the Act, the question whether the prosecutor was required to establish knowledge or awareness was unsettled.[51] Under the Act, the position is also rather complicated, but reasonably clear. By contrast with the offences in Part 1 of the Act which specifically provide for a requirement of *mens rea*,[52] no such explicit provision is made in this Part of the Act. As a result, it seems clear that the prosecutor need not establish at the outset that such was the defendant's intention or awareness. But in certain circumstances, the defendant may exculpate himself from liability either by raising doubts as to whether he had such an intention or awareness, or by establishing on a balance of probabilities the defence that he lacked *mens rea*. The point can be shown by the juxtaposition of two subsections of section 18, which provide:

"(4) In proceedings for an offence under this section it is a defence for the accused to prove that he was inside a dwelling and had no reason to believe that the words or behaviour used, or the written material displayed, would be heard or seen by a person outside that or any other dwelling."

"(5) A person who is not shown to have intended to stir up racial hatred is not guilty of an offence under this section if he did not intend his words or the written material to be, and was not aware that it might be, threatening, abusive or insulting."

The pattern established by these subsections is repeated in later sections in this Part of the Act. It will be observed that the first subsection is couched in the language of "defence."[53] This would seem to cast a burden of proof upon the defendant to establish, on a balance of probabilities,[54] that he comes within the scope of the section, which is in any event couched in very

---

[51] The Bill originally included a clause to the effect that intention or awareness was required to be proved by the prosecutor, but this was removed; cl. 19(2). The better view of the pre-Act law was that expressed by Smith and Hogan, p. 745, that the defendant's unawareness of the effects of his speech, however reasonable, was no defence, and that it was no answer for the defendant to show that he reasonably failed to appreciate the effects of what he was saying. *Malik* [1968] 1 W.L.R. 353, 1 All E.R. 582 is perhaps to the contrary. The defendant, a West Indian immigrant, claimed that he was using words which had, for him, a different significance, and this was left to the jury by the trial judge.

[52] See 6–13.

[53] *Carr-Briant* [1943] K.B. 607. See now *Hunt* [1986] 3 W.L.R. 1115.

[54] See Glanville Williams, "Offences and Defences" [1982] 2 L.S. 236–238.

restricted terms. A defence is available only where the defendant was in his own or another's house, and he failed to realise and had no reason to be aware that he would be overheard.

The second subsection, by contrast, places an evidential burden on the defendant (or the "accused," as the Act somewhat anachronistically refers to him) to assert that he did not intend, and was not aware of the impact that his conduct was having or might have. That is, if the prosecutor proves that the words or material were in fact threatening, abusive or insulting, and if the defendant wishes to assert that he did not realise that this was so, the onus is upon him to raise the issue. It is then for the prosecutor to prove that the defendant did so intend or was aware. In the case of displayed material, for example, it would be open to a shopkeeper prosecuted for displaying a magazine entitled "The British Heritage" to show that he believed that it was concerned with the stately homes of England rather than the rascist propaganda that it actually does contain.

Where the defendant is aware of the contents, however, as he generally will be with prosecutions under this section, the prosecutor must show that the defendant was aware that others might find his words to be threatening, abusive or insulting.

The intent to incite racial hatred

9–11   The defect in the Act which the reintroduction of the intention to incite **9–11**
racial hatred was intended to remedy was that where the recipient of the material was for one reason or another unlikely to be moved to racial hatred, no offence was committed.[55] Once manufactured and distributed, the material may always find its way to the hands of others who are less equable, so that its effect may be to stir up racial hatred indirectly. It is not wholly clear that the Act has the effect intended for it. A person who distributes inflammatory material to equable recipients can argue with some plausibility that he intended to display his contempt for the views of the recipient, or was seeking to indicate in forcefully graphic terms that he held a different point of view from the one espoused by his audience. Where he is addressing the converted, so to speak, he can say that his intention may have been to reinforce or confirm views already held rather than to stir up hatred. It would be unfortunate if the courts were to permit these arguments to prevail. So far as the arguments about those who already hold rascist views are concerned, there is a possibility that they will be stirred to action by what is said or written. Even if that were not so, the words of Lawton L.J. in *Relf*[56] on the cumulative effect of the constant repetition of lies should be borne in mind.

The intention of stirring hatred is not confined to the purpose of doing so.[57] In the Canadian case *Buzzanga*[58] the defendants were convicted of wilfully promoting hatred against the French-Canadian group of which

[55] White Paper, para. 6.6. The examples given are of clergymen or Members of Parliament.
[56] (1979) 1 Cr.App.R.(S) 111, 9–02.
[57] The meaning of intention is discussed in 3–15.
[58] (1979) 49 C.C.C. (2d) 369.

they were themselves members. They had distributed a pamphlet in support of a French language school, intending by their pamphlet to create "controversy, furor and an uproar" as a means of precipitating government action. It was held that the defendants were guilty of wilfully promoting racial hatred if they foresaw that hatred was a certain or morally certain consequence of what they were doing, even though it was not their purpose to promote hatred.

Whereby racial hatred is likely to be stirred up

9–12 Strictly speaking, this alternative "mental" element is not a *mens rea* **9–12** requirement at all, although it is properly enough described as a fault element. The assessment to be made is an objective one. The reference to "all the circumstances" was not included in the Bill, but had been in earlier legislation, and was reinstated for fear that the courts might read into the omission a legislative intention that was not truly held. Presumably, it must include the audience that might be expected to be subjected to the words or material, as well as the audience who were actually present.[59] The time and place are also factors that might have some bearing on whether or not racial hatred was likely. A fair and accurate report of an event by a newspaper would also be the less likely to fall foul of the legislation because of the place in which it is published.

It may be doubted, however, whether there would be anything in the nature of a public good or public interest defence available as a result of this provision, much less a defence that the words uttered were true. If their tendency is that they are likely or intended to stir up racial hatred, that is sufficient.

4. PUBLISHING OR DISTRIBUTING MATERIAL

Background

9–13 The conduct struck at by section 19 was made an offence in the 1965 **9–13** legislation, and was a more frequently prosecuted form of incitement to racial hatred than the utterance of words.

Section 19(1) reads as follows:

"A person who publishes or distributes written material which is threatening, abusive or insulting is guilty of an offence if—

(a) he intends thereby to stir up racial hatred, or
(b) having regard to all the circumstances racial hatred is likely to be stirred up thereby."

The threatening, abusive or insulting character of the material, and the mental elements have already been considered, and readers are referred to earlier sections of the book.

---

[59] *Jordan* v. *Burgoyne* [1963] 2 Q.B. 744, which is discussed above, 1–08.

Distributes or publishes

9–14   The activities struck at by the section are further defined in section 19(3)   9–14
as follows:

> "References in this Part to the publication or distribution of written
> material are to its publication or distribution to the public or a section
> of the public."

Under previous legislation, it was a defence for the publisher to show that
his intention was to publish only to members of a private association or
group of which the publisher or distributor was a member.[60] In practice,
this provided a shield behind which those whose intention it was to distribute material generally were able to disguise their activities.[61] That
exemption has now been removed, and it may be wondered what is
achieved by leaving in the Act references to the audience whom the
defendant addresses,[62] rather than penalising publication or distribution to
the public at large. Publication to a single person is, impliedly, insufficient
to constitute the offence. It may be argued that this is an appropriate
restriction, since the law catches only those who disseminate or broadcast
their propaganda on a wide scale, and not those whose correspondence is
entirely private. Members of an association are clearly a "section of the
public," and distribution to them is within the ambit of the law.

How large a group, though, is "the public, or a section of the public"?
Would it be enough, for example, that a person published material to a
handful of his neighbours urging them to make life difficult for a black person who has recently moved into the neighbourhood? The matter was considered by the Court of Appeal in *Britton*[63] where a youth had left
pamphlets late one evening in the porch of the house of a single member of
Parliament whom he believed to be responsible for bringing coloured
immigrants into Britain. The court concluded that this was not a publication to the "public" generally, or to a section of the public, even taking
into account the fact that the M.P. was accompanied at his home by three
members of his family. No change made in the Act affects this, and on this
point, *Britton* would seem still to represent the law. The decision has been
criticised,[64] it being said that the section of the public to whom publication
is in fact made is not a matter of concern. As a criticism of the courts, this
seems misconceived or at least misplaced. If Parliament had meant to say
that any distribution or publication should suffice, it could very easily have
said so; the courts are bound to make sense of the words that Parliament
has in fact used.

---

[60] And see s.29 which, although it refers to "distribute" and "publish" does not further define
those terms.
[61] See A. Dickey "Prosecutions Under the Race Relations Act 1965, s.6 (Incitement to Racial
Hatred)" [1968] Crim.L.R. 489.
[62] By comparison with s.4, for example. The language of the section, "public, or a section of
the public" is also to be found in the Race Relations Act 1976; s.20 (discrimination in the
provision of goods, facilities or services to the public or a section of the public).
[63] [1967] 2 Q.B. 51.
[64] M. Partington, "Race Relations Act 1965: A Too Restricted View?" [1967] Crim.L.R. 497;
Supperstone, p. 18.

In *Britton*, the actions of the defendant took place late at night, and at some distance from the street, and the court took the view that these facts militated against calling this a distribution, although it said that had there been evidence that the documents were visible to whoever passed by, this might amount to publication, with which the particular defendant had not been charged.[65] A person "publishes" an article when he sells it, or otherwise distributes it by giving it away, letting it on hire or lending it.[66]

Ignorance of contents

9–15 A publisher or distributor may very well be unaware of the contents of what he is circulating, although he might be thought to have some obligation to ascertain what is contained in what he is peddling. To meet this, there is a "no negligence" defence[67] available to the publisher in section 19(2), which reads: **9–15**

> "In proceedings for an offence under this section it is a defence for an accused who is not shown to have intended to stir up racial hatred to prove that he was not aware of the content of the material and did not suspect, and had no reason to suspect, that it was threatening, abusive or insulting."

The conditions for the application of the defence are cumulative rather than alternatives, so that if the publisher fails to meet any one of them, the defence fails.

It is not enough for the defendant to show that he was aware of the contents of what he was distributing or publishing, but did not himself think that it was insulting if the jury or magistrate should come to the conclusion that he suspected or had grounds to suspect otherwise. This is in contrast to section 18, which permits the defendant to claim that he was not aware that his words were threatening, abusive or insulting.[68]

5. THEATRES

Background

9–16 Theatrical performances were brought within the ambit of the criminal laws relating to racial hatred by the Theatres Act 1968, which terminated the Lord Chamberlain's role as the official censor. The Act was not amended by the Race Relations Act 1976, which meant that the mental element required for the commission of the offence remained restricted to intention to cause racial hatred, as opposed to the likelihood that racial **9–16**

---

[65] It is open to the prosecutor to allege publication or distribution in a single count, since the offence created by the section is regarded as a single count for the purposes of an indictment or information; s.27(2). The situation envisaged by the court would almost certainly amount to a display under s.18.

[66] *Cp*. the Obscene Publications Act 1959, s.1(3).

[67] This is similar to the defence to be found in the Obscene Publications Act 1959, s.2(5) and 1964, s.11(3)(*a*); Misuse of Drugs Act 1971, s.28; Contempt of Court Act 1981, s.3(2).

[68] 9–10.

hatred would be stirred up. To date, there have been no prosecutions for this version of the offence of inciting to racial hatred.

The legislation is aimed principally at those who present or direct plays rather than at the person who actually performs them; the latter commits an offence only if without reasonable excuse he performs otherwise than in accordance with the director's instructions.[69]

The offence defined

9–17   Section 20(1) provides: 9–17

"If a public performance of a play[70] is given which involves the use of threatening, abusive or insulting words or behaviour, any person who directs the performance is guilty of an offence if—

(a) he intends thereby to stir up racial hatred, or
(b) having regard to all the circumstances (and in particular, taking the performance as a whole) racial hatred is likely to be stirred up thereby."

The section requires little comment since it is couched in terms so similar to the offences already considered. There is, however, one slightly unfortunate addition to the section, namely the phrase that requires the performance to be assessed "as a whole." This was the phraseology employed in the Theatres Act 1968, but when the Bill was hurriedly amended, it was decided to bring the Theatres Act terminology into line with the remainder of the Act, and substitute "having regard to all the circumstances." This would probably have been sufficient to enable the courts to assess the performance as a whole, but the Bill was nevertheless further amended in the House of Lords so that both expressions now appear. The unfortunate side effect is that the Act appears not to require as assessment of the utterance as a whole elsewhere in the Act, especially in relation to sections 21 and 22.

Exempted performances

9–18   Certain performances that would qualify within the definition of plays[71]   9–18
are expressly exempted. These are rehearsals, and performances given solely or primarily for the purpose of making a recording or to enable the performance to be broadcast or included in a cable programme, unless it was attended by persons other than those participating for such purposes. This restates the previous law,[72] and it may be supposed that, in the situ-

---

[69] Section 20(4)(a).
[70] As defined in the Theatres Act 1968, s.18, which is made to apply by s.20(5). S.18 provides that " 'play' means (a) any dramatic piece, whether involving improvisation or not, which is given wholly or in part by one or more persons actually present and performing and in which the whole or a major proportion of what is done by the persons performing, whether by way of speech, singing or acting, involves the playing of a role; and (b) any ballet given wholly or in part by one or more persons actually present and performing, whether or not it falls within paragraph (a) of this definition." " 'Public performance' includes any performance in a public place within the meaning of the Public Order Act 1936 which the public or any section thereof are permitted to attend, whether on payment or otherwise."
[71] Last note.
[72] Theatres Act 1968, s.7.

ations envisaged, there are good reasons why the conduct should not be regarded as criminal. It might be necessary to witness a rehearsal before an asscssment of the overall impact of the play can be made, and if the purpose of the performance is so that it can be publicly reproduced on a different occasion, the circumstances in which that publication will take place will have a bearing on the offensive character of the artefact in question. Given that the decision has now been taken by Parliament to extend the law to cover recordings, broadcasts and cable programmes, it may be wondered whether the exemption for these should have been automatically carried over into the new law.

Persons to whom the section applies

9–19   The section applies to "presenters" and "directors," but not to actors   **9–19**
unless the latter depart from the script, in which case they become "directors" for the purposes of the Act.[73] Nor can the performer be guilty of an offence by aiding and abetting the director; the ordinary principles of complicity are expressed not to apply.[74] Why this denial of individual autonomy should be permitted, when it is not in the case of a person who uses the offending words under section 22 (cable broadcasting services) is unclear. The original Theatres Act 1968 exemption may well have been devised with obscene plays in mind where the editorial judgment of the director may well be decisive. It is no defence for the director to say that he was absent when the play was performed,[75] unless he can take advantage of the special defence that he did not know, and had no reason to suspect, that the performance would involve the use of the offending words or behaviour.[76]

Defences

9–20   Section 20(2) affords defences as follows: **9–20**

> "If a person presenting or directing the performance is not shown to have intended to stir up racial hatred, it is a defence for him to prove
>
> (a) that he did not know and had no reason to suspect that the performance would involve the use of the offending words or behaviour, or
> (b) that he did not know and had no reason to suspect that the offending words or behaviour were threatening, abusive or insulting, or
> (c) that he did not know and had no reason to suspect that the circumstances in which the performance would be given would be such that racial hatred would be likely to be stirred up."

[73] Sections 20(4)(a)(b).
[74] Section 20(4).
[75] Section 20(4)(c).
[76] 9–20.

6. FILMS, SOUND TAPES, VIDEOS AND RECORDS

Background to and definition of offence

9–21 The extent to which the newer means of communication might fall within **9–21**
the terms of the offences relating to written material was problematic.
There was no real evidence before the Standing Committee that such
material was currently being produced or in circulation, but the fear was
expressed that, if the "private member's club" defence were to be removed
from the most common form in which such material was currently produced, namely books, magazines and pamphlets, it would not be long
before such clubs began to produce their propaganda in new media.
Because of the uncertainties, and to forestall the predicted developments,
it was decided at the Committee stage of the Bill to redraft it to ensure that
these were explicitly within the new law. Accordingly, section 21 states:

> "(1) A person who distributes, or shows or plays, a recording of visual
> images or sounds which are threatening, abusive or insulting is
> guilty of an offence if—
>> (a) he intends thereby to stir up racial hatred, or
>> (b) having regard to all the circumstances racial hatred is likely
>> to be stirred up thereby.
> (2) In this Part, 'recording' means any record from which visual
> images or sounds may, by any means, be reproduced; and refer-
> ences to the distribution, showing or playing of a recording are to
> its distribution, showing or playing to the public or a section of
> the public."

Technically a showing of such a film in private to members of a rascist club
or group would fall within the terms of the section, since the showing
would be to a section of the public.[77] This is not positively expressed to be
the law, unlike section 18, which expressly provides that the offence may
take place in private as well as in public, and affords a private dwelling
exemption. It is also unlike section 20, which requires the "public performance" of a play. In the absence of any legislative indication one way or
the other, it must be assumed that the offence may be committed in public
and in private. But there would be no power of entry without a warrant[78] if
it were suspected that such an offence was taking place, even though there
is such a power for the less serious offence under section 4.[79]

There is a defence that the distributor, displayer or player who had no
intention to stir up racial hatred was ignorant of, and had no reason to suspect that the contents of the item in question were threatening, abusive or

---

[77] 9–14 (distributes or publishes).
[78] A search warrant could be obtained under s.24(1), since the police who know that such a
recording is being played or film shown must by definition have reasonable grounds for suspecting that a person has in his possession a recording that would fall within the terms of
s.23.
[79] PACE, s.17(1)(c)(i) as amended. No offence under this section would be committed in the
circumstances envisaged, unless the the audience were at least likely to be provoked into
immediate violence, which is unlikely in the circumstances.

insulting,[80] and the section does not apply where the showing or playing of the recording is solely for the purpose of inclusion in a cable programme service.[81]

7. BROADCASTS AND CABLE BROADCASTS

Background and definition

9–22 Cable broadcasting is a relatively new phenomenon. Whereas ordinary television is transmitted through the airwaves generally, cable television is, as its name implies, transmitted via cable into those premises equipped to receive it. It was envisaged by Parliament that the services might be developed in a more selective way, becoming available only to those who chose to have such a facility, and it was contemplated that there would not be the same obligations of good taste and balance that are required of existing television broadcasters.[82] Section 22 is in all its essentials virtually identical to the provision in the Cable and Broadcasting Act 1984.[83] It provides:

    "(1) If a programme involving threatening, abusive or insulting visual images or sounds is broadcast, or included in a cable programme service, each of the persons mentioned in subsection (2) is guilty of an offence if—

        (a) he intends thereby to stir up racial hatred, or

        (b) having regard to all the circumstances racial hatred is likely to be stirred up thereby.

    (2) The persons are—

        (a) the person providing the broadcasting or cable programme service,

        (b) any person by whom the programme is produced or directed, and

        (c) any person by whom offending words or behaviour are used."

The defences

9–23 The statute affords a number of defences, which are intended to reflect the degree of control that the various participants might have over the transmission of the programme. In the case of the cable service operator, and the producer and director of the programme in question, the defendant must show that he neither knew nor reasonably suspected that the programme would contain the offending words, or, if he did know, that he had no reasonable opportunity to remove the offending words.[84] In addition, it is open to the producer or director to show that he did not know or reasonably suspect that the offending programme would be included in a cable

---

[80] Section 21(3); 9–15 (ignorance of contents).
[81] Section 21(4). Cable broadcasting is specifically dealt with in s.22.
[82] See the White Paper, *The Development of Cable Systems and Services* Cmnd. 8866 (1983). And see the Report by the Information Technological Advisory Panel, *Cable Systems* (1982).
[83] Section 27.
[84] Section 22(3).

programme, or that in the context of the broadcast the programme would probably provoke racial hatred.[85] So far as the performer is concerned, he has the defence that he did not know and had no reason to suspect that a programme involving the use of the offending material would be included in a cable broadcast, or that the circumstances in which such material was included would be such that racial hatred would be likely to be stirred up.[86] All of these defences apply only where the person is not shown to have intended to stir up racial hatred, and all of the participants have the defence that they had no reason to suspect that the material was threatening, abusive or insulting.[87]

In addition an exemption is afforded for the British Broadcasting Corporation and the Independent Broadcasting Authority, or for any immediate re-transmission of a programme broadcast by either of those authorities.[88] The reason for this is not only that these organisations are inherently unlikely to broadcast such material, but also that they are subject to different controls as to the content of what they broadcast.[89]

8. POSSESSING RACIALLY INFLAMMATORY MATERIAL

Background

9–24   The offence of possessing racially inflammatory material is new. Difficulty had been experienced in making the previous law work, because it depended on the need to prove a particular act of distribution, not to members of a club or association of which the defendant himself was a member.   **9–24**

Section 23 is very similar in terms to the other sections in this Part. It provides as follows:

> "(1) A person who has in his possession written material which is threatening, abusive or insulting, or a recording of visual images or sounds which are threatening, abusive or insulting, with a view to—
>
> > (a) in the case of written material, its being displayed, published, distributed, broadcast or included in a cable programme service, whether by himself or another, or
> > (b) in the case of a recording, its being distributed, shown, played, broadcast or included in a cable programme service, whether by himself or another, is guilty of an offence if he intends racial hatred to be stirred up thereby or, hav-

---

[85] Section 22(4).
[86] Section 22(5).
[87] Section 22(6).
[88] Section 22(7). And see s.23(4).
[89] In the case of the B.B.C., the matter is governed by the Annex to the Royal Charter, Cmnd. 8313, and for the I.B.A. the Broadcasting Act 1981, s.4(1)(*a*) of which requires the Authority to ensure that, so far as is possible, nothing is included in its programmes which offends against good taste or decency or is likely to encourage crime or lead to disorder or be offensive to public feeling. For the extent to which these obligations are legally enforceable, see *Att-Gen ex rel. McWhirter* v. *Independent Broadcasting Authority* [1973] Q.B. 269; *R.* v. *Independent Broadcasting Authority ex p. Whitehouse* [1984] *The Times*, April 14.

ing regard to all the circumstances, racial hatred is likely to be stirred up thereby."

(2) For this purpose regard shall be had to such display, publication, showing, playing, broadcasting or inclusion in a cable programme service as he has, or it may reasonably be inferred that he has, in view."

Subsection 2 is rather oddly tacked on, and provokes the question "for what purpose"? The answer would seem to be for the purpose of ascertaining the possessor's intention, and for deciding whether in all the circumstances, racial hatred is likely to be stirred up.

In applying subsection 2, the quantity of material is one of the factors that the tribunal can bear in mind when assessing the defendant's intention, or the likelihood that racial hatred will be stirred up. Large quantities of the same pamphlet might the more readily suggest that the defendant's purposes were not wholly innocent ones. By contrast, a person who has been handed a single leaflet in the street is clearly outside the ambit of the section. Where material is possessed for legitimate educational or research purposes, or in a library, there is clearly no intention to incite racial hatred. Whether or not racial hatred is likely to be stirred up may depend in part on the circumstances in which and to whom the library will make the material available. As with the offence under section 22 (cable and broadcasting), the section does not apply to the BBC or the IBA[90]

The power of search

9–25 Extensive powers of entry, search and seizure are associated with the possession offence by virtue of section 24. Nothing is actually said in the Act to the effect that the object of the search may be siezed, but this must be read subject to the powers of seizure conferred by PACE. Section 19 of that Act, in particular, confers general powers of seizure. Under that section, the constable would be empowered to seize only if it is "necessary" to do so in order to prevent the evidence being concealed, altered, lost or destroyed.   **9–25**

Exemptions for Reporting

9–26 Fair and accurate reports of proceedings in Parliament[91] are expressly exempted from the operation of this Part of the Act,[92] which also does not apply·   **9–26**

> "where the matter consists of or is contained in a fair and accurate report of proceedings publicly heard before a court or tribunal exercising judicial authority, provided the report is published contemporaneously with those proceedings or, if it is not reasonably practicable or would be unlawful to publish a report of them contemporaneously, is

[90] Section 23(4).
[91] See *Wason* v. *Walter* (1868) L.R. 4 Q.B. 73; and see P. M. Leopold, "Freedom of Speech in Parliament" [1981] P.L. at 41.
[92] Section 26(1). The provision is in terms very similar to s.3 of the Law of Libel Amendment Act 1888.

published as soon as publication is reasonably practicable and lawful."[93]

As the provisions are framed, they are not quite defences; the section merely says that the offences cannot be committed when they represent a fair and accurate report. At most, therefore, there is an evidential burden on the defendant, and it would be for the prosecutor to establish beyond reasonable doubt that the report was unfair or inaccurate, or that the proceedings were not before a tribunal exercising judicial authority.

---

[93] The courts have a number of powers to suppress the contemporaneous reporting of their proceedings. See in particular the Contempt of Court Act 1981, s.4.

CHAPTER 10

ASSAULTING OR OBSTRUCTING A CONSTABLE IN THE EXECUTION OF HIS DUTY

1. INTRODUCTION

The offences outlined

A number of offences frequently encountered in the field of public order prohibit interference with a police officer in the execution of his duty. Assaulting a constable, or obstructing or resisting him in the execution of his duty are all specific statutory offences. Although augmented now by police powers to give instructions in the control of processions and assemblies[1] and the new crime of offensive conduct[2] it seems likely that they will continue to be of immense practical importance. The offences are to be found in section 51 of the Police Act 1964, which provides as follows:

> "(1) Any person who assaults a constable[3] in the execution of his duty, or a person assisting a constable in the execution of his duty, shall be guilty of an offence and liable on summary conviction to imprisonment for a term not exceeding six months or to a fine not exceeding level 5 on the standard scale or to both.
>
> (3) Any person who resists or wilfully obstructs a constable in the execution of his duty, or a person assisting a constable in the execution of his duty, shall be guilty of an offence and liable on summary conviction to imprisonment for a term not exceeding one month or to a fine not exceeding level 3 on the standard scale or to both."

All the offences are triable summarily only.[4]

2. COMMON INGREDIENTS OF THE OFFENCES

The scope of the policeman's duty

One element common to all forms of the offence is that the forbidden conduct must take place when the policeman is acting "in the execution of his duty," which raises the questions; what duties are imposed upon a

---

[1] Chap. 8.

[2] Chap. 7

[3] Every police officer in England and Wales, except the Commissioner and Assistant Commissioners of police of the Metropolis holds the office (as opposed to the rank) of constable; *Lewis* v. *Cattle* [1938] 2 K.B. 454. Furthermore, prison officers while acting as such have by virtue of their appointment all the powers, authorities and protection protection and privileges of a constable; Prison Act 1951, s.8. The jurisdiction of police forces other than "maintained" ones under the Police Act 1964, such as the British Transport Police, the Parks and Gardens Police and the Ministry of Defence Police is essentially territorial. When they are outside the jurisdictional limits, they are not "constables" for the purposes of the offences under consideration. For a list, see the Prosecution of Offences Act 1985 (Specified Police Forces) Order 1985, S.I. 1985/1956.

[4] Until the Criminal Law Act 1977, the offence of assault on a constable was triable either way, although the defendant had no right to elect jury trial; *Woolwich JJ. ex p. Toohey* [1967] 2 A.C. 1. See further 10–11.

policeman, and how do they come to be imposed for these purposes? The broad answers are that the duties of the policeman are manifold, and they arise both by the operation of statute and the common law.

Even though the offences under consideration have a statutory source, they have been the subject of a good deal of judicial development, reflecting the gradual and incremental changes in the social and legal functions that the police force has been expected to undertake since its inception.[5] The courts have rarely appeared constrained by the fact that, as they have developed the law by extending the constable's duties, they have in effect considerably broadened the ambit of the criminal law.[6] Even now, the categories of duty cannot be regarded as being closed[7]; they have been held to include a general duty to enforce the law,[8] to detect and prevent crime and to bring the offender to justice,[9] to prevent harm to persons and property[10] and to preserve evidence.[11] In the light of this ever-expanding catalogue, it can be asked what limits there are to the scope of the policeman's duty. The answer to that depends in turn on the precise nature of the duty, which is the subject of the next section.

The nature of the policeman's duty

10–03   For the jurist, the word "duty" has a number of possible meanings. **10–0.**
When used in any rigorous sense, it bears connotations of obligation, and in its pristine Hohfeldian sense, it is the strict correlative of a right.[12] So far

[5] See generally, L. H. Leigh, *Police Powers in England and Wales* (2nd edn., 1985) Chaps. I and II. See also M. D. A. Freeman, "Law and Order in 1984" (1984) 37 C.L.P. 174.

[6] The seminal discussion of the point is to be found in the excellent article by T. C. Daintith, "Disobeying a Policeman—A Fresh Look at Duncan v. Jones" (1966) P.L. 248. See also K. W. Lidstone, "A Policeman's Duties Not To Take Liberties" [1975] Crim.L.R. 617. For an even more general list of duties than the courts have acknowledged to exist, see the Royal Commission on the Police, *Final Report*, Cmnd. 1728 (1962), para. 59 which speaks of "a duty to befriend anyone who needs their help." This degree of vagueness should give the courts pause for thought when they contemplate the scope of s.51. The police also have, according to the Report, a duty to "maintain law and order," which is a mandate of alarming breadth when allied to the criminal offence under consideration.

[7] *Waterfield* [1964] 1 Q.B. 164; *Rice* v. *Connolly* [1966] 2 Q.B. 414. In *X.* v. *M.P.C.* [1985] 1 W.L.R. 420, 1 All E.R. 890, it was held that the policeman's duty to detect and prevent crime extends to foreign jurisdictions, since the nature of modern crime frequently extends across international boundaries.

[8] *R.* v. *M.P.C. ex p. Blackburn* [1968] 1 All E.R. 673; *R.* v. *M.P.C. ex p. Blackburn (No. 3)* [1973] Q.B. 241; *Prebble* (1858) 1 F. & F. 325, 175 E.R. 748. In some circumstances, it can be an indictable offence for the constable to fail to prevent the commission of a crime; *Dytham* [1979] Q.B. 722.

[9] *Betts* v. *Stevens* [1910] 1 K.B. 1; *Glasbrook Bros.* v. *Glamorgan C.C.* [1925] A.C. 270; *Dibble* v. *Ingleton* [1972] 1 Q.B. 480.

[10] *Hoffman* v. *Thomas* [1974] 1 W.L.R. 374; *Johnson* v. *Phillips* [1976] 1 W.L.R. 65, [1975] 3 All E.R. 682; *Saunders* [1978] Crim.L.R. 98. For a discussion of whether or not the duty can enable a policeman to instruct the citizen to disregard the law, see U. Ross, "Two Cases on Obstructing a Constable" [1977] Crim.L.R. 187. And see *Police* v. *Amos* [1977] 2 N.Z.L.R. 564.

[11] *R.* v. *Lushington ex p. Otto* [1894] 1 Q.B. 420; *Ghani* v. *Jones* [1970] 1 Q.B. 693.

[12] The classic exposition is W. N Hohfeld's *Fundamental Legal Conceptions as Applied in Judicial Reasoning*. See G. W. Paton and D. P. Derham (eds.) *Jurisprudence* (4th ed., 1972), p. 291 *et seq*. For an analysis in these Hohfeldian terms, see T. Gibbons, "The Offence of Obstruction: Obtructing a Constable—The Emergence of a New Duty to Co–Operate with the Police" [1983] Crim.L.R. 21.

as the scope of the duty in the offences of assault, resistance and obstruction is concerned, the law has developed in such a way that the obligation is not confined to duties *stricto sensu*, *i.e.* something that the officer is compelled by law to do. Rather, the courts have held that it is enough if the constable has a power to act as he does, and that he is not acting illegally in the exercise of that power at the time of the act complained of.

The precise nature of the policeman's duty was explicitly before the court in *Coffin* v. *Smith*.[13] The police had been called to a youth club where they had been asked by one of the supervisors to assist in excluding trespassers before the evening's festivities got under way. The appellants left when requested by the police to do so, but remained loitering outside the door of the club. One of the appellants was asked to move, but he declined. After several further requests, the male appellant began to move off, but then returned and punched the policeman in the chest. The argument on appeal from the ruling of the justices that there was no case to answer—a decision that Donaldson L.J. confessed to having initially found "prima facie perverse and incomprehensible"—was that a police officer is not acting in the execution of his duty if he is doing something that he is not compelled by law to do. The argument was that in this instance, the police were under no obligation to assist a person to eject a trespasser from his premises, and hence were not acting in the execution of their duty when the constable was assaulted. The Divisional Court held that the appeal must succeed, taking the view that the police officers were acting in the execution of their duty when they assisted the youth leader to eject the appellants and others from the youth club.[14] It was conceded by the court that this finding was on a strict view irrelevant, since there was a break between the clearing of the premises and the assault with which the appellant had been charged, which was a separate incident. Even at the later stage, the police were continuing to act within the execution of their duty, the general duty of the police to preserve the peace. "In a word," as Donaldson L.J. put it:

"a police officer's duty is to be a keeper of the peace and to take all

[13] (1980) 71 Cr.App.R. 221, not following *Prebble* (1885) 1 F. & F. 325, 175 E.R. 748; *Roxburgh* (1871) 12 Cox C.C. 8. In *Prebble*, it was held that there was no duty on a policeman to assist a publican to remove persons from an inn if there was no prospect of a breach of the peace, and Bramwell B. said "it would have been otherwise had there been a nuisance or disturbance of the public peace, or any danger of a breach of the peace." In the sufragettes case, *Despard* v. *Wilcox* (1910) 102 L.T. 103. it is plain that the court took the view that the duty must be specific and arise from statute or other legal source, there the duty to prevent obstructions of the highway.

[14] The police are entitled to assist a landowner to eject trespassers where the exercise of the right of self–help is likely to lead to a breach of the peace; *Coffin* v. *Smith* (last note); *Allen* v. *Police* [1961] N.Z.L.R. 732. That being so, it is not wholly clear why s.39 of the Act was considered to be necessary. Whether the police can be said to be under a duty to act when there is no likelihood of a breach of the peace, or when the persons to be ejected are not trespassers (as in *R.* v. *Chief Constable of Devon and Cornwall, ex p. Central Electricity Generating Board* [1982] Q.B. 458) is more problematic. And see *Ansell* v. *Thomas* [1974] Crim.L.R. 31 where it was held that where the police were assisting in the removal of a person believed to be a trespasser at the behest of the occupiers, the latter were responsible for the conduct of the police, and answerable in damages.

necessary steps with that in view. These officers, just like ordinary officers on the beat, were attending a place where they thought that their presence would assist in keeping the peace. . . . They were simply standing there on the beat in the execution of their duty when they were assaulted."

The conclusion at which the justices had arrived was therefore incorrect, but in view of the time that had elapsed between the hearing and the appeal, the case was not remitted to the magistrates.

There are a number of difficulties with this judgment. To begin with, there was no evidence from either of the policemen concerned that he feared a breach of the peace. Indeed, one of the lay witnesses said that he considered a breach of the peace unlikely even if the police had not been there. If the circumstances are such that the likelihood of a breach of the peace is obvious, there need be no direct evidence on the matter.[15] But in this case, the evidence seemed to go the other way, and was the express reason why the magistrates dismissed the charges. A possible basis for the decision, it is suggested, is that in instructing the appellants to leave the spot outside the premises, the police were acting to prevent an offence as they have a duty to do, namely to require the appellant to stop obstructing the highway. Failure to comply with that instruction might give rise to a charge of obstructing the police in addition to that of obstructing the highway.[16] That issue was not, however, raised in the case, and cannot formally be regarded as the reasoning underpinning the decision.

The principal importance of the decision, however, lies in the support that it affords to the proposition that it is not necessary for the duty of the policeman to be found in a specific rule of the common law or statute. According to the court, it was sufficient that the police were "standing there on the beat in the execution of their duty" for liability to attach. The court approached the issue in accordance with the judgment of the Court of Criminal Appeal in *Waterfield and Lynn*[17] (a prosecution for assaulting a constable in the execution of his duty) where Ashworth J. stated the law as follows:

"In the judgment of this court it would be difficult, and in the present case it is unnecessary, to reduce within specific limits the general terms in which the duties of police constables have been expressed. In most cases it is probably more convenient to consider what the police constable was actually doing and in particular whether such conduct was prima facie an unlawful interference with a person's liberty or property. If so, it is then relevant to consider whether (a) such conduct falls within the general scope of any duty imposed by statute or recognised

---

[15] *Joyce* v. *Hertfordshire Constabulary* (1984) 80 Cr.App.R. 298 (a prosecution under s.5 of the 1936 Act).
[16] Contrary to the Highways Act 1980, s.137 (Chap. 11); *Kavanagh* v. *Hiscock* [1974] Q.B. 600. The demonstrator is committing a criminal offence, and the officer undoubtedly has a duty to prevent the commission of crime; *Pankhurst* v. *Jarvis* (1909) 22 Cox C.C. 228; *Tynan* v. *Balmer* [1967] 1 Q.B. 91, [1966] 2 All E.R. 133; *Donaldson* v. *Police* [1968] N.Z.L.R. 32.
[17] [1964] 1 Q.B. 164; *Williams* v. *Police* [1981] N.Z.L.R. 108.

at common law and (b) whether such conduct, albeit within the general scope of such a duty, involved an unjustifiable use of powers associated with the duty."

On this analysis, the constable's duty is a defeasible one. The issue for the court to decide is whether or not the constable is doing anything that constitutes a prima facie interference with the person's liberty, person or property, as by detaining him, searching him or otherwise touching him, or constraining his behaviour in some other way. If the court comes to the conclusion that there is such an interference, it must then decide whether or not the constable has lawful justification for his conduct, which can be found either in statute[18] or the common law.

Purporting to apply these principles in *Coffin* v. *Smith*, the court concluded that the police were in this case on duty (since they were in uniform), and were doing nothing prima facie unlawful. It was not therefore necessary to ask whether or not the conduct was justifiable or otherwise. The ruling that the police were not doing anything which was prima facie an unlawful interference with a person's liberty or property is surely questionable. Being constrained upon penalty to leave the place where one would prefer to remain is surely such an interference, calling for justification. It may well be that the police did have justification in their reasonable fear that a breach of the peace would ensue if they did not remain where they were, and if they did not issue instructions to the appellants to leave.

In deciding the second of tests posed by the court in *Waterfield*, the court will consider not merely whether or not the power exists, but whether it has been properly exercised, and hold that, if the manner in which an admitted power is exercised is improper, it takes the constable outside the execution of his duty again. If he is trespassing,[19] or seeking to detain and question a person when he has no authority to do so,[20] or challenging another to a fight,[21] his conduct will be outside the scope of his duty, and any assault on him cannot come within the terms of section 51(1).[22] The improper exer-

---

[18] In particular now, the powers conferred by P.A.C.E.

[19] *Davis* v. *Lisle* [1936] 2 All E.R. 213; *McArdle* v. *Wallace* [1964] Crim.L.R. 467; *Robson* v. *Hallett* [1967] 2 All E.R. 407; *Bailey* v. *Wilson* [1968] Crim.L.R. 617; *Jones and Jones* v. *Lloyd* [1981] Crim.L.R. 340.

[20] *Kenlin* v. *Gardner* [1967] 2 Q.B. 510 *Pedro* v. *Diss* [1981] 2 All E.R. 59. *Cf. Squires* v. *Botwright* [1972] R.T.R. 462, discussed by D. Lanham, "Arrest, Detention and Compulsion" [1974] Crim.L.R. 288; *Ludlow* v. *Burgess* (1971) 75 Cr.App.R. 227, [1971] Crim.L.R. 238; *Kay* v. *Hibbert* [1977] Crim.L.R. 226; *Donnelly* v. *Jackman* [1970] 1 W.L.R. 562, 1 All E.R. 987; *Bentley* v. *Brudzinski* (1982) 75 Cr.App.R. 217; *Weight* v. *Long* [1986] Crim.L.R. 746. P.A.C.E., s.1 gives the police certain powers of detention for the purposes of search, but there are still no general powers to detain for questioning; see *Daniel* v. *Morrison* (1979) 70 Cr.App.R. 142 for an illustration of where powers under a previous Act were properly exercised; and see *McBean* v. *Parker* [1983] Crim.L.R. 399; *Hamilton* [1986] Crim.L.R. 187. See also *Lodwick* v. *Saunders* (1984) 80 Cr.App.R. 304 on the power to stop a vehicle for the purposes of traffic control under s.159 of the Road Traffic Act 1972. And see *Geen* [1982] Crim.L.R. 604, where it was held that a power to stop and search under the Misuse of Drugs Act 1971 included a power to stop, ask questions and search.

[21] *Whiteside* v. *Gamble* [1968] Crim.L.R. 560.

[22] Although it might still be an ordinary assault. But see 10–11.

cise of a power of arrest will have a similar effect. In *Lowe*,[23] for example, the policeman had said when arresting "that's enough, you're locked up." It was held that this was insufficient information to give an arrestee, and the constable who arrested in those circumstances had gone beyond the scope of his duty since he was exercising his admitted power improperly. A constable who gives inadequate reasons for conducting a search that he would otherwise be entitled to undertake is also acting outside the scope of his duty.[24] If more force than is necessary is used by the policeman, that too will take him outside the scope of the duty.

The characterisation of the policeman's duty adopted in *Coffin* equates the nature of the policeman's duty with his merely being on duty,[25] which is a related but essentially different concept. On the view there adopted, duty becomes a purely temporal concept. That is, it is sufficient that the constable is assaulted during his working hours, and the policeman's "duty" becomes "whatever the police officer considers to be necessary for doing the job."[26] Not every act that he performs in the course of his daily police routine can be "in the execution of his duty" within the contemplation of the statute. When a constable gives directions to a tourist, for example, or rescues a stranded cat from a tree, he is performing the sort of social service that the police are nowadays expected to undertake. If a passerby were to decline to lend the constable his map or his ladder to assist, he may be wilfully obstructing the constable[27]; but he would not be obstructing the constable in the execution of his duty. If only because the offence is defined in terms of "duty" the concept must be in some way limited to the ways that the law obliges the constable to act, in however attenuated or weak a sense of that word.[28]

The potential for the undesirable development of the line of reasoning adopted in *Coffin* is illustrated by the decision of the Supreme Court of Canada in *Moore*.[29] The defendant cycled through a red light and refused when requested to do so, to give his name and address to the police. He was arrested for[30] and charged with obstructing a constable in the

---

[23] [1986] Crim.L.R. 49. And see *da Costa-Small* v. *Kirkpatrick* (1979) 68 Cr.App.R. 168 (seeking to execute an arrest in a civil matter when warrant not in policeman's possession). But see *Nicholas* [1987] Crim. L.R. 000.

[24] *Brazil* v. *Chief Constable of Surrey* (1983) 77 Cr.App.R. 209; *Swales* v. *Cox* [1981] Q.B. 849.

[25] In *Betts* v. *Steven* [1910] 1 K.B. 1, Bucknell J. speaks of five policemen "on duty in the ordinary sense of that term."

[26] T. Gibbons, above n. 12, at p. 25.

[27] Arguably, there can be no liability in obstruction cases for omissions as opposed to positive acts of obstruction; see 10–12.

[28] See Smith and Hogan, *Criminal Law: Cases and Materials* (3rd ed., 1986), p. 372; "the relevant duty must relate to something which the constable is required, authorised or empowered to do."

[29] (1978) 43 C.C.C. (2d) 83, 90 D.L.R. 112; distinguished in *Guthrie* (1982) 69 C.C.C. (2d) 216. For a trenchant criticism of the decision, see A. Grant, (1979) 17 Osgoode Hall L.J. 459–468.

[30] There is no power of arrest for obstruction of a constable in England, *Gelberg* v. *Miller* [1961] 1 All E.R. 291, 1 W.L.R. 153; *Wershof* v. *M.P.C.* [1978] 3 All E.R. 540, although the police sometimes act as though there were; *Tynan* v. *Balmer* [1967] 1 Q.B. 91; *Stunt* v. *Bolton* [1972] R.T.R. 435; *Foster* v. *Atard* (1986) 83 Cr.App.R. 113. See 10–15.

execution of his duty, and his conviction was upheld by the Supreme Court of Canada. It cannot be doubted that the constable was "on duty" when he stopped the cyclist, and he was no doubt under some sort of obligation to stop the cyclist to enable him to bring the defendant before the court ultimately. But the cyclist was under no obligation to give the constable his name and address, and although the constable is perfectly at liberty to ask his questions, the citizen is under no obligation to answer them.[31] If a person is convicted in such circumstances, his right to remain silent is abrogated and set at nought. Jurisprudentially, the effect is that the offence has become obstructing a constable in the use of his powers, and that is not what the section prohibits. For these reasons, *Coffin* is perhaps better seen as a case in which the Divisional Court, contrary to the evidence, concluded that the situation was such that a breach of the peace was likely, and that the officers were seeking to prevent that at the time when the assault took place. Their active presence was intended to cause the appellants to leave the scene.[32]

One important question remains unsettled, namely, whether there can be a conviction for assault on a constable when the constable is not actually on duty in the technical sense that he has reported for his shift at the requisite time.[33] In *Albert* v. *Lavin*[34] it was assumed that the defendant was guilty of assaulting in the execution of his duty an off-duty policeman who was seeking to prevent a breach of the peace. Is it possible to extrapolate from this decision, and to say that an offence is committed whenever the constable is seeking to exercise a statutory power of arrest such as, for example, the power of arrest conferred by section 5?[35] The argument for saying that there should be liability in such circumstances is that a constable does not cease to have certain general duties because he happens to be "off duty" for the time being. When he sees an arrestable offence being committed, or an offence that carries a conditional power of arrest, he would be in dereliction of his duty if he did not intervene to prevent the misconduct.[36] He is therefore at much at risk from violence in his office of constable out of uniform and office hours as he is in them. If, as was argued earlier, the notion of duty should be seen as functional rather than purely

---

[31] *Rice* v. *Connolly* [1966] 2 Q.B. 414. Under P.A.C.E., s.25, the constable would now have a power of arrest, since the summons procedure cannot be made to work if he does not know the miscreant's name and address. But that is because Parliament considered that the initiating mechanism for the prosecution of the cycling offence is defective in the absence of such a power, and not because there has been an obstruction of the constable. See *Nicholas* [1987] Crim. L.R. 474. In *Ricketts* v. *Cox* (1981) 74 Cr.App.R. 298, a person who declined to answer questions in virulently abusive terms was held to be guilty of obstruction. This undercuts the *Rice* v. *Connolly* principles and diminishes the right to remain silent. See K. W. Lidstone, "Obstructing Freedom" [1983] Crim.L.R. 29.

[32] Viewers of the television series "One Man and His Dog" will be familiar with the shepherding effect of an entirely stationary dog. To say that the dog is merely present and nothing more does not capture the dynamic effect of the animal's presence.

[33] See Glanville Williams, (1982) 146 J.P.N. at p. 103.

[34] [1982] A.C. 546.

[35] Chap. 7.

[36] In *Dytham* [1979] Q.B. 722, the defendant constable was about to go off duty when the incident in respect of which he failed to act occurred.

temporal, it should therefore extend to all situations where the constable is engaged in obligatory police work. If the person whose liberty is interfered with does not know that the person who constrains him is a constable and believes that he is under attack, he will have the defence that, since he acted in self defence, he committed no assault.[37]

The duty to preserve the peace

10–04   There can be no doubt at all that the constable has a well-established **10–0·** duty to preserve the peace.[38] The powers that exist to enable him to carry out this task are expressly preserved by the Act,[39] and it is essential to consider their scope in some detail. They may be summarised as follows: if it appears that facts existed from which a constable could reasonably have anticipated a breach of the peace,[40] as a real and not as a remote possibility, and the constable did in fact anticipate such a breach, he is under a duty to take steps (whether by arrest or otherwise)[41] as he reasonably thinks are necessary to prevent the breach of the peace from occurring or, as it may be, from continuing. A person who makes the task of the constable more difficult when he is seeking to carry out that duty is obstructing the constable in the execution of his duty.

These principles were established in a series of cases, of which the most important—because it broke the ground in the first place—is the decision in the Divisional Court of *Duncan* v. *Jones*.[42] The appellant, in accordance with her previously announced intention, was about to address a meeting to be held across the street from the entrance to an unemployed training centre, attracting a crowd of some 30 people. She was told by the Chief Constable of the district (who was accompanied by the Inspector who became the respondent in the appeal) that a meeting could not be held on the spot, but could be held some 175 yards distant, around the corner. It was not alleged by the inspector that there was any obstruction of the highway, nor that any person present at the gathering had either committed, incited or provoked a breach of the peace. Some 15 months earlier, however, a meeting had been held at the same spot, and after that meeting, a disturbance took place at the training centre (although the report of the

---

[37] 10–10.

[38] *Duncan* v. *Jones* [1936] K.B. 218; *Thomas* v. *Sawkins* [1935] 2 K.B. 249; *McGowan* v. *Chief Constable of Kingston-Upon-Hull* [1968] Crim.L.R. 34. And see *Burton* v. *Power* [1940] N.Z.L.R. 305. But see *Forbutt* v. *Blake* (1980) 51 F.L.R. 465 below, n. 65).

[39] Section 40(4).

[40] As to what constitutes a breach of the peace, see *Chief Constable of Devon and Cornwall, ex p. Central Electricity Generating Board* [1982] Q.B. 458, 3 All E.R. 826; *Howell* [1982] Q.B. 416, [1981] 3 All E.R. 383, *Albert* v. *Lavin* [1982] A.C. 546, discussed 10–06.

[41] In *King* v. *Hodges* [1974] Crim.L.R. 424, taking hold of a person's elbow in an attempt to persuade her to move from one place to the other was held to be conduct within the policeman's duty. But see *Collins* v. *Wilcock* [1984] 1 W.L.R. 1172, 3 All E.R. 374; *Weight* v. *Long* [1986] Crim.L.R. 746. In *Humphries* v. *Connor* (1864) 17 I.C.L.R. 1, the constable removed a provocative orange lily from the plaintiff's lapel. And see *Hickman* v. *O'Dwyer* [1979] Crim.L.R. 309.

[42] [1936] 1 K.B. 218; *Dass* v. *Rennie* [1961] Crim.L.R. 396.

case gives no indication of the scale or the cause of the previous disturbance). It was accepted that the Chief Constable and the inspector actually and reasonably apprehended that a breach of the peace would result if the meeting of July 30, 1934, the subject of these proceedings, were held. The justices found that the appellant must have known of the possibility that a breach of the peace was a probable consequence of her conduct, and that she was not unwilling that this should come about. Because of the apprehension of a breach of the peace on the part of the inspector, it was held, there arose a duty on him to prevent a breach of the peace, and because the appellant had sought to hold the meeting in defiance of his instructions, she was guilty of obstructing him in the execution of his duty.

This went further than previous decisions, which had hitherto required some independent illegality in the conduct of the person whose conduct was called in question. The unlawfulness was generally to be found in the offence of unlawful assembly, but it might also have been another offence such as nuisance caused by obstruction of the highway. Neither of these was alleged against the defendant in this case. The effect of the decision, therefore, was to create an entirely new class of criminal behaviour, dependent on the instructions of a constable who feared a breach of the peace. This may well be a socially beneficial outcome, but it sets the criminal law dangerously at large unless the exercise of the powers thereby conferred is the subject of careful scrutiny by the courts.

Although the general principles underlying the decision have several times been endorsed by the superior courts, the decision itself has never been the subject of a direct challenge, and its implications have not been fully confronted by the higher courts.[43] Further, it may be doubted whether the Chief Justice of the day fully appreciated the implications of his decision for freedom of speech in public. Lord Hewart C.J., in the course of his judgment said:

"There have been moments during the argument in this case when it appeared to be suggested that the court was being confronted with a grave case involving what is called a right of public meeting. I say 'called' because English Law does not recognise any special right of public meeting either for a political or any other purpose. The right of assembly, as PROFESSOR DICEY puts it (LAW OF THE CONSTI-TUTION (8TH Edn.) p. 499), is nothing more than a view taken by the courts of individual liberty of speech. If I thought that the present case raised the question which has been held in suspense by more than one writer on constitutional law—namely, whether an assembly can properly be held to be unlawful merely because the holding of it is expected to give rise to a breach of the peace on the part of persons opposed to those who are holding the meeting—I should wish to hear much more argument before expressing an opinion. It seems to me that this case does not even touch that important question."

---

[43] At the time when the case was decided, there was no right of appeal from the Divisional Court on appeal from magistrates.

Why his Lordship should have concluded that the facts did not give rise to the issue is unclear, but subsequent events have shown that the decision has been of much greater importance for the scope of the right of public meeting than his Lordship imagined it would be. In *Piddington* v. *Bates*[44] the power was employed to enable the police to station no more than two pickets at the entrance to a factory. It was held that the defendant who had sought to push through the police cordon was committing the offence of obstructing a constable in so doing. The same power has been used to control potentially unruly crowds going to football matches, and to turn back would-be picketing miners at some distance from the scene where they wished to express their displeasure.[45] As sections 12 and 14 of the Public Order Act 1986 implicitly recognise, these are powers of considerable constitutional significance, since they involve the imposition of conditions on persons who are engaging in otherwise perfectly lawful behaviour. The law, as established in *Duncan* v. *Jones*, gives the police insufficient guidance as to when and against whom they should exercise their powers of control. In practice, it may well be, that the police give effect to the spirit of the decision in *Beatty* v. *Gilbanks*[46] that a man should not be held to commit an unlawful act when he does an act that is otherwise lawful merely because those who oppose him respond with violence or the threat of it. To what extent they are under a legal obligation to do so will be the subject of the following section.

Reviewing the constable's decision

10–05   Where the peace is threatened, the law confers upon the constable a very wide range of powers to take preventive action. At its broadest, it has been said:

> "every citizen in whose presence a breach of the peace is being, or reasonably appears to be about to be, committed has the right to take reasonable steps to make the person who is breaking or threatening the peace refrain from doing so; and those reasonable steps in appropriate cases will include detaining him against his will."[47]

What steps are reasonable in any particular case will obviously depend on the circumstances in which the policeman (or the citizen) finds himself, but these might include requiring trespassers to leave,[48] requiring a speaker to move from his chosen spot, or to desist from speaking altogether,[49] calling for quiet when noise seems likely to provoke a breach of the peace[50]; in short, anything that is necessary to prevent the breach from occurring. As

---

[44] [1961] 1 W.L.R. 162, [1960] 3 All E.R. 660.
[45] *Moss* v. *McLachlan* [1985] I.R.L.R. 76.
[46] (1882) 9 Q.B.D. 308; 1–09.
[47] *Per* Lord Diplock in *Albert* v. *Lavin* [1982] A.C. 546.
[48] *Chief Constable of Devon and Cornwall ex p. Central Electricity Generating Board* [1982] Q.B. 458.
[49] As in *Duncan* v. *Jones* [1936] K.B. 218.
[50] *Howell* [1982] Q.B. 416.

sanctions in the event of non-compliance, the peace keeper has powers of arrest,[51] or detention short of arrest.

From the foregoing, it will be apparent that the prospect of a breach of the peace licenses what would otherwise be unlawful conduct on the part of the policeman, and the question arises as to how carefully, and on what grounds, the courts will give guidance as to the use of the powers, and subject their use to review. This inquiry cannot be conducted in isolation from the general developments that have occurred in connection with judicial review of executive authority, an area in which the courts have been extremely active.[52] The courts have themselves shown a willingness recently to subject the decisions of the police to the general principles developed in other areas of the law.[53] A policeman may be able to restore the public calm without having to resort to an arrest. On the other hand, the decision to arrest may sometimes be the line of least resistance rather than the only realistic course of action. To what extent is the constable guided by the law as to how he should exercise his discretion?

In two respects, it is open to the courts to insist that the constable's decision must be a reasonable one; there must first be reasonable grounds on which the constable is entitled to rely in deciding in the first place whether or not a breach of the peace is likely to occur. Once he has come reasonably to the conclusion that this will happen, the question whether his decision to issue the particular instructions that he gave was a reasonable one in the circumstances is subject to a further test of reasonableness. There is authority for saying that the courts (in practice usually the magistrates) can and should intervene at both of these potential control points. In *Piddington* v. *Bates*,[54] Lord Parker C.J. said:

> "It seems to me the law is reasonably plain. First, the mere statement by a constable that he did anticipate that there might be a breach of the peace is clearly not enough. There must exist proven facts from which a constable could reasonably have anticipated a breach of the peace. Secondly, it is not enough that his contemplation is that there is a remote possibility but there must be a real possibility of a breach of the peace."

In *Albert* v. *Lavin*[55] the question posed for the House of Lords was "whether a constable who reasonably believes that a breach of the peace is about to take place is entitled to detain any person without arrest to prevent that breach of the peace in circumstances which appear to him to be proper." In answering that question in the affirmative, Lord Diplock

---

[51] Discussed in 2–18.

[52] See 8–08 for a brief outline of the principles of judicial review.

[53] In *Mohammed-Holgate* v. *Duke* [1984] A.C. 437 the House of Lords introduced the so-called "Wednesbury" principles principles of reasonableness developed in the administrative law context into the area of police powers. See M. Dockray (1984) 47 M.L.R. 727. For further discussion of these developments, see Christopher Ryan and Katherine Williams, "Police Discretion" [1986] P.L. 285, and D. G. T. Williams, "Criminal Law and Administrative Law: Problems of Procedure and Reasonableness" in P. F. Smith (ed.) *Criminal Law: Essays in Honour of J. C. Smith* (1987) 170 at 176.

[54] [1961] 1 W.L.R. 162, [1960] 3 All E.R. 660.

[55] [1982] A.C. 546.

insisted that the word "reasonable" should also appear in front of the verb "appear."

When they exercise powers of review, the courts are not attempting to decide whether or not the original decision was right or wrong. They are deciding whether or not the decision was properly arrived at, taking into account all relevant factors, and not taking into account irrelevant ones. The question for the courts was whether or not the decision was one at which the individual official could reasonably have arrived. What factors may the policeman take into account in deciding whether or not a breach of the peace is likely? What should he bear in mind in deciding what instructions to issue?

Some of these issues were tested in the case of *Moss* v. *McLachlan*[56] in which a group of picketing miners travelling in convoy were stopped by a police cordon on the M1 motorway and requested to turn back. The incident took place in the course of the miners' strike, within several miles of four collieries, and the policeman in charge said that he had reason to fear that a breach of the peace would occur if the miners continued on their journey. When they declined to do as requested and sought to push through the police cordon, the appellants were arrested, and later convicted of obstructing the police in the execution of their duty. On appeal, it was argued for the miners that the instructions to turn back were unlawful, and the police had no power to require them to turn back. Consequently, it was argued, the police were not acting in the execution of their duty at the time of the arrests.

The argument for the appellants was that there was no evidence from which the police could reasonably have apprehended an imminent breach of the peace. Their contention was that the constable must have a specific fear in mind; "he must be able to say which pit, which miners and when," and that it must have been clear from the words and deeds of the appellants themselves (and the others associated with them on the spot) that a breach of the peace would ensue. The Divisional Court expressed its conclusion in the following terms:

> "the situation has to be assessed by the senior police officers present. Provided they honestly and reasonably form the opinion that there is a real risk of a breach of the peace in the sense that it is in close proximity both in place and time, then the conditions exist for reasonable preventive action including, if necessary, the measures taken in this case."

In making his assessment that a breach was likely to occur, the senior policeman was entitled to take into account not only the conduct of the appellants themselves, and that of the people by whom they were accompanied, but also what they had heard and seen on television and read in the newspapers about the way in which the miners' strike was conducted, "and to exercise their common sense and judgment on that material" as well as

---

[56] [1985] I.R.L.R. 76. For a strikingly similar case, see *Police* v. *Newnham* [1978] 1 N.Z.L.R. 844.

what they saw with their own eyes. All of this was relevant material, properly considered by the police.[57]

As to the argument that, in order for the duty to take action to arise, the breach of the peace must be "imminent," the Court cited the opinion of Lord Parker C.J. to the effect that the police must anticipate "a real, not a remote, possibility" of a breach of the peace before they are justified in taking preventive action. In this respect too, the court is exercising its power of review, by identifying more closely for the police the questions that they must ask themselves in deciding whether or not they are entitled to take preventive action.[58]

Imminence must be a relative concept, and will ordinarily involve close proximity in terms of place and time. The breach will usually take place in the very presence of the constable who carries out the arrest. But it need not do so. If a person were to announce to a policeman that he was about to go to the house of his sworn enemy and beat the living daylights out of him, it would not make sense if the law were that the policeman had to follow the suspect to the *locus in quo* and only then arrest him. His powers of prevention must arise before that point is reached.

Where the second point of review is concerned, namely whether the actions taken by the constable were reasonable in the light of his apprehensions, the courts are diffident about interfering, for a number of reasons. Again, it must be remembered, the courts exercise a power of review rather than a power of appeal. Public disorder incidents are frequently transitory and fleeting events; the constable has to make quick decisions as to what course of action to adopt for the best. In *G.* v. *Chief Constable for Stroud*[59] the Divisional Court made the point that in deciding whether or not the constable's decision was a reasonable one, full allowance must be made for the circumstances in which the police find themselves in emergencies. For these reasons, it might well be that the courts will be reluctant to interfere with the judgment of the policeman on the spot, especially if he is an experienced officer. Sometimes, the prospect of a breach of the peace may form the basis of pre-planned preventive action. In *Moss* v. *McLachlan*[60] for example, the setting up of road blocks, etc., was clearly part of a coordinated police strategy, not wholly governed by the decisions of the policeman on the spot (although, as the quote from *Moss* v. *McLachlan* illustrates, it was the assessment of the senior police officers present that was being made the subject of review). Even allowing for the reluctance of

[57] In a slightly different context, it has been held that the intended victim of the conduct in question must also be taken into account. Where the object of the offending behaviour was a policeman who, because of his training, was unlikely to be provoked into causing a breach of the peace, the policeman's conclusion that a breach of the peace was about to occur was a decision to which he could not reasonably have come; *Marsh* v. *Arscott* (1982) 75 Cr.App.R. 211; above 6–11. And see *Hickman* v. *O'Dwyer* [1979] Crim.L.R. 309.

[58] Another excellent example of judicial review of the exercise of police powers may be found in the application of guidelines for search; the constable is expected to satisfy himself that the policy guidelines were met before conducting his search, and a policy of searching each and every person who came into a police station was a wrongful exercise of powers; *Lindley* v. *Rutter* [1981] Q.B. 128; *Brazil* v. *Chief Constable of Surrey* [1983] 1 W.L.R. 1155.

[59] [1987] Crim.L.R. 269.

[60] [1985] I.R.L.R. 76.

the courts to subject operational police decisions to judicial review,[61] it may be apparent that the police have failed to take into account in their decision making a relevant consideration, or have taken into account an irrelevant one, which would leave the decision open to review.

What factors should inform the decision making of the police in this difficult area? The denial of the importance of freedom of speech by the Chief Justice in *Duncan* v. *Jones*[62] suggests that it is open to the constable to take the surest means to prevent a breach of the peace, and can take whatever steps he chooses. Since that case was decided, the nature of constitutional guarantees has subtly changed in the constitution of the United Kingdom, which has since become a signatory to the European Convention on Human Rights,[63] Article 11 of which guarantees to citizens of the signatory countries a right to freedom of assembly. Although it is a matter of emphasis and weighting rather than clear-cut law, it might be argued that this also alters police responsibilities. For example, where disrupters of a public meeting are themselves behaving unreasonably, and possibly illegally,[64] there should be some sort of obligation to proceed first against the disrupters rather than the speakers, if that can be done. If there were a obligation on the police to operate a policy of protecting those first into the forum, freedom of speech would be the better preserved. The correctness of the decision in *Duncan* v. *Jones* has been doubted in Australia,[65] where it was pointed out that the effect of the decision is that "members of Parliament could be forbidden to address hostile audiences during election campaigns." For these reasons, it is possible to hope that the House of Lords might, if called upon to do so, reconsider the decision in a way that makes it plain that the right to freedom of speech in public is not wholly dependent upon the discretion of the policeman on the spot—important though that will undoubtedly always be—but is guided by rules and principles that recognise, *inter alia* the importance of freedom of speech in public, and the fact that the person interfered with was going about his otherwise lawful business.

In so far as it remains possible to approach the problem as a matter of principle, the law should be that, if a person is acting in a way that is independently lawful, his conduct should not become unlawful merely because

---

[61] 1–10.

[62] Above, n. 42. In *Piddington* v. *Bates* [1961] 1 W.L.R. 162, 3 All E.R. 660, Lord Parker C.J. went even further than that, saying; "I think that a police officer charged with the duty of preserving the Queen's peace must be left to take such steps as on the evidence before him he thinks are proper." This non-interventionist stance is out of tune with more recent decisions, which are replete with references to the reasonableness or otherwise of the policeman's decision.

[63] 1–07. In the House of Lords, an undertaking was given by the Home Office spokesman that a circular would be issued to the police reminding them of the importance of this Article in the implementation of the new offence created by s.5. See the Home Office Circular No 11/1987, para. 11, which honours this undertaking in relation to processions and assemblies.

[64] Public Meeting Act 1908; 7–12.

[65] *Forbutt* v. *Blake* (1980) 51 F.L.R. 465 (Supreme Court of the Australian Capital Territories). Two points may be noted; the penalty for the offence in that State is two years rather than the six months available in this country, and Connor A.C.J. took the view that a binding over order was available as a sanction and might have been (he expressed no concluded view on the point) the better alternative course of action.

he fails to obey the instructions of a policeman. If the actor intends to provoke a breach of the peace (which will often be independently criminal, by virtue of sections 4 and 5 in any event), it should be open to the policeman in the last resort to require him to desist.[66] Even here, the test of imminence discussed in *Moss* v. *McLachlan* suggests that there must be a clear and present danger[67] that the conduct in which he is engaging will give rise to a breach of the peace, and it is demonstrable that the constable has no reasonable alternative course of action open to him other than to ask the speaker to desist, as by, for example, calling for assistance.[68] As Professor E.C.S. Wade put it so powerfully several years ago:

> "a police officer should be grateful if he could point to a clear cut instruction that he was only to stop a meeting if some incident at the meeting itself, whether caused by the speaker and his supporters or by the opposition present at the meeting place, led him to suppose that disorder was inevitable and could not be averted by any other means."[69]

If this were not the case, it would be open to a constable to ask a member of parliament or other prominent person to stop speaking (or never even to begin his address), and a failure to do so would constitute an offence. Disruptive persons would succeed in their objects, and that is not something that the law should permit.

Breach of the peace

Although "breach of the peace" forms a cornerstone of public order law, it is surprisingly difficult to say what the concept entails with any degree of precision.[70] Because of the association between "peace" and "quiet," there is a natural tendency to suppose that a breach of the peace is "any behaviour that disturbed or tended to disturb the tranquility of the citi-

---

[66] As in *Wise* v. *Dunning* [1902] 1 K.B. 167.

[67] The "clear and present danger" test was propounded by Justice Holmes as the point at which the First Amendment protection of freedom of speech ran out. As he put it in *Schenck* v. *U.S.* 249 U.S. (1919), "the question . . . is whether the words used are used in such circumstances and are of such a nature as to create a clear and present danger that they will bring about the substantive evils that Congress has a right to prevent. It is a question of proximity and degree."

[68] There is authority for the proposition that the police must be able to show that there was no other course of action reasonably open to them. In *Londonderry Justices* (1890) 28 L.R. (Ir) 440, is to be found in O'Brien J. said; "if danger arises from where the exercise of lawful rights resulting in a breach of the peace, the remedy is the presence of sufficient force to prevent that result, not the legal condemnation of those who exercise those rights."

[69] "Police Powers and Public Meetings" (1938) 2 M.L.R. 177.

[70] Glanville Williams, "Arrest for Breach of the Peace" [1954] Crim.L.R. 578. For a discussion of some of the older decisions, see L. H. Leigh *op. cit.*, p. 185 *et seq.* It is difficult to know how much weight should be attached to some of these decisions. The lack of precision prompted the Law Commmission to decide that, where it could, Parliament should replace breach of the peace with a clearer notion such as violence; Report, paras. 5–14 *et seq.* But the Government preferred not to define the police powers precisely because of their useful open-endedness; White Paper, para. 6.13.

zenry."[71] But if any legal expression is a term of art, breach of the peace is one of them. Recently, the courts have refined the concept, and established very clearly that it is allied to harm, actual or prospective, against persons or property.

The leading modern authority is undoubtedly the decision of the Court of Appeal in *Howell*.[72] The defendant had been told by the police to leave the scene outside a party where he had been swearing and shouting, which he grudgingly did, continuing to use foul language. Watkins L.J. said:

> "even in these days when affrays, riotous behaviour and other disturbances happen all too frequently, we cannot accept that there can be a breach of the peace unless there has been an act done or threatened to be done which either actually harms a person, or in his presence his property, or is likely to cause such harm, or which puts someone in fear of such harm being done."

By tethering the law to the notion of harm rather than peace and quiet, this definition[73] places the law on a more stable footing in the world of facts, and reduces some of the areas of uncertainty that formerly surrounded it. Thus, merely shouting and swearing is not itself a breach of the peace,[74] although (as in this case) it was conduct likely to give rise to a breach of the peace on the part of another, and there could be an arrest for it on that footing. Subsequently, it has been held that, even where such conduct causes alarm, it is not sufficient to amount in itself to a breach of the peace.[75] Threats to property in a person's presence are themselves a breach.[76]

Unfortunately, later observations of the Civil Division of the Court of Appeal in *R. v. Chief Constable of Devon and Cornwall, ex p. Central Electricity Generating Board*[77] throw a certain amount of doubt on aspects of this definition. There, a group of protesters prevented the officers of the C.E.G.B. from conducting surveys for the purposes of ascertaining the suitability of the site for the construction of a power plant. In doing that, they were committing an offence, but not an arrestable one. It is unclear whether or not the protestors were trespassers.[78] The Court held that the Chief Constable, who had been unwilling to lend the assistance of his men to help move the protesters, should not be compelled by mandamus to do

---

[71] See the American *Model Penal Code and Commentaries*, (1980) Part II, Vol. 3, p. 325. And see Moriarty's *Police Law*, (24th ed., 1981), which asserts that "any interruption of that peace and good order which ought to prevail in a civilised country is a breach of the peace," at p. 220.

[72] [1982] Q.B. 416.

[73] Followed in *Parkin* v. *Norman* [1983] Q.B. 92.

[74] Although it is an offence under s.28 of the Town Police Clauses Act 1847, and would as such give rise to a power of arrest if the general arrest conditions in PACE, s.25 2–17 are satisfied.

[75] *G.* v. *Chief Constable for Stroud* [1987] Crim.L.R. 269.

[76] It is also an offence under the Criminal Damage Act 1971, s.2.

[77] [1982] Q.B. 458; A. T. H. Smith, [1982] P.L. 212.

[78] Lord Denning quotes in his judgment a passage from the evidence to the effect that the farmer on whose land the demonstrations were taking place had asked the demonstrators to leave, so that their continued presence would be as trespassers. But the Chief Constable of the day took a different view; in his *Law and Disorder* (1984) at 182 says that the farmer

otherwise. He had concluded that there was no likelihood of a breach of the peace, largely, it would seem, because the protesters had emphasised that theirs was to be a peaceful event. But the Court took the view that, even if the police had made an error of judgment about that matter, the application for the mandamus was misconceived. Neither the court nor a Chief Constable could compel an officer to do acts which can only lawfully be done if the officer himself with reasonable cause suspects that a breach of the peace has occurred or is imminently likely to occur. It is the judgment of the officer about that matter that is crucial.

So far as the definition of what constitutes a breach of the peace is concerned, however, the decision is less satisfactory. Although *Howell* was cited to the Court, none of the three judgments refers to that decision, and Templeman and Denning L.JJ. made remarks that were at variance with it. Lord Denning said that:

> "the conduct of these people, their criminal obstruction, is itself a breach of the peace. There is a breach of the peace whenever a person who is lawfully carrying out his work is unlawfully and physically prevented by another from doing it."

There is no reference here to the likelihood of harm. Lord Denning may have reasoned that a person who is obstructed is likely to use force on the obstructor and harm him. But if force were used, it would be lawful force, and that could not itself be a breach of the peace, which implies illegality.[79] True, the lawful use of force might then be met with unlawful resistance which would in turn be likely to give rise to harm to the person whose use of force was justified in the first place. It can hardly be said, even using this attenuated chain of reasoning, that the harm is "likely," more especially when the protesters had made plain their aversion to the use of force of any kind.

3. ASSAULTING A CONSTABLE

"Assaults or resists"

Technically, an assault is either the application of force to the person of another, or the threat to apply it in such a way as to cause the other to fear or apprehend that he is about to be subjected to force.[80] As a general principle, the status of a person made the subject of an assault is a matter to be considered by the tribunal as an aggravating factor in sentencing, rather than an ingredient in the substantive description of the offence. An excep-

---

"declined to remove the protesters from his land." "The result of this ploy was that the protesters were not trespassers on his land and for that reason could not be forcibly removed."

[79] This is implicit in the reasoning of the court in *Marsh* v. *Arscott* (1982) 75 Cr.App.R. 211, where the defendant's conduct provoked the police into arresting him. But the mere use of force in such situations could not be a breach of the peace, since it was lawful for the police to arrest in such circumstances. *McBean* v. *Parker* (1983) 147 J.P. 205, [1983] Crim.L.R. 401. And see *Lowe* [1986] Crim.L.R. 49; Glanville Williams, (1982) 146 J.P. at 219.

[80] See G. Williams, *Text*, Chap. 8; Smith and Hogan, (5th ed.) pp. 352–354.

tion is made in this instance because the policeman's task in maintaining law and order exposes him to a greater risk of attack than other members of the public. He has a duty to involve himself in "trouble" in order to prevent it. The separate offence exists as a warning that "those who are minded to assault police officers should appreciate that they run a real risk of a sentence of immediate imprisonment."[81] The existence of the offence is, therefore, of both practical and symbolic significance.

Resisting a constable is the least commonly encountered form of the three special police offences, resistance and obstruction being virtually synonymous for these purposes. To resist an arrest might also involve an obstruction and an assault, although it has been held that merely pulling away from another is not an assault for the purposes of the offence of assault with intent to resist an arrest.[82]

The mental element for assault on a constable

10–08   It has long been established that under section 51 (1), it is not encumbent **10–0** upon the prosecutor to establish that the defendant was aware that his victim was a policeman.[83] If a person assaults another who turns out to be a policeman, he can be convicted of assaulting a constable in the execution of his duty even though he had no knowledge that the other was a policeman, or even the means of such knowledge.[84] This seems a particularly harsh result where the person assaulted was in plain clothes, and it may be doubted whether it can be justified in principle.[85] Even if it is true that policemen require special protection in the course of their duties because of the proactive roles that we expect them to undertake, it does not follow that the person who assaults them without justification should be marked as having committed what is, in reality, an aggravated form of assault.

If the prosecutor were required to prove that the assailant knew or was reckless about the question whether his victim was a policeman, it might occasionally be that the assailant would escape conviction of the section 51 charge. Even here, if the defendant has (for example) used more force than was reasonably necessary, he can (if appropriately charged)[86] be convicted of the offence of simple assault. To some extent, the potential harshness of the strict liability rule is mitigated by the fact that, if a person acts in what he takes to be self-defence when he is confronted by another whom

---

[81] 14th Report of the C.L.R.C., *Offences Against the Person* Cmnd. 7844, (1980) para. 171.
[82] *Sherriff* [1969] Crim.L.R. 260.
[83] *Forbes* v. *Webb* (1865) 10 Cox 362; *Maxwell and Clanchy* (1909) 2 Cr.App.R. 26. The decision was followed by the High Court of Australia in *Reynhoudt* (1962) 107 C.L.R. 381, Aus.L.R. 381 which is powerfully criticised by Colin Howard in "Assaulting Policemen in the Execution of their Duty" (1963) 79 L.Q.R. 247. And see *Simpson* [1978] 2 N.Z.L.R. 221, where it was held that it is necesary to prove an awareness that the person assaulted is a constable. Glanville Williams, *C.L.G.P.*, pp. 193–194.
[84] In the remarkable case of *McBride* v. *Turnock* [1964] Crim.L.R. 456, it was held that a person was guilty of this offence where he aimed an unlawful blow at his antagonist, and accidentally hit a policeman.
[85] See the useful discussion on this in the 14th Report of the C.L.R.C., para. 167, which recommends a change in the law. See also the Report to the Law Commission, *Codification of the Criminal Law* (1985) clause 78.
[86] See further below, 10.11.

he does not realise to be a constable, he has a good defence to the charge, because he is not guilty of an assault.[87] This is a convoluted way of achieving a just result, and the law should be that the defendant should be proved to have realised that he was dealing with a policeman, or was reckless about the matter.

Where the defendant does realise that he is confronted by a policeman, it is not necessary for the prosecutor to show that he is aware that the latter is acting in the execution of his duty. This means that it is no defence that the defendant believes that the policeman is acting outside the scope of his duty, even if he reasonably so thought.[88] This second feature of the rules relating to *mens rea* is more readily defensible in terms of social policy than is the rule just considered. If a person knows that he is confronted by a policeman and comes to the conclusion, wrongly, that the policeman is acting outside the scope of his duty, he acts at his peril if he chooses to use force to escape from his predicament. This can work hardship, since the scope of the constable's duty is often unclear, and the person charged may very reasonably believe that he is being falsely dealt with. A person who is wrongly accused will know that he has not done that of which he is suspected, example, and may be indignant at being the object of suspicion. But he can rarely know whether or not the policeman has good grounds for acting as he does, and in so far as there is a conflict between the citizen and the policeman, the reasonable suspicions of the policeman must take priority. In *Fennell*[89] a father sought to secure the release of his son who had been arrested for participating in an affray. He hit one of the policemen on the jaw, and claimed in his defence that he had believed, on reasonable grounds, that his son was not guilty of the offence of which he was suspected, and had therefore been wrongfully arrested. Had the detention of the son been unlawful, Fennell would have been justified in acting as he did. His defence was, therefore, that on the facts as he reasonably believed them to be, his use of force would not have been unlawful, and he was entitled to be acquitted according to the ordinary principles governing criminal liability. Holding that the defence was not available the court in effect classified the defendant's belief that the arrest was unlawful as a mistake of law, which could not avail him for these purposes. As Scarman L.J. expressed the point in a slightly different context:

> "if you choose at the street side to act the part of Hampden, you have got to be right. There is a Latin maxim *ignorantia juris non excusat*, and, although these words are variously translated and variously applied in our law, they are remarkably applicable to someone who chooses to act in a challenging way towards a policeman on the street."[90]

---

[87] 10–10.
[88] *Bentley* (1850) 4 Cox C.C. 406; *Fennell* [1971] 1 Q.B. 428. And see *Barrett* (1980) 72 Cr.App.R. 212 on use of unreasonable force to resist a bailiff.
[89] Last note.
[90] *Reid* [1973] 3 All E.R. 1020 at p. 1025.

Self defence against wrongful police conduct

10–09   Where a person is actually being made the subject of an unlawful attack   **10–6**
by another, he is entitled to act in self-defence, and use force to do so. His
conduct does not amount to an assault, since his use of force is lawful.[91]
These principles hold good even where one of the participants is a policeman; self-defence against unlawful interference by a policeman is not an
assault.[92] English law does not recognise the continental doctrine of *rebel-
lion*[93] which requires a person to acquiesce in the unlawful use of official
force against him, seeking such civil remedies as may be available subsequently. In this country, a person may use preventive force where a
policeman wrongfully insists upon attempting to do that which is unlawful.

The amount of force that a person is entitled to use depends in part on
what the policeman is seeking to do. Professor Williams criticises the
attitude of some courts as being that a person may use "only force that is so
mild as to be ineffective."[94] The difficulty is that once violence is resorted
to at all, it tends to become part of an escalating spiral; violence begets
violence, and one object of the law is to prevent the resort to violence.
Where the wrongful conduct of the police is the initiating event, this would
seem to justify the citizen in engaging in increasingly spirited acts of resistance. Yet common sense dictates that there can be very few police actions
which a person would be entitled to resist at all costs, including if "necessary" the use of fatal force.[95] The law therefore sets a point (although an
extremely unclear one) at which the citizen is not entitled to resist
further,[96] and must be expected to endure the indignity or invasion, seeking relief subsequently when he can substantiate that he has been the victim of a police mistake.[97] Suppose, for example, that the police seek to
remove a person's clothing,[98] or to take fingerprints when they are not
authorised to do so,[99] or persistently seek to question a person who makes
it plain that he has no wish to answer,[1] or seek to enter a house when they

---

[91] See 3–13.

[92] *Marsden* (1868) L.R. 1 C.C.R. 131; *Kenlin* v. *Gardner* [1967] 2 Q.B. 510; the point was also
assumed by the House of Lords in *Albert* v. *Lavin* [1982] A.C. 546. See A.A.S. Zucker-
man, "Assault or not Assault" (1972) 88 L.Q.R. 246.

[93] G. Williams, "The Requisites of a Valid Arrest" [1954] Crim.L.R. 6.

[94] *Text* at 512.

[95] The question whether a person is guilty of homicide when he resists an unlawful arrest with
fatal force is very unclear. The older cases treated this as provocation, reducing murder to
manslaughter. But it has been said that "if the unlawful arrester shows an intention of himself killing or inflicting serious harm, the victim may in self-defence reply in kind"; G. Williams, n. 93, at p. 11.

[96] This is implicit in the numerous suggestions in the decided cases that, where there has been
a challenge to the policeman's technical authority, there should nevertheless be a charge of
simple assault where the reaction of the citizen is unjustifiable. See *Bentley* v. *Brudzinski*
(1982) 75 Cr.App.R. 217.

[97] One would advance this point with greater confidence if it were not for the fact that civil
proceedings against the police are as expensive and personally harrowing as they are likely
to be.

[98] *Lindley* v. *Rutter* [1981] Q.B. 128; *Brazil* v. *Chief Constable* [1983] 1 W.L.R. 1155.

[99] *Jones* [1978] 3 All E.R. 1098, 67 Cr.App.R. 166 (a good example of the escalation that follows when tempers are lost).

[1] *Donnelly* v. *Jackman* [1970] 1 W.L.R. 562, 1 All E.R. 987.

have no search warrant or a defective one.[2] Concern for the physical welfare of the police and the person resisting (since the police are likely to be able to muster the greater force ultimately) both dictate that a point must arise at which further resistance is not only unwise but improper. It is difficult to say how much force is permissible, and the universal but anodyne expression "as much as is reasonably necessary" does not give sufficient guidance as to the true state of the law.[3]

If the police were to use excessive force in exercising an admitted power,[4] they would be acting unlawfully, and their victim would be entitled to use reasonable force preventively.

There are several reason why the courts insist that the police should observe the set limits to their powers. The first is that since the person against whom the powers are being improperly exercised is entitled to resist such use, he is in principle entitled to know sufficient to enable him to make a judgment about whether it would be right to do so. This is a consideration of principle rather than practical reality, since the relevant law is often obscure, and unlikely to be at the fingertips of the qualified lawyer let alone the layman. Perhaps more important in practice, is the fact that police powers often involve invasions of the individual's privacy, dignity and integrity; their use can involve offence and humiliation, and the courts wish to insist that this should not be caused without legal justification. Sometimes, the courts will push this rather far. In *Richards and Leeming*,[5] for example, the police were summoned to a house by an emergency call indicating that one of the occupants of a house was being badly assaulted. When they arrived at the house, they saw a man whom they had good reason to suppose to be the assailant washing blood from himself. The police sought to enter, giving as the reason a wish to make sure that the feared victim was safe and unhurt. Surprisingly, no power is conferred for this purpose, either by statute or by the common law, although there was ample authority to enter to arrest if there were sufficient grounds to suspect that an offence had been committed. It was held that the very considerable force—the defendants injured four policemen—used to try to prevent the police from entering was justified. The notion that a person's home is his castle will not be eroded without explicit justification.

A further reason that may be advanced for insisting that police interference of whatever kind must be legally justified is that it is an understandable human reaction to respond with some indignation to an allegation or suspicion believed by its object to be unjustified. The fact that the subject believes himself to be been falsely suspected will not necessarily protect

---

[2] *Richards* v. *Leeming* (1985) 81 Cr.App.R. 125.
[3] See L. H. Leigh, (1967) 30 M.L.R. 340.
[4] See, *e.g.* PACE, s.117 of which says that where the Act confers a power that may be exercised without consent, the policeman "may use reasonable force, if necessary, in the exercise of the power."
[5] (1985) 81 Cr.App.R. 125. In *Syce* v. *Harrison* [1980] Crim.L.R. 649, the defendant refused to admit police who were in possession of a defective search warrant, and tampered with evidence when the police went to secure a fresh warrant. Her conviction of obstruction was quashed, since she was perfectly entitled to refuse permission, and had not obstructed the police when they did return with a warrant in the proper form.

him from criminal liability if he should over-react. In this sense, the use of police powers may create provocative incidents, and even if the law cannot treat such conduct as being unlawful provocation,[6] such incidents should be avoided wherever possible.

It is not entirely clear whether an onlooker or third person is entitled to use force to assist another to resist unlawful police conduct. In principle, it would seem he should be able to do so; where the attacker is a citizen, the bystander may certainly intervene, both on grounds of private defence, and the prevention of crime.[7] In a New Zealand decision,[8] it was held that the police are in a different position, so that the associate of the police "victim" was guilty of assaulting the police in the execution of their duty, even though, *viz-à-viz* the victim they were acting outside the execution of their duty.

Mistaken self-defence

10–10   A problem arises when a person makes a mistake about the circumstances by which he is confronted and supposes himself to be under attack when in truth he is not. There is then a question whether he is guilty of an offence if the mistake he makes is an unreasonable one, or whether any mistake will exculpate. It has already been seen that, if the defendant knows that his assailant was a policeman, it will not avail him as a defence if he mistakenly thinks that the policeman was exceeding his powers.[9]

Where, however, the defendant is unaware that he is confronted by a policeman and believes himself to be entitled to use force, the situation is different. The effect of his mistake is that he is not guilty of assault. If the facts actually were as he believed them to be, he would be entitled to act as he did.[10] This reasoning applies where a person goes to the aid of another whom he believes to be under attack. In *Gladstone Williams*[11] the defendant was on a bus when he witnessed what he believed to be an attack by a large man on another, smaller youth. He went to the youth's "assistance," only to find later that he had assaulted a policeman who had seen the youth committing an offence. It was held that Williams was not guilty, since had the facts been as he believed them to be, he would have been acting in defence of the other. Furthermore, the Court held that the direction that the mistake must, to exculpate, be based on reasonable grounds[12] had been overtaken by later developments.[13] This was subsequently followed

---

[6] See Paul G. Chevigny, "The Right to Resist an Unlawful Arrest" (1969) 78 Yale L.J. 1128, who advances this as a continuing rationale.
[7] *Duffy* [1967] 1 Q.B. 63.
[8] *Williams* [1981] N.Z.L.R. 108. The decision is perhaps at variance with the cases on mistaken belief discussed in the next section. But in them, the defendant was unaware that the person with whom he interfered was a policeman, whereas the defendant in *Williams* undoubtedly did know.
[9] 10.08
[10] *Geen* [1982] Crim.L.R. 604.
[11] (1983) 78 Cr.App.R. 276. And see *Jackson* [1985] R.T.R. 257.
[12] In *Mark and Mark* [1961] Crim.L.R. 173, it was held that the mistake must be based on reasonable grounds.
[13] See above 3–13.

in *Ansell* v. *Swift*[14] where the defendant who had been lawfully protecting his brother in a fight hit a policeman who sought to restrain him. The defendant thought that he was being attacked when he acted, and it was held that self-defence was available to him. The prosecutor sought to rely on the words of Winn L.J. in *Kenlin* v. *Gardner*[15] that self defence was not available against an assault that was justifiable in law, as for instance a lawful arrest. But the remarks were *obiter* in that case, since the interference was unlawful. The report of *Ansell* does not disclose whether or not the defendant was aware that his assailant was a policeman, but it would seem that he did not. Had the defendant been aware, it is submitted, he would have had no defence, since he would then have been making a mistake as to whether or not the policeman was justified in seeking to restrain him, and whether he was therefore acting in the execution of his duty. If the policeman had approached him from behind, for example, and the defendant had acted without seeing who confronted him, he should have the defence, as *Williams* and *Ansell* hold. This has the apparently anomalous result that both the policeman and the defendant are using force lawfully. The difference is that whereas the policeman is justifed in acting as he does, the citizen is merely excused from criminal liability on the grounds that he lacks *mens rea*.

Section 51(1) and other assaults

Assault on a constable is one of a group of offences with a somewhat   complicated family connection.[16] The offence of "common assault," as it is known, is triable either way, and punishable with six months when tried summarily, but with one year's imprisonment if tried on indictment.[17] Paradoxically, assaulting a constable contrary to section 54(1) of the Police Act 1964,[18] which would appear to be an aggravated form of the offence is triable summarily only. If the trial takes place before the magistrates and they come to the conclusion that the offence under section 54(1) is not made out, they are presently unable to convict of the offence of simple assault[19] unless there is an additional information charging the common assault. Prosecutors rarely adopt this course since the addition of the extra charge gives the defendant the choice of jury trial.[20] The offence of assault

---

[14] [1987] Crim.L.R. 194.

[15] [1967] 2 Q.B. 510.

[16] Edward Griew, "Common Assault and the Statute Book" [1983] Crim.L.R. 710.

[17] The Criminal Justice Bill 1987, clause 25, contained a proposal to make the offence triable summarily only, in which case the difficulties encountered in this area would have disappeared. This part of the Bill was lost when a General Election was called.

[18] Above, para. 10–1.

[19] *Lawrence* v. *Same* [1968] 2 Q.B. 93. For criticism of the law from the prosecutor's perspective, see B. G. Coase, (1980) 144 J.P.N. 441.

[20] See Dunn L.J. in *McBean* v. *Parker* (1983) 147 J.P. 205 at 207; and see Donaldson L.J. in *Bentley* v. *Brudzinski* (1982) 75 Cr.App.R. 217 at 226, who speaks of the "attendant expense" of a jury trial, and who asks that the police (and now Crown Prosecutors) should nevertheless consider charging assault when the reaction of the citizen has been wholly unjustifiable, and there is likely to be a technical challenge to the policeman's authority. And see *R.* v. *Ramsgate JJ. ex p Warren and others* [1981] 2 All E.R. 129, where it was held that it is open to the prosecutor to offer no evidence on the more serious charge if the defendant elects jury trial.

with intent to resist arrest—whether by a policeman or a civilian—remains indictable, and punishable with two years' imprisonment.[21]

Where the hearing is by way of complaint upon the complaint of the party aggrieved, contrary to section 42, the justices have the option whether or not they will accept jurisdiction.[22]

The question of whether the offence under section 51 should be triable summarily only is controversial, for reasons examined by the C.L.R.C.[23] Since magistrates often imprison persons convicted of assaulting policemen,[24] but not of simple assault, the propriety of excluding jury trial seems questionable.

4. OBSTRUCTING A CONSTABLE

The meaning of obstruction

10–12   When the offence of obstructing a constable[25] was first enacted by Parliament, it seems reasonably clear that it was intended to refer to physical obstruction only. The argument that it was confined to physical obstruction and threats was rejected in *Bastable* v. *Little*.[26] As a result, what amounts to obstruction may depend on what the policeman is seeking to do. In *Hinchcliffe* v. *Sheldon*[27] Lord Goddard said:

> "obstructing, for the present purposes, means making it more difficult for the police to carry out their duties."

As will be presently discussed, this enlarges the notion of obstruction further than is warranted.

The mere intention to obstruct is insufficient. In *Bennett* v. *Bale*[28] the defendant had invited a person to tell lies to disguise what he believed had been the commission of a licensing offence. The person thus solicited happened to be an under-cover police officer. In fact, no offence had been

---

[21] O.A.P.A., s.38. If the relevant intention to evade arrest cannot be proved, a conviction for common assault was still available to the jury; *Wilson* [1955] 1 W.L.R. 493.

[22] *R.* v. *Harrow JJ. ex p. Osaseri* [1986] Q.B. 589. The penalty is then two months' only.

[23] 14th Report, *Offences Against the Person* Cmnd. 7844, (1980), paras 173–177.

[24] In *Jones* [1978] 3 All E.R. 1098, 67 Cr.App.R. 166, Pain J. makes the point that assaulting the police is "a serious charge and a person convicted of it must in the ordinary way expect to be deprived of her liberty."

[25] See R. C. Austin "Obstruction—The Policeman's Best Friend?" (1982) C.L.P. 187. Later parliamentary offences include the offence created by the Misuse of Drugs Act 1971, s.23(4)(*a*). See *Forde* (1985) 81 Cr.App.R. 19, where the destruction of self-incriminating evidence was treated as an obstruction.

[26] [1907] 1 K.B. 59; *Betts* v. *Stevens* [1910] 1 K.B. 1. *Cf.* the Scottish law; *Curlett* v. *M'Kechnie* 1938 S.C.J. 176, where it has been held that obstruction means physical obstruction; J. A. Coutts (1956) 19 M.L.R. 411.

[27] [1955] 1 W.L.R. 1207. And see *Lewis* v. *Cox* [1985] 1 Q.B. 509. In the former decision, the obstruction was physical; the defendant had barred the door to the police to prevent them from entering while the evidence of an offence was being dispersed.

[28] [1986] Crim.L.R. 404.

committed, so that the assistance sought could not actually have impeded the police. It was held that the conviction should be quashed.[29]

One qualification that should be made to the general formula that Lord Goddard laid down in *Hinchcliffe* v. *Sheldon* is that it appears to make a person guilty of obstructing by omission, and the view may be expressed that this is not the law.[30] By being uncooperative, a person might very well make the task of the constable more difficult, but it may be doubted whether he commits obstruction. If a constable were to ask for a ladder to rescue a cat from a tree, the person who declined to lend his assistance would commit no offence thereby. There is no general legal duty to cooperate with the police to assist their investigations.[31]

It may, however, be difficult to draw a line between acts and omissions for these purposes. In *Stunt* v. *Bolton*[32] a man refused to hand over to the police the keys of a car which was causing an obstruction of the highway. He was adjudged guilty of the offence of obstruction.

A refusal to answer police questions is plainly not an offence under section 51(3). In *Rice* v. *Connolly*,[33] the landmark decision establishing that this is the law, it was said that this was so because a refusal to answer questions was not "wilful," an expression that their Lordships interpreted to mean "without lawful excuse." Wilfulness is more obviously part of the *mens rea* than of the *actus reus*. A refusal to answer police questions undoubtedly makes the policeman's job more difficult when the person interrogated knows the correct answers, and the suspect intends to make the task of the police more difficult, in the sense that he is fully aware that he is doing so.

It has been held, however, that refusing to answer questions in abusive terms may amount to obstruction.[34] The correctness of this decision may be doubted. Offensive lack of cooperation may make the task of the con

---

[29] There is no doubt that the defendant was seeking to obstruct the police, and would have been guilty of an attempt, even though what he was seeking to do was impossible; *Shivpuri* [1987] A.C. 1. In the Magistrates' court, he could not be convicted of the offence unless expressly charged with it.

[30] C.L.R.C. 7th Report, *Felonies and Misdemeanours* Cmnd. 2659 (1965), para. 42. See the discussion of *Dibble* v. *Ingleton* [1972] 1 Q.B. 480 by Glanville Williams, [1972] C.L.J. at 193. Thomas Gibbons, "The Offence of Obstruction: (1) Obstructing a Constable—The Emergence of a New Duty to Co-Operate with the Police" [1983] Crim.L.R. 21; K. W. Lidstone, "Obstructing Freedom" [1983] Crim.L.R. 29.

[31] See generally M.E. Bennun, "The Duty to Assist the Police—some Aspects" in Lasok, Jaffey, Perrott and Sachs, (eds.), *Fundamental Duties* (1980).

[32] [1972] R.T.R. 435, Crim.L.R. 561; *Liepins* v. *Spearman* [1986] R.T.R. 24, [1985] Crim.L.R. 229. These decisions may be contrasted with *Umeh* [1979] Crim.L.R. in which the police declined to return keys to the driver on the grounds that the driver did not have a proper licence. The justification offered was therefore that the police were acting to prevent the commission of an offence. The car owner's friend did have a licence, and could have driven, in which case the refusal on the part of the police to comply with the owner's request would appear to be tortious, taking the police outside the execution of their duty.

[33] [1966] 2 Q.B. 414. There are statutory exceptions to this common law principle, notably the Official Secrets Act 1939, s.1; the Road Traffic Act 1960, ss.161, 162, 164, 165, 167, 168; PACE, s.25 and the Public Order Act 1986, s.5. Prevention of Terrorism (Temporary Provisions) Act 1984, s.11.

[34] *Ricketts* v. *Cox* (1981) 74 Cr.App.R. 298 see [1982] Crim.L.R. 184 and 484, the latter being critically commented upon in Smith and Hogan, p. 369 n. 13.

stable more unpleasant, but it does not make it any more difficult than would a civilised refusal to help. In such circumstances, the policeman could perhaps more appropriately proceed under sections 4 or 5 of the Act.

A policeman's job is made more difficult if a person physically obtrudes so as to prevent the policeman from arresting a third person,[35] and it has been held that such conduct constitutes obstruction. The logic of this has been held to extend to the situation where the person interposes by advising his friend of his legal rights; the courts have held that this too amounts to obstruction.[36]

The mental element in obstruction: wilfully

10–13   Parliament has used the expression "wilfully" to denote the mental element in the obstruction offence. This is a word that changes its meaning according to context, and it is dangerous to generalise by reference to decisions on other statutes.[37] The courts decided readily enough that in this instance the offence is one requiring proof of *mens rea*; "the gist of the offence to my mind lies in the intention with which the thing is done," as Darling J. put it.[38] What is actually meant by intention is more problematic, and will be approached in stages.

By contrast with the offence of assaulting the police in the execution of their duty,[39] it is clear that the prosecutor must show that the defendant was aware that the person obstructed was a constable.[40] So far as the attitude to his obstruction is concerned, the essence is that it must be shown that the defendant has deliberately brought about the state of affairs that makes it more difficult for the police to do their duties, and is aware that he has done so. To what extent is it necessary for the prosecutor to show that it was the purpose of the defendant to make the task of the police the more difficult? The authorities on the issue are discordant. In *Willmott* v. *Atack*[41] the defendant intervened as the police were in the course of effecting an arrest because he believed that he would be able to persuade the person being arrested to cooperate. His actions in doing so in fact obstructed the police. It was held by the Divisional Court that his appeal against conviction of the obstruction offence must be allowed. According to the court, it was not enough that the defendant deliberately did some act that had the effect, objectively assessed, of obstructing the police. Croom-Johnson J. said that

"there must be something in the nature of a criminal intent of the kind

---

[35] *Pounder* v. *The Police* [1970] N.Z.L.R. 1080.
[36] *Steele* v. *Kingsbeer* [1957] N.Z.L.R. 552 (see I. D. Campbell [1958] Crim.L.R. 100). Where the person being arrested makes a request for information it has been held that to respond is not necessarily to obstruct wilfully; *Dash* v. *Police* [1970] 2 N.Z.L.R. 273.
[37] See *Sheppard* [1981] A.C. 394.
[38] *Betts* v. *Stevens* [1910] 1 K.B. 1, at p. 8. *Bastable* v. *Little* [1907] 1 K.B. 59. And see *Hammerley* v. *Scandrett* [1921] N.Z.L.R. 455; "unless the thing be done deliberately, and with the intention of obstructing the constable, it is not 'wilfully' obstructing him."
[39] 10–08.
[40] *Ostler* v. *Elliott* [1980] Crim.L.R. 584.
[41] *Willmott* v. *Atack* [1977] Q.B. 498.

which means that it is done with the idea of some form of hostility to the police with the intention of seeing that what is done is to obstruct, and that it is not enough merely to show that he intended to do what he did and that it did in fact have the result of the police being obstructed."

Leaving aside for the time being the question of "hostile intent,"[42] it is plain that it is not enough that the defendant deliberately does an act that has the incidental effect of obstructing the police; he must also have some notion that he is obstructing and causing the police difficulties. The question is whether he is in addition permitted to say that, although he was aware that he was causing difficulties, he was doing so from the best of intentions. Croom-Johnson J. plainly thought that he is; one of the reasons advanced for accepting the contentions of the appellant was that, if the law were otherwise, the "well meaning" defendant who went to the aid of the police and accidentally obstructed them would be guilty of an offence. By implication, the law should not seek to produce such an undesirable result. A citizen is hardly encouraged to do his civic duty as he sees it if he is guilty of committing an offence should events backfire on him.

It is not clear from the report in *Willmott* v. *Atack* whether the police had made it plain that they did not want the defendant's "help," and, if so, what impact that has on the state of the law. In *Hills* v. *Ellis*[43] the defendant was outside a football match where he witnessed a policeman arresting a person whom he believed to be faultless. Thinking that the police were arresting the wrong man, he attempted to attract the arresting policeman's attention, and seized his arm for this purpose, since he could not make himself heard over the hubbub. He was warned by another constable that he was liable to be arrested for obstruction if he persisted, which he did.[44] His motives, clearly, were of the best, but the court held that this was irrelevant. His deliberate act was in fact obstructing the police who were making a lawful arrest, and that was sufficient *mens rea*. The court might equally have said that the defendant also realised that what he was doing was obstruction, since the police had told him so. In those circumstances, he could not argue that he did not mean to obstruct, or that he was unaware that his conduct was obstructing. It may be, then, that there is a distinction between the two cases and that, notwithstanding the later doubts expressed in *Hills* v. *Ellis*, *Willmott* v. *Atack* should be taken to stand for the proposition that a person who interferes with the police intending to help them is not guilty of a wilful obstruction.

It is not clear what Croom-Johnson J. had in mind when he said that there was a requirement of "hostile intent," and the observation has been doubted and explained subsequently. In *Hills* v. *Ellis*, this was interpreted to mean that the act of the defendant must in some way be "aimed at" the police, even if there need be no hostility towards them. This requirement

---

[42] Hostile intent is discussed further below, *infra*.
[43] [1983] Q.B. 680.
[44] There is no power of arrest for obstruction; 10–15.

was satisfied in *Hills* v. *Ellis* itself. But the element caused difficulties in *Lewis* v. *Cox*[45] A friend of the defendant was arrested and placed in the back of a police van. The defendant opened the door, to ask his friend where he was being taken. Before he received any answer, the arresting policeman shut the door, warned him that he would be arrested for obstruction if he persisted and went back to the driver's seat. The defendant was arrested when he again opened the door to find out from his friend where he was being taken. His argument that his conduct was not in any sense "aimed at" the policeman, as apparently required by the earlier decision, was accepted by the justices, who dismissed the prosecution. The prosecutor's appeal was allowed. The court said that, although in some circumstances the question whether the conduct was "aimed at" the police may be "not unhelpful," that was not an essential ingredient of the offence. Rather:

> "the simple facts which the court has to find are whether the defendant's conduct in fact prevented the police from carrying out their duty, or made it more difficult for them to do so, and whether the defendant intended that conduct to prevent the police from carrying out their duty or to make it more difficult to do so."

Here, because it could be inferred that the defendant knew that the police could not drive off while the van door was still open, he was aware that he was obstructing the police, and intended therefore to do so. The court distinguished between the defendant's intention and his motive, treating the latter as being irrelevant, and cited McCullogh J. in *Moore* v. *Green*[46]:

> "What is meant by 'an intention to obstruct'? I would construe 'wilfully obstructs' as doing deliberate actions with the intention of bringing about a state of affairs which, objectively regarded, amount to an obstruction as that phrase was explained by Lord Parker C.J. in *Rice* v. *Connolly i.e.* making it more difficult for the police to carry out their duty. The fact that the defendant might not himself have called the state of affairs an obstruction is, to my mind, immaterial. That is not to say that it is enough to do deliberate actions which, in fact, obstruct; there must be an intention that those actions should result in the further state of affairs to which I have been referring."

In other words, what would appear to be required is some awareness on the part of the defendant that he was making the task of the police a more difficult one, and this element may have been lacking in *Wilmott* v. *Atack*, which would explain why the appeal was allowed. It was present in abundance in *Lewis* v. *Cox* because of the police warnings. If the police can show that they have issued a warning, it might seem the defence that the actor's conduct was not "wilful" will hardly ever avail.

---

[45] [1985] 1 Q.B. 509.
[46] Citing McCullough J. in *Moore* v. *Green* [1983] Q.B. 667 at 671, who had said that motive and emotion are alike irrelevant in the criminal law.

Intoxication and wilfulness

0–14   Although there appears to be no authority on the point, principle dic-   **10–14**
tates that the offence of wilful obstruction is a specific intent offence.[47] If
that is so, the defendant cannot be convicted if he raises doubts as to
whether or not he realised that the person with whom he was dealing was a
policeman, or that he did not realise that what he was doing would make
the task of the policeman more difficult. There appears to be little direct
authority on the point, but in *Lewis* v. *Cox*[48] Webster J. said that even taking into account the fact as found by the magistrates that the defendant was
intoxicated and that his intoxication affected his actions, they must still
inevitably have inferred that the defendant intended to obstruct. This suggests that it is general practice for the courts to admit evidence of intoxication as a defence to the charge where this negatives the requisite *mens rea*.
Although it is dangerous to generalise about matters of fact, it may be
asserted that it will require a considerable degree of intoxication before a
defendant can plausibly make such claims. If he is so intoxicated, he is
almost certainly guilty of the offence of being either drunk and disorderly
or drunk in a public place.[49]

Arrest for Obstruction

10–15   Whenever the issue of whether or not there is a power of arrest for   **10–15**
obstructing a constable in the execution of his duty has been explicitly considered by the courts, they have held that no such power exists.[50] The authorities appear to be ignored in practice with impunity,[51] perhaps because
there is frequently an power of arrest in situations in which the police at
present exercise the "power." A policeman has a power of arrest for
breach of the peace,[52] and can issue instructions in order to prevent a
breach of the peace. If his instructions are disobeyed and he continues to
fear a breach of the peace, he can therefore arrest, for a breach of the
peace, the person who refuses to comply, and either seek to have the person bound over, or prosecuted for obstructing a constable in the execution
of his duty.

---

[47] Within the category laid down by the House of Lords in *Majewski* [1977] A.C. 443.
[48] Above, n. 45.
[49] Considered in 7–13.
[50] *Gelberg* v. *Miller* [1961] 1 W.L.R. 153, 1 All E.R. 291; *Wershof* v. *M.P.C.* [1978] 3 All
E.R. 540, 68 Cr.App.R. 82.
[51] Most recently, see *Foster* v. *Atard* (1986) 83 Cr.App.R. 214; *Liepins* v. *Spearman* [1986]
R.T.R. 24.
[52] 2–18.

CHAPTER 11

OFFENCES ON THE HIGHWAY

1. INTRODUCTION

Usage of the highway

11–01   The highway is perhaps the most regulated area whose use citizens   **11–01**
generally enjoy; where a meeting, procession, demonstration or picket[1]
takes place in a street, it does so subject to a large number of laws controlling the proper use of the highway. The various statutory and common law
offences governing the matter will be the subject of this chapter. At the
outset, however, the legal status of the highway and the public's right to
use it should be described. In essence, a highway is not a road, as might be
imagined, but "a way over which there exists a right of passage, that is to
say a right for all of Her Majesty's subjects at all seasons of the year freely
and at their will to pass and repass without let or hindrance."[2] By contrast,
"if there is no regular way, but people merely go where they like, there is
no highway."[3] The highway includes not merely the carriageway, but all
the geographical space over which rights of passage exist, including foot-
paths, pedestrian precincts and other areas dedicated to public passing. If
the space has been dedicated for any purpose other than passing to and fro
(fishing, perhaps) it is not a highway. What matters is the dedication. If a
highway is temporarily impeded, as by the setting up of a road block under
section 4 of PACE, the road remains a highway, notwithstanding that the
public right of passage is temporarily suspended.[4]

Technically, a highway is private property[5] that has been dedicated to
the public for the limited purpose of passing and repassing. It follows as a
matter of general principle that any use other than passing and repassing is
not authorised, and is prima facie a trespass, however unlikely it may be
that the local authority or other owner will take action in respect of it. The
law recognises that there must be permissible uses reasonably associated

---

[1] The offences that might be committed by obstructing the highway in the course of a picket
are separately considered further in 12–02.
[2] 21 Halsbury's *Laws of England* (4th ed.) paras. 1–8, citing *Ex p. Lewis* (1888) 21 Q.B.D.
191. There is no statutory definition of the expression "highway" in the Highways Act,
although the natural meaning of the term is somewhat extended by the Act, s.328. It is for
the magistrates to determine whether or not the space in question is a highway; *Ogden ex p.
Long Ashton R.D.C.* [1963] 1 All E.R. 574; *Brandon* v. *Barnes* [1966] 1 W.L.R. 1505, 3 All
E.R. 296. In *R.* v. *Andrews, ex p. Cheshunt Urban District Council* (1962) 60 L.G.R. 211,
proceedings were instituted on indictment in anticipation of a claim that the land in question was not a highway, in the mistaken belief that the magistrates would have no jurisdiction to try the issue if that were so. And see *Armstrong* v. *Whitfield* [1974] Q.B. 16.
[3] Halsbury, last note.
[4] *Dubbins* (1986) *The Times*, May 22 and 19.
[5] Where the highway is to be maintained at public expense, it vests in the local authority;
Highways Act 1980, ss.1, 263, 265–267. Highways not publicly owned are presumed to
belong to the adjoining landowners, unless there is evidence to the contrary.

with the right of passage.[6] Pausing for breath, or stopping to tie up one's shoe lace are perfectly legitimate uses of the highway, as are stopping to talk to friends or waiting for friends[7] or queuing to get into a shop,[8] so long as these are within reasonable limits. One consequence of this, so far as the law of public disorder is concerned, is that a procession is prima facie lawful, since the participants are merely exercising *en masse* rights that they possess individually, whereas a static meeting has a more questionable status.[9] The logic of this distinction is open to question.[10] There can be no doubt that a procession usually does in fact cause an obstruction, and the purpose for which the crowds process is not purely passage to and fro. They seek to draw attention to the cause that they are promoting. The mere fact that there is movement along the highway will not necessarily prevent an obstruction from taking place. Suppose, for example, that a truck were to be driven along the crown of the road in such a way that other vehicles could not pass.[11] It seems that even though the truck is moving it may cause an obstruction in fact, and there is no reason to conclude that it cannot cause an obstruction in law also. Obstruction can be caused, in other words, by the unreasonable exercise of an admitted right of passage and re-passage. What saves the procession from the taint of illegality is that by custom processions for religious, political and other ceremonial and celebratory purposes are a time honoured use to which the highway is put, and are prima facie therefore a reasonable use of the highway.[12]

Obstruction at common law

11–02   There is some authority for the proposition that obstruction of the high-   **11–02**
way is a common law offence in its own right. It is very rarely, if ever, prosecuted and as with many common law offences, there are considerable

---

[6] *Harrison* v. *Duke of Rutland* [1893] 1 Q.B. 142; *Hickman* v. *Maisey* [1900] 1 Q.B. 753; *M'Ara* v. *Edinburgh Magistrates* [1913] S.C. 1059. See also *Hadwell* v. *Righton* [1907] 2 K.B. 345, 348.

[7] *Bierton* [1983] Crim.L.R. 392 (Southwark Crown Court).

[8] *Cp. Fabbri* v. *Morris* [1947] 1 All E.R. 315; *Dwyer* v. *Mansfield* [1946] 1 K.B. 437.

[9] In *Lowdens* v. *Keaveney* (1903) 2 I.R. 82, it is claimed that there is a "marked distinction" between a moving crowd and a stationary assembly. A. L. Goodhart, "Public Meetings and Processions" (1936) 6 Camb.L.J. 161; E. C. S. Wade, "The Law of Public Meeting" (1938) 2 M.L.R. 177; E. R. H. Ivamy, "The Right of Public Meeting" (1949) C.L.P. 183. See also P. Wallington, "Injunctions and the Right to Demonstrate" (1976) 35 Camb.L.J. 82; H. Carty, "The Legality of Peaceful Picketing on the Highway" [1984] P.L. 600. The arguments for and against the existence of a right of public meeting are discussed at length in *Supperstone*, at p. 44.

[10] See D. G. T. Williams, "Protest and Public Order" (1978), *The Cambridge/Tilburg Law Lectures*, First Series at pp. 32–33. The distinction is preserved in the Act, in the sense that there can be a ban on processions, but not on static assemblies. To some extent, Parliament has reduced the significance of the distinction by conferring powers to impose conditions on static assemblies too under s.14 of the Act.

[11] *Norton* v. *Lees* (1921) 85 J.P.N. 500, 87 J.P.N. 675. It was reported that, during the miners' strike, a convoy of 150 cars travelled down a motorway in South Yorkshire at five M.P.H., blocking the way. A number of the drivers were arrested for obstruction. *The Times*, March 28, 1984.

[12] *Lowdens* v. *Keaveney* [1903] I.R. 82, *Melbourne Corp* v. *Barry* (1922) 31 Cth.L.R. 174. *Clarke (No. 2)* [1964] Q.B. 315.

doubts about its existence and exact scope. In the case commonly regarded as authority for the existence of the offence,[13] Lord Parker C.J. cites no precedent for his views, and it may well be that what he had in mind was the much better attested offence of public nuisance, which clearly can be committed by obstructing the highway.[14] Supperstone suggests that only a highway authority may proceed by way of indictment.[15] The point may be that the highway authority has a statutory duty to take action (including legal proceedings) to prevent obstructions and to preserve public rights,[16] which means that the authority should, if necessary, bring a prosecution for public nuisance. It does not follow from this that there is an independently existing indictable offence of highway obstruction.

There is also some question about whether or not the standard of proof is the one that ordinarily applies in criminal cases (beyond reasonable doubt), or some lesser burden.[17] In the light of these uncertainties, the opinion may be expressed that the sooner Parliament acts to rid us of so vestigial an offence the better.

2. The Highways Act 1980

Definition, sentence and power of arrest

11–03　　　Very commonly encountered in the public order context is the summary statutory offence under the Highways Act 1980, section 137(1), which provides that:

> "If a person, without lawful authority or excuse, in any way wilfully obstructs the free passage along a highway he is guilty of an offence and liable to a fine not exceeding [level 3 on the standard scale]."[18]

Until PACE, the offence was arrestable where a constable saw the person committing it.[19] Now, however, a power of arrest is available only where the general arrest conditions of that Act are satisfied. In context, this means that the constable can arrest if he has reasonable grounds for believing that a non-arrestable offence has been committed or is about to be or is in the process of being committed, it appears to him that the summons procedure is impracticable or inappropriate, and that there are reasonable grounds for believing that (*inter alia*) the arrest is necessary to prevent the

---

[13] *R* v. *Andrews, ex p. Cheshunt Urban District Council* (1962) 60 L.G.R. 211.

[14] Below, 11–08.

[15] At p. 82. And see G. Flick, *Civil Liberties in Australia* (1981) who points out that, in the absence of an express statutory provision conferring locus standi on a local authority, the authority stands in no better position to bring proceedings than an ordinary individual, who must show either private nuisance to himself, or prove special damage; pp. 93–94.

[16] Highways Act 1980, s.130.

[17] See the discussion of the point by Lord Parker C.J. in *Andrews*, above n. 2.

[18] Criminal Justice Act 1982, ss.38, 46. See 2–08. Mention should also be made of the obstruction offences under the Town Police Clauses Act 1847, s.28 and the Metropolitan Police Act 1839, s.54(6). Under s.52 of the last-mentioned Act, the Metropolitan Police Commissioner may make an order prohibiting, *inter alia* "obstruction" to the free passage of members to and from Parliament, but the courts have interpreted this to mean actual obstruction; *Papworth* v. *Coventry* [1967] 2 All E.R. 41.

[19] Highways Act, s.137(2) repealed by PACE 1984, s.26, Sched. 7.

suspect causing an unlawful obstruction of the highway.[20] No warning need be given prior to the arrest, although it may be argued that the giving of a warning may be relevant to the reasonableness or otherwise of the user. It is permissible to use reasonable force to prevent the continuation of the offence.[21]

What constitutes an obstruction?

11–04   According to the O.E.D., to obstruct is "to interrupt or render difficult   **11–04**
the progress or passage of" a person or thing. In the context of obstructing the highway, it means the continuous physical occupation of a portion of the highway which appreciably diminishes the space available to the public for passing and repassing.[22] The legal principle underlying the use of the highway is that members of the public are entitled to use it, and the whole of it, for the purposes of passing and re-passing, and for any uses reasonably incidental thereto. Any usage of the highway at variance with this is prima facie an obstruction.

Despite some suggestions to the contrary, it is well established that for an offence under this section,[23] there need not be proved an actual obstruction in the sense that any particular person or persons were inconvenienced.[24] The fact that people were inconvenienced is no more than a factor having a bearing on the reasonableness or otherwise of the user of the highway[25]— if obstruction to free passage is proved, it is no defence that others were not inconvenienced.[26] In *Homer* v. *Cadman*[27] the defendant marched to a place on the highway with a band and addressed the crowd which had gathered for upwards of an hour. It was held that his conduct constituted an obstruction notwithstanding that there was sufficient free space for others to pass. The magistrate had found as a fact that no person could have gone across that part of the highway where the appellant

---

[20] PACE, s.25(3)(*d*)(v), for the full text of which see 2–17. In *Cooper* v. *M.P.C* (1985) 82 Cr.App.R. 238, the defendant who was under observation by the police was not warned that his conduct was regarded as being an obstruction before he was arrested. Since the question whether there was an obstruction is one of fact and a matter for judgment, this looks like an oppressive use of the power of arrest, and in similar circumstances the courts might now take the view that the police have no reasonable grounds to believe that the arrest is necessary when a warning to desist would or might do.

[21] *Reed* v. *Wastie* [1972] Crim.L.R. 221.

[22] *Hayward* v. *Mumford* (1907) 7 Cth.L.R. 133 at 138.

[23] By contrast, see public nuisance; 11–09.

[24] The contrary was suggested in *Gill* v. *Carson and Nield* [1917] 2 K.B. 674. But see *Scarfe* v. *Wood* [1969] Crim.L.R. 265.

[25] *Nagy* v. *Weston* [1965] 1 All E.R. 78, 1 W.L.R. 280; *Cooper* v. *M.P.C.* (1985) 82 Cr.App.R. 238.

[26] In *Read* v. *Perrett* (1876) 1 Ex.D. 349, 41 J.P. 135, (a prosecution under the Metropolitan Police Act 1839), the magistrates declined to hear evidence from passers-by that they were not inconvenienced on the grounds that this was irrelevant. And see *Dunn* v. *Holt* (1904) 73 L.J.K.B. 341; *Stewart* [1961] N.Z.L.R 680 says that there need not be an actual obstruction, although there was proof in that case that passing pedestrians had been forced to circumnavigate the defendant.

[27] (1886) 55 L.J.M.C. 110, 16 Cox C.C. 51; *Lowdens* v. *Keaveney* (1903) 2 I.R. 82. *cf. Aldred* v. *Miller* (1924) J.C. 117 (High Court of Justiciary). And see *Arrowsmith* v. *Jenkins* [1963] 2 Q.B. 561.

and his band were without "considerable inconvenience and danger," and this was held to be sufficient.

Where an obstruction is a minimal one, the principle of *de minimis* (the law will not concern itself with trifles) applies.[28] It is open to the court to dismiss a prosecution on the grounds that the amount of space actually taken of that which was available was negligible, or that the obstruction, although total, was merely transient. Since the obstruction that must be proved is notional in the sense that it need not be proved that any particular person was obstructed, the *de minimis* principle may be of limited application. For example, a juggler may take up only a small amount of the available space, but he takes up the whole that he does in fact occupy, and this is clearly enough to constitute the offence if the magistrates conclude that this is an unreasonable user of the highway.[29]

On many occasions, it has been held that the question whether or not there has been an obstruction is one of fact.[30] This means that once facts are found upon which the magistrates could come to the conclusion that an obstruction may have been committed, the decision that there was an obstruction will not be reviewed by the higher courts.

Without lawful authority or excuse[31]

11–05   The section envisages the possibility that the obstruction might be perpetrated with authority or excuse. A person has lawful authority when he is in fact authorised by some agency having the authority to do so[32] to cause an obstruction, as when he has a permit to run a market stall, or a food hawker's licence.[33] An excuse, by contrast, is that the use of the highway, although obstructive, is a reasonable use notwithstanding. Although section 137 says nothing in terms about the reasonableness of use of the highway, it is plain that a reasonable user of the highway cannot amount to an

---

[28] *Wolverton v. Willis* [1962] 1 All E.R. 243 (Town Police Clauses Act 1847, s.28); *Seekings v. Clarke* (1961) 59 L.G.R. 268; *Hinchon v. Briggs* (1963) 61 L.G.R. 615. English law, unlike the Indian, has no clearly defined rule to cope with the *de minimis* principle. See [1978] Crim.L.R. 525.

[29] In *Hertfordshire C.C. v. Bolden* [1986] *The Times*, magistrates dismissed a prosecution on the grounds that an obstruction was *de minimis*. The obstruction in that case occupied fully half of the available footpath, and the Divisional Court held that the magistrates finding was quite untenable.

[30] *Dunn v. Holt* (1904) 73 L.J.K.B. 341; *Nagy v. Weston* [1965] 1 W.L.R. 280, 1 All E.R. 78; *Absalom v. Martin* [1974] R.T.R. 145; *Hipperson v. District Electoral Registration Officer* [1985] 1 Q.B. 1060.

[31] See generally, R. I. E. Card, "Authority and Excuse as Defences to Crime" [1969] Crim.L.R. 359, 415.

[32] The courts have held that it is no defence that the local authority has informally licensed what is being done; *Redbridge London Borough Council v. Jacques* [1970] 1 W.L.R. 1604; *Cambridgeshire and Isle of Ely County Council v. Rust* [1972] 2 Q.B. 426 (D.C.); *Brook v. Ashton* [1974] Crim.L.R. 105; *Pugh v. Pidgen* (1987) *The Times*, April 2. For criticisms of this line of cases, see A. J. Ashworth, "Excusable Mistake of Law" [1974] Crim.L.R. 652 and A. T. H. Smith, "Ignorance and Mistake of Law in Anglo American Criminal Law" (1985) 14 Anglo-American L.R. 3.

[33] Under the Local Government (Miscellaneous Provisions) Act 1982 s.3 and sched. 4, for example, or the Food Act 1984, s.66.

offence under the section, and that there is no requirement of permanent movement upon the highway. Reasonable use amounts to lawful excuse.[34]

The rule is that where the stopping is part and parcel of passing and re-passing on the highway and is ancillary to it, there is no obstruction within the meaning of the Act.[35] Stopping to deliver letters or milk, or to talk to friends, or to look into a shop window are examples of such accepted uses of the highway. If it is not so incidental, then it may be an obstruction. If it is an obstruction, then the further question arises as to whether or not the obstruction is unauthorised or unreasonable. Each will be considered in turn.

Conduct is authorised when there is a rule of the common law or a stat-ute permitting what is done. The police are authorised to set up road blocks by the PACE,[36] and these must be regarded as authorised. They also have statutory powers to require vehicles to stop,[37] which would be regarded as unauthorised when done by private individuals.[38] There are also common law police powers to require that drivers should stop, deriv-ing from the duty to prevent a breach of the peace.[39] Private citizens may sometimes be licensed to effect obstructions, especially where this is necessary for building works,[40] or to sell food on the highway.[41] But the courts are jealous of the powers thus conferred. They have held, for example, that the supposed "right to picket" conferred by the Trade Dis-putes Act 1906 and its successors does not confer on pickets any right to stop strike breakers in order to seek to persuade them not to cross picket lines.[42] It can be predicted with some confidence that the courts will hold that, where notice of a procession has been given under section 11 of the 1986 Act, this does not amount to lawful authority for the purposes of this section. If the defendant is doing no more than complying with conditions that may have been imposed upon the procession, his claim that he was not acting wilfully would have a ring of plausibility about it.

Longstanding usage will not necessarily give rise to lawful authority. If the practice in question prevailed before dedication, there is no offence, since the dedication takes effect subject to the prescriptive rights.[43] The principle is that once a highway, always a highway, and the mere fact that the public have condoned a particular usage over a period of years will not necessarily prevent the conduct in question from being an offence.[44]

---

[34] In *Nagy* v. *Weston* [1965] 1 W.L.R. 280, 1 All E.R. 78, Lord Parker C.J. equated lawful excuse with reasonable user. He said in response to defence counsel's argument that it must be proved "first, that the defendant had no lawful authority or excuse, and secondly that the user to which he was putting the highway was an unreasonable user. For my part I think that excuse and reasonableness are really the same ground."

[35] *Hirst* v. *Chief Constable for West Yorkshire* (1987) 151 J.P. 304.

[36] Section 6.

[37] Section 159.

[38] *Broome* v. *D.P.P.* [1974] A.C. 587.

[39] As in *Moss* v. *McLachlan* [1985] I.R.L.R. 76, (1984) 149 J.P. 167.

[40] *Harper* v. *G. N. Haden and Sons Ltd* [1933] Ch. 298.

[41] Above, n. 33.

[42] *Broome* v. *D.P.P.* [1974] A.C. 587.

[43] *Spice* v. *Peacock* (1875) 39 J.P. 581.

[44] *Gerring* v. *Barfield* (1864) 16 C.B.(N.S.) 597, 143 E.R. 1261, 11 L.T. 270.

To decide whether or not an obstruction is reasonable and therefore excused, it is necessary to have regard to such matters as the length of time for which the obstruction continues, the place where it occurred, the purpose for which it was done and whether it caused an actual as opposed to a potential obstruction.[45]

The application of these principles has been tested in a series of recent cases. In *Waite* v. *Taylor*[46] a juggler in a pedestrian precinct was held to be guilty of the offence because he occupied part of the available space for passing and re-passing. The Court held that the law was that where the stopping could not be said to be part and parcel of the use of the highway, then the obstruction was an unreasonable one. But in *Hirst* v. *Chief Constable of West Yorkshire*,[47] the Divisional Court disagreed that the correct test had been applied. Rather, it was said, the proper approach was to ask whether what was being done was incidental to the rights of passing and repassing. Only if it was not was the conduct an obstruction. Once it had been decided that there was an obstruction, there was the further question as to whether or not the obstruction was reasonable, having regard to the needs of the other users, the time of day and so forth. Since the magistrates had not posed the questions for themselves in these terms, the convictions were quashed. The decision is of considerable importance in the field of public disorder, since the judgment of Otton J. in particular affirms that one of the factors to be taken into account in deciding what is or is not reasonable is the fact that the defendants were exercising rights of assembly and demonstration. Citing *Beatty* v. *Gillbanks*[48] and stressing the need for peace and good order, Otton J. said that the analysis permitting reasonableness to qualify the commission of the obstruction would permit the balance properly to be struck, and that " 'freedom of protest on issues of public concern' would be given the recognition it deserves."

Where a person is behaving in a way that is at variance with his rights to pass and repass, but other citizens can go about their business without having to take evasive action, the conduct of the person obstructing is more readily seen to be reasonable. If persons are standing aimlessly about, that may more readily be construed as obstruction even though it cannot be shown that particular individuals have been inconvenienced by the conduct.

The question whether or not the user is reasonable must be assessed in the light of whether or not the person obstructing is using the highway as a highway. In an unreported decision,[49] it was held that where a picket blocked the entrance to a hospital where he was in dispute with his employers, the question whether he was behaving reasonably did not arise, since he was not using the highway as a highway, for the purposes of passing and repassing. The magistrates had dismissed the prosecution on the

[45] *Nagy* v. *Weston* [1965] 1 W.L.R. 280, 1 All E.R. 78. *Bierton* [1983] Crim.L.R. 392 (Southwark Crown Court).
[46] (1985) 149 J.P. 551.
[47] (1987) 151 J.P. 304.
[48] (1882) 9 Q.B.D. 308. See 1–08–1–09.
[49] *Jones* v. *Bescoby* (1983) CO/161/83. The decision is cited in *Hirst*, n. 47.

grounds that the conduct was not unreasonable, having regard to the brevity of the obstruction. The decision is inconsistent with the later case of *Hirst*. Whether or not the conduct is incidental to the right of passing and re-passing is treated in the later case as going to the question whether or not there is an obstruction at all, whereas the approach adopted by the court precludes the question whether or not the conduct was reasonable at all. Otherwise, as the court said in *Hirst*, stopping to talk to one's friends in the street for 20 minutes or so, when one could as easily go to a nearby coffee shop, might be treated as an obstruction, since it is not incidental to the rights of passage and re-passage.

By long established custom, people park cars overnight in the street where there is no off-street parking which, provided that the vehicle affords no actual obstruction, is commonly regarded as a reasonable use. If the person obstructing is using the highway as an integral part of his business, as for example by using it for parking his trailers,[50] or providing a service as by setting up shop, or a hot-dog stand[51] or providing entertainment,[52] then even though nobody is obliged to take steps to avoid the activity, the obstruction may be accounted unreasonable, since the activity is not reasonably incidental to the use of the highway as such. For this reason, doubts have been expressed on the question whether a static meeting on the highway can ever be lawful.[53]

It has been held that to erect a permanent bollard, even though done with the intention of protecting one's own property, is an offence, the desire to protect oneself and others not amounting to lawful excuse for these purposes.[54] Where the defence is that one has engaged in such conduct on previous occasions without official interference, the courts are less sympathetic than might be expected. In *Arrowsmith* v. *Jenkins*[55] there was evidence that the defendant had held highway meetings in the same place on previous occasions. This was held not to amount to an excuse. Similarly, where the defence was that others were engaging in precisely the same conduct as the person singled out for prosecution, it was held that such apparently discriminatory enforcement did not afford a defence, although the court plainly approved when the magistrates granted what amounted to an absolute discharge.[56]

---

[50] *Nelmes* v. *Rhys Howells Transport Ltd* [1977] R.T.R. 266.
[51] *Pitcher* v. *Lockett* (1966) 64 G.L.R. 477, Crim.L.R. 283; *Waltham Forest L.B.C.* v. *Mills* [1980] R.T.R. 201, Crim.L.R. 243.
[52] *Waite* v. *Taylor* (1985) 149 J.P. 551.
[53] In his Red Lion Square Report, Lord Scarman said: "a procession, which allows room for others to go on their way is lawful; but it is open to question whether a public meeting held on a highway could ever be lawful, for it is not in any way incidental to the right of passage"; at para. 122. But see *Burden* v. *Rigler* [1911] 1 K.B. 337, which held that a static meeting that did in fact permit members of the public to pass was not necessarily unlawful. Ironically, the ruling permitted the court to convict under the Public Meetings Act 1908, s.1.
[54] *Dixon* v. *Atfield* [1975] 1 W.L.R. 1171, 3 All E.R. 265; *Campadonic* v. *Evans* (1966), 200 E.G. 857.
[55] [1963] 2 Q.B. 561. See also *Cooper* v. *M.P.C.* (1985) 82 Cr.App.R. 238, where the defendant's conviction for identical conduct had been quashed four times within the space of a year by the Crown Court.
[56] *Dunning* v. *Trainer* (1909) 101 L.T. 421.

The mental element—wilfully

11–06   It must be shown that, in causing the obstruction, the defendant acted   **11–0**
"wilfully." This means that, where the defendant is genuinely unaware that
what he is doing may result in obstruction, he commits no offence. Thus in
Eaton v. *Cobb*[57] the defendant flung open his car door in the path of an
oncoming cyclist, having first checked in his mirror and concluded that the
way was clear. Even if he had not checked, it is difficult to see that his conduct could properly have been accounted wilful, since he was not then
actually aware that his conduct would be an obstruction. The point is not
wholly free from doubt, since the courts are apt to interpret "wilfully" differently in different contexts,[58] but the use of the term wilfully should
denote that a person is guilty of this offence only if it is proved that his conduct was deliberate, and that he intended by it to obstruct, or was aware
that his conduct was likely to obstruct. If a person stops his car or truck
temporarily (for example to unload) and it will not start when he returns,
he does not commit wilful obstruction.[59]

It has been held that it is no defence that the person obstructing believed
that he was entitled to hold a meeting on the highway.[60] This was to make a
mistake of law which, as a matter of general principle, affords no defence.
The rule is a harsh one if it is applied without warning, and the decision in
which it was uttered is one of considerable importance for public order law.
Because of the terseness of the reported judgment, its limits are unclear.
The defendant was addressing a gathering that had the effect of blocking
the pavement and carriageway completely for a brief period, and partially
for just under an hour. Meetings had been held on the same spot before,
on which occasions the police had helped to officiate. On the occasion in
question, there was no evidence that the police had asked the speaker to
stop speaking, and there was evidence that she had cooperated with the
police in clearing a path for pedestrians and through traffic when requested
to do so. Although it could undoubtedly be said that she intended to cause
an obstruction in the sense that she intended that the crowd should gather
around her, it may be doubted whether in the circumstances her conduct in
causing the obstruction was properly described as "wilful." Had it been
shown that the police had asked her to desist, the conclusion of wilfulness
would have seemed more appropriate. Of course, an obstruction could be
wilful where there had been no request to desist, as where a person puts a
bollard in the centre of the road.[61] But where no contemporaneous objection is taken by those whose official function it is to preserve the way free
from obstruction, it is unduly restrictive of freedom of speech for the courts

---

[57] [1950] 1 All E.R. 1016.
[58] See Webster J. in *Lewis* v. *Cox* [1985] 1 Q.B. 509, who makes this point in connection with
wilfully obstructing a police constable. In *Sheppard* [1981] A.C. 394, the House of Lords
held that the expression referred to both intention and recklessness. For discussion, see J.
C. Smith and Hogan, p. 111; G. Williams, *C.L.G.P.* p. 459; In *Gabriel* v. *Enfield L.B.C.*
[1971] R.T.R. 265, it was said, erroneously it is submitted, that the offence was one of
"absolute liability."
[59] *Waring* v. *Wheatley* (1951) 115 J.P. 630.
[60] *Arrowsmith* v. *Jenkins* [1963] 2 Q.B. 561.
[61] *Dixon* v. *Atfield* [1975] 1 W.L.R. 1171, 3 All E.R. 265.

to hold that the obstruction is wilful when the speaker acts in reliance on that official, and perfectly proper, connivance. A person who is not warned that his conduct is regarded as being an unreasonable user of the highway in the course of a procession or demonstration has no reason to know that he is in danger of overstepping the permitted use. However, it has been held that even where a person acts in reliance on official advice, he has no defence to the charge of obstruction.[62]

Lord Parker C.J.'s observation in the case that the act should be done "intentionally as opposed to accidentally, that is, by an exercise of his or her free will" may well have misled the magistrates in *Lewis* v. *Dickson*.[63] The defendant was a gateman who was working to rule as a result of instructions from officials of the union of which he was a member in the course of a dispute with his employers. His instructions were to stop and search every car, as a result of which traffic blocked the roads leading to the entrance to the works. He refused upon request to desist, but the magistrates found that he had not committed the offence of wilful obstruction because he was acting under instructions; his actions, it was said, did not amount to wilfulness as it was not exercised by free will. Unsurprisingly, the case was remitted to the magistrates to consider whether, in all the circumstances, the undoubted obstruction was reasonably caused. So far as the mental element of the offence was concerned, there could be no doubt that the act was a deliberate, intentional and non-accidental one, as a result of which the traffic was caused to build up, and there could be no defence of lack of wilfulness in the circumstances.

The burden of proof

11–07   In order for the prosecutor to set up his case, he must show that there   **11–07**
was an in fact obstruction in the form of conduct that is not incidental to the ordinary user of the highway. Must the prosecution show that the use is unreasonable as part of its case from the outset, or is reasonable user a defence, placing the burden on the defendant? The cases are not wholly clear on the point. In *Nagy* v. *Weston*[64] Lord Parker C.J. says that "it has to be proved that there was no lawful authority," and "it is undoubtedly true . . . that there must be proof that the use in question was an unreasonable use." This was taken slightly further in *Absalom* v. *Martin*[65] where magistrates took the view that since there was no evidence of unreasonable user of the highway by the defendant (having regard to the defendant's business as a bill poster and the fact that he was parked for only a very short period of time), they should dismiss the prosecution. No reference

---

[62] *Cambridgeshire and Isle of Ely County Council* v. *Rust* [1972] 2 Q.B. 426. *Cf.* the Baton Rouge case, *Cox* v. *Louisianna* 379 U.S. 559 (1965), in which it was held that the due process clause of the American Constitution precluded the conviction of demonstrators for demonstrating "near" a courthouse when they were complying with police advice as to where they were entitled to stand.
[63] [1976] R.T.R. 431.
[64] [1965] 1 W.L.R. 280, 1 All E.R. 78.
[65] [1974] R.T.R. 145. *Gatland* [1968] 2 Q.B. 279, was cited to, but not by, the Court.

was made in either case to the predecessor of Magistrates' Court Act 1980,[66] which places the burden on the defendant to prove the existence of any "exception, exemption, proviso, excuse or qualification." Since the issue of reasonableness arises as part of "lawful excuse" this would point to reasonableness as a defence, with an evidential burden on the defendant once it has been shown that his conduct does in fact cause a wilful obstruction to establish on the balance of probabilities[67] that his conduct was reasonable.[68]

3. PUBLIC NUISANCE

Introduction

11–08   Public nuisance is a curious hybrid creature, being both a common law   **11–08**
misdemeanour[69] and a tort.[70] Notwithstanding that the purposes of the proceedings are entirely different in character, being punishment and compensation respectively, the rule is that once the plaintiff in a civil action has proved the crime of public nuisance, he can maintain an action in tort by showing also that he has suffered particular damage.[71] Having regard to the different purposes of the proceedings, it is quite likely that the criminal and the civil courts will come to quite different conclusions as to what is, for example, a reasonable user of the highway. Civil proceedings may be

---

[66] The Magistrates' Courts Act 1952, s.81 (last note). In *Gatland* v. *M.P.C.* it was held that in a prosecution for depositing an object on the highway to the danger of other passengers without lawful authority, the burden is on the defendant. The decision was recently approved by the House of Lords in *Hunt* [1987] 1 All E.R. 1 at 19 [1986] 3 W.L.R. 1115. In *Stewart* [1962] N.Z.L.R. 680, the New Zealand equivalent of s.101 was held to apply to the offence of obstructing the highway. On the other hand, it has been held that once evidence of a reasonable excuse emerges, it is for the prosecution to eliminate the existence of the defence to to satisfaction of the court; *Clarke* [1969] 2 All E.R. 1008.

[67] *Carr-Briant* [1943] K.B. 607.

[68] See the commentary to *Hirst and Agu* v. *Chief Constable of West Yorkshire* [1987] Crim.L.R. 330.

[69] More accurately, perhaps, a series of misdemeanours grouped together under the generic term nuisance. Activities such as securing the release of a mental patient *Soul* (1980) 70 Cr.App.R. 295, making obscene telephone calls *Norbury* [1978] Crim.L.R. 435, or hoax ones *Madden* [1975] 1 W.L.R. 1379, 3 All E.R. 155, obstructing rights of way on the highway (*infra*) and brothel keeping *Thompson-Schwab* v. *Costaki* [1956] 1 W.L.R. 335 and *Tan* [1984] Q.B. 1053 have very little in common with one another. The offences are triable either way; Magistrates' Court Act 1980, sched. 1.

[70] R. A. Buckley, *The Law of Nuisance* (1981). The importance of this, in connection with demonstrations, is that civil proceedings are available to supplement the controls exercisable in the criminal law. See *Hubbard* v. *Pitt* [1976] Q.B. 142; *Thomas* v. *N.U.M.* [1986] Ch. 20; *News Group Newspapers* v. *SOGAT '82* [1986] I.R.L.R. 337. See P. Wallington, "Injunctions and the Right to Demonstrate" (1976) 35 C.L.J. 82; Hazel Carty, "The Legality of Peaceful Picketing on the Highway" [1986] P.L. 600. And see Chap. 12.

[71] Street *Tort* (7th ed., 1983), Chap. 13; *Harper* v. *Haden* [1933] Ch. 298. In *Tynan* v. *Balmer* [1967] 1 Q.B. 91, picketing a factory was held to be a common law nuisance, from which failure to desist could amount to the obstruction of a constable in the execution of his duty. Would this reasoning apply if the obstruction were merely tortious? It is not, presumably, part of the constable's duty to prevent the commission of a tort if this is unlikely to lead to a breach of the peace.

brought by, or on the relation of the Attorney-General,[72] which would appear to be the most appropriate form of proceedings where the nuisance is an ongoing one. The law clearly is that a single act may be indictable.[73]

The Law Commission did not consider the law of nuisance as part of its review of the common law public order offences, partly because of the diversity of forms that the offence might take. Instead, it expressed the hope that prosecutors would not feel the need to resort to the offence in public order situations.[74] That sentiment is echoed, but the fact is that the form of public nuisance that consists of the obstruction of the highway has been prosecuted as recently as 1964,[75] and a prosecutor may be tempted to feel that if a person were to incite a massive obstruction,[76] the penalty provided for by the statutory offence of obstructing the highway[77] is insufficient. It is proposed therefore briefly to describe the offence.

Although in theory the offence is punishable with imprisonment for life, in practice the maximum should not exceed two years' imprisonment unless the case is a serious one.[78]

Definition and scope of public nuisance

11–09   Sir James Stephen defined public nuisance in his *Digest* as follows: 11–09

> "an act not warranted by law or an omission to discharge a legal duty, which act or omission obstructs or causes inconvenience or damage to the public in the exercise of rights common to all His Majesty's subjects."[79]

---

[72] As in *Att.-Gen.* v. *Gastonia Garages* [1977] R.T.R. 219.

[73] *Att.-Gen.* v. *P.Y.A. Quarries Ltd.* [1957] 2 Q.B. 169 at 192, *per* Denning L.J. Lord Denning says that "an isolated act may amount to a public nuisance if it is done under such circumstances that the public right to condemn it should be vindicated." There is a degree of circularity evident in the reasoning that is undesirable in the criminal law context.

[74] Report, para. 1.8. Such an expression of hope might possibly affect prosecution policy, but it can of course have no effect on the law itself. Until the offence is abolished, it must be considered as part of the law. A prosecutor minded to proceed at common law would do well to bear in mind the observations of John G. Fleming, who says that the concept of nuisance has become "so amorphous as to defy rational exposition" and that it has "become a catch-all for a multitude of ill-assorted sins"; *The Law of Torts* (6th ed., 1983), at p. 378. These animadversions indicate that the offences are themselves offensive to the principle of legality. See J. R. Spencer, (1984) 148 J.P.N. 805, and the reply by J. N. Spencer, (1985) 149 J.P. 678.

[75] *Clark No. 2* [1964] Q.B. 315.

[76] The so-called Stop the City demonstrations in 1983–84, may be an example of this. See the White Paper, para. 5.9, which gives these as examples of "serious disruption to the life of the community" for the purposes of ss.12 and 14 of the 1986 Act.

[77] In *Clark (no. 2)* [1964] Q.B. 315, the defendant seems to have done little more than organise into a disruptive procession a large group of people who had gathered in central London. A charge under s.11(7)(*a*) would now, perhaps, be more appropriate, although the penalty available is a great deal less than the 18 months' imprisonment imposed at first instance in *Clark* itself.

[78] *Morris* [1951] 1 K.B. 394; *Higgins* [1952] 1 K.B. 7.

[79] (9th ed., 1950), Art. 235. And see Pratt and Mackenzie, *Law of Highways* (21st ed.), p. 112; "any wrongful act or omission upon or near a highway, whereby the public are prevented from freely, safely and conveniently passing along the highway." *Archbold*, para. 27–46 offers a definition of even greater vagueness and breadth.

The courts have put a number of glosses on this definition, and there is authority for saying that, in the criminal law at least, the obstruction must be actual as opposed to potential,[80] it must be substantial,[81] it must be unreasonable, and a conviction should be quashed if the jury are not given the opportunity to say whether or not the obstruction is unreasonable,[82] a considerable number of persons must be affected so that the obstruction is truly public,[83] and the whole is subject to the application of the *de minimis* rule.[84]

It is plain that not every obstruction is a nuisance. It must be unlawful. A person is free to block the highway for the purposes of repairing his house (indeed he commits a public nuisance if he allows his house to fall into disrepair so that it becomes a danger to the public),[85] and it must follow that he is entitled to take at least reasonable steps to repair his property, even though these might mean inevitable interference with the rights of the public.[86] Where a person causes a crowd to gather, he may be guilty of an offence if he causes actual inconvenience.[87]

Indictments for public nuisance for organising disruptive public meetings and processions appear to be rare, and of comparatively modern origin. In *Clark (No. 2)*[88] the defendant organised a procession of some 2,000 people, blocking the streets of central London. The report does not disclose either the duration of the obstruction, nor the time of day at which it occurred. The trial judge neglected to tell the jury that, for a conviction for incitement to commit nuisance, it had to be proved that the obstruction was unreasonable.[89] But in *Moule*[90] it appears to have been established that sitting down on the highway is prima facie an unreasonable obstruction. The decision surely requires the qualifications that the person must sit down with the intention[91] of disrupting and obstructing the traffic, and

---

[80] *Bartholomew* [1908] 1 K.B. 554; *Stinson* v. *Browning* (1866) 35 L.J.M.C. 152; *Dymond* v. *Pearce* [1972] 1 All E.R. 1142 and *Trevett* v. *Lee* [1955] 1 W.L.R. 113, 117. The latter two are both civil cases.

[81] *Ward* (1836) 4 Ad. & E. 384, 111 E.R. 832; *Train* (1862) 3 F. & F. 22, 176 E.R. 11.

[82] *Clark No. 2* [1964] 2 Q.B. 315.

[83] *Madden* [1975] 1 W.L.R. 1379, 3 All E.R. 155.

[84] *Ward* (1836) 4 Ad. & E. 384 at 387, 111 E.R. 832.

[85] *Watts* (1703) 1 Salk 357, 91 E.R. 311. In *Jacobs* v. *London County Council* [1950] A.C. 361, it was said that a nuisance may be defined, in relation to highways, as "any wrongful act or omission upon or near a highway, whereby the public are prevented from freely, safely, and conveniently passing along the highway." Prosecutorial diffidence about relying upon such general descriptions of wrongdoing is perhaps illustrated by the fact that, although the definition would cover lighting fires adjacent to a highway, Parliament should have felt it necessary to enact the Highways (Amendment) Act 1986. And see *Stinson* v. *Browning* (1866) 35 L.J.M.C. 152.

[86] *Jones* (1812) 3 Camp. 230, 170 E.R. 1364. If the person obstructing has a licence as required under Highways Act 1980, s.169, it is difficult to see that he can commit the offence; and see *Hayter* v. *Hayden* [1933] 2 Ch. 298.

[87] *Carlile* (1834) 6 C. & P. 636, 172 E.R. 1397; *Gray* (1864) 4 F. & F. 73, 176 E.R. 472.

[88] *Clarke (No. 2)* [1964] 2 Q.B. 315.

[89] Following *Lowdens* v. *Keaveney* [1903] 2 I.R. 82.

[90] [1964] Crim.L.R. 303; 108 S.J. 100; *Adler* [1964] Crim.L.R. 304.

[91] In *Walker* v. *Horner* (1875) 45 L.J.M.C. 34, Lord Cockburn C.J. expresses the view that evidence of wilfulness is required for the indictment.

must in fact disrupt.[92] Although it is difficult to be dogmatic when the decisions are so briefly reported, the courts appear to have had little regard to the other qualifications with which the offence is hedged about, and the view may be taken that, should there be any attempt to revive this form of the offence, its constituent ingredients should be scrutinised with considerable care by the courts.

The mental element

1–10
Since it is so rarely prosecuted in modern times, it is difficult to be confident about the precise mental element in public nuisance. In the older cases, there is some authority to the effect that it is not necessary to establish that it was the defendant's object to create a nuisance.[93] This is reinforced by the point that, since the civil action involves establishing that the crime has been committed, something less than intention or advertent recklessness will suffice. This may be one respect in which the tort and the crime diverge. In *Walker* v. *Horner*[94] Cockburn C.J. expressed the view that wilfulness was required for proceedings on indictment. **11–10**

4. MISCELLANEOUS OFFENCES[95]

Introduction

11–11
As A. P. Herbert's wise Lord Chancellor once observed: **11–11**

"there is no conduct in a public thoroughfare which cannot be easily be brought into some unlawful category, however vague."[96]

In addition to those offences already considered, the following may be noted. There are no doubt others. Under the Motor Vehicles (Construction and Use) Regulations 1978,[97] it is an offence for a person in charge of a motor vehicle or trailer to cause or permit the vehicle to stand on the road so as to cause any unnecessary obstruction thereon. This has been held to require proof of an unreasonable user.[98] Street collecting without a permit is an offence under the Police, Factories, etc., (Miscellaneous Provisions) Act 1919, and regulations made thereunder,[99] and might possibly

---

[92] As in *Bartholomew* [1908] 1 K.B. 554.
[93] *Moore* (1832) 3 B. & Add. 184, 110, E.R. 68.
[94] (1875) 1 Q.B.D. 46, 45 L.J.M.C. 34.
[95] Peter Thornton, *Public Order Law* (1986), Chap. 6 contains a useful section on these offences.
[96] *Enghein and Others* v. *The King* in A. P. Herbert, *Misleading Cases*.
[97] Road Traffic Act 1972, s.178, S.I. 1978, No. 1017, reg. 122.
[98] *Langham* v. *Crisp* [1975] Crim.L.R. 652; *Nelmes* v. *Rhys Howells Transport* [1977] R.T.R. 266. Since the terms of the regulation prohibit "unnecessary obstruction," the burden of proof would appear to be on the prosecutor to establish that the use was unnecessary. *Cf.* the Highways Act 1981, s.137(1); 11–07.
[99] Such as the Street Collections (Metropolitan Police District) Regulations 1979 (1979 S.I. No. 1230) reg. 4; *Meaden* v. *Wood* [1985] Crim.L.R. 678 (collecting for striking miners).

constitute begging under the Vagrancy Act 1824, section 3.[1] Leaving litter lying about falls within the terms of the Litter Act 1983, section 1.[2]

The use of the Highways Act 1981 to prevent people setting up trading stalls is supplemented by such provisions as the Local Government Act 1972, which authorises local authorities to enact by-laws for "the prevention and suppression of nuisances,"[3] and more explicitly by the licensing mechanisms of the Food Act 1984,[4] the Local Government (Miscellaneous Provisions) Act 1982,[5] and the Pedlars Act 1871, which authorises the police to issue pedlars' licenses without which it is an offence to trade.

If the public sexual offences are thought to fall within the realms of public disorder, they include the offences of soliciting by either females[6] or males,[7] and, since 1985, Parliament has legislated for the particular form of nuisance known as kerb crawling.[8]

---

[1] *Pointon* v. *Hill* (1884) 12 Q.B.D. 306. In *Mathers* v. *Penfold* [1915] 1 K.B. 514, it was held that a worker on strike did not commit this offence when soliciting contributions for his union, which was regarded as being a charitable purpose.
[2] In *Witney* v. *Cattanach* [1979] Crim.L.R. 461, it was held that "leaves" in the Litter Act 1958 did not mean "abandons," so that where the defendant had deposited a quantity of scrap metal on the side of the road for a considerable period of time, this was held to amount to the offence.
[3] Sections 235 and 237.
[4] Part IV. See especially s.64.
[5] Section 3, sched. 4.
[6] Street Offences Act 1959, s.1.
[7] Sexual Offences Act 1956, s.32.
[8] Sexual Offences Act 1985, s.1. *Hughes* v. *Holley* (1987) 151 J.P. 304 (bind over).

Introduction

12–01   With the exception of the offence under section 7 of the Conspiracy and   **12–01**
Protection of Property Act 1875, to be dealt with in this chapter, there is no
criminal law dealing specifically with picketing.[1] Order is preserved on the
picket line through the police use of powers associated with offences such
as obstruction of the highway or of a police constable in the execution of
his duty.[2] Where violence breaks out, the general offences against public
order, which are the principal subject of this book can be used, supplemented where appropriate by the offences against persons and property.

In the legal regulation of picketing, there is a complex overlap between
the criminal and the civil law. A full description of the latter is outside the
scope of this work, but it may be summarised as being based on the premise that workers in dispute with their employers are at liberty to withdraw
their own labour, to seek to persuade others to do so, and to persuade
others not to deal with their employers. Certain immunities from civil liability are afforded to further the accomplishment of these objectives. The
law does not immunise so-called secondary picketing, which means in
essence picketing by a person not at his own place of work. Lord Denning
summarised the law thus:

"If employees are in dispute with their own employer, they are at
liberty to picket *his* place of work or black, (*i.e.* refuse to handle)
goods in *his* premises or coming into or from *his* premises. But they
are not to be at liberty to picket the premises of other commercial
firms with whom their employer has commercial contacts, or other
traders, and with whom their employer has commercial contacts, or
with other traders, and with whom neither they nor their employers
are in dispute."

The consequences of engaging in wrongful secondary picketing are matters
for the civil law[3] rather than the criminal, and it is no task of the police to
prevent secondary picketing as such. Their role is the preservation of the
peace, even when they are acting is support of officers of the Court in
enforcing a Court Order. When mutually conflicting "rights" are asserted,

---

[1] Section 7 is not confined in its operation to industrial disputes, as was pointed out by Chitty
L.J. in *Wilkins* v. *Lyons* [1899] 1 Ch. at 272.
[2] See generally R. Kidner, "Picketing and the Criminal Law" [1975] Crim.L.R. 256; J. E.
Trice, "Methods of and Attitudes to Picketing" [1975] Crim.L.R. 271. Peter Wallington,
"Some Implications for the Policing of Industrial Disputes" [1987] Crim.L.R. 180.
[3] The relevant civil law is highly complex and constantly evolving, with successive govern-
ments making changes; Lord Denning once described the legislation as "the most tortous I
have ever come across"; *Hadmore Productions Ltd* v. *Hamilton* [1982] 1 A.C. 191. For an
account of the law, see Lord Wedderburn, *The Worker and the Law* (3rd ed. 1986); J. C.
Wood and I. T. Smith, *Industrial Law* (1986) Chap. 9.

as they are apt to be in industrial disputes, it may sometimes be difficult for the police to avoid the appearance of partiality. The rights to strike and to work can clash in their implementation.[4]

The area is one in which the exercise of police discretion plays a larger role than is usual even in public order offences generally. It is for the police to say, for example, how many may stand on a picket line in a place where they might seek to persuade those crossing the picket line not to do so. A further illustration of the point is that the ritual trials of strength character-ised by one writer as "pushing and shoving"[5] are tolerated within certain limits, notwithstanding that such conduct may be an assault.[6]

The application of the general criminal law

12–02   Section 16 of the Employment Protection Act 1980 provides for what is **12–0** known as the "peaceful picketing" exemption.[7] The principal impact of the section has been on the civil law,[8] but the apparently unqualified words "it shall be lawful" would seem to mean that the conduct impugned should not be considered criminal either. However, the courts have interpreted the section (and its predecessors[9]) to confer immunity only for liability that might otherwise attach under the Conspiracy and Protection of Property Act 1875, to be considered shortly.[10] No exemption is afforded from other offences. Thus, stopping vehicle drivers in an attempt to persuade them not to cross the picket line may constitute an offence under the Highways Act 1980, section 137 if the conduct in question is unreasonable.[11] In that case, the defendants had spoken to the drivers of the vehicles seeking entry, and had obstructed for a period of five minutes, even after the drivers had made their wishes plain. The magistrates had come to the the the conclusion that this was, in the circumstances, a reasonable user of the highway. In the House, it was claimed for the pickets that this conclusion was correct, since the right to communicate peacefully must carry with it a right to stop others to require them to listen. No such right was given,

---

[4] For a development of the point, see P. Wallington, "Policing the Miners' Strike" [1985] I.L.J. 145.

[5] R. Geary, *Policing Industrial Disputes: 1893 to 1985* (1985) Chap. 5.

[6] The point is stated somewhat cautiously, because it is possible that the consent of the police would technically constitute a defence to a charge of assault.

[7] 12–11.

[8] See *Thomas* v. *N.U.M.* [1986] Ch. 20; S. Lee and S. Whittaker, (1986) 102 L.Q.R. 35.

[9] For the history, see F. A. R. Bennion, "Mass Picketing and 1875 Act" [1985] Crim.L.R. 65. See also J. Finkelman, "The Law of Picketing in Canada" (1937) 2 Univ. of Toronto L.J. 67.

[10] 12–03 Discussion of the scope of the exemption conferred from criminal liability under s.7 is also deferred; 12–11.

[11] *Broome* v. *D.P.P.* [1974] A.C. 587. See G. S. Goodwin-Gill, (1975) 91 L.Q.R. 173, who argues that such stopping is unlawful only when it is an unreasonable user of the highway. It would be unreasonable if the drivers had made it plain on previous occasions that they were not prepared to stop, or if the numbers of pickets were such that is would be danger-ous for them to do so, or if the drivers were preceding in a convoy, which might make polic-ing the picket line particularly difficult were several trucks to be stopped. It is suggested that a requirement of reasonableness is in any event in accordance with the common police practice of allowing a small number of pickets to stop vehicles to speak with drivers. See J. Wood and I. T. Smith *op. cit* at p. 461.

according to the House, and the ruling of the magistrates was incorrect. It has also been held that pushing past a police cordon in order to join a picket line when the police have decided that the numbers already on the line are sufficient can amount to obstruction of a constable in the execution of his duty, so long as there is a reasonable apprehension on the part of the police that a breach of the peace will otherwise be occasioned, and this is a reasonable course for the police to adopt.[12] This in effect enables the police to form a cordon in such a way as to prevent pickets from physically stopping a driver.[13] In *Piddington v. Bates*,[14] in which these rules were first laid down, no attempt was made by the court to square this result with the wording of the section apparently conferring the immunity. Later decisions are more explicit; even trespassing in breach of by laws is not within the protection conferred by the Act.[15]

2. THE CONSPIRACY AND PROTECTION OF PROPERTY ACT 1875, SECTION 7

Background

–03   Throughout much of the nineteenth century, the courts were hostile to   **12–03** the aims and methods of trade unionists. The crime of conspiracy in particular was deployed as a weapon against strikers in dispute with their employers, and the judges were apt to pay scant regard to legislation that sought to legalise combinations of workmen.[16] A balance of sorts was eventually struck in the legislation of 1875, the most important provision of which was section 7.[17]

Prosecutions under this Act have not been frequent in recent years, principally, it may be supposed, because in serious cases of intimidation the penalty has been thought by prosecutors to be inadequate,[18] and there was

---

[12] *Piddington v. Bates* [1961] 1 W.L.R. 162, [1960] 3 All E.R. 660. In *Tynan v. Balmer* [1967] 1 Q.B. 91, pickets circling in the street who were committing a common law nuisance were instructed to desist, and their failure to do so was held to be obstruction of the police in the execution of their duty. A better basis for the decision it is submitted, is that the pickets were also in breach of the criminal law of obstructing the highway, which the police have a clear duty to prevent.

[13] *Kavanagh v Hiscock* [1974] Q.B. 600.

[14] Note 12.

[15] *British Airports Authority v. Ashton* [1983] 3 All E.R. 6, following *Larkin v. Belfast Harbour Commrs* (1908) 2 I.R. 214.

[16] The decisions in *Druitt* (1867) 10 Cox C.C. 600 and *Bunn* (1872) 12 Cox C.C. 316 were particularly notorious, and were repudiated by Lord Coleridge C.J. in *Gibson v. Lawson* [1891] 2 Q.B. 545. See P. Wallington, "Criminal Conspiracy and Industrial Conflict" (1975) 4 I.L.J. 69. And see Citrine's, *Trade Union Law* (3rd Ed. 1976), at p. 558.

[17] Section 5, which makes it an offence "wilfully and maliciously" to break a contract knowing or having reasonable cause to believe that the probable consequences of doing so would be to endanger life or cause serious bodily harm or expose property to serious injury remains extant, although it is today never prosecuted.

[18] The offence was punishable on summary conviction with imprisonment up to three months and a fine not exceeding level 2. The inadequacy of the penalty no doubt prompted the prosecutor in *Jones* (1974) 59 Cr.App.R. 120 to bring a charge of conspiracy to intimidate, since the penalty for conspiracy was at large. Sentences of three years' and two years' imprisonment were imposed. These provoked a "bitter reaction" which resulted in part in the penalty for conspiracy being limited in the Criminal Law Act 1977 to that available on the substantive charge; see E. Griew, *The Criminal Law Act 1977* (1978) General note.

no specific power of arrest associated with the offence.[19] In spite of these supposed defects, the offence was frequently prosecuted in the course of the miners' strike.[20] The penalty was increased by the 1986 Act,[21] the offences[22] now carry a power of arrest, and it may be anticipated that the Act may be used more frequently in appropriate cases.

The Act provides:

> "Every person who, with a view to compel any other person to abstain from doing or to do any act which such other person has a legal right to do or to abstain from doing, wrongfully and without legal authority:—
> (1) uses violence to or intimidates such other person or his wife or children, or injures his property; or
> (2) persistently follows such other person about from place to place; or
> (3) hides any tools, clothes or other property owned or used by such other person, or deprives him of or hinders him in the use thereof; or
> (4) watches or besets the house or other place where such other person resides, or works, or carries on his business, or happens to be, or the approaches to such house or place; or
> (5) follows such other person with two or more other persons in a disorderly manner through any street or road."

commits an offence. Prosecutions under the Act are summary only.[23]

The mental element—with a view to compel

12–04   All of the offences created by the section are governed by the opening   **12–**
phrase, which requires that the defendant should act with a view to compel; it is this element which, it has been held, is the unifying feature of the various offences.[24] This requires more than the intention to persuade; there must be an element of compulsion or force in the defendant's mind. It has been said that the words "with a view to" refer to purpose rather

---

[19] Section 40(2), Sched. 2.

[20] According to J. Percy-Smith and P. Hillyard, "Miners in the Arms of the Law: A Statistical Analysis" (1985) 12 Jo. Law Soc. 345, there were 275 charges brought under the Act, mainly for watching and besetting.

[21] This has been increased by the Act to six months or a fine not exceeding level 5 on the standard scale; s.40(2), Sched. 2.

[22] It has been held that the section creates one offence for the purposes of the rules against duplicity; *Clarkson* v. *Stuart* (1894) 32 S.L.R. 4; *Wilson* v. *Renton* (1909) 47 S.L.R. 209; *Att.-Gen.* v. *O'Brien* (1936) 70 I.L.T.R. 101; *Hardy* v. *O'Flynn* (1948) I.R. 343. But see *Edmondes* (1895) 59 J.P. 776. See Bennion, *Statutory Interpretation* 744–746.

[23] Until the Criminal Law Act 1977, the offence was triable either way. Where prosecutions were on indictment, the courts required a considerable degree of specificity in the indictment; it must, *e.g.* specify the acts which the defendant is alleged to have sought to compel the victim to do or abstain from doing; *Mackenzie* [1892] 2 Q.B. 519. In *Smith* v. *Moody* [1903] 1 K.B. 56, it was held that an indictment alleging that the defendant "did injure the property of . . . T.M.W." was held to be insufficiently specific. See also *Hulme* (1913) 9 Cr.App.R. 77. In *Elsey* v. *Smith (Procurator Fiscal)* [1983] I.R.L.R. 292, the charges are more detailed than is customary in modern prosecutions.

[24] *The State* v. *O'Flynn* [1948] I.R. 343.

than motive.[25] Generally, a person acts "purposely" when he wants something to exist or occur,[26] and it would be no defence that a person sought to improve working conditions if the method of accomplishing that objective involved the wrongful compulsion of another.[27] Whether or not the compulsion is actually effective to compel is immaterial, since the question is the intention with which the defendant acts.[28]

Wrongfully and without lawful authority

12–05 All compulsion is not itself wrongful,[29] and it must be shown that the **12–05** compulsion was of such a character before an offence under this section is proved. There is an outstanding question whether the conduct complained of must be independently unlawful, or whether it is sufficient that the conduct falls within one of the species referred to in the remainder of section 7, and has no legally accepted justification.[30] There are conflicting Court of Appeal authorities on the point.[31] The critical point of the controversy is that merely attending a picket might be an offence if the act is not required to be independently wrongful, i.e. tortious. Where in a criminal case there are conflicting authorities in the Court of Appeal, the generally accepted rule is that the interpretation of the law that most favours the defendant is the one that should be preferred[32]; it can hardly be said that, in such a situation, the law is left incapable of dealing with the lacuna that might be created by such an interpretation.

Such other person

12–06 In *Lyons* v. *Wilkins*[33] it was held that harassing one person with a view to **12–06** compelling another was within the mischief of the section. According to the Court of Appeal, the words "such other person" could be read to refer to "any other person," rather than the person whom it was sought to compel. It is an offence, therefore, to intimidate a workman with a view to compelling his employer, or vice versa. This is a somewhat forced reading of a criminal provision, and it has been persuasively argued that the case is wrongly decided, and should not be followed.[34]

---

[25] *Lyons* v. *Wilkins* (1899) 1 Ch., at 270.
[26] This is the definition given in the Law Commission Draft Code, Law Com. No. 143, cl. 22(*a*).
[27] *Allied Amusements* v. *Reaney* (1936) 3 W.W.R. 129.
[28] *Agnew* v. *Munro* (1891) 28 S.L.R. 335.
[29] *Gibson* v. *Lawson* [1891] 2 Q.B. 545.
[30] See F. A. R. Bennion, [1985] Crim.L.R. 64 and, for an opposing point of view, H. Carty, [1986] P.L. 600.
[31] *Lyons and Sons* v. *Wilkins* (1896) 1 Ch. 811, (1899) 1 Ch. 255 suggests that the second interpretation is the better one, whereas *Ward Lock and Co. Ltd.* v. *The Operative Printers' Society* (1906) 22 T.L.R. 327 prefers the former view.
[32] *Taylor* [1950] 2 K.B. 368; *Gould* [1968] 2 Q.B. 65.
[33] [1899] 1 Ch. 255; followed in *Charnock* v. *Court* (1899) 2 Ch. 35.
[34] M. A. Hickling, *Citrine's Trade Union Law* (3rd ed.; 1967) at 537. See also F. A. R. Bennion [1985] Crim.L.R. at 67.

Section 7(1); intimidates

12–07   Although violence and intimidation are juxtaposed in section 7(1) in a
manner that makes them appear to be alternatives, the courts originally
held that intimidation requires an element or threat of personal violence.[35]
Thus, it is not intimidation to threaten to deprive a workman of his liveli-
hood,[36] or to black an employer's business.[37] Whether these decisions survive the ruling of the House of Lords decision in *Rookes* v. *Barnard*[38] that
the tort of intimidation extends to threatened breaches of contract is perhaps questionable, and in *Jones*[39] it was said that the offence was not confined to the use or threat of violence. Might it be said, for example, that
presence in very large numbers amounts to intimidation? In *Bonsall*[40]
Judge Woods spoke of the "terror that their very numbers convey" in connection with a charge of besetting, and his reasoning would appear to apply
to the charge of intimidation also. A person may clearly intimidate by
means other than explicit threats. To intimidate is to cause another to fear;
but quite what he must fear (if it is not violence) is unclear. It has been said
that what is meant by intimidation is a matter for the jury,[41] now—since
the offence is triable summarily only, a matter of fact for the magistrates.

For the offence to be committed under this section, there must be evidence that the victim of it was actually put in fear, even though it need not
be shown that the intimidation had the desired effect.[42] The threat may be
by words or gestures.[43]

Persistent following

12–08   The use of violence is not a constituent of the offence under subsection
(2), and the following need not be in any sense disorderly.[44] This may be
contrasted with subsection (5), which requires more than one person, and
disorderly conduct. The distinction is that subsection 2 requires persistence. This was held to be satisfied in a case where the defendant had disen-
gaged himself from a group of pickets at the factory gates, and followed an
emerging worker through three streets, making no attempt to speak to the

---

[35] *McKeevit*, Liverpool Assizes 1890, December 16th. The decision is unreported, but
referred to by Cave J. in *Gibson* v. *Lawson*[1891] 2 Q.B. 545, at 550.
[36] *Gibson* v. *Lawson* last note. *Cf.* however *Judge* v. *Bennett* (1887) 4 T.L.R. 103, 52 J.P. 247
where it was held that it was intimidation to inform an employer in terms sufficiently forceful to make him afraid that his shop would be picketed.
[37] *Curran* v. *Treleavan* [1891] 2 Q.B. 560; *Wood* v. *Bowron* (1867) L.R. 2 Q.B. 21.
[38] [1964] A.C. 1129.
[39] *Jones* (1974) 59 Cr.App.R. 120.
[40] [1985] Crim.L.R. 150.
[41] *Baker* (1911) 7 Cr.App.R. 89.
[42] *McCarthy* [1903] 2 I.R. 146. As Lord O'Brien L.C.J. acknowledges, this may greatly narrow the scope of the offence in practice, since it may result in persons who are intimidated
declining to testify to the fact, or asserting that they were not put in fear. *Cf.* however,
Agnew v. *Munro* (1891) 28 S.L.R. 335, which appears to suggest that it is not necessary that
a person be put in fear. So far as the *actus reus* of the offence is concerned, it is suggested
that the decision is incorrect, as being inconsistent with the natural meaning of the section.
[43] *Kennedy* v. *Cowie* [1891] 1 Q.B. 771.
[44] *Wilson* v. *Renton* (1909) 47 S.L.R. 209.

worker, and on one occasion overtaking him.[45] Following a person in a car would be sufficient, if done with a view to compel. In a recent Scottish case,[46] it was held that the following in a car was in a disorderly manner when striking employees followed some working fellow employees in a way that appears to have given rise to altercations between the parties. The High Court of Justiciary found that there was sufficient material on which the Sheriff was entitled to find that the following was disorderly.

Hiding tools

2–09   In a civil case,[47] it was held that it is not a breach of subsection (3) to deprive a person of the use of his tools or hinder him in their use if the deprivation or hindrance is effected without violence or threats of violence. It is difficult to find any warrant for this in the wording of the Act itself, and it may be doubted whether the interpretation is correct, and whether it was in any event necessary for the decision. The defendants were officials of a miners' union. They pointed out to their fellow-employee who was responsible for distributing miners' lamps that two members of a rival union were not, by virtue of an arrangement with the employer, entitled to be given lamps. The judge in an application for an injunction took a broad view of the statute, saying that it was concerned to prevent violence or the threat of it, which was certainly not present in this case. But he also concluded that the defendants did not act with a view to compelling the plaintiff "victims" to join a union but rather to prevent a strike, and that would on its own have been fatal to a prosecution. It may also be doubted whether the conduct of the defendants really amounted to a deprivation or hindrance within the contemplation of the Act which, even if it does not contemplate the use or threat of violence, might readily be interpreted to refer to a physical deprivation or hindrance; that may, indeed, be what the judge had in mind.

12–09

Watching or besetting

2–10   The application of subsection 4 is a matter of some considerable delicacy, since it comes close to striking at peaceful picketing.[48] Watching may involve little more than attending the place of the picket, even if it is interpreted to mean persistent watching.[49] It has been held that what constitutes "watching" is a matter for the jury,[50] subject to the usual caveats that the evidence must be capable of giving rise to the conclusion that the defendants were guilty of such conduct. "Besetting," defined in the

12–10

---

[45] *Smith* v. *Thomasson* (1891) 16 Cox C.C. 740; *Wall* (1907) 21 Cox C.C. 401.
[46] *Elsey* v. *Smith (Procurator Fiscal)* [1983] I.R.L.R. 292.
[47] *Fowler* v. *Kibble* [1922] 1 Ch. 140. If the prosecutor is able to prove the intent permanently to deprive there may be a conviction of theft; *Warner* (1970) 55 Cr.App.R. 93.
[48] In *J. Lyons and Sons* v. *Wilkins* (1896) 1 Ch. 811, the Court of Appeal held that this was the law, subject to the exemption afforded by the peaceful picketing exemption.
[49] This was the interpretation adopted by Palles B. in his instruction to the jury in *Wall* (1907) 21 Cox C.C. 401.
[50] *Att.-Gen.* v. *O'Brien* (1936) 70 I.L.T.R. 101, now of course, a matter of fact for the magistrates to decide, since the proceedings are summary only.

O.E.D. to mean "to set about, to close around, hem in, surround or occupy a place" is similar to watching, although its application to persons who were strikers occupying their own place of work and preventing entry to would-be workers in *Galt* v. *Philp*[51] was somewhat novel. Hitherto, it appears to have been applied only to persons standing outside the object of the picket, whether it be a ship,[52] a theatre,[53] or a railway station.[54]

It shall be lawful: the immunity conferred by section 16

12–11   Section 16 of the Employment Protection Act 1980 confers an exemption   **12–1**
for peaceful picketing in the following terms:

> "It shall be lawful for a person in contemplation or furtherance of a trade dispute to attend—
> (a) at or near his own place of work; or
> (b) if he is an official of a trade union, at or near the place of work of a member of that union whom he is accompanying for the purpose only of peacefully obtaining or communicating information, or peacefully persuading any person to work or abstain from working."

As has already been seen,[55] the courts insist that the protection afforded by the peaceful picketing exemption does not confer any immunity from the general criminal law. It applies only to what might otherwise constitute an offence under section 7. Even then, the courts have insisted that the exemption afforded be fairly strictly confined, and the Act itself confers only fairly limited protection. Picketing other than at one's own place of work is not protected unless one is a trade union official, and watching or besetting another's house is unlawful.[56] The section does not licence trespass, including the criminal trespass involved in breaches of bylaws.[57]

The exemption is available only where the purposes of those present is peaceful persuasion. Congregating in very large numbers with a view physically to prevent people from getting to work across a picket line is almost certainly not within the terms of the exemption, since there is a very strong inference to be drawn that the purpose of the presence is something more than mere persuasion.[58] In *Tynan* v. *Balmer*[59] the view was taken that the circling manoeuvre would in any event hinder rather than help the purposes of peaceful persuasion, and the defendants were in reality there to do more than persuade.

---

[51] *Galt (Procurator Fiscal)* v. *Philp* [1984] I.R.L.R. 156.
[52] *Farmer* v. *Wilson* (1900) 69 L.J.Q.B. 496.
[53] *Toppin* v. *Feron* (1909) 43 I.L.T.R. 190.
[54] *Charnock* v. *Court* (1899) 2 Ch. 35.
[55] 12–02.
[56] *Wall* (1907) 21 Cox. C.C. 401.
[57] *Larkin* v. *Belfast Harbour Commissioners* (1908) 2 I.R. 214; *British Airports Authority* v. *Ashton* [1983] 1 W.L.R. 1079; 3 All E.R. 6.
[58] *Young* v. *Peck* (1912) 29 T.L.R. 31 "assembling in large numbers and throwing eggs" at the informant. *Thomas* v. *N.U.M* [1986] Ch. 20; *Bonsall* [1985] Crim.L.R. 150.
[59] [1967] 1 Q.B. 91, above, n. 12.

CHAPTER 13

POSSESSION OFFENCES

Introduction

3–01 Because of their potential for causing harm, certain types of articles and **13–01** objects may not be possessed, either in public or at all, or subject only to controlled conditions such as the possession of a licence. The aim of this chapter is to describe the principal offences that fall into this category.[1] As with many of the public order offences, their ultimate purpose is to prevent harm to persons or property, but each has distinct public order connotations too. Section 4 of the Public Order Act 1936, made it an offence to have an offensive weapon at a public meeting. This was repealed by the Act[2] since it was largely covered by the Prevention of Crime Act 1953, which the first part of this chapter describes. The public order implications of the Firearms Act 1968 are, perhaps, obvious enough, but is is worth noting in passing that the chief officer of police may revoke a firearm certificate if he is satisfied that the holder is of "intemperate habits or unsound mind"[3] and a shotgun certificate if satisfied that the holder "cannot be permitted to possess a shot gun without danger to the public safety or to the peace."[4] The offences under the Explosives Substances Acts 1893 were enacted to deal with Fenian terrorism[5]—there was a spate of bombings in London around that period, whereas the Sporting Events (Control of Alcohol Etc.) Act 1985, as amended by the Act, is an attempt to legislate for the problems associated with football hooliganism by supplementing the existing legislation on the misuse of alcohol in public.[6]

1. OFFENSIVE WEAPONS

The offence defined

13–02 Section 1 of the Prevention of Crime Act 1953 (in this section referred to **13–02** as the Act) provides as follows:

> 1.–(1) Any person who without lawful authority or reasonable excuse, the proof whereof shall lie on him has with him in any public place any offensive weapon shall be guilty of an offence, and shall be liable—
>
> (a) on summary conviction, to imprisonment for a term not exceed-

---

[1] It is also an offence to possess anything with intent to destroy or damage property; Criminal Damage Act 1971, s.3. A conditional intent will suffice; *Buckingham* (1976) 63 Cr.App.R. 159. Where a person possessed a can of paint with which he intended to wipe out National Front slogans, it was held that this did not amount to an intent to do damage; *Fancy* [1980] Crim. L.R. 171.

[2] Section 40(3), Sched. 3.

[3] Firearms Act 1968, s.30(1)(*a*).

[4] Firearms Act 1968, s.30(2); *Ackers* v. *Taylor* [1974] 1 W.L.R. 405, 1 All E.R. 771.

[5] K. R. M. Short, *The Dynamite War* (1979).

[6] 7–13.

219

ing three months or a fine not exceeding the statutory maximum or both;

(b) on conviction on indictment, to imprisonment for a term not exceeding two years or a fine, or both.

There is no express power of arrest for the offence,[7] although an arrest will be lawful if the general arrest conditions are satisfied,[8] and in any event the constable has power to seize the offensive weapon in question.[9] Upon conviction, the court has the power to order forfeiture or disposal of the weapon.[10]

The courts have pointed out on numerous occasions that, where the weapon has actually been used in an assault, it may not be wise to bring the additional charge. The multiplication of counts in the indictment merely causes jury confusion, and the offence is, in its rationale, an incohate one.[11]

The meaning of an offensive weapon

13-03   Section 1(4) provides a definition of offensive weapon in the following   **13-0.**
terms:

" 'offensive weapon' means any article made or adapted for use for causing injury to the person, or intended by the person having it with him for such use by him [or by some other person]."[12]

A weapon can therefore be or become offensive for the purposes of the section in two[13] different ways. Some weapons are offensive *per se* because they have been made for the purpose of causing injury, or have been adapted for that purpose. Alternatively, any article at all that has the potential of causing injury is an offensive weapon if the possessor has it with him with the intention of causing injury. The question whether an article is an offensive weapon *per se* or otherwise is of great practical

---

[7] Section 1(3) was repealed by PACE, sched. 7. The shortcomings of the previous law were exposed in *Forbes* [1984] Crim.L.R. 482.

[8] See 2-17.

[9] PACE, s.1(6), (7) and (9). This appears to be the combined effect of the sections. Subsection (6) says that he may confiscate "if in the course of such a search the constable discovers a prohibited article." This language is hardly apt to describe the common situation where the constable's attention is drawn to the miscreant because he is brandishing the offensive weapon in the first place. Since the rationale of the offence is so clearly preventive, it would be absurd if the police were unable to seize weapons obviously offensive.

[10] Section 1(2).

[11] *Ohlson* v. *Hylton* [1975] 1 W.L.R. 724, 2 All E.R. 490; *Bates* v. *Bulman* [1979] 1 W.L.R. 1190, 3 All E.R. 170, (1978) 68 Cr.App.R. 21. See generally the article by A. J. Ashworth, "Liability for Carrying Offensive Weapons" [1976] Crim.L.R. 725.

[12] The bracketed words were added by the Public Order Act 1986 section 40(2) and Sched. 2, to bring the definition into line with that in PACE, s.1(9).

[13] *Flynn* (1985) 82 Cr.App.R. 319; Glanville Williams, *Text*, p. 508. Some commentators have said that there are three categories of offensive weapon, breaking down the categories of weapons offensive *per se* into two; Smith and Hogan, p. 397; Supperstone, p. 149. But this seems unnecessarily complicated. A. J. Ashworth, "Liability for Carrying Offensive Weapons" [1976] Crim.L.R. 725 limits the categories to two.

importance because it has a bearing on the burden of proof. If the weapon is offensive *per se* and the prosecutor proves that the defendant had it with him in a public place, the burden shifts to the defendant to prove that he had lawful authority or reasonable excuse,[14] and the prosecutor is relieved of the burden of proving that the defendant had it with him with the intention of causing injury.[15] This leads to unfortunate procedural complications, since the question of the category to which the article in question belongs is a said to be a matter of fact for the jury,[16] qualified by the fact that in the interests of the uniform administration of justice, it is open to a judge to take "judicial notice" that certain articles (such as flick knives) fall necessarily into one category or the other.[17]

The section creates only one offence, which covers both categories of weapon, and it is not necessary for the prosecutor to include two counts in the indictment. Nor is it necessary that the jury should be satisfied unanimously that the weapon falls into one category or the other, so long as they are given a careful direction in the light of the differing burdens of proof.[18]

Articles offensive per se

3–04   An article falls into the category of being offensive *per se* when it is   **13–04**
"made or adapted for use for causing injury to the person." The definition is unfortunate, since it apparently refers to the intention of a maker whose identity is generally unknown, and whose purpose may not be generally apparent either. The fact is that the most lethal seeming weapon is perfectly safe in the hands of one (such as a museum keeper) whose intentions are entirely peaceable. Secondly, many lethal weapons can be used and have therefore been made for purposes other than injuring persons—shotguns, which are frequently used for killing animals being the most obvious of these[19]—and cannot therefore be said to be made or adapted for the purpose of causing injury to the person. Conversely, as the Act recognises, almost any article can become dangerous if the person who has possession of it intends to cause mischief with it. So the category is an artificial one, and not surprisingly it causes difficulty. Even without the distinction drawn by the Act, there would be a strong common sense inference that a person in public with knuckledusters, coshes and flick knives has at least a con-

---

[14] *Petrie* [1961] 1 W.L.R. 358, 1 All E.R. 466, 45 Cr.App.R. 72; *Brown* (1971) 55 Cr App R 478. The general rule is that, whenever a persuasive burden is placed on the defendant, he must discharge it on the balance of probabilities rather than beyond reasonable doubt; *Carr-Briant* [1943] K.B. 607; *Morton* v. *Confer* [1963] 1 W.L.R. 763, 2 All E.R. 765. See *Swayland* (1987) *The Times*, April 15.

[15] *Davies* v. *Alexander* (1970) 54 Cr.App.R. 398.

[16] *Williamson* (1978) 67 Cr.App.R. 35. As the Court of Appeal pointed out in *Simpson* [1983] 1 W.L.R. 1494, 3 All E.R. 789, 78 Cr.App.R. 116, "If it is to be left in each case to a jury to decide whether or not a flick knife is an offensive weapon *per se*, the identical weapon may be the subject of different decisions by different juries."

[17] *Gibson* v. *Wales* (1983) 76 Cr.App.R. 60; *Simpson* last note (flick knives).

[18] *Flynn*, above, n. 13.

[19] *Hodgson* [1954] Crim.L.R. 379; *Gipson* [1963] Crim.L.R. 281; *Sparks* [1965] Crim.L.R. 113.

ditional intention[20] to use them in a dangerous way if he has the opportunity to do so. Lord Widgery C.J. described what Parliament was seeking to do in *Ohlson* v. *Hylton*[21] as follows:

> "This is a case in which the mischief at which the statute is aimed appears to me to be very clear. Immediately prior to the passing of the 1953 Act the criminal law was adequate to deal with the actual use of weapons in the course of a criminal assault. Where it was lacking, however, was that the mere carrying of offensive weapons was not an offence.[22] The long title of the Act reads as follows: 'An act to prevent the carrying of offensive weapons in public places without lawful authority or reasonable excuse.' Parliament is there recognising the need for preventive justice where, by preventing the carriage of offensive weapons in a public place, it reduced the opportunity for the use of such weapons."

That being so, and in the light of the difficulties earlier expressed, it is perhaps a pity that Parliament did not specify a list of such articles, to be supplemented by Order if necessary. It follows from the rationale as explained in *Ohlson* v. *Hylton* that, where as in that case the defendant (a carpenter) had seized a hammer from his bag of tools and assaulted his victim with it that he was not guilty of the offence, since the weapon was neither offensive *per se*, nor did the defendant have it with him for the purpose of causing harm to the person. It also follows from the rationale, as Lord Widgery himself pointed out, that where the weapon actually is used, an additional count may well do nothing except add to the complexity of the case.[23]

The following have been held to be in the class of offensive weapons *per se*. Sword sticks,[24] coshes,[25] knuckledusters,[26] revolvers,[27] and daggers.[28] It has even been held in a civil case that a police truncheon is a weapon that is offensive *per se*, since it can have no other purpose than the infliction of harm upon the person.[29] On the other hand, apparently offensive objects such as a machete and a strong catapult have been held not to come within this category, since neither had been made or adapted for the purpose of causing injury to the person.[30]

The accurate characterisation of flick knives illustrates many of the diffi-

---

[20] Which has been held to be sufficient for these purposes; *Allamby* [1974] 1 W.L.R. 1494, 3 All E.R. 126.

[21] [1975] 1 W.L.R. 724, 2 All E.R. 490.

[22] Except, that is, under the Public Order Act 1936, s.4.

[23] In *Ohlson* v. *Hylton*, above, n. 11. See also *Humphreys* (1977) 68 Cr.App.R. 28, *Ashworth* [1976] Crim.L.R. 725.

[24] *Davies* v. *Alexander* (1970) 54 Cr.App.R. 398.

[25] *Jura* [1954] 1 Q.B. 503; *Petrie* [1961] 1 W.L.R. 358, 45 Cr.App.R. 72.

[26] *Petrie*, last note.

[27] *Petrie*, above n. 25.

[28] Subject, presumably, to doubts of the kind expressed by Macbeth as to the nature of the implement that he saw in front of him. *Macbeth*, Act II.i. A sheath knife is not offensive *per se*, being the kind of thing boy scouts and even brownies might possess; *Williamson* (1978) 67 Cr.App.R. 35.

[29] *Houghton* v. *Chief Constable for Greater Manchester* (1987) 84 Cr.App.R. 319.

[30] *Southwell* v. *Chadwick* (1987) *The Times*, January 6.

culties entailed in the notion of offensive weapons *per se*. In *Allamby*[31] it was unhesitatingly said that such knives are offensive *per se*. More doubts were expressed in *Gibson* v. *Wales*[32] where the argument was advanced that flick knives are sometimes used for purposes other than causing harm to the person, in occupations where it might sometimes be necessary to have one hand occupied while the knife was made ready for use. Parliament had, in fact controlled the importation, manufacture and sale of flick knives by the Restriction of Offensive Weapons Acts 1959 and 1961,[33] but it had not specifically criminalised the possession of them. It was inferred from this that Parliament left the gap because it believed it to be covered by the section under consideration. As McCullogh J. put it, "whether a flick knife is an article made for use for causing injury to the person is a question of fact, but in my judgment it is a question which admits of only one answer; it is." Whether or not there can be a matter of fact that admits of only one answer, when counsel is able to suggest reasons other than the causing of harm to the person that might have been in the mind of the maker is problematic.[34] Furthermore, for the court to rule authoritatively that an instrument is offensive *per se* involves the judges in deciding an issue of fact. A way out of the dilemma was found in *Simpson*[35] where the court adopted the device of taking "judicial notice" of the fact that flick knives are offensive *per se*. This slightly dubious stratagem does not avoid the difficulty that judges are still deciding jury issues, but it has the considerable merit that uniform justice is more likely to be achieved (as Lord Lane, C.J. remarked, "this is one of the areas where there is great scope for unevenness in the administration of the law. If it is to be left to the jury to decide whether or not a flick knife is an offensive weapon *per se*, the identical weapon may be the subject of different decisions by different juries"). Nor does it have the disadvantage of leaving the innocent possessor entirely without a defence. If he has the weapon for a purpose that is not related to causing harm of the person, he has the opportunity of persuading the jury of his innocence.

Articles adapted for use

3–05 It is suggested that articles "adapted for use" do not form a separate **13–05** category of offensive weapon. The consequence of this reading of the Act is that it does not matter whether it was the defendant or somebody else who adapted the article, and need not therefore be proved that the defendant adapted the article with the purpose of using it to cause harm to the

---

[31] [1974] 1 W.L.R. 1494, 3 All E.R. 126, 59 Cr.App.R. 189. In *McCogg* [1982] Crim.L.R. 685, counsel was permitted to address the jury on the issue, and managed to persuade the jury that such knives may have other legitimate uses. In the light of later cases, he should not have been.

[32] [1983] 1 W.L.R. 393, 1 All E.R. 869.

[33] The nature and use of flick knives is discussed by A. Popkiss, then Chief Constable of Nottinghamshire in [1959] Crim.L.R. 640.

[34] See *Archbold*, (41st ed., Third Supplement). In the preface to the 42nd ed., the editors of that august work wave the white flag, conceding that the argument is lost.

[35] [1983] 1 W.L.R. 1494, 3 All E.R. 798, 78 Cr.App.R. 116; reinforced by the Scottish opinion as expressed in *Tudhope* v. *O'Neill* (1982) S.L.T. 360.

person. Since it does not matter who made the article in question, it is difficult to see why it should be relevant who adapted it either. Of course, if it can be proved that the defendant did adapt it with the intention of using it to cause harm to the person, he is in any event caught by the second part of the section. What of the article accidentally "adapted," as when a bottle is accidentally broken?[36] It is difficult to see that this comes within the terms of the section, so that if it is to be treated as offensive, it can only be so because of the intention with which it is possessed.

Articles not per se offensive

13-06 Articles that do not fall into the first category of offensive weapons *per se* can be treated as offensive where the prosecutor can show that the possessor had the thing with him with the intention of causing injury.[37] Although this turns on the intention with which the defendant acted, the legal situation is one of those rare cases where, without the requisite intention, the defendant does nothing wrong, and there is technically no *actus reus*.[38] The defendant's intention to cause injury will convert the implement into an offensive weapon,[39] however inoffensive its maker's intention may have been. Furthermore, an article is capable of moving from one category to the other (*i.e.* from inoffensive to offensive) from moment to moment, so that the particulars of time and place alleged in the indictment might well be material. If, for example, a person has gone abroad with a kitchen knife to attack a particular person, he has with him an offensive weapon. After he has accomplished his purpose, the same implement is no longer an offensive weapon, since the person carrying it no longer has the requisite intention.[40]

A conditional intention, that is, an intention to use a thing if the situation arises may well be sufficient for these purposes.[41] The courts have been reluctant to permit a person to arm himself by way of self-defence.[42] Yet the intention of such a person would be to use the thing only if attacked, which, it may safely be assumed, he hopes not to be. This must be distinguished from another situation. Suppose a demonstrator has a placard at the end of a heavy stick. If the policeman were to ask, "would

[36] The juxtaposition of "made and adapted" is discussed in *Maddox* v. *Storer* [1963] 1 Q.B. 451. In *Wood* v. *M.P.C.* [1986] 2 All E.R. 570 (1986) 83 Cr.App.R. 145, where the defendant picked up a piece of glass that had been accidentally broken during a scuffle, it was held that he did not come within the terms of the Vagrancy Act 1824, since he did not have the weapon with him as a premeditated act.
[37] *Petrie* [1961] 1 W.L.R. 358, 1 All E.R. 466.
[38] A.C.E. Lynch, "The Mental Element in the *Actus Reus*" (1982) 98 L.Q.R. 109.
[39] Subject to what is said below about the instantaneously formed intention 13-06.
[40] *Allamby and Medford* [1974] 1 W.L.R. 1494, 3 All E.R. 126, 59 Cr.App.R. 189.
[41] In *Buckingham* (1976) 63 Cr.App.R. 159, it was said that a person who carried a jemmy with the intention of using it only if necessary was nevertheless guilty of the offence under the Criminal Damage Act 1971. But that may be distinguished from the situation where the person agrees when asked that he would use the implement. In *Buckingham*, the defendant had decided that he would use the jemmy, provided that the appropriate conditions presented themselves. See generally, K. Campbell, "Conditional Intention" (1982) Legal Studies 77.
[42] 13-13.

you use this if attacked," the answer (and perhaps the sensible answer) is "yes I would," in which case the article might thereafter become an offensive weapon,[43] even though the person carrying it had no intention of so using it until it was suggested to him that it could be put to such a use. In the latter situation, it is suggested the conduct does not fall within the mischief at which the section is aimed, as described by Lord Widgery C.J. in *Ohlson* v. *Hylton*.[44] An awareness that one might use an article as a weapon where the occasion demanded it is not the same thing as an intention to use it for such purposes, and the statute plainly requires that intention be proved.

It appears not to have been expressly decided whether the thing must be at least capable of causing injury to the person, but it is arguable that this is a restriction on the ambit of things that could be offensive. Even though it is not necessary to be able to call the thing a "weapon" in the hands of the person who intends to use it as such (because of the stipulative definition in section 1(4)), it must be possible to establish that what the defendant intends to do would amount to injury if carried out.[45] A question arises, for example, as to whether a tin of pepper could amount to a weapon for these purposes, supposing that a woman kept a pot handy in case she were attacked. Whether the discomfort which she intends to inflict would amount to injury may be a matter of some doubt.[46] Injury to the person does not include injury to the person's clothing, so that an intention to splash a person with ink or paint should not convert the bottle or tin into an offensive weapon.[47] Furthermore, even if it could be said that a person who intended to splash another with paint should have realised that it might cause injury (*e.g.* by getting into the victim's eyes), mere recklessness is not enough. It must be shown that the person possesses the object intending[48] to use it for the purpose specified.

Subject to these qualifications, however, "any article" is capable of being an offensive weapon. A list will illustrate what has in the past been possessed with the relevant intention. It includes sheath knives,[49] kitchen knives,[50] spanners and other tools,[51] sports equipment,[52] razors,[53] articles of clothing (especially studded belts and heavy boots)[54] and so forth. Dem-

[43] See M. D. A. Freeman, *The Police and Criminal Evidence Act 1984* (1985) p. 60–22.
[44] 13–04.
[45] This may be implicit in the line of cases deciding that, except in rare situations, the intention to intimidate is not in itself a sufficient intention; 13–07.
[46] The C.L.R.C. has committed itself to the proposition that "injury" is impossible to define since it "is a word in ordinary use in the English language, is readily understood and will cause little problem of interpretation." 14th Report, *Offences Against the Person* (1980), para. 154. Professor Glanville Williams disagrees, and offers a definition that would probably exclude such relatively transient discomfort.
[47] Supperstone, p. 150, n. 12 says that it has been held that paint was regarded as being an offensive weapon.
[48] The recent decisions as to the meaning of intention are discussed 3–15.
[49] *Williamson* (1977) 66 Cr.App.R. 35.
[50] *Rapier* (1980) 70 Cr.App.R. 17.
[51] *Dayle* (1974) 58 Cr.App.R. 28.
[52] *Petrie* [1961] 1 W.L.R. 358, 1 All E.R. 466.
[53] *Petrie*, last note.
[54] *McMahon* v. *Dollard* [1965] Crim.L.R. 238.

onstrators in possession of banners and placards might also find themselves the object of police suspicion. An article is not offensive unless the person who has it with him actually intends to use it to injure, but a policeman would have good reason to suspect that it is a prohibited article and confiscate it if he concludes that the person who has it intends to use it.

The intention to intimidate as the intention to injure

13–07   It has been held that the intention to intimidate another is not a suf-   **13–07** ficient intention to injure unless the intimidation is of a sort that is capable of producing injury through the operation of shock, and the Court of Appeal has held that it may be better altogether if the trial judge avoids using the word "intimidate" in the course of his summing up in case the jury misunderstand the point.[55] In *Woodward* v. *Koessler*[56] the defendant's explanation of his original possession of a sheath knife was that he intended to use it to force the door of a cinema. When accosted by the elderly caretaker, however, he brandished it in a threatening manner. The justices dismissed the prosecution on the basis that the intention to frighten the elderly man was not an intention to injure him. Lord Goddard C.J. in the Divisional Court considered that such a narrow interpretation would "drive a coach and four through this useful Act." His judgment has, however, been restrictively distinguished in subsequent cases. In *Edmonds*,[57] the Court of Appeal expressed the view that any reference to "frightening" in a direction on the operation of section 1(4) must make it plain that the frightening must be of a kind which is capable of producing injury through the operation of shock. As the Court of Appeal pointed out in *Rapier*,[58] affirming what was said in *Edmonds*, "circumstances giving rise to that situation must be exceedingly rare."

    It has been suggested that, as a consequence, some thought should be given to amending the legislation in such a way as to catch the person who has an intention to intimidate.[59] It may be pointed out in response that in all of the cases giving rise to this difficult problem, an assault was committed, so the gap in the law is not as great as might be feared. The real lacuna in the law arises where a person goes intending to intimidate with but not otherwise use the implement in question. Those cases too might be thought to be exceedingly rare.

"Has with him"

13–08   The courts tend to treat the question of whether a person has the thing   **13–08** with him as though it were the equivalent of and identical to the question of whether or not a person is in possession. In truth, the two concepts are really rather different,[60] in a way that has a fundamental bearing on the

---

[55] *Rapier* (1979) 70 Cr.App.R. 17.
[56] [1958] 1 W.L.R. 1255, 3 All E.R. 557.
[57] [1963] 2 Q.B. 142.
[58] Above, n. 55.
[59] J. C. Smith, [1980] Crim.L.R. 48; A Samuels, (1985) 149 J.P.N. at 746.
[60] In *Murphy* [1971] N.I. 193, it was held that the phrase denoted a more personal form of possession. And in *Kelt* (1977) 65 Cr.App.R. 74, Scarman L.J. is emphatic that the difference between the two "cannot be a merely semantic distinction, it must be a distinction of

operation of the Act. For certain purposes, a person is said to be in possession of anything that is in his house (at least if he realises that it has been put there), but that is not to say that he has it with him, either in public or anywhere else. The purpose of the section under consideration is not to prevent people from owning or possessing offensive weapons, but to stop them bringing such articles into the public arena in such a way that harm is more likely to occur.

There is a minor ambiguity in the drafting of the section. It is not clear whether it is the defendant, the weapon or both which must be in the public place. Supperstone suggests that if the weapon were left in nearby private premises, this might satisfy the section, the question being one of "ease and immediacy of access to the weapon."[61] The section seems to be genuinely ambiguous on the point, since the expression might grammatically refer to either the weapon or the defendant. Without wishing to rely too heavily on the presumption that the benefit of any such ambiguity should be given to the defendant,[62] it may again be pointed out that if the defendant uses the weapon in any way, he is almost certainly guilty of an assault. The gist of the section is not that the defendant is preparing a weapon for use but is carrying it in the public domain, and although this may require artificial distinctions to be drawn, this need not be done at the expense of setting free altogether a person who attempts to use a weapon.

Where an article is not one that is offensive *per se*, it must be shown that the intention to use it existed before the occasion to use violence actually arises. This is because until the intention to use the article is formed, it is not an offensive weapon. The additional explanation for the point is that the actor must have the offensive weapon in public with him. The point is sometimes difficult to apply in practice, but was established in principle in *Jura*,[63] which illustrates the point well. The defendant was at a shooting gallery and in possession of an air rifle when he became annoyed with his companion. He turned the gun on her and fired, hitting her and wounding her slightly. The Court held that he had a lawful excuse for being in possession of the rifle, and that the mere unlawful use of the article did not lead to the conclusion that he had it with him with the intention of causing harm to the person.

That principle was applied in the leading decision in *Ohlson v. Hylton*.[64] The appellant was a carpenter by trade who, on the way home from work, became involved in a fracas. He had with him a bag of the tools of his trade, including a hammer which he took out and used to assault his protagonist. At first instance, it was held that he was guilty of the offence, but the Crown Court allowed his appeal on the grounds that there was insufficient time between taking the hammer from the brief case intending to use it and the injury for it to be said that the defendant was carrying an

---

substance. The legislature must have had it in mind that, in regard to those offences where it is an offence for the person to have with him a firearm, there must be a very close physical link and a degree of immediate control over the weapon."

[61] *Op. cit.* at 153.
[62] See generally Glanville Williams, *Text*, pp. 11–18.
[63] [1954] 1 Q.B. 503. See also *Police* v. *Smith* [1974] 2 N.Z.L.R. 32.
[64] [1975] 1 W.L.R. 724, 2 All E.R. 490.

offensive weapon with him. This was at variance with several earlier decisions, including *Woodward* v. *Koessler*[65] in which Donovan J. rejected a submission that the words "having it with him" meant having taken the weapon out (*i.e.* into the public domain) with him with the initial intention of using force against another. In the course of giving his judgment, he said:

> "If it is found that the person did, in fact, make use of it for the purpose of causing injury, he had it with him for that purpose, and I think that is good enough."

These observations had been applied in subsequent decisions,[66] but were considered by Lord Widgery C.J. to be too wide in their application. The effect was that, whenever a person actually used a weapon inoffensive *per se* (if one may use such an expression), he would be guilty of the additional offence. This is not what Parliament had intended to punish, as evidenced by the Long Title of the Act, which makes it plain that the mischief of the Act is carrying offensive weapons in public, and not using them. The prosecutor's appeal was consequently dismissed.

The difficulties do not quite end there. What of the person who spontaneously arms himself with a weapon, whether to defend himself or otherwise. In *Harrison* v. *Thornton*[67] a Divisional Court held that a man committed the offence when he picked up a stone with the intention of intervening to stop a fight. This was consistent with what had been said in *Woodward* v. *Koessler*, but not, so later courts have held, with the intention of the framers of the Act as explained by Lord Goddard in *Jura*.[68] In *Dayle*[69] it was held that a man who took a jack from the boot of his car to throw at his adversary did not have the jack with him with the requisite intent. In *Humphreys*,[70] a decision of the Court of Appeal, a man who had taken from his pocket a pen-knife in the course of a fight was held to be not guilty of the offence, because the jury had not been properly directed that had he formed the intention *ad hoc*, he would not have had with him an offensive weapon. This was followed in *Bates* v. *Bulman*[71] where the appellant had been handed a knife by a companion in the course of a fight. The justices rejected a submission that there was an insufficient lapse of time between his being handed the knife and his use of it. The principle would therefore seem to be that, where a person is charged with carrying an inoffensive weapon *per se* under section 1(4) of the Act, he commits no offence if he uses an article that he already has with him, not having previously intended to use it to cause harm to another. Nor does he commit an offence

---

[65] [1958] 1 W.L.R. 1255, 3 All E.R. 577.
[66] *Powell* [1963] Crim.L.R. 511; *Harrison* v. *Thornton* [1966] Crim.L.R. 388, 68 Cr.App.R. 28. The latter report was published some 10 years after the case was decided.
[67] Last note.
[68] [1954] Q.B. 503.
[69] [1974] 1 W.L.R. 181, [1973] 3 All E.R. 1151.
[70] (1977) 68 Cr.App.R. 28.
[71] [1979] 3 All E.R. 170. And see *Wood* v. *M.P.C.* 2 All E.R. 570, (1986) 83 Cr.App.R. 145, a prosecution under s.4 of the Vagrancy Act 1824, where it was held that the defendant did not commit a similar offence when he spontaneously armed himself with glass that had broken during an altercation.

where he takes the object up with such a purpose. As a matter of principle, it should not even matter if he arms himself with a weapon that is offensive *per se* for immediate use, since he would still be able to say that he did not have it with him until the occasion arose on which he used it.

It is suggested that what is necessary under the Act is that there should be some break between the time or the place of the initiating incident, and the person's arming himself with the weapon. Suppose, for example, that an incident took place outside a man's house as a result of which he rushed inside and picked up a carving knife. Even though the break in time and location might be a short one, he would be guilty of the offence.[72]

Joint custody

13–09 Where one person is found to have control of a weapon in circumstances making it appear that others might use it, but that the possessor himself would not, no offence would be committed unless the weapon was offensive *per se*. A minor change to the Act effected by the 1986 Act[73] alters this, so that such a person would now be guilty. This alteration might also now cover the situation where a weapon is found in what appears to be the joint control of a group, for example where the weapon is found in a car containing several people. So long as it can be said that they have the weapon with them, all those who knew that the weapon was in the car could be convicted, even if it was clear that only one member of the group intended to use the weapon.[74]

In a public place

13–10 The question whether or not the defendant is in[75] a public place is one for the jury,[76] guided by the words of section 1(4), which provides:

> "In this section, 'public place' includes any highway and any other premises or place to which at the material time the public have or are permitted to have access, whether on payment or otherwise."

---

[72] In *O'Leary* (1986) 82 Cr.App.R. 341, it was held that a person committed aggravated burglary contrary to the Theft Act 1968, s.10, when he armed himself only after he had entered the house, by picking up a knife, the definition of "weapon of offence" being very similar to the one under consideration. If the policy of the Theft Act is the same as that of the Prevention of Crime Act, namely to prevent people going armed, this seems a somewhat harsh reading, since the offence is punishable with life imprisonment. The defendant had picked up the knife before being accosted by the householders, and to that extent was going armed.

[73] Section 40(2), Sched. 2(2) adds the words "or by some other person."

[74] This is a matter of evidence and inference; *McGuire and Page* [1963] Crim.L.R. 572. Mere knowledge of the existence of the weapon is not sufficient to establish the commission of the *actus reus*; *Searle* [1971] Crim.L.R. 592; *Bellerby* v. *Carle* [1983] 2 A.C. 101.

[75] For a discussion of whether it is the weapon, the defendant or both which must be in the public place, see 13–08, n. 61.

[76] *Elkins* v. *Cartlidge* [1947] 1 All E.R. 829; *Waters* (1963) 47 Cr.App.R. 149; *Theodolou* [1963] Crim.L.R. 573. The definition is very similar to that in the Public Order Act 1936, s.9 (as amended), and the authorities that have collected around that section are of some assistance in interpreting section 1(4). But each definition must be separately considered in its own context, having regard to the mischief that the statute seeks to suppress; *Woods* v. *Lindsay* (1910) S.C. (J.) 88. S.9 also includes a definition of "private premises." See also the

The best evidence that a place is public is that the public do in fact use the location as such.[77]

The courts have held that the following are not public places: a public house car park bearing the notice that it was for the use of patrons only, was held not to be a public place one hour after closing time.[78] A shop car park, long after the shop had been closed was no longer public,[79] in *Edwards and Roberts*[80] it was held that lawful access through the garden to a private house did not make the garden a public place since persons entering enjoyed access *qua* visitors rather than as members of the public. In contrast, the staircase adjoining a block of flats on a housing estate was held to be public since there was nothing to stop the public from entering the staircases.[81]

The mental element

13–11 The element of intention that converts an otherwise innocent article into an offensive weapon was considered earlier.[82] That does not complete the description of the mental element required for the offence, since in *Cugullere*[83] the Court of Criminal Appeal held that the expression "has with him in any public place" means "knowingly" has with him. If the defendant's intention is to use the thing with the intention of causing injury, he almost by definition has the necessary knowledge. But it is possible that a person has an offensive weapon slipped into his pocket by an escaping rogue, or is a passenger in a car that has such a weapon in the glove compartment, so that he has no idea that he has it with him. It would seem contrary to principle to make such a person guilty of an offence.

What would be the significance of a claim by the defendant that he did not realise that the article that he had in his possession was an "offensive weapon"? Suppose, for example, that a sailor carried a flick knife with him on a boat because occasionally he needed to have access to a sharp blade to save himself in a hurry. Could he argue that he did not realise that it was an offensive weapon? In principle, it would seem the answer must be no—the defendant is making a mistake of or is ignorant as to the law which, as we have seen, makes it a matter of judicial notice that the flick knife is *per se* offensive.[84] In that case, the sailor's recourse must be to argue (and to persuade the jury) that he had a reasonable excuse for what he was doing.[85]

There is a different problem, which is the problem of "forgotten knowledge." Normally, if a person took what he knew to be an offensive weapon

definition of "public place" in s.16 of the 1986 Act, which is wider than the expression under consideration, since it refers to the presence of the member of the public "by virtue of express or implied permission."

[77] *Pugh* v. *Knipe* [1972] Crim.L.R. 247.
[78] *Sandy* v. *Martin* [1974] R.T.R. 263, Crim.L.R. 258.
[79] *Marsh* v. *Arscott* (1982) 75 Cr.App.R. 211.
[80] (1978) 67 Cr.App.R. 228.
[81] *Knox* v. *Anderton* (1983) 76 Cr.App.R. 156.
[82] See 13–06.
[83] [1961] 1 W.L.R. 858, 45 Cr.App.R. 108.
[84] See 13–04 above.
[85] See 13–13.

into the public domain, it would be no defence for him to say that, at the time when he was apprehended, he had forgotten that it was with him. The issue arose in *Russell*[86] where the defendant's car was searched by the police and found to contain a cosh in the form of a piece of rubber hose filled at one end with metal. His defence at the trial appears to have been (the facts are not very clearly stated) that he found the cosh when he was doing some work on the car (having bought it second-hand, presumably) threw it under the front seat, and then forgot about it. This defence was not put to the jury, since the judge interpreted the Act to mean that it was enough that the defendant had the cosh with him physically in a public place. His conviction was quashed by the Court of Appeal, which expressed the view that:

> "It would be wrong to hold that a man knowingly has a weapon with him if his forgetfulness of its existence or presence in his car is so complete as to amount to ignorance that it is there at all."

There are a number of difficulties with this judgment, and it has subsequently been doubted by the Court of Appeal in *Martindale*,[87] a prosecution for possessing drugs. There, the Court cited a passage from an earlier case[88] indicating that, once a person had knowingly come into possession of drugs, he could not be heard to say that he lost possession of them merely because he had put them in a drawer and forgotten all about them. That case had not been cited to the Court in *Russell*, and Lord Lane C.J. expressed the view that if it had been, he doubted whether *Russell* would have been decided in the way that it was.

There are, however, considerable differences between the two offences which Lord Lane did not consider, and since there are apparently contradictory authorities of equal status, the matter must be examined more closely.[89] It is illegal to possess the specified drugs *tout court*, whereas the possession of offensive weapons is not, as such, an offence. It becomes an offence only when the person has a weapon with him in public. Had Russell kept the cosh in a drawer of his house (for protection against burglars or otherwise), he would not have committed any offence. The Report does not disclose where the car was at the time when Russell discovered the cosh. If it had been in a private garage, he might genuinely be able to say that he did not realise that he had it with him in public at any stage. Of course, he ought to have thought about the matter, but that is a very different thing from saying that he did do so. Alternatively, suppose that he had had lawful authority or reasonable excuse when he first put the cosh into his car,[90] but then forgot about it when the danger was passed? In both of these hypotheticals, the claim that he was unaware that he had the weapon with him at the time is different from the claim that he was not in possession of the weapon. He was not charged with being in possession of the weapon; the offence is having it with him in public. Whereas drugs must be

---

[86] (1984) 81 Cr.App.R. 315.
[87] [1986] 1 W.L.R. 1042, 3 All E.R. 24, (1985) 84 Cr.App.R. 31.
[88] *Buswell* [1972] 1 W.L.R. 64, 1 All E.R. 57.
[89] *Young* v. *Bristol Aero Co. Ltd.* [1984] K.B. 718; *Gould* [1968] 2 Q.B. 65, Q.B. 618.
[90] *Evans* v. *Wright* [1964] Crim.L.R. 466.

permanently in somebody's possession unless they have been effectively abandoned, it is not the case that a person having once possessed himself of an offensive weapon permanently has it with him in public until he abandons it.

There is a qualification to be made to the foregoing. At the time when he threw the cosh under the front seat, Russell presumably knew that he would be driving in public. To that extent, he might be said to have been wilfully blind to the consequences of what he was doing.[91] It is suggested that this should suffice for liability. To express the point in terms of principle, if a person takes up an offensive weapon knowing that he will in the future have it with him in public, he cannot be heard to say that, when he has it with him in public that he lacks the necessary mental element for the offence.

Lawful authority[92]

13–12   Before the 1953 Act, there was no general offence[93] of being armed with   **13–12** an offensive weapon in public. Now, it would seem that having such a weapon in public is prima facie unlawful, and the person who has the weapon must be able to point to some legal justification for what he is doing. His possession must be "supported by law."[94] In *Bryan* v. *Mott*[95] Lord Widgery C.J. expressed the view that the term applies to "those people who from time to time carry an offensive weapon as a matter of duty—the soldier with his rifle and the police officer with his truncheon." The authority may be statutory in origin, or can it arise from the common law as the courts deem it to be.[96] It has been held that security men cannot wear truncheons as a matter of routine and plead lawful excuse,[97] and it would seem *a fortiori* that they could not plead that they acted with lawful authority.

Reasonable excuse

13–13   The categories of reasonable excuse are not closed, since whether or not   **13–13** conduct is excused is a matter for the jury.[98] One plea met with considerable frequency is that the possession of the weapon was necessary for the purposes of self-defence, and the courts have developed certain guidelines that assist the judge in directing the jury as to whether or not the defence might be available. Indeed, if the evidence is such that no reasonable jury

---

[91] *Westminster City Council* v. *Croyalgrange* (1986) 83 Cr.App.R. at 164.
[92] See generally R. I. E. Card, "Authority and Excuse as Defences to Crime" [1969] Crim.L.R. 359.
[93] Under the Public Order Act 1936, s. 4, it was an offence to possess such a weapon at a public meeting. Brandishing the weapon might have been charged as an affray, although modern practice was not to charge that species of the offence.
[94] *Per* Napier J. in *Crafter* v. *Kelly* [1941] S.A.S.R. 237 at 244.
[95] (1976) 62 Cr.App.R. 71. The definition is very similar to that in the Public Order Act 1936, s.4(2), repealed.
[96] The issue is explored more fully by Helen Beynon in "The Ideal Civic Condition" [1986] Crim.L.R. 580 and 647. See especially at 592.
[97] *Spanner* [1973 Crim.L.R. 704.
[98] *Leer* [1982] Crim.L.R. 310.

could decide that there was a reasonable excuse, the judge would be entitled to refuse to leave the issue at all. In *Evans* v. *Hughes*[99] the principle was established that the defence is available only if the defendant believed and that there actually was "an imminent particular threat affecting the particular circumstances in which the weapon was carried." The application of that principle has caused some difficulties especially where the person claiming it is under constant threat, perhaps because of the hazardous nature of his calling (for example, the guard of a van ferrying cash from place to place). The principle to which he is equally subject is that citizens who are under constant threat are expected to seek police protection. In *Bradley* v. *Moss*,[1] for example, an unpopular youth who had been chased and threatened with assault on previous occasions by older youths, and who was then assaulted after the incident for which he was prosecuted, was held to have no defence even though the incidents had been reported to the police. What appears to have told against the defendant was that he had armed himself with a length of steel (10½ inches long), a two foot length of cycle chain, a metal clock weight and a studded glove. The court took the view that he need not have carried all four weapons for self defence. Whether he would have had the defence had he used only one of the implements is a matter of some conjecture, but it is at least arguable that the nature of the weapon should have some bearing on whether or not the carrier has an excuse. Suppose, for example, that a woman were regularly to carry an acrosol spray can for use in the event of her being attacked which, when used, could cause injury to her attacker's eyes? Even though the law does not sanction the routine carrying of weapons, it would be a harsh ruling that she was precluded from asking the jury whether in their opinion what she was doing was without reasonable excuse. Certainly, the nature of the weapon can be used against the defendant. In *Pittard* v. *Mahoney*[2] the defendant had equipped himself with a ball and chain when several of his friends had been attacked. It was held that this fact could be taken into account in addition to other factors such as the imminence of the threat. A ball and chain, one might surmise, falls into the category of weapons offensive *per se*.

As has been pointed out on more than one occasion,[3] it is common practice for guards of security vans regularly to go about armed with truncheons when they collect money. The practice is connived at, even though it appears to be in breach of the often repeated warnings given by the

---

[99] [1972] 1 W.L.R. 1452, 3 All E.R. 412, 56 Cr.App.R. 813; *Peacock* [1973] Crim.L.R. 639; *Taylor* v. *Mucklow* [1973] Crim.L.R. 750; *Giles* [1976] Crim.L.R. 253. And see *Henman* [1987] Crim.L.R. 333 and commentary.

[1] [1974] Crim.L.R. 430.

[2] [1977] Crim.L.R. 169. *Peacock* [1973] Crim.L.R. 639. In *Attorney-General's Refce (No. 2 of 1983)* (1984) 78 Cr.App.R. 183, 187, it was held that a defendant in possession of petrol bombs might still be able to plead self defence for the purposes of the Explosive Substances Act 1883.

[3] Smith and Hogan p. 400 raise the point rhetorically, whereas Bevan and Lidstone, *A Guide to the Police and Criminal Evidence Act 1984* (1985), p. 44, assert the point more unequivocally.

courts against going abroad armed as a matter of routine. It might be argued that, so long as the business in question is a well organised one which employs and trains its staff adequately, there is no real prospect that the weapons will be used other than in self-defence. Such conduct is thus outside the mischief at which the Act is really aimed. In the absence of such obvious signs of self-protection, it might be argued, there really would be a permanent threat to the carriers of such weapons.[4] It is perhaps otherwise with the commonly met plea that a young man goes armed in case he is attacked by the members of a rival gang. It has been held that the plea of self-defence is not available to persons engaged in equally hazardous callings such as that of the taxi-driver,[5] who may very well have to deal with violent customers late at night. Presumably bus drivers and train guards are equally placed, and not entitled to equip themselves for self protection.

2. FIREARMS

Outline of offences

13–14   The licensing and control of firearms is a large subject, the details of **13–1** which are beyond the scope of this work.[6] The Firearms Act 1968 creates a number of serious offences. It is an offence to purchase, acquire or possess a firearm[7] or ammunition without a firearms certificate.[8] The Act dis-

---

[4] In *Evans* v. *Wright* [1964] Crim.L.R. 466, the defendant had collected wages from the bank for his employees and then left his weapons (a knuckleduster and a truncheon) in the car afterwards. It was held that the question whether he had an excuse had to be answered at the time when he had the weapons in public with him, and the appeal failed. The court said, apparently, that if the weapons had been found on him as soon as he returned from the bank, the excuse might have been reasonable. *A fortiori*, it must be available when he is on his way to the bank or on his way back to pay the employees.

[5] *Grieve* v. *Macleod* (1967) S.L.T. 70, [1967] Crim.L.R. 424.

[6] See generally P. J. Clarke and J. W. Ellis, *The Law Relating to Firearms* (1981); G. Sandys-Winch, *Gun Law* (4th ed., 1985).

[7] The word "firearm" is extensively defined in s.57 as being "a lethal barrelled weapon of any description from which any shot, bullet or other missile can be discharged, and includes (a) any prohibited weapon, whether it is such a lethal weapon or not." In *Read* v. *Donovan* [1947] 1 K.B. Lord Goddard expressed the view that "lethal" meant no more than "capable of causing injury," but this seems a dubious interpretation of a criminal provision which, on a more natural interpretation means capable of causing death. In *Moore* v. *Gooderham* [1960] 3 All E.R. 575, the observation was doubted. And see *Heron* v. *Flockhart* [1970] Crim.L.R. 166; *Seamark* v. *Prowse* [1980] 1 W.L.R. 698; *Thorpe* [1987] 1 W.L.R. 383, 2 All E.R. 108. Antiques are outside the scope of the Act if they are possessed "as a curiosity or ornament"; s.58(2). What constitutes an antique is a matter of fact for the jury. *Richards* v. *Curwen* (1977) 65 Cr.App.R. 95, 3 All E.R. 426; *Burke* (1978) 67 Cr.App.R. 220; *Bennett* v. *Brown* (1980) 71 Cr.App.R. 109. In *Howells* [1977] Q.B. 614, it was held that it is no defence that the possessor believes that he has an antique if it is in reality a fake.

[8] Section 1. As to the meaning of "possession," see *Sullivan* v. *Earl of Caithness* [1976] Q.B. 966. And see *Hall* v. *Cotton* [1986] 3 W.L.R. 681. It has been held that it is no defence that the person does not realise that he is in possession of what is, technically, a firearm; *Hussain* [1981] 2 All E.R. 287, it being sufficient if the defendant knowingly has in his possession an article that is in fact a firearm; applying *Warner* [1969] 2 A.C. 256.

tinguishes between firearms, shotguns,[9] and prohibited weapons,[10] the latter of which may be possessed only by persons who have secured the consent of the Defence Council. Restrictions are also imposed upon those who may possess and be sold firearms; persons with certain criminal records,[11] and juveniles[12] may not acquire or be given firearms.

Analytically, several of the offences occupy the borderline between public order or safety, and offences against the person. Thus, section 16 makes it an offence for a person to have in his possession any firearm or ammunition with intent to endanger life, or to enable another to endanger life.[13] Under section 17, a person commits an offence if he uses or attempts to make use of a firearm or imitation firearm with intent to resist or prevent the lawful arrest or detention of himself or another person. There is a presumption that, if a person has such an object in his possession at the time of his committing an offence or being arrested therefor, he had it for an unlawful object unless he is able to establish otherwise.[14] Three offences, similar in character to the offensive weapons offences considered earlier in this chapter must, however, be noted in slightly greater detail. They proscribe carrying a firearm with criminal intent,[15] carrying a firearm in a public place,[16] and trespassing with a firearm.[17]

Section 18—carrying a firearm with intent

13–15 Section 18 provides as follows: **13–15**

> (1) It is an offence for a person to have with him a firearm[18] or imitation firearm with intent to commit an indictable offence, or to resist arrest or prevent the arrest of another, in either case while he has the firearm or imitation firearm with him.

[9] Smooth bore, with a barrel of not less than 24 inches in length. In *Hucklebridge, Att.-Gen.'s Refce (No. 3 of 1980)* [1980] 1 W.L.R. 1284, 3 All E.R. 273, it was held that a rifle from which the barreling had been removed was a shot-gun, even though the weapon was incapable of firing shot, and remained capable of firing bullets.

[10] Section 5(1) defines these. Machine guns fall into the category. In *Jobling* [1981] Crim.L.R. 625, it was held that an automatic that had been altered in such a way that it could fire only single shots was not within the definition, even though the weapon could be re-converted very simply. In *Pannell* (1982) 76 Cr.App.R. 53, it was held that the offence was committed where the weapon could not fire because of a temporary fault. These decisions are inconsistent, and in *Clarke* [1986] 3 All E.R. 846, it was held that *Pannell* must be taken to have overruled the earlier decision.

[11] A person who has been sentenced to more than three years' imprisonment may never possess a firearm; s.21; *Davies v. Tomlinson* (1980) 71 Cr.App.R. 279.

[12] Sections 22–24.

[13] See *Bentham* [1973] Q.B. 357. The intention may be to commit an offence elsewhere than in England; *El Hakkaoui* [1975] 1 W.L.R. 396. In *Norton* [1977] Crim.L.R. 478, it was held that the intention to commit suicide was not a relevant intention within the scope of the section.

[14] Firearms Act 1968, s.17(2). Currently, the offence under s.17 is punishable with 20 years' imprisonment.

[15] Section 18.

[16] Section 19.

[17] Section 20.

[18] Because of doubts about the application of the Act to imitation firearms, the 1982 Firearms Act makes it plain that the Act does apply. The question for the jury is whether the thing looked like a firearm at the time the defendant had it with him. They are not concerned

(2) In proceedings for an offence under this section proof that the accused had a firearm or imitation firearm with him and intended to commit an offence, or to resist or prevent arrest, is evidence that he intended to have it with him while doing so.

It has been held in *Houghton*[19] that the offence may be committed where the person in possession of the firearm has no pre-conceived intention of using it before he actually does so. This appears to be at variance with the offences relating to offensive weapons, to which it bears a very close resemblance. The defendant in that case, who had been drinking, fell asleep in a taxi. The driver, being unable to wake his passenger, drove him to a police station. Upon being wakened, the defendant drew an imitation firearm and threatened the taxi driver with it. The jury were directed that it did not matter that the defendant did not form any intention of using the weapon before he actually drew it, and the defendant was convicted. His appeal was dismissed, the view being taken that the direction was correct. This decision seems to be inconsistent with *Kelt*[20] which holds that the important question is not the intention with which the weapon was used, but why the defendant had the thing with him—why, in the wording of the side note to the section he was 'carrying' it in the first place. The court distinguished the offensive weapons decisions[21] by saying that the 1968 Act was concerned not simply with the carrying of firearms, but also with their use. But that is not what the Act says; in terms, it is concerned with a form of possession by a person who intends to use it, and there was no evidence that Houghton had any such intention, apart from the fact that he did so use it. The two decisions seem to be irreconcilable, and it is submitted that *Kelt* is for the reasons given by the court in that case, the better one.

In *French*[22] it was held that it is perfectly proper for prosecutors to add a firearms count to a robbery charge, and for the sentence to take account of this aggravating element, so long as the overall sentence reflected the totality of the wrongdoing.

Section 19: Carrying firearms in a public place

13–16 Section 19 provides: **13–16**

"A person commits an offence if, without lawful authority or reasonable excuse (the proof whereof lies on him) he has with him in a public place a loaded shot gun or loaded air weapon, or any other firearm (whether loaded or not) together with ammunition suitable for use in that firearm."

---

with what it looks like at any other time. *Debreli* [1964] Crim.L.R. 53; *Morris* (1984) 79 Cr.App.R. 104. In *Freeman* (1970) 54 Cr.App.R. 251, it was held that a starting pistol was an imitation for these purposes. *Titus* [1971] Crim.L.R. 279.
[19] [1982] Crim.L.R. 112.
[20] [1977] 1 W.L.R. 1365, 65 Cr.App.R. 74.
[21] Discussed 13–08.
[22] (1982) 75 Cr.App.R. 1. And see *Faulkener* (1972) 56 Cr.App.R. 594.

In *Ross* v. *Collins*[23] it was held that the possession of a shot-gun licence did not constitute 'lawful authority' for the possession of a loaded shot-gun in a public place. Given the width of the definition of 'public place,'[24] this would seem to extend the potential scope of the offence considerably.

Lawful authority and reasonable excuse can arise either by the operation of the common law or by statute. Self-defence, for example, might be an example of the former. In *Taylor* v. *Mucklow*[25] the defendant sought to argue that he had a reasonable excuse of this nature when the contractor whom he had employed to undertake work for him began to demolish the work when a dispute as to payment arose. The defendant produced a loaded airgun and threatened the builder with it. The justices took the view that there was no real danger to the defendant's house (as opposed to the extension which was the object of the dispute) and convicted. On appeal, it was held that the true question for the justices was whether or not the use of such force was reasonable in all the circumstances, and the court refused to interfere with the conviction, saying that for anyone to argue nowadays that a loaded firearm was a suitable way of restraining the kind of bad temper exhibited by the builder was to show a lack of appreciation of modern trends and dangers.[26]

Section 20: Trespassing with a firearm

3–17   Section 20 provides that: **13–17**

> "A person commits an offence if, while he has a firearm with him, he enters or is in any building or part of a building as a trespasser and without reasonable excuse (the proof whereof lies on him).
>
> (2) A person commits an offence if, while he has a firearm with him, he enters or is on land as a trespasser and without reasonable excuse (the proof whereof lies on him)."

When the trespasser[27] enters a building with the intention of committing an offence, he is also in all probability guilty of committing aggravated burglary, which carries a penalty of life imprisonment.[28] By contrast, the offences under section 20(1) carries five years,[29] and 20(2) on summary conviction only with three months.[30]

---

[23] [1982] Crim.L.R. 368.
[24] "Public place" is defined in s.57(1) in terms identical to the Prevention of Crime Act 1953, s.1(4) and the authorities on that section discussed in 13–10 are relevant here. In *Anderson* v. *Miller* (1977) 64 Cr.App.R. 178, it was held that it includes behind the counter of a shop.
[25] [1973] Crim.L.R. 750. And see *Cousins* [1982] Q.B. 526; a person may have a lawful excuse for threatening to kill which would not be available were he to carry out his threat.
[26] *Cp. Hussey* (1924) 18 Cr.App.R. 160.
[27] The meaning of trespass is considered in 14–15.
[28] Theft Act 1968, s.10(2).
[29] Firearms Act 1968, s.51(1).
[30] Firearms Act 1968, s.51(2) and sched. 6, Part I.

3. EXPLOSIVE SUBSTANCES

Background

13–18　　The offences created by the Explosive Substances Act 1883 were created **13–1** as the result of Fenian and anarchist bombings in London in the 1880s to supplement existing legislation.[31] Three offences were created: causing explosions likely to endanger life or cause serious injury to property[32]; attempting or conspiring to cause a dangerous explosion, or possessing explosives with intent to endanger life or cause injury to property; and making or possessing explosives under suspicious circumstances. The courts regard the offences as particularly serious ones, attracting long terms of imprisonment.[33] In its review of the law of criminal damage, the Law Commission did not consider the possession of explosives, taking the view that this should be dealt with as part of a review of the offences relating to public order. In the event, the law was untouched by the Public Order Act 1986, although it has been the subject of relatively recent amendment in the light of the more recent atrocities associated with the Irish political situation. The political connotations of the offences are indicated by the fact that no proceedings can be instituted without the leave of the Attorney-General.[34]

The offences defined

13–19　　Section 3(1) of the Explosive Substances Act 1883 (as amended) reads as **13–1** follows:

"A person who in the United Kingdom or a dependency[35] or (being a citizen of the United Kingdom and Colonies)[36] elsewhere unlawfully and maliciously—

(b) makes or has in his possession or under his control an explosive substance with intent by means thereof to endanger life, or cause serious injury to property, whether in the United Kingdom or the Republic of Ireland, or to enable any other person so to do, shall, whether any explosion does or does not take place, and whether any

---

[31] Principally that found in the Offences Against the Person Act 1861, ss.28, 29, 30 and 64. Evidentiary and procedural considerations apart, these might seem comprehensive enough to have coped.

[32] Section 2. This section is not further considered here. Nor is s.3(1)(*a*), which is committed by doing an act with intent to cause, or conspiring to cause by an explosive substance an explosion of a nature likely to endanger life or cause serious injury to property, whether in the U.K. or in the Republic of Ireland.

[33] *Byrne* (1975) 62 Cr.App.R. 159; *Gerald* (1981) 3 Cr.App.R.(S) 162; *Coughlan* (1976) 63 Cr.App.R. 33 (conspiracy).

[34] Section 7. *Cain and Schollick* (1975) 61 Cr.App.R. 186; *McLaughlin* (1983) 76 Cr.App.R. 42. In *Elliott* (1984) 81 Cr.App.R. 115, it was held that proceedings are not "instituted" within the meaning of the section until the defendant is brought before the court to enter a plea.

[35] " 'Dependency' means the Channel Islands, the Isle of Man and any colony other than a colony for whose external relations a country other than the United Kingdom is responsible"; s.3(2).

[36] See now the British Nationality Act 1981.

injury to person or property is actually caused or not, be guilty of an offence and on conviction on indictment shall be liable to imprisonment for life,[37] and the explosive substance shall be forfeited."

Section 4(1):

"Any person who makes or knowingly has in his possession or under his control any explosive substance, under such circumstances[38] as to give rise to a reasonable suspicion that he is not making it or does not have it in his possession or under his control for a lawful object, shall, unless he can show that he made it or had it in his possession or under his control for a lawful object, be liable to imprisonment for a term not exceeding fourteen years, and the explosive substance shall be forfeited."

The offences can be charged in the alternative. In either case, it is essential for the prosecutor to prove that the person charged had the substance in his possession or control, and that he knew that the substance was an explosive one. The difference between the two sections is that, for a prosecution under section 3, the prosecutor must in addition be able to show the intention to endanger life or to cause injury to property, whereas under section 4, the onus passes to the defendant to explain his possession.

Possession or control

3–20 To establish the requisite possession or control for the purposes of both sections 3(*b*) and 4, it is necessary for the prosecutor to show that the defendant was aware that the explosive substance existed.[39] He must also be able to show that the defendant had acquired and retained possession of the explosives. This may be difficult where the explosives are simply found on premises which he occupies or over which he exercises or is able to exercise control. In such circumstances, it should be shown that he has accepted the presence of the substance on the premises, or connived at their remaining there. The defendant must be in a position to exercise practical control over the disposition of the substance in question,[40] and this is not proved merely by knowledge of the presence of the substance and its character.[41] In addition, a person may be guilty of the offence by aiding and abetting another in his possession.[42]   **13–20**

---

[37] The penalty was increased from 20 years' to life by the Criminal Law Act 1977, s.33, sched. 12.

[38] Suspicious circumstances would include the fact that the place of storage of the explosives was not registered under the Explosives Act 1875, and that the possessors did not hold a certificate for keeping such explosives.

[39] *Hallam* [1957] 1 Q.B. 569; *Ashton-Rickardt* [1978] 1 W.L.R. 37, 1 All E.R. 173.

[40] *Black* v. *H.M. Lord Advocate* [1974] S.L.T. 247. *Bellerby* v. *Carle* [1984] A.C.

[41] *Rutter and White* [1959] Crim.L.R. 288. This caused considerable difficulty in Northern Ireland, as a result of which the Northern Ireland (Emergency Provisions Act) 1978 s.9 was passed; *Whelan* [1972] N.I. 153. This gives the court a discretion to require a person to prove that he had no control over explosives or weapons discovered on premises habitually used by him. See *Killen* [1974] N.I. 220.

[42] This would be so as a matter of general principle; *McCarthy* [1964] 1 W.L.R. 196, 48 Cr.App.R. 86. And see s.5.

Explosive substances

13–21   What constitutes an "explosive substance" is far wider than the natural   **13–2**
meaning of those words might lead one to expect, because of the defi-
nitions in section 9, and the Explosives Act 1875, section 3. The 1883 Act
does not itself define "explosive" any further, but section 9 says that
"explosive substance" shall be deemed to include any materials used for
making any explosive substance, and in *Wheatley*[43] it was held that this
should be construed in accordance with the terms of the 1875 Act. Under
this, the term "explosive" means

> "gunpowder, nitroglygerine, dynamite, gun-cotton, blasting powders,
> fulminate or mercury or of other metals, coloured fires and every
> other substance, whether similar to those mentioned or not, use or
> manufactured with a view to producing a practical effect by explosion
> or a pyrotechnic effect; and (2) includes fog-signals, fireworks,[44] fuses,
> rockets, percussion caps, detonators, cartridges, ammunition of all
> description, and every adaptation or preparation of an explosive as
> above defined."

It has been held that this includes petrol bombs.[45]
   In addition to this extended definition, the remainder of section 9 must
be considered. The provides that "explosive substance" shall be deemed to
include "any apparatus, machine, implement or materials used, or
intended to be used, or adapted for causing, or aiding in causing, any
explosion in or with any explosive substance; also any part of such apparatus, machine, or implement."
   On the strength of this definition, it has been held that the section
applies to a shot-gun[46] and a pistol,[47] neither of which one would ordinarily
think of as being an explosive substance.

The mental element—knowledge

13–22   It is plain that, for a conviction under this section, mere suspicion as to   **13–2**
the nature of the substance is insufficient to give rise to liability. In *Hallam*[48] Lord Goddard C.J. said that the prosecution must prove "(i) that the
prisoner knew that he had the substance in his possession or under his control and also (ii) that he knew it was an explosive substance."

Lawful object

13–23   The lawfulness of the defendant's object may operate to exclude him   **13–2**
from liability under this Act, even though in arming himself, the defendant
might commit other offences. In *Fegan*[49] it was held that this expression

---

[43] *Wheatley* [1979] 1 W.L.R. 144, 1 All E.R. 954, 68 Cr.App.R. 287.
[44] See 13–29 possession at football matches.
[45] *Bouch* [1983] Q.B. 246; *Elliott* (1984) 81 Cr.App.R. 115.
[46] *Downey* [1971] N.I. 224.
[47] *Fegan* (1971) 78 Cr.App.R. 189.
[48] [1957] 1 Q.B. 569, overruling *Dacey* (1939) 27 Cr.App.R. 86. See also *Stewart and Harris*
    (1959) Cr.App.R. 29; *McVitie* [1960] 2 Q.B. 483.
[49] (1971) 78 Cr.App.R. 189.

means for a lawful object and nothing else. That is, it is not enough for the possessor to show that he had no unlawful object; instead, he must be able to establish what his object actually is, and show that it is a lawful one. For example, if he possesses explosives for self defence, the prospect of an imminent attack must be real and not fanciful, and genuinely anticipated. Furthermore, it must be a threat which could not reasonably be countered by different means, such as calling for the assistance of the police. This might not be possible where the possessor is in an area where riots have occurred. In *Attorney-General's Refce. (No 2 of 1983)*[50] the defendant was acquitted by a jury after a direction on the availability of self-defence to a charge under section 4. After his shop had been looted during a riot, he made a number of petrol bombs for use in self-defence if necessary. Counsel for the Attorney-General argued that the defence should not have been left to the jury at all, since this would in effect allow a man to "write his own immunity" for acts done in preparation for violence to be used by him in the future. According to this argument, acts done in self defence may be done spontaneously, but not lawfully prepared for in advance. The court declined to accept the arguments, saying that if the defendant could satisfy the court on a balance of probabilities that his object was to protect himself or his family against an imminent apprehended attack, and to do so by means that he believed were no more than those reasonably necessary to meet the force used by his attackers, he could plead self defence.

The House of Lords has held that there is no defence where a person who is charged under section 4 asserts that he intends to export the explosive substance that he has manufactured, and that he therefore has a lawful object in the United Kingedom.[51] To escape conviction, he must also be able to show that he has a lawful purpose outside the United Kingdom. In view of the preceding subsection, which specifically limits the punishable intention to one of causing injury in the United Kingdom or Northern Ireland, this is perhaps questionable as an interpretation of Parliament's policy. But equally, since Parliament has said nothing about the matter in the latter subsection, it is open to the courts to reason that Parliament must have intended that for reasons of comity an intention to make explosives for an unlawful purpose beyond the jurisdiction should also be punishable in this country.

Burden of proof

13–24   In prosecutions under subsection (3)(b) the burden of proof is on the   13–24 prosecution throughout. It is otherwise under the section 4. Notwithstanding the seriousness of the offence created by that provision, the burden of proof is placed on the defendant to show that his possession or control was for a lawful object.[52] Before that obligation arose, the prosecutor would be required to prove that the defendant was in fact in possession or control of

---

[50] [1984] Q.B. 456.
[51] *Berry* [1985] A.C. 246.
[52] Section 4(1). In *Berry* [1985] A.C. 246, Lord Roskill thought it significant that the defendant and his spouse were given by s.4(2) the right to testify on their own behalves a right not generally available until the Criminal Evidence Act 1898.

the substance in question. Thereafter, the defendant must discharge his burden on the balance of probabilities.[53]

4. ALCOHOL AND FIREWORKS

Background

13–25   The phenomenon commonly referred to as "football hooliganism"[54]   **13–2**
prompted the creation of a cluster of offences controlling the possession of alcohol, and being drunk at a football match, or on the way to or therefrom. The offences are couched in considerable detail; the principal purpose of this part is to give an overview rather than a detailed appraisal of the relevant law, the text of which is to be found in Appendix 2.

     The White Paper's discussion of the phenomenon was truncated, to say the least, the Government apparently taking the view that specific legislation was necessary to cope with the problem.[55] This was rapidly forthcoming, and the Sporting Events (Control of Alcohol, Etc.) Act 1985, modelled upon Scottish legislation,[56] was speedily enacted.[57] Immediately after its enactment, however, the Act required amendment, principally to extend its provisions to persons travelling to matches on certain non-public transport, and these changes have been effected by the Public Order Act 1986.[58] Linked as it is to certain types of public or communal transport, the legislation is not a complete solution. There is nothing to prevent a group of "fans" from proceeding on foot and consuming alcohol on the way, arriving in the drunken condition that the legislators would wish to prevent.

The legislation outlined

13–26   The 1985 legislation prohibits public drunkenness[59] at, or in certain   **13–2(**
vehicles on the way to or from a prescribed football match.[60] In addition, the Act makes it a strict liability offence to possess alcohol on certain types of public transport, or knowingly to cause or permit a person to possess alcohol on these vehicles on the way to or from[61] designated matches, or to possess alcohol at such fixtures.

---

[53] *Berry* [1985] A.C. 246; *Att.-Gen.'s Refce. (No. 2 of 1983)* [1984] Q.B. 456.
[54] See 1–11 at n. 12. See 2–09 for a discussion of exclusion orders.
[55] White Paper, para. 6.20. It is fair to say that it had been the subject of a great many studies before the White Paper. They are listed by the Inquiry into Crowd Safety and Control at Sports Grounds, *Final Report* Cmnd. 9710 (1986).
[56] Criminal Justice (Scotland) Act 1980, Part V.
[57] See D. J. Birch, "Bottles, Booze and Bobbies" (1985) 149 J.P.N. 596.
[58] Section 40(1), Sched. 1.
[59] Whether such legislation is not otiose in view of the offences considered in 7–13 may be doubted. There is, however, an additional power of arrest; s.7(2).
[60] The legislation applies to all "designated sporting events" (defined in s.9(3)), but the government's intention was that only football matches should be covered initially. See Sports Grounds and Sporting Events (Designation) Order 1985, S.I. 1151. But the legislation is permissive, and could be extended to other sporting events; s.37, P.O.A. 1986. In Scotland, the equivalent Designation Order includes rugby internationals at Murrayfield.
[61] Within periods designated by the Act; s.9(4). As a rule of thumb, two hours before and one hour after the event.

The alcohol legislation is supplemented by two provisions having slightly different public order purposes. One prohibits the possession at a sports ground of articles and containers that are capable of being used as offensive weapons, but which it is particularly difficult to prove are intended to be used as such.[62] The other, which is aimed at reducing the fire risk at football stadiums, and which was added by the 1986 legislation, prohibits persons from taking fireworks and other items such as distress flares, fog signals and fumigation devices[63] into grounds. All of the offences created by the Act are triable summarily, and punishable with fines only.[64]

Extensive provision is made in the Act enabling magistrates to grant licences for the sale of alcohol[65] at sports grounds, and provision is also made for appeals from refusals.[66] The police are given a power to require a bar to be closed for a specified period, failure to comply with which amounts to an offence.[67]

Specified vehicles

3–27   The 1985 Act applied to public service vehicles[68] a term that includes   **13–27**
coaches and buses, and trains ("railway passenger vehicles"). Only those vehicles being used for the principal purpose of carrying passengers to or from designated sporting events are covered.[69] Scheduled services are therefore excluded, notwithstanding that at least part of the mischief at which the Act is aimed is the conduct of persons on public transport generally.[70] Specially chartered buses and trains were included. The 1986 Act added minibuses,[71] defined as non public service vehicles made or adapted for the carriage of eight or more persons, and being used for the purpose of carrying two or more passengers for the whole or part of a journey to a designated event. So a group of six or seven travelling in a large private car can possess and drink alcohol, whereas two or more in a minibus cannot. With such particularistic legislation, there are bound to be anomalies.

Alcohol offences

3–28   The offences in connection with alcohol are: **13–28**
1. being drunk on a designated vehicle,[72] or at or whilst trying to enter a designated sports ground, or in any area of a designated sports ground from which the play may be directly viewed[73];

---

[62] See 13–06.
[63] Section 2A.
[64] See s.8.
[65] Sections 3 and 4. Notwithstanding the title of the Act, the offences are defined in terms of "intoxicating liquor," a phrase that is to be interpreted in accordance with the Licensing Act 1964; s.9(7). This would exclude drugs and solvents.
[66] Section 5, extensively added to by the 1986 Act.
[67] Section 6(2).
[68] As defined by the Passenger Vehicles Act 1981, s.1(1); s.1(5).
[69] Section 1(1)(b).
[70] In the case of scheduled train services, the British Rail Byelaws, Art. 3 prohibits the possession of alcohol on designated services.
[71] Section 1A.
[72] Section 1(4) and 1A(4).
[73] Section 2(2).

2. possessing[74] alcohol on such a vehicle, or at or whilst trying to enter a designated ground[75];

3. knowingly[76] causing[77] or permitting[78] a person to possess alcohol on a specified vehicle. The latter offence can be committed by the operator, or the servant or agent of the operator.[79]

Possessing containers and fireworks

13–29   A person who without lawful authority possesses a designated article in   **13–2** or whilst trying to enter a designated ground or in any area of a ground from which the event may be directly viewed commits an offence.[80] The objects prohibited are defined by section 2(3) of the Sporting Events (Control of Alcohol etc.) Act 1985 as being

> "any article capable of causing injury to a person struck by it, being—
> (a) a bottle, can or other portable container (including such article when crushed or broken) which—
> (i) is for holding any drink, and
> (ii) is of a kind which, when empty, is normally discarded or returned to, or left to be recovered by, the supplier, or
> (b) part of an article falling within paragraph (a) above; but does not apply to anything that is for holding any medicinal product (within the meaning of the Medicines Act 1968).

This is amplified in the 1986 Act, section 2A(3) which prohibits smoke bombs;

> "any article or substance whose main purpose is the emission of a flare for purposes of illuminating or signalling (as opposed to igniting or heating) or the emission of smoke or a visible gas; and in particular it applies to distress flares, fog signals, and pellets and capsules intended to be used as fumigators or for testing pipes, but not to matches, cigarette lighters or heaters."

A hip-flask or thermos flask would not fall within the containers definition,

---

[74] Section 1(3) and 1A(3).

[75] Section 2(1).

[76] *Roper* v. *Taylor's Central Garages (Exeter) Ltd.* [1951] 2 T.L.R. 284; *Ross* v. *Moss* [1965] 2 Q.B. 396.

[77] The word "knowingly" in the section clearly governs "causes," which precludes argument about whether or not the section requires *mens rea*. It is possible that the courts would hold that this includes suspecting that the intoxicating liquor is possessed, in addition to having absolute knowledge that it is. It has been held that the use of the word "cause" denotes a requirement of proof of a positive act; *Price* v. *Cromack* [1975] 1 W.L.R. 988, 2 All E.R. 113.

[78] The courts have been anything but consistent in interpreting the expression "permits," but have generally held that it requires knowledge of the conduct or state of affairs permitted. A person can hardly be said to permit that of which he is not aware. In any event, the use of the word "knowingly" in ss.1(2) and 1A(2) would appear to be conclusive.

[79] Sections 1(2) and 1A(2).

[80] Section 2(3), 2A(3).

since it is not thrown away or returnable. This would still not permit the carrying of intoxicating liquor, which is expressly prohibited by the 1985 Act, section 2. The 1986 Act also extends the prohibitions to fireworks.[81]

Enforcement provisions

The Act confers powers to enter grounds and parts thereof, to search **13–30** designated vehicles and persons, and arrest where the police have reasonable grounds to believe that an offence is being or has been committed.[82] It is unclear whether the restrictions imposed by PACE apply,[83] so that, for example, the police would have to give reasons for a search in each individual case if challenged at the entrance to the ground, or when searching a vehicle. Since the police cannot genuinely have reasonable grounds for suspecting everybody who enters a football ground, it may still be necessary for them to rely on "consent" to search as a condition of admission to the ground.

---

[81] Section 2A(4). It may be noted that the Explosive Substances Act 1883 also forbids the possession of fireworks. It was perhaps though that the penalty was rather too severe for the conduct in question.

[82] Section 7.

[83] D. Birch questions whether there will automatically be sufficient grounds for reasonable suspicion to search vehicles; (1985) 149 J.P.N. 596.

CHAPTER 14

MISCELLANEOUS OFFENCES

1. QUASI-MILITARY ORGANISATIONS

Introduction

14–01   A number of offences proscribe setting up private armies, and the adop-   **14–0**
tion by civilians of military and quasi-military organisation and parapher-
nalia. Some of these offences such as the Unlawful Drilling Act 1819 wear
a dated air. Under the Unlawful Oaths Acts 1797 and 1812, for example, it
remains an offence punishable with imprisonment for five years, to admin-
ister, assist in or be present at the administration of an oath to disturb the
public peace or belong to an association formed for such a purpose. Law
reform in the area is long overdue.[1] Modern terrorists frequently adopt the
tactics of military organisation, even to the point of calling themselves
armies,[2] and special legislation has been devised to deal with them.

The Prevention of Terrorism (Temporary Provisions) Act 1984

14–02   Undoubtedly the most important modern provision aimed at para-mili-   **14–0:**
tary activities is the Prevention of Terrorism (Temporary Provisions) Act
1984, which as its title implies deals with problems generated by terrorism.[3]
This is supposed to be emergency legislation, first enacted in 1974,[4] and
modelled on the Northern Ireland (Emergency Provisions) Act 1973. It
creates a number of criminal offences associated with such conduct. These
include powers to proscribe organisations,[5] making membership of such an
organisation an offence.[6] It is also an offence to solicit or invite financial or

---

[1] In its Working Paper No. 72, *Treason, Sedition and Allied Offences* (1977) para. 95, the
Law Commission said that these Acts, which were "ripe for repeal or restatement in
modern form" could "more conveniently be dealt with in the context of offences against
public order." Homer, it would seem, may have nodded.

[2] Both organisations currently proscribed in Britain, below, n. 5 adopt this style. In 1969,
members of the Free Wales Army were prosecuted under the Public Order Act 1936, s.2.
See D. G. T. Williams, [1970] 28 Camb. L.J. 103.

[3] The expression "terrorism" is very broadly defined in s.14(1) to mean "the use of violence
for political ends, and includes any use of violence for the purpose of putting the public or
any section of the public in fear." Interpreted literally, this would appear to suggest that
many offences of riot, violent disorder or affray are also acts of terrorism. For prosecutions
under s.10 and 11, however, the acts of terrorism must be "connected with Northern Irish
affairs"; s.10(5). The C.L.R.C. has recommended that terrorism as such should not be
made a separate offence; 14th Report, para. 125.

[4] Although based on the Prevention of Violence (Temporary Provisions) Act 1939.

[5] Section 1(3), (4), sched. I. Currently, the Irish Republican Army and the Irish National
Liberation Army are proscribed.

[6] Section 1(1)(*a*) says "belongs or professes to belong."

other[7] support for such an organisation,[8] or to arrange or support a meeting, public or private, of three or more persons, in support of such an organisation.[9] Because of the seriousness of the offences,[10] knowledge is required that the organisation is proscribed.[11]

A further offence, that of displaying support for a proscribed organisation, is committed by the wearing in a public place[12] of any item of dress[13] or carrying or displaying any article (such as lapel badges) indicating membership or support of such an organisation.[14]

Two offences refer directly to acts of terrorism. Section 10 makes it an offence to contribute to acts of terrorism by soliciting money or other property for, or making it available for acts of terrorism, or accepting it, intending that it shall be applied for or in connection with the commission, preparation or instigation of acts of terrorism.[15] There is also a misprision-type offence, imposing in effect a legal duty to assist the police where a person has acquired information[16] about terrorism.[17] If the person knows or believes that the information might be of material assistance[18] in preventing the commission by another of an act of terrorism, or in securing the apprehension, prosecution or conviction of another[19] he commits an offence if he fails without reasonable excuse[20] to disclose that information to the proper authorities.[21]

In addition, the Act confers powers on the Home Secretary to make exclusion orders, and confers wide powers of arrest and detention upon the police. The operation and efficacy of this legislation has been the subject of

---

[7] This will include services such as food and accommodation.

[8] Section 1(1)(*b*).

[9] Section 1(1)(*c*).

[10] All the offences under s.1 are punishable with imprisonment for five years, s.1(2)(*b*).

[11] Smith and Hogan, at p. 794–5 take the view that the defendant here must be shown to "know [or be wilfully blind to] the facts which constitute the organisation a proscribed organisation but he need not know that it is by law proscribed." Given that there are only two such organisations, and that it must be a notorious matter that they are so proscribed, the problem may not one of great practical moment. But if a person could say that he was unaware that the organisation was proscribed, is he in principle making a mistake of law? In *Lim Chin Aik* [1963] A.C. 160, a man's unawareness that he was a prohibited immigrant was held to exculpate.

[12] Defined in s.2(3) as for offensive weapons. See 13–10.

[13] This goes wider than the uniforms offence under the Public Order Act 1936, s.1.

[14] Section 2(1).

[15] The offence is punishable with five years' imprisonment on trial on indictment; s.10(3)(*b*).

[16] Rumours and gossip do not count as "information" for these purposes; *Sykes* [1962] A.C. 528. The Act does not impose any obligation on the individual to make inquiries.

[17] Misprision was abolished by the Criminal Law Act 1967, s.5.

[18] A claim by a person that he did not realise that information that he had was of relevance will frequently carry credibility, since a person who does not have a full picture will be unaware of how what he does know relates to what is known to, say, the authorities. In *Wilde* [1960] Crim.L.R. 116, Slade J. said that what was required for misprision was "concealment of knowledge of the commission of a felony which a reasonable person would regard as sufficiently serious to report to the police."

[19] The privilege against self-incrimination means, obviously enough, that the defendant would not commit an offence by not informing against himself.

[20] Section 11. the offence is punishable with five years' imprisonment; s.11(2)(*b*).

[21] See 13–13.

three important recent reviews,[22] to which readers are referred for further detail.

Prohibition of quasi-military organisations

14–03   Section 2 of the Public Order Act 1936 provides as follows: 14–0

"(1) If the members or adherents of any association of persons, whether incorporated or not, are—

(a) organised or trained or equipped for the purpose of enabling them to be employed in usurping the functions of the police or of the armed forces of the Crown; or

(b) organised and trained or organised and equipped either for the purpose of enabling them to be employed for the use or display of physical force in promoting any political object, or in such mannner as to arouse reasonable apprehension that they are organised and either trained or equipped for that purpose;

then any person who takes part in the control or management of the association, or in so organising or training as aforesaid any members or adherents thereof, shall be guilty of an offence under this section:

Provided that in any proceedings against a person charged with the offence of taking part in the control or management of such an association as aforesaid it shall be a defence to that charge to prove that he neither consented to nor connived at the organisation, training, or equipment of members or adherents of the association in contravention of the provisions of this section."

"(6) Nothing in this section shall be construed as prohibiting the employment of a reasonable number of persons as stewards to assist in the preservation of order at any public meeting held upon private premises, or the making of arrangements for that purpose or the instruction of the persons to be so employed in their lawful duties as such stewards, or their being furnished with badges or other distinguishing signs."

The offences are punishable after trial on indictment with imprisonment for two years,[23] and no prosecutions may be brought without the consent of the Attorney-General.[24]

---

[22] *Review of the Operation of the Prevention of Terrorism (Temporary Provisions) Acts 1974 and 1976,* Cmnd. 7342, (1978) (chaired by Lord Shackleton); *Review of the Operation of the Prevention of Terrorism (Temporary Provisions) Act 1976* Cmnd. 8803, (1983) (chaired by Lord Jellicoe). Equivalent Northern Ireland legislation was examined in *The Review of the Operation of the Northern Ireland (Emergency Provisions) Act 1978* Cmnd. 9222, (1983) (chaired by Sir George Baker). See Clive Walker, *The Prevention of Terrorism in British Law* (1986); D. Bonner, *Emergency Powers in Peacetime* (1985), Chap. 4.

[23] Section 7, as amended by the Criminal Law Act 1977, s.28(2), 32(1). Where the trial is summary, the maximum penalty is six months'. In *Fell* [1974] Crim.L.R. 673, the defendant was sentenced to 12 years' when he was convicted of this offence and conspiracy to damage buildings.

[24] Section 2(2).

For a criminal provision, the section generates a large number of questions. What are the "functions of the police" for the purposes of section 2(1)(*b*)? They cannot be the same as the duties of the police as that phrase is understood for the purposes of the offence of obstruction.[25] Private security forces do not seem to fall within the scope of these offences, although such persons are not permitted to wear weapons.[26] Yet such organisations certainly duplicate the work of the police, as do vigilante groups, and neighbourhood watch schemes. The legal answer must be that none of these organisations seeks to "usurp" the functions of the police, in the sense of adversely performing or appropriating those functions.

Under section 2(1)(*b*), the question arises, what is a "political object"? Presumably the objectives of the Salvation Army are not considered as being "political" for these purposes, nor those of the scouting movement. In *Jordan and Tyndall*[27] it was held that for a prosecution under section 2(1)(*b*), there need be no evidence of specific training with a view to confronting particular opponents before a jury could conclude that the activities of the defendants gave rise to a reasonable apprehension of their training for the use or display of force. In a direction which the Court of Criminal Appeal described as being "lucid, accurate and beyond criticism," the trial judge directed that "reasonable apprehension" meant "an apprehension or fear which is based not upon undue timidity or excessive suspicion or still less prejudice but one which is founded on grounds which to you appear to be reasonable. Moreover the apprehension or fear must be reasonably held by a person who is aware of all the facts . . . You must try to put yourselves in a position of a sensible man who knew the whole of the facts."

The Unlawful Drilling Act 1819

14-04 Prosecutions for this offence are extremely rare,[28] and there have been   **14-04**
occasions in this century when they could have been brought but were not.[29] The Act, for all its antiquated language, remains law. It provides that a person commits an offence if he attends a meeting or assembly for the purpose of training or drilling or being trained or drilled in the use of arms, or the practice of military exercises, movements or "evolutions," without lawful authority from either the monarch, the Lieutenant or two Justices of the Peace. Unlike section 2, no political object need be established, the statute saying that such conduct is "dangerous to the peace and security of his Majesty's liege subjects and of his government." This would

---

[25] 10-02/3.
[26] *Spanner* [1973] Crim.L.R. 704. See Hilary Draper, *Private Police* (1978) for a description of the activities of some of the private security forces in existence.
[27] [1963] Crim.L.R. 124.
[28] The last reported prosecutions would appear to have been in *Hunt* (1848) 3 Cox C.C. 215; *Gogarty* (1849) 3 Cox 306.
[29] Bailey, Harris and Jones, *Civil Liberties: Cases and Materials* (1985). (2nd ed.), p. 130. It would seem that the defendants in *Jordan and Tyndall* [1963] Crim.L.R. 124 could have been prosecuted with this, but were in fact proceeded against under s.2.

make unlawful any attempt to set up a private army on some pretext such as assisting the government in a time of crisis if necessary. It has been suggested that the section might be repealed, apparently without replacement.[30] A better course, it is suggested, is that it should be amalgamated with section 2 and brought up to date.

Wearing uniforms

14–05   Wearing uniforms might be seen as symbolic of the introduction of force   **14–05** and violence into the political system, in place of reason and argument. As a result of the Fascist marches in the 1930s, in which the participants adopted black shirts by way of a uniform, Parliament enacted the Public Order Act 1936, section 1 of which reads:

> "1. Prohibition of uniforms in connection with political objects
>
> (1) Subject as hereinafter provided, any person who in any public place or at any public meeting wears uniform signifying his association with any political organisation or with the promotion of any political object shall be guilty of an offence:
> Provided that, if the chief officer of police is satisfied that the wearing of any such uniform as aforesaid on any ceremonial, anniversary, or other special occasion will not be likely to involve risk of public disorder, he may, with the consent of a Secretary of State, by order permit the wearing of such uniform on that occasion either absolutely or subject to such conditions as may be specified in the order."

No proceedings may be taken without the consent of the Attorney-General.[31]

A number of prosecutions were brought under the Act shortly after it was enacted.[32] Indeed, this section was contemporaneously regarded as being the principal purpose of the Act,[33] although section 5 ultimately had a great deal more impact on the control of public disorder. More recently, a prosecution was brought against members of the Irish Republican Army.[34] The appellants were convicted of the offence, when they had paraded at a funeral wearing black berets and dark glasses.

A person committing the offence may be arrested without warrant,[35] and the penalty on summary conviction is 3 months' imprisonment and a level 4 fine.[36]

---

[30] C. Walker, *The Prevention of Terrorism in British Law* (1986) at 241.

[31] Section 1(2).

[32] *Wood* (1937) 81 Sol.Jo. 108; *Charnley* (1937) 81 Sol.Jo. 108. See also (1937) Sol.Jo. 509; E. R. H. Ivamy, [1949] C.L.P. 184–187.

[33] J. Baker, *The Law of Political Uniforms, Public Meetings and Private Armies* (1937) says, "the most important provision in the new Act is, probably, the one which prohibits the wearing of political uniforms in public."

[34] *O'Moran* [1975] Q.B. 864. See now the Prevention of Terrorism (Temporary Provisions) Act 1984, s.2.

[35] Section 7(3).

[36] Section 7(2).

2. Trespass Offences

Background

14–06   Unlike many other jurisdictions,[37] the United Kingdom has no general   **14–06**
law of criminal trespass.[38] By tradition, trespass to land has been in the
province of the civil rather than the criminal law.[39] But it has historically
set its face against the forcible occupation, acquisition or dispossession of
land, principally on public order grounds. The Forcible Entry Acts
1381–1623 sought to force even the owner of land to go to the courts to
recover his land rather than resort to unbridled self-help. Offences created
by these obsolescent provisions were revived in the early 1970s to penalise
squatting and occupations by students and industrial workers,[40] and even
in one case persons gatecrashing a party.[41] The modern successors to these
repealed provisions, are the subject of this part. They are now to be found
in the Criminal Law Act 1977; using violence for the purpose of entry, as
supplemented by a trespass offence enacted by section 39 of the Public
Order Act 1986.

Using violence for the purposes of entry

14–07   Although trespass by a single individual did not constitute a criminal   **14–07**
offence, the House of Lords confirmed, in the context of the occupation of
an embassy by protesters, that conspiracy to trespass was an offence at
common law.[42] This was at variance with the stand taken by the Law Commission that the element of combination should not make criminal for
several that which was not criminal for one.[43] The result was that Parliament enacted two offences to replace conspiracy to trespass[44] and the

---

[37] As for example, the Trespass (Scotland) Act 1865; American Model Penal Code, s.221.2.
Trespass Act 1968, New Zealand; *Folley* v. *Police* (1975) 1 N.Z. recent Law (N.S.) 326;
Police v. *Cunard* [1975] 1 N.Z.L.R. 511.

[38] There are a number of specific trespass offences, frequently protecting public property; see
for example the Official Secrets Act 1911, s.1; *Chandler* [1964] A.C. 763 (trespassing on a
prohibited place). By-laws made under the Military Lands Act 1892, such as the R.A.F.
Greenham Common by-laws 1985, No. 485, and R.A.F. by-laws No. 1340 serve the same
purpose. The offences are catalogued by Glanville Williams, *Text* p. 915–916.

[39] See the Law Commission Working Paper No. 54, *Offences of Entering and Remaining on
Property* (1974); D. W. Elliott, "Offences of Entering and Remaining on Property" [1974]
Crim.L.R. 501; A. Dashwood and J. E. Trice, [1976] Crim.L.R. 500; Change was again
canvassed by the Home Office in a Consultation Paper, *Trespass on Residential Premises*
(1983), issued after a man entered the Queen's bedroom at Buckingham Palace. A Criminal Trespass Bill was published, but not ultimately passed by Parliament.

[40] *Robinson* [1971] 1 Q.B. 136; *Mountford* [1972] 1 Q.B. 28.

[41] *Brittain* [1972] 1 Q.B. 357.

[42] *Kamara* [1974] A.C. 104.

[43] Parliament gave effect to this policy in the Criminal Law Act 1977, s.5. See the *Report on
Conspiracy and Criminal Law Reform* (1976) Law Com. No. 76; A. M. Prichard, "Squatting—the Law and the Mythology" (1976) 40 Conv.(N.S.) 255; A. T. H. Smith, "Squatting
and Sitting-In" [1977] Crim.L.R. 139.

[44] The Act also creates, s.9, the offences of trespassing on a foreign mission, in compliance
with the U.K.'s treaty obligations under the Vienna Convention on Diplomatic Relations
signed in 1961, as set out in the schedule to the Diplomatic Privileges Act 1964, and trespassing with a weapon of offence; s.8.

ancient statutes and common law offences of forcible entry. Section 6 (1) of the Criminal Law Act 1977 creates a summary offence[45] as follows:

> "Subject to the following provisions of this section, any person who, without lawful authority, uses or threatens violence for the purpose of securing entry into any premises for himself or any other person is guilty of an offence, provided that—
> (a) there is someone present on those premises at the time who is opposed to the entry which the violence is intended to secure; and
> (b) the person using or threatening the violence knows that that is the case."

The offence carries a power of arrest without warrant by a constable in uniform of anybody whom he, with reasonable cause, suspects to be guilty of the offence,[46] and an associated power of entry and search.[47]

An exemption from liability is afforded for the "displaced residential occupier,"[48] since it was felt that no offence should be committed by the householder who, coming home from holiday, for example, discovered that his property had been made the subject of a squat. Otherwise, however, the policy behind the Act is that it should be no defence that the person using the force was entitled to possession of the premises in question.[49] The "main purpose of the offence," according to the Law Commission, is "to prevent breaches of the peace."[50] The resulting law is complicated,[51] and to date, there have been no reported prosecutions under it. One possibility for this is that the offence is defined in terms of using or threatening violence, so that either an assault or an offence under one of the public order offences carrying the same or even a higher penalty is almost invariably available, and in the light of this, prosecutors have preferred to steer clear of so complicated an offence.

Uses or threatens violence

14–08   The terminology in which the conduct constituting the offence is couched is very similar to that in the 1986 Act.[52] The offence is committed by the use or threat of violence for purpose of entry, rather than by entering forcibly, which was the essence of the previous law. Violence towards property as well as towards persons is included,[53] although missile throwing is not specifically referred to.[54] For prosecutors, the fact that the con- **14–08**

---

[45] The maximum penalty is six months' imprisonment, whereas the Law Commission had recommended an offence punishable with two years'.
[46] Section 6(6), which was preserved by PACE, s.26, sched. 2. See also ss.7(11), 8(4), 9(7) and 10(5), all of which are also preserved.
[47] Section 11.
[48] Section 6(3).
[49] Section 6(2).
[50] Para. 2.54.
[51] For an extended analysis and discussion of some of these difficulties, see A. M. Prichard, *Squatting* (1981), part 3.
[52] Sections 1(1), 2(1) and 3(1).
[53] Section 6(4)(*a*).
[54] *Cf.* 1986, s.8.

duct is expressed in alternative terms may give rise to problems of duplicity.[55]

The Law Commission offered a definition of violence which may be at variance with the ordinary meaning of that word. It said that "any application of force to the person" would be covered, although the term "carries a somewhat restricted meaning in relation to property."[56] It is suggested that these words must be seen in the context of an attempt to enter property. An application of force to the person would only be "violence" when accompanied by such an intention. The Commission also said that forcing a lock was not violence since it is "unlikely of itself to cause a breach of the peace." This appears to confuse conduct that is itself a breach of the peace (which forcing a lock is probably not)[57] and conduct that is likely to provoke such a breach. If a person on the premises is opposed to the entry and is prepared to use force to prevent it, a breach of the peace is quite likely to be occasioned by those seeking entry,[58] whatever method of entry they adopt.

Concern was expressed during the passage of the Act that it was susceptible of an interpretation making gathering in large numbers (and hence picketing, or sitting-in) punishable as such. It must be shown that there is a purpose of entry that is to be accomplished by violence and although it might be possible to infer such a purpose when there are large numbers, the inference is by no means an inevitable, or even, it might be said, an obvious one. Large numbers might very well congregate outside premises without any wish to enter them.

Premises

14–09   Parliament, on the advice of the Law Commission, was principally concerned with residential accommodation in framing the definition of the place in which the offence could be committed. As the Bill progressed, drafting was permitted to become more and more complex. The purpose of the actor must be to enter "premises," and there must be somebody on the premises who is opposed to the entry. "Premises" is defined[59] to mean

> "any building, any part of a building under separate occupation, any land ancillary to a building, the site comprising any building or buildings together with any land ancillary thereto."

At its broadest, therefore, any land on which a building is situated and is

---

[55] Contrary to rr. 12(1) and 100 of the Magistrates' Courts Rules 1981. The offence is not insulated from such objections as has been provided for the offences created by the Public Order Act 1986, ss.7(2) and 27(2). There are precedents for saying that even though the statute uses the expression disjunctively, only one offence is created; *Thompson* v. *Knights* [1947] K.B. 336 *Griffiths* v. *Freeman* [1970] 1 W.L.R. 659. But see *Bastin* v. *Davies* [1950] 2 K.B. 579.

[56] Para. 2.61.

[57] This is the distinction that McCullogh J. said in *Marsh* v. *Arscott* (1982) 75 Cr.App.R. 211 underlay s.5 of the Public Order Act 1936.

[58] This is on the assumption that, in resisting entry, the occupier is using lawful force, which cannot itself amount to a breach of the peace.

[59] Section 12(1)(*a*).

"ancillary to" the building can be the subject of the offence. If it were a person's home, the offence could start at the front gate. The location of need not necessarily be a residence, as is made plain by the further definition of building, which includes any "structure" other than a movable one, and any movable structure, vehicle or vessel designed or adapted for use for residential purposes. Any non-movable structure will suffice, whatever purposes it is currently being put to, so long as there is a person in it or on the land ancillary to it which the person is seeking to enter. An allotment, for example, on which a man has his shed, could be premises for these purposes. Even though the shed is movable, in the sense that it could be moved, it has not been made for shifting from one place to another, which is what appears to be contemplated by the section.[60] Where the building is movable, it must have been constructed or adapted for residential purposes before it can qualify. Oddly, therefore, it would seem that a large marquee is outside the protection conferred by the statute.[61] Gatecrashers at a party being held in such premises[62] are therefore not caught, although if they used or threatened violence to gain entry to an adjacent house or garden, they would be within the ambit of the section.

Person opposed to entry

14–10   Consistently with the public order rationale of the offence, there must be someone present on the premises at the time who is opposed to the entry which the violence is intended to secure.[63] It is unclear whether the person must be confronting the would-be entrants, making his opposition plain, or whether it would suffice that he was on the property and would object when he discovers what is occurring. It is submitted that the latter is the better interpretation. If a person is in fact on the premises and opposed, there is a risk to the peace, whether the risk materialises or otherwise. Conversely no offence is committed under this section if the entrant waits until the occupier of the house or other premises has left and then effects his entry.   **14–10**

Without lawful authority

14–11   The use of this expression here causes considerable doubts, since it is very unclear what rights the person entitled to possession enjoys.[64] Section 6(2) makes it plain that the right to possess is not, as such, lawful authority. It says: **14–11**

> "the fact that a person has any interest in or right to possession or occupation of any premises shall not . . . constitute lawful authority

---

[60] Smith and Hogan, at p. 755.

[61] Prichard, *op. cit.* at p. 81.

[62] One can use the expression easily enough of a marquee, but that is irrelevant for the purposes of interpreting the section, since the definition of "premises" is stipulative. It does not say that "premises includes" but that it "means."

[63] Section 6(1)(*a*).

[64] What rights has an owner to enter his own property to re-possess his own chattels, for example? See Prichard, *op. cit.* at p. 66.

for the use or threat of violence by him or anyone else for the purpose of securing his entry into those premises."

If, for example, workers were locked out of their place of employment by their fellow employees on strike, they could be guilty of this offence notwithstanding that they were entitled to be on the premises. The interests of public order are deemed to be such that they take precedence over the right to work in such circumstances, even though the strikers might themselves be committing an offence by what they are doing.[65]

It should be noticed that what is required is not simply authority to enter the premises in question, but authority to use force to do so. A bailiff might very well have authority to enter premises, but he will not invariably have authority to use force to permit him to do so. It would in such circumstances be lawful to resist his entry by the use of force,[66] and he might very well be guilty of this offence by using or threatening force when he had no such authority. Where he does have authority, because he is engaged in executing any process issued by the court in possession proceedings, it is an offence to resist him in the execution of his duties.[67]

It will be noted that the expression is not juxtaposed, as is often the case, with the other words "or excuse." This suggests that there must be an actual authority, and that a belief in authority, even if based on reasonable grounds, will not afford any defence.[68]

The mental element

14–12 Three elements go to make up the *mens rea* for this offence. It must be proved that the defendant acted with the purpose of entry for himself or another. Second, it must be established that he intentionally or recklessly used or threatened the violence for the purpose of doing so,[69] and third, the defendant must know that there is a person on the premises opposed to his entry. Where the offence takes the form of threats, there can be little doubt about the existence of this third element. If violence is actually used, it would not matter that the owner or occupier is unaware that the violence has occurred—the Act in effect creates a summary offence of trespass on residential premises. Forcing a window for the purposes of getting into a house for a sleep, or to talk to one of the occupants would be an offence under the section.

The use of the word "purpose" is not common in English criminal law, and its use here suggests that it is not enough that the defendant realises that, as a result of what he is doing, another will be permitted to enter. It connotes a state of mind akin to desire, as opposed merely to the realisation that something will almost certainly happen. Once the purpose of

14–12

---

[65] As in *Galt* v. *Philp* [1984] I.R.L.R. 156 (s.7, Conspiracy and Protection of Property Act 1875).
[66] *Vaughan* v. *McKenzie* [1969] Q.B. 558. For a useful compendium and discussion of powers of entry, see Richard Stone, *Entry, Search and Seizure* (1985). See also D. Feldman, *The Law Relating to Entry, Search and Seizure* (1986).
[67] Criminal Law Act 1977, s.10.
[68] *Barrett and Barrett* (1980) 72 Cr.App.R. 212.
[69] Unlike s.6 of the 1986 Act, the section is not explicit on this point, but it is suggested that the new Act merely states what is in any event implicit.

achieving entry has been established, nothing further need be shown. There need be no intention to occupy the premises, either permanently, or at all.[70]

It is not necessary that the person on the premises should actually oppose the entry, so long as he would have opposed it had he been aware of it. That being so, it must be sufficient that the defendant knows or suspects that somebody is on the premises, and realises that the person would probably object if he knew what was occurring. This will not ordinarily cause a prosecutor any difficulty, since most owners do object to the violent entry of their premises. But if a person mistakenly blunders into another's house,[71] no offence would be committed under this section.

The defence for a displaced residential occupier

14–13   Although as a general rule, it is no defence for the person seeking to   **14–1**
enter that he has a right to possession of the property,[72] an exception is made for the person who has been excluded from his own home. If he manages to gain entry without using violence, he would then be entitled to use force to repel the trespassers when they return, or to evict them.[73] If he cannot, and decides to resort to force, he commits no offence under this section in resorting to violence because of the specific exemption, although he can, apparently, be prosecuted with any other offences that he may have happened to commit, such as an assault or, it would seem, an affray.[74] If such a person used no more force than was reasonable[75] (pushing the door sufficiently hard to overcome the resistance of the trespassers), it would be a hard magistrate who would impose a severe sentence for such conduct.

The defence which must be proved is:

> "(a) that at the time of the alleged offence he or any other person on whose behalf he was acting was a displaced residential occupier of the premises in question: or
> (b) that part of the premises in question constitutes premises of which he or any other person on whose behalf he was acting was a displaced residential occupier and that the part of the premises to which he was seeking to secure entry constitutes an access of which he or, as the case may be, that other person is also a displaced residential occupier."

Who is a "displaced residential occupier" is further defined:

---

[70] Section 6(4)(*b*).

[71] As in *Jaggard* v. *Dickinson* [1981] Q.B. 527.

[72] Section 6(2).

[73] *Hussey* (1924) 18 Cr.App.R. 160. If the initial entry of the trespasser was peaceable, force may not be used by the displaced residential occupier until he has requested the trespasser to depart, and given the trespasser a chance to comply; *Robson* v. *Hallett* [1967] 2 Q.B. 939; *Kay* v. *Hibbert* [1977] Crim.L.R. 226.

[74] Above, Chap. 5.

[75] Unusually, it would seem that the protection afforded by the subsection is complete, in the sense that there is no requirement that the displaced residential occupier should use only reasonable force. That being so, it is perhaps as well that the immunity conferred is from liability under s.6 only.

"any person who was occupying any premises as a residence immediately before being excluded from occupation by anyone who entered those premises or any access to those premises, as a trespasser is a displaced residential occupier of the premises . . . so long as he continues to be excluded from occupation of the premises by the original trespasser or by any subsequent trepsasser."

The prolixity of it all is such that it is hardly to be wondered that prosecutors do not seem to employ the statute with any frequency.

A person who himself entered as a trespasser, or who derives his entitlement to occupy through such a person does not qualify as a displaced residential occupier.[76] Once he has been ousted, he commits an offence under this section if he seeks to re-enter violently. There must be entry as a trespasser,[77] so that a tenant who holds over after the tenancy has terminated is protected in the sense that he cannot commit this offence, even though he becomes a trespasser when his right to remain expires.

If a person is excluded from the use of part of his premises, he can be regarded as a displaced residential occupier for these purposes, and can employ violence to regain possession of the part from which he has been barred.

Criminal Law Act 1977, section 7: refusing to leave "premises"

14–14 An offence of very limited application under section 7 is committed by a person who:

"is on any premises as a trespasser after having entered as such . . . if he fails to leave those premises on being required to do so by or on behalf of—
(a) a displaced residential occupier of the premises; or
(b) an individual who is a protected intending occupier of the premises."

Where a person has been locked out of his own house by a trespasser, he can, as has been seen, use force to get it back if he chooses to do so.[78] If he chooses not to do so, he can summon the assistance of the police to help him[79] to eject the trespasser, who is committing an offence under section 7.

Who is a trespasser?

14–15 The concept of trespass is a civil law notion, encountered in the law of tort, although it is also met with increasing frequency in the criminal law.[80] Any entry on to the land or into the building of another, without authority express or implied, is a trespass, whether the person deliberately intrudes,

---

[76] Section 12(6).
[77] The meaning of "trespass" is considered in 14–15.
[78] 14–13. That is, he does not commit the offence under s.6. Does he commit other offences such as an assault? The point has not been decided, but it would appear that he does.
[79] The offence carries a power of arrest similar to that available under s.6.; s.7(11). The offence is triable summarily only, and punishable with six months' or a fine.
[80] Principally in the law of burglary, as to which see J. C. Smith, *The Law of Theft* (5th ed., 1986), at 167.

or is reckless or negligent about it. If the owner or some person authorised by the owner[81] consents, there is no trespass.[82] It is generally assumed that a person has an implied licence to enter the property of another to speak to him, or to deliver letters and similar purposes.[83] A member of the householder's family is capable of giving permission for these purposes,[84] although it would seem that if the permission is given in order to enable the entrant to steal, he is a trespasser.[85] Once the owner effectively withdraws his consent, the trespass begins, although for most purposes the person trespassing must be given a reasonable period of grace in which to conduct his retreat.[86] Entry by deceit amounts to trespass,[87] so that if a man entered while the householder was out, claiming to be a friend of the householder, he would be a trespasser. Even so, no offence would be committed under section 7 if he refused to leave when the householder returned, since the householder is not a displaced residential occupier, which bears the same meaning for the purposes of this offence as it does under section 6, previously considered.[88]

The protected intending occupier

14–16   Section 7 provides a definition in exhaustive detail of who is a protected intending occupier, and how he must establish a claim to be such. Essentially, he is a person who has just bought a house freehold, or on a 21-year lease, or who has managed to reach the top of the council housing list. If he can produce a document, signed by a J.P. (or in the case of a council house, from the authority) that authenticates his claim, he is a protected intending occupier, and could invoke the assistance of the police.[89] The section is of no use to a developer who has finished building his housing estate and discovers that the squatters have moved in before he has managed to sell.

Defences

14–17   The section affords the person who fails to comply with a request to leave the premises with several defences. It is a defence for the trespasser to prove that he believed that the person requiring him to leave was not himself a displaced residential occupier, or someone acting on such a per-

---

[81] In *Jones and Jones* v. *LLoyd* [1981] Crim.L.R. 341, it was held that a party guest has an implied permission from the host to invite the police to enter for the purposes of checking the story given by the guest.

[82] *Snook* v. *Mannion* [1982] Crim.L.R. 602.

[83] *Morris* v. *Beardmore* [1981] A.C. 446. The licence can be revoked, as it was in that case, in which event policemen were trespassers, and as such acting outside the execution of their duty.

[84] *Collins* [1973] 1 Q.B. 100.

[85] This would seem to be the best explanation of the decision in *Jones and Smith* [1976] 1 W.L.R. 672 3 All E.R. 54 where it was held that the son of the household committed burglary when he entered late one night with an accomplice and stole a television set.

[86] *Boyle* [1954] 1 Q.B. 292.

[87] *Robson* v. *Hallett* [1967] 2 Q.B. 939.

[88] 14–13.

[89] The documentation requirements are included because of police concerns that title to property is frequently a matter of debate. There is an air of unreality about them.

son's behalf.[90] It would seem that the belief need not be a reasonable one, although, since the burden is on the defendant, if it is not a reasonable one, it is likely to be disbelieved. There is also a defence if the premises form part of premises used for mainly non-residential purposes, and the trespasser was not on the part used primarily for residential purposes.[91] Finally, if the person claiming to be the displaced residential occupier is unable to produce the authenticating documentation when requested by the trespasser to do so, there is a defence,[92] even though the trespasser knows that he is thwarting a displaced residential occupier.

Public Order Act 1986, section 39; refusing to leave non-residential property

-18 In the years immediately preceding the Act, several incidents occurred **14–18** involving large incidents of mass trespass, committed by groups such as Hell's Angels, "hippies" and similar groups.[93] While the Bill was in Parliament, a group styling itself the Peace Convoy trespassed on the Somerset farm of a Mr Attwell with a cluster of vehicles of over 100 buses, trucks, caravans and other assorted vehicles.[94] This triggered the introduction in the House of Lords of the clause that eventually became section 39, ineptly referred to in the marginal note as "power to direct trespassers to leave land." The section in truth creates a limited form of trespass offence. It is somewhat more widely drafted than would strictly have been necessary to penalise the mischief that inspired its creation, since it can be committed by a group of two people only. It will have no application to residential squatting, nor to industrial disputes where there is no intention to reside on the premises occupied.

It is questionable whether such an offence was really necessary. Civil proceedings are available to expel the trespassers,[95] and the conduct complained of must almost invariably amount to criminal damage,[96] which is arrestable, an offence under section 5 of the Public Order Act 1986 which is arrestable under certain circumstances, or a cause of a breach of the peace where the occupier indicates that it is his intention to remove the

---

[90] Section 7(6).

[91] Section 6(7).

[92] Section 6(8)(a).

[93] For a somewhat partisan account of this and the other recent trespass legislation, see P. Vincent-Jones, "Private Property and Public Order: The Hippy Convoy and Criminal Trespass" (1986) 13 Jo. Law and Soc. 343.

[94] It is an offence under the Road Traffic Act 1972 s.36 to drive a motor vehicle without lawful authority off a road upon any common land, moor land or other land of whatsoever description, subject to an exception for the purpose of parking.

[95] Under R.S.C. Order 113 in the High Court, and Ord. 24 in the County Court. Since January 12, 1987, the procedure has been streamlined even further following a review by the Lord Chancellor, *Summary Proceedings for Possession of Land* (1986). It may be noted that the offence cannot be committed until the actors have actually trespassed, and the law of attempt cannot be used to prevent the trespassers from entering in the first place, since the police cannot issue directions until the trespass has taken place.

[96] *Gayford* v. *Chouler* [1898] 1 Q.B. 316 (damage to the grass); *Salisbury Mags Court, ex p. Mastin* (1986) 84 Cr.App.R. 249.

trespassers by force if necessary.[97] Against this, however, it may be said that the civil remedy is neither quick enough, nor cheap, even if costs are awarded against the wrongdoers.

The offence defined

14–19   Section 39(2) reads as follows: 14

> "If a person knowing that such a direction[98] has been given which applies to him—
>> (a) fails to leave the land as soon as reasonably practicable, or
>> (b) having left again enters the land as a trespasser within the period of three months beginning with the day on which the direction was given,
>
> he commits an offence and is liable on summary conviction to imprisonment for a term not exceeding three months or a fine not exceeding level 4 on the standard scale, or both."

The power to issue directions

14–20   Before the senior police officer can issue an instruction to the tres-   14
passers, there are a number of stringent conditions that must be satisfied. There are in total four such conditions. The first two must be satisfied in every case, and the latter are in the alternative. They are: (1) that the senior police officer[99] must reasonably[1] believe that two or more people have entered land as trespassers,[2] and are present there with the intention of residing there for a period; and (2) that reasonable steps have been taken by or on behalf of the occupier to ask them to leave. Unless both of these conditions have been satisfied, the directions cannot validly be issued, and no offence can be committed. If those two conditions are established, however, the senior police officer must reasonably believe; either (3) that any of the trespassers had caused damage to property on the land, or used threatening, abusive or insulting language towards the occupier, a member of his family or his agent; or (4) that those persons have between them brought 12 or more vehicles on to the land.

Two points may be noted. In property law generally, land includes buildings forming part of the land. The Act alters this rule, providing that land does not include buildings unless they are agricultural buildings[3] or sched-

---

[97] 10–03.

[98] The circumstances in which the police may issue a direction are considered in the following section.

[99] The "senior police officer" is defined to mean "the most senior in rank of the police officers present at the scene"; s.39(5) *cf.* s.14(2)(*b*).

[1] The use of the word "reasonably" means that the decision of the officer concerned is subject to judicial review, and would require him to be able to point to reasons for arriving at the decision that he did in fact reach.

[2] The meaning of "trespassers" is considered in 14–15.

[3] S.39(5), as defined by the General Rate Act 1967, s.26(4). Essentially non-dwellings, used solely in connection with agricultural operations.

uled monuments.[4] Furthermore, land forming part of a highway[5] (bridle-ways, etc.) is not included.

3. HARASSMENT OF TENANTS

Outline of offences

21   To prevent unscrupulous landlords from evading the protection afforded   **14–21**
to tenants by the Rent Act 1977,[6] the Protection From Eviction Act 1977
creates two overlapping offences of (1) unlawful eviction or attempted
eviction, section 1(2), and (2) harassment of a residential occupier, section
1(3).[7]

The Act has been described as "the modern expression of the timeless
social sentiment which abhors the forcible eviction of a man and family
from their home."[8] As such, the existence of the legislation performs an
important symbolic function, stating what society is not prepared to tolerate. Its implementation is in practice more problematic. Although the Act
has very clear public order connotations, its principal aim is to protect a
person's right to remain in his own house, which is essentially a property
right. The determination of such rights is often a complex question of the
civil law, especially where these are complicated by disputed factual issues.
Furthermore, there is no specific power of arrest associated with the
offences. That being so, the police are reluctant to intervene in disputes[9] as
to entitlement to reside in the property further than is necessary to preserve public order.[10] Since a person who is in fact in occupation generally
has a right to remain unless there is a court order otherwise, it may be possible to collect evidence after the event so that the harm actually done by
the defendant is properly labelled by a prosecution under the Act rather
than under one of the public order offences.

---

[4] S.39(5), as defined by the Ancient Monuments and Archaeological Areas Act 1979. Essentially, this is done by way of schedule compiled by the Secretary of State for the Environ-
ment.

[5] 11–01.

[6] As the long title indicates, the Act consolidates s.16 of the Rent Act 1957 and Part III of the
Rent Act 1965.

[7] A. Arden and M. Partington, *Quiet Enjoyment* (2nd ed., 1985); *Housing Law* (1983)
p. 852; A. J. Ashworth, "Protecting the Home Through the Criminal Law" (1979) J. Social
Welfare Law 76.

[8] K. Gray and P. Symes, *Real Property and Real People* (1981) 469. For a study of the evolu-
tion of the legislation see D. Nelken, *The Limits of the Legal Process. A Study of Landlords, Law and Crime* (1983).

[9] According to Arden and Partington, "as a matter of policy, the police do not prosecute in
cases of unlawful eviction and harassment"; *op. cit.* at 72. The decision whether or not to
bring a prosecution is now a matter for the Crown Prosecution Service rather than the
police, and a decision by the police not under any circumstances to pursue clear cases of
such harassment or eviction would be susceptible to a challenge by way of judicial review,
under the principles in *R.* v. *M.P.C. ex p. Blackburn* [1968] 2 Q.B. 118. Prosecutions are in
practice initiated by local authorities.

[10] The new offences under ss.4 and 5 of the 1986 Act are likely to be of significance and relevance here.

Protection from eviction

14–22 Section 1(2) of the Act provides as follows:

> "If any person unlawfully deprives the residential occupier of any premises of his occupation of the premises or any part thereof or attempts to do do he shall be guilty of an offence unless he proves that he believed, and had reasonable cause to believe, that the residential occupier had ceased to reside in the premises."

The offence is triable either way, punishable on summary conviction by a level 5 fine or 6 months' imprisonment, and on conviction on indictment by an unlimited fine and/or two years' imprisonment.[11] A sentence is likely to be severe where the victim of the offence is single and elderly, or has been in residence for a long period, or where the harassment is prolonged.[12]

Any person may be guilty of the offence. Although it is to be found in the successor to the Rent Acts, the offence is not confined to commission any landlords, but may be committed by others on his behalf,[13] or by a neighbour or a creditor with purposes of his own to serve. Persons who harass neighbours from racist motives might very well be guilty of one or other of these offences if they act with the intention of driving out their victims.[14] Nor need the eviction be forcible; it is enough if the locks are changed while the occupier is absent in such a way as to bring his occupation of the premises to an end.

The residential occupier

14–23 Protection is afforded not just to tenants *stricto sensu*, but to any "residential occupier," defined in section 1(1) to mean:

> "a person occupying the premises as a residence, whether under a contract or by virtue of any enactment or rule of law giving him the right to remain in occupation or restricting the right of any other person to recover possession of the premises."

---

[11] S.1(4) as amended by the Criminal Justice Act 1982, s.46.

[12] As to the liability of companies, see s.1(6) which provides that where an offence under this section is committed by a company, with the consent or connivance of, or attributable to any neglect on the part of any director, manager, secretary or other similar officer of the company or person purporting to act in such a capacity, both the company and the individual can be guilty; *A.M.K. (Property Management) Ltd.* [1985] Crim.L.R. 600. The provision is strictly unnecessary, since such persons would almost certainly be guilty as a matter of general principle, but it serves to make it plain that it is not possible to shelter behind the corporate veil.

[13] The possibility is canvassed in the Third Report from the House of Commons Home Affairs Committee, *Racial Attacks and Harassment* Session 1985–86 (1986) H.C. 409, Recommendation 14. And see the Government reply, *Racial Attacks and Harassment* Cmnd. 45, (1986). Curiously, though, the section does not appear to apply where the occupier is a freeholder.

[14] In *Bokhari* (1974) 59 Cr.App.R. 303, a total sentence of two years' imprisonment on three counts of harassment imposed on a defendant of previous good character was upheld on appeal. And see *Spratt* [1978] Crim.L.R. 102 (six months) and *Brennan* [1979] Crim.L.R. 603 (custodial sentence correct in principle).

This will include not only contractual and statutory tenants and sub-tenants, but contractual licensees and service occupants. Squatting tres-passers generally have no rights under legislation or at common law, and it would not therefore seem to be an offence under this section for the owner or his agent to evict the squatter, who cannot be a residential occupier. It may nevertheless be an offence to use violence to enter for the purposes of evicting such persons unless the person exercising the force is himself a dis-placed residential occupier.[15] The question whether this amounts to a restriction on the right to recover possession of the premises has not been decided, but it would be most odd if this were the case, since it would catch the true owner who waited until the squatter had gone out for the day and then entered peacefully and changed the locks.

The mere fact that a person may be a trespasser does not conclude the issue, since section 3(1) of the Act provides that eviction without due process is prohibited in certain circumstances. When these circumstances arise (as when a tenancy comes to an end, for example), the tenant who holds over is a "residential occupier" within the terms of section 1(1). In *Blankley*[16] it was held that the supposed victim was not a tenant but a contractual licensee who had been given reasonable notice to quit. He therefore enjoyed no right to remain, and a verdict of not guilty was directed. A different result would be arrived at today, since the licensee continues to enjoy the status of "residential occupier" until a court order is obtained. It is questionable whether the offence can be committed against persons such as members of the residential occupier's household,[17] since none of these technically has a right to remain. Deserted spouses have, since 1981, had a right to remain by virtue of the Matrimonial Homes Act 1983, section 1. Since they are in occupation by virtue of an enactment, they are residential occupiers within the meaning of the section.

"Premises"

4-24 Unlike the Criminal Law Act 1977,[18] the Act does not define "premises" **14-24**
any further. It seems probable that "premises" includes any premises inhabited by a residential occupier, not simply a dwelling house.[19] The occupancy of a single room is sufficient, and it would be enough that the tenant or occupier was excluded from any part of his premises, such as a lavatory.[20]

---

[15] Criminal Law Act 1977 s.6(1)(3).

[16] [1979] Crim.L.R. 166 and 248 (a prosecution under the previous legislation).

[17] *Cp.* s.1(3), which makes specific reference to harassment of the members of the residential occupier's household.

[18] Criminal Law Act 1977, s.12(2).

[19] *Norton* v. *Knowles* [1969] 1 Q.B. 572. The word "premises" would probably be sufficiently wide to protect caravan dwellers, at least where the caravan has become immobile and part of the land on which it rests. But in any case, such persons are offered express statutory protection: Caravan Sites Act 1968 s.3. See *Hooper* v. *Eaglestone* [1977] L.G.R. 308, 34 P. & C.R. 311, [1978] Crim.L.R. 761.

[20] *Thurrock U.D.C.* v. *Shina* (1972) P. and C. R. 205.

Unlawfully deprives . . . of his occupation

14–25   It is not sufficient that the occupier is temporarily excluded from his   **14–2!**
premises; he must actually be deprived of his occupation. But it is sufficient
that he has been deprived only temporarily. The cases make the point
plainer. In *Yuthiwattana*[21] the victim lost the key to the front door of the
house in which he occupied a separate bed-sitter, and the owners of the
premises declined to give him a replacement. This forced him to rely on
being granted admission to the front door of the house, and on one
occasion he was refused admission to the house, in consequence of which
he was forced to sleep elsewhere for the evening. This event formed the
basis of the prosecution for unlawful eviction. The conviction was quashed
on appeal on the grounds that the conduct was insufficient to constitute a
deprivation of occupation. In interpreting the Act, the court looked at the
heading to Part I of the Act, which refers to "unlawful eviction and harassment." The word "eviction" does not appear in the definition of the
offence, but the court took the view that this indicated the sort of mischief
at which the statute was aimed, so that the unlawful deprivation of occupation must have the character of an eviction. That would have been a sufficient basis on which to allow the appeal, but the court went on to say,
obiter that the decision of the Court of Appeal in *Commissioner of Crown
Lands* v. *Page*[22] that "eviction" carries a requirement of permanence does
not apply in this context. The deprivation did not have to be permanent,
but it had to be more than the temporary deprivation of a person who was
still in occupation. A later decision confirms that the test is not so much the
length of time for which a person is in fact excluded, but rather whether or
not the deprivation was designed to evict the occupier.[23] An analogy with
theft might be helpful. If a person appropriates property, and at that time
he has the intention permanently to deprive the other of his property, it is
immaterial if he later repents and replaces the property. Similarly, if under
the Act, a landlord is persuaded to re-admit the person he has evicted, this
may be grounds for leniency at the sentencing stage, but does not preclude
the commission of the offence itself.

The question whether the conduct amounted to an attempt appears not
to have been considered in *Yuthiwattana*. Unusually and unnecessarily[24]
the attempt to evict is specifically included within the section.[25]

It remains to be decided whether deprivation is a single or a continuing
act. The problem arises in a case like *Davidson-Acres*,[26] where the landlord changed the locks on the front door of a house in which the complain-
ants were tenants. They had left some belongings behind when they went
away for a period of ten days, but the landlord claimed that he believed

---

[21] (1984) 80 Cr.App.R. 55.
[22] [1960] 2 Q.B. 274.
[23] *Costelloe* v. *London Borough of Camden* [1986] Crim.L.R. 249.
[24] Unnecessarily, because by virtue of the Criminal Law Act 1967, s.6(3), the attempt is
    included within the allegation of the full offence.
[25] Which reinforces the overlap between this offence, and the offence of harassment con-
    sidered *infra*.
[26] [1980] Crim.L.R. 50.

these to have been rubbish. His defence was that he believed that they had left permanently. The trial judge directed the jury to convict, taking the view that at the time when the deprived couple returned, the defendant had no reasonable grounds for his asserted belief that the couple had departed for good.[27] In quashing the conviction, the court said that the question of intention should have been left to the jury. The court appears also to have said that the question of whether the deprivation occurred when the locks were changed as opposed to when the couple returned was also a matter for the jury. This would seem to be a matter of the proper constuction of the statute, for the court to decide rather than a matter for the jury in each case. Although the point is far from simple, it is suggested that the better view is that the offence is not a continuing one.[28] If the landlord does an act that effectively evicts the occupier, and does so with an innocent belief, he should not thereafter be guilty of an offence when he learns the truth. He may, in the meantime, for example, have re-let the premises in question, and would not then be in a position to let the occupiers back in.

The deprivation must also be unlawful. This means that, where it is lawful for a landlord to regain possession without first obtaining a court order, he cannot commit the offence under section 1(2).

The intent

14–26   Section 1(2) is framed in a way that would make it appear that the section is one that imposes strict liability, since it provides the defence that the person who deprives "proves that he believed, and had reasonable cause to believe, that the residential occupier had ceased to reside in the premises." No intention to evict is expressly called for by the Act. But in *Davidson-Acres*[29] it was held that it must be shown that the landlord acts with the intention of forcing the residential occupier to leave. This necessarily includes knowledge on the part of the landlord that the person with whom he is dealing is a residential occupier, and any mistake as to the status of the occupier will prevent a conviction. In the civil case of *McCall* v. *Abelesz*[30] where services were originally discontinued without the landlord's knowledge, his subsequent hopeful inertia was held by Ormrod L.J. to be insufficient material to warrant an inference of *mens rea* being drawn. It is also a defence for the defendant to be able to show on a balance of probabilities that he did not realise on reasonable grounds that the person evicted was a residential occupier.[31]

---

[27] The mental element is further considered in 14–28.

[28] In *Ahmad* (1986) 84 Cr.App.R. 64, it was held that the offence of harassment cannot be committed by an omission, the decision of the House of Lords in *Miller* [1983] 2 A.C. 161 being of no application.

[29] [1980] Crim.L.R. 50. According to A. J. Ashworth, the courts should hold that intention or recklessness is required as a matter of general principle; *op. cit.* n. 7 at p. 78.

[30] [1976] Q.B. 585.

[31] Section 1(2) 14–22. Technically, the defence is required to prove this, and the magistrates should not accede to a submission of no case at the end of the prosecutor's case until they have heard what the defendant has to say. *Westminster City Council* v. *McGraw and Marks* (1974) 232 E.G. 712.

Harassment

14–27

"(3) If any person with intent to cause the residential occupier of any   **14–27**
premises

    (a) to give up the occupation of the premises or any part
       thereof; or

    (b) to refrain from exercising any right or pursuing any rem-
       edy in respect of the premises or part thereof

does acts calculated to interfere with the peace or comfort of the residential occupier or members of his household, or persistently withdraws or witholds services reasonably required for the occupation of
the premises as a residence, he shall be guilty of an offence."

The section creates two different forms of offence, being; (1) acts calculated to interfere wth peace or comfort, and (2) persistent witholding of
services. It is unclear whether this creates two separate offences, but arguably it does so.[32]

Threats of violence and acts of damage clearly constitute harassment of
the kind indicated in the subsection.[33] Apart from that, it is not wholly
clear what constitutes an act "calculated to interfere with peace or comfort," but typically it might include banging on the ceiling of shared accommodation, slamming doors, verbal abuse, removing possessions and
entering the premises without permission. "Calculated to interfere" means
no more than likely to so interfere,[34] but because of the mental element of
the offence,[35] it is necessary to distinguish deliberate harassment from irritation caused where people have to live in multiple occupation of accommodation not originally designed for that purpose. Harassment normally
consists of a series of acts spreading over a period, and the section specifies
that it is committed by a person who "does acts." Whether a single incident
can amount to harassment has not been authoritatively decided. An "act"
may in truth be a number or series of acts, depending on the point of view
of the person describing the incident in question.

It has been held, however, that the offence cannot be committed by way
of omission. In *Ahmad*[36] the defendant had done a number of acts intending to repair the property in question. Unknown to him, his tenant
objected. It was held that he committed no offence in failing to repair
immediately the damage that had been done. The acts that had been done
were done innocently, and a failure to make them good could not be
brought within the terminology of "does acts."

Where the offence is committed by witholding services, the conduct

---

[32] See 2–05.
[33] Such threats probably amount to substantive offences in their own right; assault and criminal damage respectively. Behaviour of this kind may also give rise to civil liability. In *Drane*
v. *Evangelou* [1978] 1 W.L.R. 455, 2 All E.R. 437, where the landlord evicted the occupier
and declined to admit him for a period of ten weeks in defiance of a court order to do otherwise, exemplary damages were awarded "to teach a wrongdoer that tort does not pay."
[34] *A.M.K. Property Management Ltd.* [1985] Crim.L.R. 600.
[35] Below 14–28.
[36] (1986) 84 Cr.App.R. 64.

must be persistent[37] and may take the form of deliberate failure to supply essential services such as gas, electricity or water, at least where the landlord is under an obligation to provide these services. If there is no such obligation, the mere failure on the landlord's part to pay the bills so that the gas or electricity is cut off should not on principle amount to an offence, even though he knows that the supplying authority will not deal directly with the occupier. To hold otherwise would be to permit the criminal law to create an obligation where the civil law holds that there is none.[38] Persistently offering payment as an inducement to quit or superior alternative accommodation may constitute harassment if done in a sufficiently objectionable manner.

The mental element in harassment

14–28 On several occasions, the courts have held that the offence under section 1(3) requires an intention to evict.[39] This means that the defendant must either desire that the occupier should leave, or realise that, as a result of what he is doing, it is virtually certain that he or she will be forced to quit. **14–28**

Where a defence is advanced to the effect that the defendant did not realise that his conduct was annoying, or that he believed that the victim was no longer or had never been a residential occupier, a question arises as to whether the belief must be based on reasonable grounds. It has been argued that there must be such grounds,[40] by analogy with the requirements under the previous subsection, and in *Phekoo*[41] the Court of Appeal *obiter* that in general this was the law, saying that the decision of the House of Lords in *Morgan*[42] was confined to decisions on the mental element in the law of rape. A differently composed court has subsequently said[43] that this view of *Morgan* is incorrect, and that any mistake that prevents the formation of *mens rea* must exculpate, whether it is based upon reasonable grounds or not. The law would seem to be that as to the occupier's status as a residential occupier a mistake need not be based on reasonable grounds. A claim by the person alleged to be guilty of the harassment that he was unaware of the effects that his conduct was having need not be reasonable

---

[37] Persistence should, where relevant, be expressly alleged in the information or indictment; *Westminster City Council* v. *Peart* [1968] L.G.R. 561, Crim.L.R. 504; *Abrol* [1972] Crim.L.R. 318.

[38] Lord Denning has suggested, *obiter*, that there may be an implied obligation to supply gas and electricity through the meters so long as the tenancy continues even in cases where there is no express undertaking: *McCall* v. *Abelesz* [1976] Q.B. 585. The law is not clear, but the weight of authority is against this view. See "Power Implied" (1976) 40 The Conveyancer (N.S.) 169. See generally, J. T. Farrand, *The Rent Act 1977, The Protection From Eviction Act 1977*, (1978) Chap. 43.

[39] *A.M.K. (Property Management) Ltd.* [1985] Crim.L.R. 600; *Schon* v. *Camden London Borough Council* (1986) 279 E.G. 859.

[40] N. Yell, 145 J.P. 664.

[41] [1981] 1 W.L.R. 1117, 3 All E.R. 84, 73 Cr.App. R. 107; M. Wasik, (1981) Conveyancer 377.

[42] [1976] A.C. 182.

[43] *Kimber* [1983] 1 W.L.R. 1118, 3 All E.R. 316, 77 Cr.App.R. 225.

either, although in practice it is likely to founder on the scepticism of the jury.

4. CONTAMINATION OF GOODS FOR SALE

Background

14–29   One of the methods increasingly used by groups of protesters to cause   **14–29**
harm to those with whose practices they disagree is by employing what
might be called consumer sabotage. Actually contaminating goods, or
threatening to do so, or claiming already to have done so can cause a
retailer considerable loss, since he may very well have to destroy all suspect
stock. Although not a great social menace in this country, there were four
such incidents in the summer of 1986.[44] Depending on the strategy that he
adopts, it is generally possible to proceed against a person who behaves in
such a way under such offences as the Criminal Damage Act 1971,[45] or for
blackmail under the Theft Act 1968.[46] If the person had contaminated
food with a lethal substance, he could be prosecuted under one of the
offences against the person,[47] and, if he succeeded in killing, with homicide. The existing law did not unequivocally and specifically condemn
such conduct,[48] and it was felt that a new offence was necessary, so that
when Parliament reconvened after the summer recess, a clause was
added to the Bill aimed directly at such conduct. The connections of such
conduct with public order are slight, especially when it is motivated by
the intention to extort. But the public alarm and anxiety which it is the
aim of the saboteurs to excite can be seen as a threat to public confidence of the kind undermined by the public order offences considered
earlier. The view may be expressed that it is in principle better that Parliament should address itself specifically to new forms of wrongdoing,
and condemn them (with an indication as to the appropriate penalty),
rather than leave it to the courts and prosecutors to amend the existing
law to make do, if necessary.

---

[44] S. Watson, "Consumer Terrorism" (1987) 137 New L.J. 84. In fact, most of the incidents
were prompted by the intention to extort money rather than out of concern for animal welfare, although one of the blackmailers claimed to have links with an animal rights group.

[45] Under s.1(2), it is an offence to damage one's own property if the actor intends or is reckless towards the endangering of life. It would be no defence, therefore, that he had bought
the item before tampering with it. Even if he could say that he hoped that nobody would be
injured, because he intended to give a warning so that the stocks would be destroyed, there
might well be an obvious risk of injury, in which case he would be reckless as that
expression was interpreted in *Caldwell* [1982] A.C. 341.

[46] Section 21. The offence can be committed by a person who acts with intent to cause loss to
another. A person who threatened that he would act unless a company changed its practices might have been able to argue that his conditional intention was insufficient, or that he
never intended to carry out his threat.

[47] Specifically, ss.23 and 24; administering poisons or noxious things.

[48] There was nothing in either the Medicines Act 1968 or the Food Act 1984 covering such
conduct.

The offences outlined

14–30   Section 38 creates in effect three new offences, which may be summarised as follows: (1) contaminating goods[49] or appearing to do so[50]; (2) threatening to contaminate, or claiming to have done so[51]; (3) being in possession of goods with a view to committing offences under (1).[52] The mental element which must be established is the intention either: **14–30**

(a) of causing public alarm or anxiety; or
(b) of causing injury to[53] members of the public consuming or using the goods; or
(c) of causing economic loss to any person by reason of the goods being shunned by members of the public; or
(d) of causing economic loss to any person by reason of steps taken to avoid any such alarm or anxiety, injury or loss

The offences are regarded as serious ones, being triable either way, and carrying a penalty of 10 years' imprisonment on conviction on indictment.[54]

There is an exemption for the person who reports in good faith that acts have been done by another which might be offences under the Act.[56] This is not strictly a defence, since the section says that the Act "does not include" such a person. At the very most, therefore, a person who does claim to have been acting from public-spirited motives has an evidentiary burden to carry.

---

[49] "Goods" are defined in s.38(5) to "include substances whether natural or manufactured and whether or not incorporated in or mixed with other goods." This will include foodstuffs, which appear to be the usual target, and other items such as car accessories and spare parts.
[50] Section 38(1).
[51] Section 38(2).
[52] Section 38(3).
[53] Injury would include, presumably, death.
[54] Section 38(4). On summary prosecution, the penalties are six months and the maximum fine; *ibid.*

APPENDIX 1

Public Order Act 1986

(1986 c. 64)

ARRANGEMENT OF SECTIONS

PART I

New Offences

PART II

Processions and Assemblies

PART III

Racial Hatred

Meaning of "racial hatred"

Acts intended or likely to stir up racial hatred

Racially inflammatory material

Public Order Act 1986

(1986 c. 64)

An Act to abolish the common law offences of riot, rout, unlawful assembly and affray and certain statutory offences relating to public order; to create new offences relating to public order; to control public processions and assemblies; to control the stirring up of racial hatred; to provide for the exclusion of certain offenders from sporting events; to create a new offence relating to the contamination of or interference with goods; to confer power to direct certain trespassers to leave land; to amend section 7 of the Conspiracy and Protection of Property Act 1875, section 1 of the Prevention of Crime Act 1953, Part V of the Criminal Justice (Scotland) Act 1980 and the Sporting Events (Control of Alcohol etc.) Act 1985; to repeal certain obsolete or unnecessary enactments; and for connected purposes.

[7th November 1986]

BE IT ENACTED by the Queen's most Excellent Majesty, by and with the advice and consent of the Lords Spiritual and Temporal, and Commons, in this present Parliament assembled, and by the authority of the same, as follows:—

PART I

New Offences

Riot.

A–01   (1) Where 12 or more persons who are present together use or threaten   A–01
unlawful violence for a common purpose and the conduct of them (taken together) is such as would cause a person of reasonable firmness present at the scene to fear for his personal safety, each of the persons using unlawful violence for the common purpose is guilty of riot.

(2) It is immaterial whether or not the 12 or more use or threaten unlawful violence simultaneously.

(3) The common purpose may be inferred from conduct.

(4) No person of reasonable firmness need actually be, or be likely to be, present at the scene.

(5) Riot may be committed in private as well as in public places.

(6) A person guilty of riot is liable on conviction on indictment to imprisonment for a term not exceeding ten years or a fine or both.

Violent disorder.

A–02   (1) Where 3 or more persons who are present together use or threaten   A–02
unlawful violence and the conduct of them (taken together) is such as would cause a person of reasonable firmness present at the scene to fear for his personal safety, each of the persons using or threatening unlawful violence is guilty of violent disorder.

(2) It is immaterial whether or not the 3 or more use or threaten unlawful violence simultaneously.

(3) No person of reasonable firmness need actually be, or be likely to be, present at the scene.

(4) Violent disorder may be committed in private as well as in public places.

(5) A person guilty of violent disorder is liable on conviction on indictment to imprisonment for a term not exceeding 5 years or a fine or both, or on summary conviction to imprisonment for a term not exceeding 6 months or a fine not exceeding the statutory maximum or both.

Affray.

A–03   (1) A person is guilty of affray if he uses or threatens unlawful violence   A–03
towards another and his conduct is such as would cause a person of reasonable firmness present at the scene to fear for his personal safety.

(2) Where 2 or more persons use or threaten the unlawful violence, it is the conduct of them taken together that must be considered for the purposes of subsection (1).

(3) For the purposes of this section a threat cannot be made by the use of words alone.

(4) No person of reasonable firmness need actually be, or be likely to be, present at the scene.

(5) Affray may be committed in private as well as in public places.

(6) A constable may arrest without warrant anyone he reasonably suspects is committing affray.

(7) A person guilty of affray is liable on conviction on indictment to imprisonment for a term not exceeding 3 years or a fine or both, or on summary conviction to imprisonment for a term not exceeding 6 months or a fine not exceeding the statutory maximum or both.

Fear or provocation of violence.

A–04   (1) A person is guilty of an offence if he—   A–04

- (*a*) uses towards another person threatening, abusive or insulting words or behaviour, or
- (*b*) distributes or displays to another person any writing, sign or other visible representation which is threatening, abusive or insulting,

with intent to cause that person to believe that immediate unlawful violence will be used against him or another by any person, or to provoke the immediate use of unlawful violence by that person or another, or whereby that person is likely to believe that such violence will be used or it is likely that such violence will be provoked.

(2) An offence under this section may be committed in a public or a private place, except that no offence is committed where the words or behaviour are used, or the writing, sign or other visible representation is distributed or displayed, by a person inside a dwelling and the other person is also inside that or another dwelling.

(3) A constable may arrest without warrant anyone he reasonably suspects is committing an offence under this section.

(4) A person guilty of an offence under this section is liable on summary conviction to imprisonment for a term not exceeding 6 months or a fine not exceeding level 5 on the standard scale or both.

Harassment, alarm or distress.

A–05   (1) A person is guilty of an offence if he—   A–05

- (*a*) uses threatening, abusive or insulting words or behaviour, or disorderly behaviour, or
- (*b*) displays any writing, sign or other visible representation which is threatening, abusive or insulting,

within the hearing or sight of a person likely to be caused harassment, alarm or distress thereby.

(2) An offence under this section may be committed in a public or a private place, except that no offence is committed where the words or behaviour are used, or the writing, sign or other visible representation is displayed, by a person inside a dwelling and the other person is also inside that or another dwelling.

(3) It is a defence for the accused to prove—

    (*a*) that he had no reason to believe that there was any person within hearing or sight who was likely to be caused harassment, alarm or distress, or

    (*b*) that he was inside a dwelling and had no reason to believe that the words or behaviour used, or the writing, sign or other visible representation displayed, would be heard or seen by a person outside that or any other dwelling, or

    (*c*) that his conduct was reasonable.

(4) A constable may arrest a person without warrant if—

    (*a*) he engages in offensive conduct which the constable warns him to stop, and

    (*b*) he engages in further offensive conduct immediately or shortly after the warning.

(5) In subsection (4) "offensive conduct" means conduct the constable reasonably suspects to constitute an offence under this section, and the conduct mentioned in paragraph (*a*) and the further conduct need not be of the same nature.

(6) A person guilty of an offence under this section is liable on summary conviction to a fine not exceeding level 3 on the standard scale.

Mental element: miscellaneous.

A–06   (1) A person is guilty of riot only if he intends to use violence or is aware   A–06 that his conduct may be violent.

(2) A person is guilty of violent disorder or affray only if he intends to use or threaten violence or is aware that his conduct may be violent or threaten violence.

(3) A person is guilty of an offence under section 4 only if he intends his words or behaviour, or the writing, sign or other visible representation, to be threatening, abusive or insulting, or is aware that it may be threatening, abusive or insulting.

(4) A person is guilty of an offence under section 5 only if he intends his words or behaviour, or the writing, sign or other visible representation, to be threatening, abusive or insulting, or is aware that it may be threatening, abusive or insulting or (as the case may be) he intends his behaviour to be or is aware that it may be disorderly.

(5) For the purposes of this section a person whose awareness is impaired by intoxication shall be taken to be aware of that of which he would be aware if not intoxicated, unless he shows either that his intoxication was not self-induced or that it was caused solely by the taking or administration of a substance in the course of medical treatment.

(6) In subsection (5) "intoxication" means any intoxication, whether caused by drink, drugs or other means, or by a combination of means.

(7) Subsections (1) and (2) do not affect the determination for the purposes of riot or violent disorder of the number of persons who use or threaten violence.

Procedure: miscellaneous.

–07   (1) No prosecution for an offence of riot or incitement to riot may be   A–07 instituted except by or with the consent of the Director of Public Prosecutions.

(2) For the purposes of the rules against charging more than one offence in the same count or information, each of sections 1 to 5 creates one offence.

(3) If on the trial on indictment of a person charged with violent disorder or affray the jury find him not guilty of the offence charged, they may (without prejudice to section 6(3) of the Criminal Law Act 1967) find him guilty of an offence under section 4.

(4) The Crown Court has the same powers and duties in relation to a person who is by virtue of subsection (3) convicted before it of an offence under section 4 as a magistrates' court would have on convicting him of the offence.

Interpretation.

–08   In this Part—   A–08

"dwelling" means any structure or part of a structure occupied as a person's home or as other living accommodation (whether the occupation is separate or shared with others) but does not include any part not so occupied, and for this purpose "structure" includes a tent, caravan, vehicle, vessel or other temporary or movable structure;

"violence" means any violent conduct, so that—

(*a*) except in the context of affray, it includes violent conduct towards property as well as violent conduct towards persons, and

(*b*) it is not restricted to conduct causing or intended to cause injury or damage but includes any other violent conduct (for example, throwing at or towards a person a missile of a kind capable of causing injury which does not hit or falls short)

Offences abolished.

A–09   (1) The common law offences of riot, rout, unlawful assembly and affray   A–09 are abolished.

(2) The offences under the following enactments are abolished—

(*a*) section 1 of the Tumultuous Petitioning Act 1661 (presentation of petition to monarch or Parliament accompanied by excessive number of persons),

(*b*) section 1 of the Shipping Offences Act 1793 (interference with operation of vessel by persons riotously assembled),

(*c*) section 23 of the Seditious Meetings Act 1817 (prohibition of certain meetings within one mile of Westminster Hall when Parliament sitting), and

(*d*) section 5 of the Public Order Act 1936 (conduct conducive to
breach of the peace).

Construction of other instruments.

A–10   (1) In the Riot (Damages) Act 1886 and in section 515 of the Merchant   A–
Shipping Act 1894 (compensation for riot damage) "riotous" and "riotously" shall be construed in accordance with section 1 above.

(2) In Schedule 1 to the Marine Insurance Act 1906 (form and rules for
the construction of certain insurance policies) "rioters" in rule 8 and "riot"
in rule 10 shall, in the application of the rules to any policy taking effect on
or after the coming into force of this section, be construed in accordance
with section 1 above unless a different intention appears.

(3) "Riot" and cognate expressions in any enactment in force before the
coming into force of this section (other than the enactments mentioned in
subsections (1) and (2) above) shall be construed in accordance with section 1 above if they would have been construed in accordance with the
common law offence of riot apart from this Part.

(4) Subject to subsections (1) to (3) above and unless a different intention appears, nothing in this Part affects the meaning of "riot" or any cognate expressions in any enactment in force, or other instrument taking
effect, before the coming into force of this section.

PART II

Processions and Assemblies

Advance notice of public processions.

A–11   (1) Written notice shall be given in accordance with this section of any   A–
proposal to hold a public procession intended—

(*a*) to demonstrate support for or opposition to the views or actions
of any person or body of persons,

(*b*) to publicise a cause or campaign, or

(*c*) to mark or commemorate an event,

unless it is not reasonably practicable to give any advance notice of the procession.

(2) Subsection (1) does not apply where the procession is one commonly
or customarily held in the police area (or areas) in which it is proposed to
be held or is a funeral procession organised by a funeral director acting in
the normal course of his business.

(3) The notice must specify the date when it is intended to hold the procession, the time when it is intended to start it, its proposed route, and the
name and address of the person (or of one of the persons) proposing to
organise it.

(4) Notice must be delivered to a police station—

    (*a*) in the police area in which it is proposed the procession will start, or

    (*b*) where it is proposed the procession will start in Scotland and cross into England, in the first police area in England on the proposed route.

(5) If delivered not less than 6 clear days before the date when the procession is intended to be held, the notice may be delivered by post by the recorded delivery service; but section 7 of the Interpretation Act 1978 (under which a document sent by post is deemed to have been served when posted and to have been delivered in the ordinary course of post) does not apply.

(6) If not delivered in accordance with subsection (5), the notice must be delivered by hand not less than 6 clear days before the date when the procession is intended to be held or, if that is not reasonably practicable, as soon as delivery is reasonably practicable.

(7) Where a public procession is held, each of the persons organising it is guilty of an offence if—

    (*a*) the requirements of this section as to notice have not been satisfied, or

    (*b*) the date when it is held, the time when it starts, or its route, differs from the date, time or route specified in the notice.

(8) It is a defence for the accused to prove that he did not know of, and neither suspected nor had reason to suspect, the failure to satisfy the requirements or (as the case may be) the difference of date, time or route.

(9) To the extent that the alleged offence turns on a difference of date, time or route, it is a defence for the accused to prove that the difference arose from circumstances beyond his control or from something done with the agreement of a police officer or by his direction.

(10) A person guilty of an offence under subsection (7) is liable on summary conviction to a fine not exceeding level 3 on the standard scale.

Imposing conditions on public processions.

-12   (1) If the senior police officer, having regard to the time or place at   **A–12** which and the circumstances in which any public procession is being held or is intended to be held and to its route or proposed route, reasonably believes that—

    (*a*) it may result in serious public disorder, serious damage to property or serious disruption to the life of the community, or

    (*b*) the purpose of the persons organising it is the intimidation of others with a view to compelling them to not to do an act they have a right to do, or to do an act they have a right not to do,

he may give directions imposing on the persons organising or taking part in the procession such conditions as appear to him necessary to prevent such disorder, damage, disruption or intimidation, including conditions as to the route of the procession or prohibiting it from entering any public place specified in the directions.

(2) In subsection (1) "the senior police officer" means—

(a) in relation to a procession being held, or to a procession intended to be held in a case where persons are assembling with a view to taking part in it, the most senior in rank of the police officers present at the scene, and

(b) in relation to a procession intended to be held in a case where paragraph (a) does not apply, the chief officer of police.

(3) A direction given by a chief officer of police by virtue of subsection (2)(b) shall be given in writing.

(4) A person who organises a public procession and knowing fails to comply with a condition imposed under this section is guilty of an offence, but it is a defence for him to prove that the failure arose from circumstances beyond his control.

(5) A person who takes part in a public procession and knowingly fails to comply with a condition imposed under this section is guilty of an offence, but it is a defence for him to prove that the failure arose from circumstances beyond his control.

(6) A person who incites another to commit an offence under subsection (5) is guilty of an offence.

(7) A constable in uniform may arrest without warrant anyone he reasonably suspects is committing an offence under subsection (4), (5) or (6).

(8) A person guilty of an offence under subsection (4) is liable on summary conviction to imprisonment for a term not exceeding 3 months or a fine not exceeding level 4 on the standard scale or both.

(9) A person guilty of an offence under subsection (5) is liable on summary conviction to a fine not exceeding level 3 on the standard scale.

(10) A person guilty of an offence under subsection (6) is liable on summary conviction to imprisonment for a term not exceeding 3 months or a fine not exceeding level 4 on the standard scale or both, notwithstanding section 45(3) of the Magistrates' Courts Act 1980 (inciter liable to same penalty as incited).

(11) In Scotland this section applies only in relation to a procession being held, and to a procession intended to be held in a case where persons are assembling with a view to taking part in it.

Prohibiting public processions.

A–13   (1) If at any time the chief officer of police reasonably believes that,   **A–1.** because of particular circumstances existing in any district or part of a district, the powers under section 12 will not be sufficient to prevent the holding of public processions in that district or part from resulting in serious public disorder, he shall apply to the council of the district for an order prohibiting for such period not exceeding 3 months as may be specified in the application the holding of all public processions (or of any class of public procession so specified) in the district or part concerned.

(2) On receiving such an application, a council may with the consent of the Secretary of State make an order either in the terms of the application or with such modifications as may be approved by the Secretary of State.

(3) Subsection (1) does not apply in the City of London or the metropolitan police district.

(4) If at any time the Commissioner of Police for the City of London or the Commissioner of Police of the Metropolis reasonably believes that, because of particular circumstances existing in his police area or part of it, the powers under section 12 will not be sufficient to prevent the holding of public processions in that area or part from resulting in serious public disorder, he may with the consent of the Secretary of State make an order prohibiting for such period not exceeding 3 months as may be specified in the order the holding of all public processions (or of any class of public procession so specified) in the area or part concerned.

(5) An order made under this section may be revoked or varied by a subsequent order made in the same way, that is, in accordance with subsections (1) and (2) or subsection (4), as the case may be.

(6) Any order under this section shall, if not made in writing, be recorded in writing as soon as practicable after being made.

(7) A person who organises a public procession the holding of which he knows is prohibited by virtue of an order under this section is guilty of an offence.

(8) A person who takes part in a public procession the holding of which he knows is prohibited by virtue of an order under this section is guilty of an offence.

(9) A person who incites another to commit an offence under subsection (8) is guilty of an offence.

(10) A constable in uniform may arrest without warrant anyone he reasonably suspects is committing an offence under subsection (7), (8) or (9).

(11) A person guilty of an offence under subsection (7) is liable on summary conviction to imprisonment for a term not exceeding 3 months or a fine not exceeding level 4 on the standard scale or both.

(12) A person guilty of an offence under subsection (8) is liable on summary conviction to a fine not exceeding level 3 on the standard scale.

(13) A person guilty of an offence under subsection (9) is liable on summary conviction to imprisonment for a term not exceeding 3 months or a fine not exceeding level 4 on the standard scale or both, notwithstanding section 45(3) of the Magistrates' Courts Act 1980.

Imposing conditions on public assemblies.

A–14   (1) If the senior police officer, having regard to the time or place at which and the circumstances in which any public assembly is being held or is intended to be held, reasonably believes that—   **A–14**

> (a) it may result in serious public disorder, serious damage to property or serious disruption to the life of the community, or
>
> (b) the purpose of the persons organising it is the intimidation of

others with a view to compelling them not to do an act they have a right to do, or to do an act they have a right not to do,

he may give directions imposing on the persons organising or taking part in the assembly such conditions as to the place at which the assembly may be (or continue to be) held, its maximum duration, or the maximum number of persons who may constitute it, as appear to him necessary to prevent such disorder, damage, disruption or intimidation.

(2) In subsection (1) "the senior police officer" means—

> (*a*) in relation to an assembly being held, the most senior in rank of the police officers present at the scene, and
>
> (*b*) in relation to an assembly intended to be held, the chief officer of police.

(3) A direction given by a chief officer of police by virtue of subsection (2)(*b*) shall be given in writing.

(4) A person who organises a public assembly and knowingly fails to comply with a condition imposed under this section is guilty of an offence, but it is a defence for him to prove that the failure arose from circumstances beyond his control.

(5) A person who takes part in a public assembly and knowingly fails to comply with a condition imposed under this section is guilty of an offence, but it is a defence for him to prove that the failure arose from circumstances beyond his control.

(6) A person who incites another to commit an offence under subsection (5) is guilty of an offence.

(7) A constable in uniform may arrest without warrant anyone he reasonably suspects is committing an offence under subsection (4), (5) or (6).

(8) A person guilty of an offence under subsection (4) is liable on summary conviction to imprisonment for a term not exceeding 3 months or a fine not exceeding level 4 on the standard scale or both.

(9) A person guilty of an offence under subsection (4) is liable on summary conviction to a fine not exceeding level 3 on the standard scale.

(10) A person guilty of an offence under subsection (6) is liable on summary conviction to imprisonment for a term not exceeding 3 months or a fine not exceeding level 4 on the standard scale or both, notwithstanding section 45(3) of the Magistrates' Courts Act 1980.

Delegation.

A–15   (1) The chief officer of police may delegate, to such extent and subject to   **A–15** such conditions as he may specify, any of his functions under sections 12 to 14 to a deputy or assistant chief constable; and references in those sections to the person delegating shall be construed accordingly.

(2) Subsection (1) shall have effect in the City of London and the metropolitan police district as if "a deputy or assistant chief constable" read "an assistant commissioner of police."

Interpretation

A–16   In this Part—   A–16

"the City of London" means the City as defined for the purposes of
the Acts relating to the City of London police;

"the metropolitan police district" means that district as defined in section 76 of the London Government Act 1963;

"public assembly" means an assembly of 20 or more persons in a public place which is wholly or partly open to the air;

"public place" means—

(*a*)any highway, or in Scotland any road within the meaning of
the Roads (Scotland) Act 1984, and

(*b*)any place to which at the material time the public or any section of the public has access, on payment or otherwise, as of
right or by virtue of express or implied permission;

"public procession" means a procession in a public place.

PART III

Racial Hatred

Meaning of "racial hatred"

Meaning of "racial hatred".

A–17   In this Part "racial hatred" means hatred against a group of persons in   A–17
Great Britain defined by reference to colour, race, nationality (including
citizenship) or ethnic or national origins.

Acts intended or likely to stir up racial hatred

Use of words or behaviour or display of written material.

A–18   (1) A person who uses threatening, abusive or insulting words or behav-   A–18
iour, or displays any written material which is threatening, abusive or
insulting, is guilty of an offence if—

(*a*) he intends thereby to stir up racial hatred, or

(*b*) having regard to all the circumstances racial hatred is likely to be
stirred up thereby.

(2) An offence under this section may be committed in a public or a private place, except that no offence is committed where the words or behaviour are used, or the written material is displayed, by a person inside a
dwelling and are not heard or seen except by other persons in that or
another dwelling.

(3) A constable may arrest without warrant anyone he reasonably suspects is committing an offence under this section.

(4) In proceedings for an offence under this section it is a defence for the
accused to prove that he was inside a dwelling and had no reason to believe
that the words or behaviour used, or the written material displayed, would
be heard or seen by a person outside that or any other dwelling.

(5) A person who is not shown to have intended to stir up racial hatred is

not guilty of an offence under this section if he did not intend his words or behaviour, or the written material, to be, and was not aware that it might be, threatening, abusive or insulting.

(6) This section does not apply to words or behaviour used, or written material displayed, solely for the purpose of being included in a programme broadcast or included in a cable programme service.

Publishing or distributing written material.

A–19   (1) A person who publishes or distributes written material which is   A–19
threatening, abusive or insulting is guilty of an offence if—

    (*a*) he intends thereby to stir up racial hatred, or

    (*b*) having regard to all the circumstances racial hatred is likely to be stirred up thereby.

(2) In proceedings for an offence under this section it is a defence for an accused who is not shown to have intended to stir up racial hatred to prove that he was not aware of the content of the material and did not suspect, and had no reason to suspect, that it was threatening, abusive or insulting.

(3) References in this Part to the publication or distribution of written material are to its publication or distribution to the public or a section of the public.

Public performance of play.

A–20   (1) If a public performance of a play is given which involves the use of   A–20
threatening, abusive or insulting words or behaviour, any person who presents or directs the performance is guilty of an offence if—

    (*a*) he intends thereby to stir up racial hatred, or

    (*b*) having regard to all the circumstances (and, in particular, taking the performance as a whole) racial hatred is likely to be stirred up thereby.

(2) If a person presenting or directing the performance is not shown to have intended to stir up racial hatred, it is a defence for him to prove—

    (*a*) that he did not know and had no reason to suspect that the performance would involve the use of the offending words or behaviour, or

    (*b*) that he did not know and had no reason to suspect that the offending words or behaviour were threatening, abusive, or insulting, or

    (*c*) that he did not know and had no reason to suspect that the circumstances in which the performance would be given would be such that racial hatred would be likely to be stirred up.

(3) This section does not apply to a performance given solely or primarily for one or more of the following purposes—

    (*a*) rehearsal,

    (*b*) making a recording of the performance, or

(*c*) enabling the performance to be broadcast or included in a cable programme service;

but if it is proved that the performance was attended by persons other than those directly connected with the giving of the performance or the doing in relation to it of the things mentioned in paragraph (*b*) or (*c*), the performance shall, unless the contrary is shown, be taken not to have been given solely or primarily for the purposes mentioned above.

(4) For the purposes of this section—

    (*a*) a person shall not be treated as presenting a performance of a play by reason only of his taking part in it as a performer,

    (*b*) a person taking part as a performer in a performance directed by another shall be treated as a person who directed the performance if without reasonable excuse he performs otherwise in accordance with that person's direction, and

    (*c*) a person shall be taken to have directed a performance of a play given under his direction notwithstanding that he was not present during the performance;

and a person shall not be treated as aiding or abetting the commission of an offence under this section by reason only of his taking part in a performance as a performer.

(5) In this section "play" and "public performance" have the same meaning as in the Theatres Act 1968.

(6) The following provisions of the Theatres Act 1968 apply in relation to an offence under this section as they apply to an offence under section 2 of that Act –

    section 9 (script as evidence of what was performed),

    section 10 (power to make copies of script),

    section 15 (powers of entry and inspection).

Distributing, showing or playing a recording.

A–21   (1) A person who distributes, or shows or plays, a recording of visual   **A–21** images or sounds which are threatening, abusive or insulting is guilty of an offence if—

    (*a*) he intends thereby to stir up racial hatred, or

    (*b*) having regard to all the circumstances racial hatred is likely to be stirred up thereby.

(2) In this Part "recording" means any record from which visual images or sounds may, by any means, be reproduced; and references to the distribution, showing or playing of a recording are to its distribution, showing or playing to the public or a section of the public.

(3) In proceedings for an offence under this section it is a defence for an accused who is not shown to have intended to stir up racial hatred to prove that he was not aware of the content of the recording and did not suspect, and had no reason to suspect, that it was threatening, abusive or insulting.

(4) This section does not apply to the showing or playing of a recording

solely for the purpose of enabling the recording to be broadcast or included in a cable programme service.

Broadcasting or including programme in cable programme service.

A–22   (1) If a programme involving threatening, abusive or insulting visual   A–22
images or sounds is broadcast, or included in a cable programme service, each of the persons mentioned in subsection (2) is guilty of an offence if—

> (*a*) he intends thereby to stir up racial hatred, or
> (*b*) having regard to all the circumstances racial hatred is likely to be stirred up thereby.

(2) The persons are—

> (*a*) the person providing the broadcasting or cable programme service,
> (*b*) any person by whom the programme is produced or directed, and
> (*c*) any person by whom offending words or behaviour are used.

(3) If the person providing the service, or a person by whom the programme was produced or directed, is not shown to have intended to stir up racial hatred, it is a defence for him to prove that—

> (*a*) he did not know and had no reason to suspect that the programme would involve the offending material, and
> (*b*) having regard to the circumstances in which the programme was broadcast, or included in a cable programme service, it was not reasonable practicable for him to secure the removal of the material.

(4) It is a defence for a person by whom the programme was produced or directed who is not shown to have intended to stir up racial hatred to prove that he did not know and had no reason to suspect—

> (*a*) that the programme would be broadcast or included in a cable programme service, or
> (*b*) that the circumstances in which the programme would be broadcast or so included would be such that racial hatred would be likely to be stirred up.

(5) It is a defence for a person by whom offending words or behaviour were used and who is not shown to have intended to stir up racial hatred to prove that he did not know and had no reason to suspect—

> (*a*) that a programme involving the use of the offending material would be broadcast or included in a cable programme service, or
> (*b*) that the circumstances in which a programme involving the use of the offending material would be broadcast, or so included, or in which a programme broadcast or so included would involve the use of the offending material, would be such that racial hatred would be likely to be stirred up.

(6) A person who is not shown to have intended to stir up racial hatred is not guilty of an offence under this section if he did not know, and had no

reason to suspect, that the offending material was threatening, abusive or insulting.

(7) This section does not apply—

(a) to the broadcasting of a programme by the British Broadcasting Corporation or the Independent Broadcasting Authority, or

(b) to the inclusion of a programme in a cable programme service by the reception and immediate re-transmission of a broadcast by either of those authorities.

(8) The following provisions of the Cable and Broadcasting Act 1984 apply to an offence under this section as they apply to a "relevant offence" as defined in section 33(2) of that Act—

section 33 (scripts as evidence),

section 34 (power to make copies of scripts and records),

section 35 (availability of visual and sound records);

and sections 33 and 34 of that Act apply to an offence under this section in connection with the broadcasting of a programme as they apply to an offence in connection with the inclusion of a programme in a cable programme service.

Racially inflammatory material

Possession of racially inflammatory material.

(1) A person who has in his possession written material which is threat- ening, abusive or insulting, or a recording of visual images or sounds which are threatening, abusive or insulting, with a view to—

(a) in the case of written material, its being displayed, published, distributed, broadcast or included in a cable programme service, whether by himself or another, or

(b) in the case of a recording, its being distributed, shown, played, broadcast or included in a cable programme service, whether by himself or another,

is guilty of an offence if he intends racial hatred to be stirred up thereby or, having regard to all the circumstances, racial hatred is likely to be stirred up thereby.

(2) For this purpose regard shall be had to such display, publication, distribution, showing, playing, broadcasting or inclusion in a cable programme service as he has, or it may reasonably be inferred that he has, in view.

(3) In proceedings for an offence under this section it is a defence for an accused who is not shown to have intended to stir up racial hatred to prove that he was not aware of the content of the written material or recording and did not suspect, and had no reason to suspect, that it was threatening, abusive or insulting.

(4) This section does not apply to the possession of written material or a recording by or on behalf of the British Broadcasting Corporation or the Independent Broadcasting Authority or with a view to its being broadcast by either of those authorities.

Powers of entry and search.

A–24   (1) If in England and Wales a justice of the peace is satisfied by infor-   A–24 mation on oath laid by a constable that there are reasonable grounds for suspecting that a person has possession of written material or a recording in contravention of section 23, the justice may issue a warrant under his hand authorising any constable to enter and search the premises where it is suspected the material or recording is situated.

(2) If in Scotland a sheriff or justice of the peace is satisfied by evidence on oath that there are reasonable grounds for suspecting that a person has possession of written material or a recording in contravention of section 23, the sheriff or justice may issue a warrant authorising any constable to enter and search the premises where it is suspected the material or recording is situated.

(3) A constable entering or searching premises in pursuance of a warrant issued under this section may use reasonable force if necessary.

(4) In this section "premises" means any place and, in particular, includes—

    (*a*) any vehicle, vessel, aircraft or hovercraft,
    (*b*) any offshore installation as defined in section 1(3)(*b*) of the Mineral Workings (Offshore Installations) Act 1971, and
    (*c*) any tent or movable structure.

Power to order forfeiture.

A–25   (1) A court by or before which a person is convicted of—   A–25

    (*a*) an offence under section 18 relating to the display of written material, or
    (*b*) an offence under section 19, 21 or 23,

shall order to be forfeited any written material or recording produced to the court and shown to its satisfaction to be written material or a recording to which the offence relates.

(2) An order made under this section shall not take effect—

    (*a*) in the case of an order made in proceedings in England and Wales, until the expiry of the ordinary time within which an appeal may be instituted or, where an appeal is duly instituted, until is is finally decided or abandoned;
    (*b*) in the case of an order made in proceedings in Scotland, until the expiration of the time within which, by virtue of any statute, an appeal may be instituted or, where such an appeal is duly instituted, until the appeal is finally decided or abandoned.

(3) For the purposes of subsection (2)(*a*)—

    (*a*) an application for a case stated or for leave to appeal shall be treated as the institution of an appeal, and
    (*b*) where a decision on appeal is subject to a further appeal, the appeal is not finally determined until the expiry of the ordinary time within which a further appeal may be instituted or, where a

further appeal is duly instituted, until the further appeal is finally decided or abandoned.

(4) For the purposes of subsection (2)(*b*) the lodging of an application for a state case or note of appeal against sentence shall be treated as the institution of an appeal.

Supplementary provisions

Savings for reports of parliamentary or judicial proceedings.

A–26 (1) Nothing in this Part applies to a fair and accurate report of proceed- **A–26** ings in Parliament.

(2) Nothing in this Part applies to a fair and accurate report of proceedings publicly heard before a court or tribunal exercising judicial authority where the report is published contemporaneously with the proceedings or, if it is not reasonably practicable or would be unlawful to publish a report of them contemporaneously, as soon as publication is reasonably practicable and lawful.

Procedure and punishment.

A–27 (1) No proceedings for an offence under this Part may be instituted in **A–27** England and Wales except by or with the consent of the Attorney General.

(2) For the purposes of the rules in England and Wales against charging more than one offence in the same count or information, each of sections 18 to 23 creates one offence.

(3) A person guilty of an offence under this Part is liable—

(*a*) on conviction on indictment to imprisonment for a term not exceeding two years or a fine or both;

(*b*) on summary conviction to imprisonment for a term not exceeding six months or a fine not exceeding the statutory maximum or both.

Offences by corporations.

A–28 (1) Where a body corporate is guilty of an offence under this Part and it **A–28** is shown that the offence was committed with the consent or connivance of a director, manager, secretary or other similar officer of the body, or a person purporting to act in any such capacity, he as well as the body corporate is guilty of an offence and liable to be proceeded against and punished accordingly.

(2) Where the affairs of a body corporate are managed by its members, subsection (1) applies in relation to the acts and defaults of a member in connection with his functions of management as it applies to a director.

Interpretation.

A–29 In this Part— **A–29**

"broadcast" means broadcast by wireless telegraphy (within the meaning of the Wireless Telegraphy Act 1949) for general reception, whether by way of sound broadcasting or television;

"cable programme service" has the same meaning as in the Cable and Broadcasting Act 1984;

"distribute", and related expressions, shall be construed in accordance with section 19(3) (written material) and section 21(2) (recordings);

"dwelling" means any structure or part of a structure occupied as a person's home or other living accommodation (whether the occupation is separate or shared with others) but does not include any part not so occupied, and for this purpose "structure" includes a tent, caravan, vehicle, vessel or other temporary or movable structure;

"programme" means any item which is broadcast or included in a cable programme service;

"publish", and related expressions, in relation to written material, shall be construed in accordance with section 19(3);

"racial hatred" has the meaning given by section 17;

"recording" has the meaning given by section 21(2), and "play" and "show", and related expressions, in relation to a recording, shall be construed in accordance with that provision;

"written material" includes any sign or other visible representation.

PART IV

Exclusion Orders

Exclusion orders.

A–30   (1) A court by or before which a person is convicted of an offence to which section 31 applies may make an order (an exclusion order) prohibiting him from entering any premises for the purpose of attending any prescribed football match there.   **A–30**

(2) No exclusion order may be made unless the court is satisfied that making such an order in relation to the accused would help to prevent violence or disorder at or in connection with prescribed football matches.

(3) An exclusion order may only be made—

(*a*) in addition to a sentence imposed in respect of the offence of which the accused is convicted, or

(*b*) in addition to a probation order or an order discharging him absolutely or conditionally.

(4) An exclusion order may be made as mentioned in subsection (3)(*b*) notwithstanding anything in sections 2, 7 and 13 of the Powers of Criminal Courts Act 1973 (which relate to orders there mentioned and their effect).

Offences connected with football.

A–31   (1) This section applies to any offence which fulfils one or more of the following three conditions.   **A–31**

(2) The first condition is that the offence was committed during any period relevant to a prescribed football match (as determined under subsections (6) to (8)), while the accused was at, or was entering or leaving or trying to enter or leave, the football ground concerned.

(3) The second condition is that the offence—

(*a*) involved the use or threat of violence by the accused towards another person and was committed while one or each of them was on a journey to or from an association football match.

(*b*) involved the use or threat of violence towards property and was committed while the accused was on such a journey, or

(*c*) was committed under section 5 or Part III while the accused was on such a journey.

(4) The third condition is that the offence was committed under section 1(3) or (4) or 1A(3) or (4) of the Sporting Events (Control of Alcohol etc.) Act 1985 (alcohol on journeys to or from certain sporting events) and the designated sporting event concerned was an association football match.

(5) For the purposes of subsection (3) a person's journey includes breaks (including overnight breaks).

(6) The period beginning 2 hours before the start of the match or (if earlier) 2 hours before the time at which it is advertised to start, and ending 1 hour after the end of it, is a period relevant to it.

(7) Where the match is advertised to start at a particular time on a particular day and is postponed to a later day, the period in the advertised day beginning 2 hours before and ending 1 hour after that time is also a period relevant to it.

(8) Where the match is advertised to start at a particular time on a particular day and does not take place, the period in that day beginning 2 hours before and ending 1 hour after that time is a period relevant to it.

Effect of order.

A–32 (1) An exclusion order shall have effect for such period as is specified in the order. A–32

(2) The period shall not be less than three months or, in the case of a person already subject to an exclusion order, not less than three months plus the unexpired period of the earlier order or, if there is more than one earlier order, of the most recent order.

(3) A person who enters premises in breach of an exclusion order is guilty of an offence and liable on summary conviction to imprisonment for a term not exceeding 1 month or a fine not exceeding level 3 on the standard scale or both.

(4) A constable who reasonably suspects that a person has entered premises in breach of an exclusion order may arrest him without warrant.

Application to terminate order.

A–33 (1) A person in relation to whom an exclusion order has had effect for at least one year may apply to the court by which it was made to terminate it. A–33

(2) On such an application the court may, having regard to the person's character, his conduct since the order was made, the nature of the offence which led to it and any other circumstances of the case, either by order terminate the order (as from a date specified in the terminating order) or refuse the application.

(3) Where an application under this section is refused, a further appli-

cation in respect of the exclusion order shall not be entertained if made within the period of six months beginning with the day of the refusal.

(4) The court may order the applicant to pay all or any part of the costs of an application under this section.

(5) In the case of an exclusion order made by a magistrates' court, the reference in subsection (1) to the court by which it was made includes a reference to any magistrates' court acting for the same petty sessions area as that court.

(6) Section 63(2) of the Magistrates' Courts Act 1980 (power to suspend or rescind orders) does not apply to an exclusion order.

Information.

A–34   (1) Where a court makes an exclusion order, the clerk of the court (in   **A–34** the case of a magistrates' court) or the appropriate officer (in the case of the Crown Court)—

    (*a*) shall give a copy of it to the person to whom it relates,

    (*b*) shall (as soon as reasonably practicable) send a copy of it to the chief officer of police for the police area in which the offence leading to the order was committed, and

    (*c*) shall (as soon as reasonably practicable) send a copy of it to any prescribed person.

(2) Where a court terminates an exclusion order under section 28, the clerk of the court (in the case of a magistrates' court) or the appropriate officer (in the case of the Crown Court)—

    (*a*) shall give a copy of the terminating order to the person to whom the exclusion order relates,

    (*b*) shall (as soon as reasonably practicable) send a copy of the terminating order to the chief officer of police for the police area in which the offence leading to the exclusion order was committed, and

    (*c*) shall, (as soon as reasonably practicable) send a copy of the terminating order to any prescribed person.

(3) References in this section to the clerk of a magistrates' court shall be construed in accordance with section 141 of the Magistrates' Courts Act 1980, reading references to that Act as references to this section.

(4) In this section "prescribed" means prescribed by order made by the Secretary of State.

(5) The power to make an order under this section shall be exercisable by statutory instrument subject to annulment in pursuance of a resolution of either House of Parliament.

Photographs.

A–35   (1) The court by which an exclusion order is made may make an order   **A–35** which—

    (*a*) requires a constable to take a photograph of the person to whom the exclusion order relates or to cause such a photograph to be taken, and (*b*) requires that person to go to a specified police station not later than 7 clear days after the day on which the order under this section is made, and at a specified time of day or between specified times of day, in order to have his photograph taken.

(2) In subsection (1) "specified" means specified in the order made under this section.

(3) No order may be made under this section unless an application to make it is made to the court by or on behalf of the person who is the prosecutor in respect of the offence leading to the exclusion order.

(4) If the person to whom the exclusion order relates fails to comply with an order under this section a constable may arrest him without warrant in order that his photograph may be taken.

Prescribed football matches.

A–36   (1) In this Part "prescribed football match" means an association football match of any description prescribed by order made by the Secretary of State.   A–36

(2) The power to make an order under this section shall be exercisable by statutory instrument subject to annulment in pursuance of a resolution of either House of Parliament.

Extension to other sporting events.

A–37   (1) The Secretary of State may by order provide for sections 30 to 35 to apply as if—   A–37

     (*a*) any reference to an association football match included a reference to a sporting event of a kind specified in the order, and

     (*b*) any reference to a prescribed football match included a reference to such a sporting event of a description specified in the order.

(2) An order under subsection (1) may make such modifications of those sections, as they apply by virtue of the order, as the Secretary of State thinks fit.

(3) The power to make an order under this section shall be exercisable by statutory instrument, and no such order shall be made unless a draft of the order has been laid before and approved by resolution of each House of Parliament.

PART V

Miscellaneous and General

Contamination of or interference with goods with intention of causing public alarm or anxiety, etc.

A–38   (1) It is an offence for a person, with the intention—   A–38

     (*a*) of causing public alarm or anxiety, or

     (*b*) of causing injury to members of the public consuming or using the goods, or

     (*c*) of causing economic loss to any person by reason of the goods being shunned by members of the public, or (*d*) of causing economic loss to any person by reason of steps taken to avoid any such alarm or anxiety, injury or loss,

to contaminate or interfere with goods, or make it appear that goods have been contaminated or interfered with, or to place goods which have been contaminated or interfered with, or which appear to have been contaminated or interfered with, in a place where goods of that description are consumed, used, sold or otherwise supplied.

(2) It is also an offence for a person, with any intention as is mentioned in paragraph (*a*), (*c*) or (*d*) of subsection (1), to threaten that he or another will do, or to claim that he or another has done, any of the acts mentioned in that subsection.

(3) It is an offence for a person to be in possession of any of the following articles with a view to the commission of an offence under subsection (1)—

(*a*) materials to be used for contaminating or interfering with goods or making it appear that goods have been contaminated or interfered with, or

(*b*) goods which have been contaminated or interfered with, or which appear to have been contaminated or interfered with.

(4) A person guilty of an offence under this section is liable—

(*a*) on conviction on indictment to imprisonment for a term not exceeding 10 years or a fine or both, or

(*b*) on summary conviction to imprisonment for a term not exceeding six months or a fine not exceeding the statutory maximum or both.

(5) In this section "goods" includes substances whether natural or manufactured and whether or not incorporated in or mixed with other goods.

(6) The reference in subsection (2) to a person claiming that certain acts have been committed does not include a person who in good faith reports or warns that such acts have been, or appear to have been, committed.

Power to direct trespassers to leave land.

A–39　(1) If the senior police officer reasonably believes that two or more persons have entered land as trespassers and are present there with the common purpose of residing there for any period, that reasonable steps have been taken by or on behalf of the occupier to ask them to leave and—　A–39

(*a*) that any of those persons has caused damage to property on the land or used threatening, abusive or insulting words or behaviour towards the occupier, a member of his family or an employee or agent of his, or

(*b*) that those persons have between them brought twelve or more vehicles on to the land,

he may direct those persons, or any of them, to leave the land.

(2) If a person knowing that such a direction has been given which applies to him—

(*a*) fails to leave the land as soon as reasonably practicable, or

(b) having left again enters the land as a trespasser within the period of three months beginning with the day on which the direction was given,

he commits an offence and is liable on summary conviction to imprisonment for a term not exceeding three months or a fine not exceeding level 4 on the standard scale, or both.

(3) A constable in uniform who reasonably suspects that a person is committing an offence under this section may arrest him without warrant.

(4) In proceedings for an offence under this section it is a defence for the accused to show—

(a) that his original entry on the land was not as a trespasser, or

(b) that he had a reasonable excuse for failing to leave the land as soon as reasonably practicable or, as the case may be, for again entering the land as a trespasser.

(5) In this section—

"land" does not include—

(a) buildings other than—

(i) agricultural buildings within the meaning of section 26(4) of the General Rate Act 1967, or

(ii) scheduled monuments within the meaning of the Ancient Monuments and Archaeological Areas Act 1979;

(b) land forming part of a highway;

"occupier" means the person entitled to possession of the land by virtue of an estate or interest held by him;

"property" means property within the meaning of section 10(1) of the Criminal Damage Act 1971;

"senior police officer" means the most senior in rank of the police officers present at the scene;

"trespasser", in relation to land, means a person who is a trespasser as against the occupier of the land;

"vehicle" includes a caravan as defined in section 29(1) of the Caravan Sites and Control of Development Act 1960;

and a person may be regarded for the purposes of this section as having the purpose of residing in a place notwithstanding that he has a home elsewhere.

Amendments, repeals and savings.

A–40   (1) Schedule 1, which amends the Sporting Events (Control of Alcohol   A–40
etc.) Act 1985 and Part V of the Criminal Justice (Scotland) Act 1980, shall have effect.

(2) Schedule 2, which contains miscellaneous and consequential amendments, shall have effect.

(3) The enactments mentioned in Schedule 3 (which include enactments related to the subject matter of this Act but already obsolete or unnecessary) are repealed to the extent specified in column 3.

(4) Nothing in this Act affects the common law powers in England and Wales to deal with or prevent a breach of the peace.

(5) As respects Scotland, nothing in this Act affects any power of a constable under any rule of law.

Commencement.

A–41   (1) This Act shall come into force on such day as the Secretary of State   A–41 may appoint by order made by statutory instrument, and different days may be appointed for different provisions or different purposes.

(2) Nothing in a provision of this Act applies in relation to an offence committed or act done before the provision comes into force.

(3) Where a provision of this Act comes into force for certain purposes only, the references in subsection (2) to the provision are references to it so far as it relates to those purposes.

Extent.

A–42   (1) The provisions of this Act extend to England and Wales except so far   A–42 as they—

(a) amend or repeal an enactment which does not so extend, or
(b) relate to the extent of provisions to Scotland or Northern Ireland.

(2) The following provisions of this Act extend to Scotland—
in Part I, section 9(2) except paragraph (a);
in Part II, sections 12 and 14 to 16;
Part III;
Part V, except sections 38, 39, 40(4), subsections (1) and (3) of this section and any provision amending or repealing an enactment which does not extend to Scotland.

(3) The following provisions of this Act extend to Northern Ireland—
sections 38, 41, this subsection, section 43 and paragraph 6 of Schedule 2.

Short title.

A–43   This Act may be cited as the Public Order Act 1986.   A–43

SCHEDULES

SCHEDULE 1

SPORTING EVENTS

PART I

England and Wales

Introduction

A–44   1. The Sporting Events (Control of Alcohol etc.) Act 1985 shall be amended as mentioned   A–44 in this Part.

Vehicles

A–45   2. The following shall be inserted after section 1 (offences in connection with alcohol on   **A–45**
coaches and trains)—

"Alcohol on certain other vehicles.

1A.—(1) This section applies to a motor vehicle which—

    (*a*) is not a public service vehicle but is adapted to carry more than 8 passengers, and

    (*b*) is being used for the principal purpose of carrying two or more passengers for the whole or part of a journey to or from a designated sporting event.

(2) A person who knowingly causes or permits intoxicating liquor to be carried on a motor vehicle to which this section applies is guilty of an offence—

    (*a*) if he is its driver, or

    (*b*) if he is not its driver but is its keeper, the servant or agent of its keeper, a person to whom it is made available (by hire, loan or otherwise) by its keeper or the keeper's servant or agent, or the servant or agent of a person to whom it is so made available.

(3) A person who has intoxicating liquor in his possession while on a motor vehicle to which this section applies is guilty of an offence.

(4) A person who is drunk on a motor vehicle to which this section applies is guilty of an offence.

(5) In this section—

    "keeper", in relation to a vehicle, means the person having the duty to take out a licence for it under section 1(1) of the Vehicles (Excise) Act 1971,

    "motor vehicle" means a mechanically propelled vehicle intended or adapted for use on roads, and

    "public service vehicle" has the same meaning as in the Public Passenger Vehicles Act 1981.".

Fireworks etc.

A–46   3. The following shall be inserted after section 2 (offences in connection with alcohol, containers etc. at sports grounds)—   **A–46**

"Fireworks etc.

2A.—(1) A person is guilty of an offence if he has an article or substance to which this section applies in his possession—

    (*a*) at any time during the period of a designated sporting event when he is in any area of a designated sports ground from which the event may be directly viewed, or

    (*b*) while entering or trying to enter a designated sports ground at any time during the period of a designated sporting event at the ground.

(2) It is a defence for the accused to prove that he had possession with lawful authority.

(3) This section applies to any article or substance whose main purpose is the emission of a flare for purposes of illuminating or signalling (as opposed to igniting or heating) or the emission of smoke or a visible gas; and in particular it applies to distress flares, fog signals, and pellets and capsules intended to be used as fumigators or for testing pipes, but not to matches, cigarette lighters or heaters.

(4) This section also applies to any article which is a firework.".

4. The following shall be inserted after section 5—

"Private facilities for viewing events.
5A.—(1) In relation to a room in a designated sports ground—

(*a*) from which designated sporting events may be directly viewed, and
(*b*) to which the general public are not admitted,

sections 2(1)(*a*) and 3(1)(*a*) of this Act have effect with the substitution for the reference to the period of a designated sporting event of a reference to the restricted period defined below.
(2) Subject to any order under subsection (3) below, the restricted period of a designated sporting event for the purposes of this section is the period beginning 15 minutes before the start of the event or (if earlier) 15 minutes before the time at which it is advertised to start and ending 15 minutes after the end of the event, but—

(*a*) where an event advertised to start at a particular time on a particular day is postponed to a later day, the restricted period includes the period in the day on which it is advertised to take place beginning 15 minutes before and ending 15 minutes after that time, and
(*b*) where an event advertised to start at a particular time on a particular day does not take place, the period is the period referred to in paragraph (*a*) above.

(3) The Secretary of State may by order provide, in relation to all designated sporting events or in relation to such descriptions of event as are specified in the order—

(*a*) that the restricted period shall be such period, shorter than that mentioned in subsection (2) above, as may be specified in the order, or
(*b*) that there shall be no restricted period.

(4) An order under this section shall be made by statutory instrument which shall be subject to annulment in pursuance of a resolution of either House of Parliament.

Occasional licences.
5B.—(1) An occasional licence which is in force for any place situated in the area of a designated sports ground, and which would (apart from this section) authorise the sale of intoxicating liquor at the place during the whole or part of the period of a designated sporting event at the ground, shall not authorise such sale.
(2) Where the sale of intoxicating liquor would (apart from this section) be authorised by an occasional licence, its holder is guilty of an offence if he sells or authorises the sale of such liquor and by virtue of this section the licence does not authorise the sale.
(3) A person is guilty of an offence if he consumes intoxicating liquor at a place, or takes such liquor from a place, at a time when an occasional licence which would (apart from this section) authorise the sale of the liquor at the place does not do so by virtue of this section.

Clubs.
5C.—(1) Subsections (3) and (5) of section 39 of the Licensing Act 1964 (clubs), and subsection (4) of that section as it applies to subsection (3), shall not apply as regards the supply of intoxicating liquor in the area of a designated sports ground during the period of a designated sporting event at the ground or as regards the keeping of intoxicating liquor for such supply; but subsections (2) to (5) below shall apply.
(2) During the period of such an event at the ground, intoxicating liquor shall not be supplied by or on behalf of a registered club to a member or guest in the area of the ground except at premises in respect of which the club is registered.

(3) A person supplying or authorising the supply of intoxicating liquor in contravention of subsection (2) above is guilty of an offence.

(4) A person who, during the period of such an event, obtains or consumes intoxicating liquor supplied in contravention of subsection (2) above is guilty of an offence.

(5) If intoxicating liquor is kept in any premises or place by or on behalf of a club for supply to members or their guests in contravention of subsection (2) above, every officer of the club is guilty of an offence unless he shows that it was so kept without his knowledge or consent.

Non-retail sales.

5D.—(1) During the period of a designated sporting event at a designated sports ground, intoxicating liquor shall not be sold in the area of the ground except by sale by retail.

(2) A person selling or authorising the sale of intoxicating liquor in contravention of subsection (1) above is guilty of an offence.

(3) A person who, during the period of such an event, obtains or consumes intoxicating liquor sold in contravention of subsection (1) above is guilty of an offence.".

Supplementary

A–48   5. In sections 2 and 3, after subsection (1) insert—   **A–48**
"(1A) Subsection (1)(a) above has effect subject to section 5A(1) of this Act."

A–49   6. In section 7(3) (power to stop and search vehicles), after "public service vehicle (within   **A–49**
the meaning of section 1 of this Act)" insert "or a motor vehicle to which section 1A of this Act applies".

A–50   7.—(1) Section 8 (penalties) shall be amended as follows.   **A–50**
(2) In paragraph (a) after "1(2)" there shall be inserted "or 1A(2)".
(3) In paragraph (b) after "1(3)" there shall be inserted ",1A(3)", after "2(1)" there shall be inserted ",2A(1)" and after "3(10)" there shall be inserted ",5B(2), 5C(3), 5D(2)".
(4) In paragraph (c) after "1(4)" there shall be inserted ",1A(4)".
(5) At the end there shall be inserted—

> "(d) in the case of an offence under section 5B(3), 5C(4) or 5D(3), to a fine not exceeding level 3 on the standard scale, and
> (e) in the case of an offence under section 5C(5), to a fine not exceeding level 1 on the standard scale.".

Minor amendment

A–51   8. Section 3(9) (notice varying order about sale or supply of intoxicating liquor) shall have   **A–51**
effect, and be taken always to have had effect, as if in paragraph (b) "order" read "notice".

PART II

Scotland

Introduction

A–52   9. Part V of the Criminal Justice (Scotland) Act 1980 (sporting events: control of alcohol   **A–52**
etc.) shall be amended as mentioned in this Part.

Vehicles

A–53   10. After section 70 there shall be inserted the following—   **A–53**

"Alcohol on certain other vehicles.

70A.—(1) This section applies to a motor vehicle which is not a public service vehicle but is adapted to carry more than 8 passengers and is being operated for the principal purpose of conveying two or more passengers for the whole or part of a journey to or from a designated sporting event.

(2) Any person in possession of alcohol on a vehicle to which this section applies shall be guilty of an offence and liable on summary conviction to imprisonment for a period not exceeding 60 days or a fine not exceeding level 3 on the standard scale or both.

(3) Any person who is drunk on a vehicle to which this section applies shall be guilty of an offence and liable on summary conviction to a fine not exceeding level 2 on the standard scale.

(4) Any person who permits alcohol to be carried on a vehicle to which this section applies and—

    (*a*) is the driver of the vehicle, or
    (*b*) where he is not its driver, is the keeper of the vehicle, the employee or agent of the keeper, a person to whom it is made available (by hire, loan or otherwise) by the keeper or the keeper's employee or agent, or the employee or agent of a person to whom it is so made available,

shall, subject to section 71 of this Act, be guilty of an offence and liable on summary conviction to a fine not exceeding level 3 on the standard scale.".

A–54   11. In section 71 (defences in connection with carriage of alcohol) for "or 70" there shall be   **A–54**
substituted ", 70 or 70A(4)".

A–55   12. In section 75 (police powers of enforcement) for "or 70" there shall be substituted ",70   **A–55**
or 70A".

A–56   13. In section 77 (interpretation of Part V)—   **A–56**

    (*a*) the following definitions shall be inserted in the appropriate places alphabetically—
      ""keeper", in relation to a vehicle, means the person having the duty to take out a licence for it under section 1(1) of the Vehicles (Excise) Act 1971;
      "motor vehicle" means a mechanically propelled vehicle intended or adapted for use on roads;"; and
    (*b*) in the definition of "public service vehicle" for the words "Part I of the Transport Act 1980" there shall be substituted the words "the Public Passenger Vehicles Act 1981";".

Fireworks etc.

A–57   14.—(1) After section 72 there shall be inserted the following—   **A–57**

"Possession of fireworks etc. at sporting events.

   72A.—(1) Any person who has entered the relevant area of a designated sports ground and is in possession of a controlled article or substance at any time during the period of a designated sporting event shall be guilty of an offence.

   (2) Any person who, while in possession of a controlled article or substance, attempts to enter the relevant area of a designated sports ground at any time during the period of a designated sporting event at the ground shall be guilty of an offence.

   (3) A person guilty of an offence under subsection (1) or (2) above shall be liable on summary conviction to imprisonment for a period not exceeding 60 days or to a fine not exceeding level 3 on the standard scale or both.

   (4) It shall be a defence for a person charged with an offence under subsection (1) or (2) above to show that he had lawful authority to be in possession of the controlled article or substance.

   (5) In subsections (1) and (2) above "controlled article or substance" means—

    (*a*) any article or substance whose main purpose is the emission of a flare for purposes of illuminating or signalling (as opposed to igniting or heating) or the emission of smoke or a visible gas; and in particular it includes distress flares, fog signals, and pellets and capsules intended to be used as fumigators or for testing pipes, but not matches, cigarette lighters or heaters; and
    (*b*) any article which is a firework.".

   (2) In section 75 (police powers of enforcement) at the end of sub-paragraph (ii) of paragraph (*e*) there shall be inserted—

"; or
      (iii) a controlled article or substance as defined in section 72A(5) of this Act.".

SCHEDULE 2

OTHER AMENDMENTS

Conspiracy and Protection of Property Act 1875 (c. 86)

A–58   1.—(1) In section 7 of the Conspiracy and Protection of Property Act 1875 (offence to inti-   **A–58**
midate etc. with a view to compelling another to abstain from doing or to do an act) for the
words from "shall" to the end there shall be substituted "shall be liable on summary conviction to imprisonment for a term not exceeding 6 months or a fine not exceeding level 5 on the
standard scale or both.".
    (2) And the following shall be added at the end of that section—
    "A constable may arrest without warrant anyone he reasonably suspects is committing an
offence under this section.".

Prevention of Crime Act 1953 (c. 14)

A–59   2. In section 1 of the Prevention of Crime Act 1953 (offence to have offensive weapon) at   **A–59**
the end of subsection (4) (offensive weapon includes article intended by person having it for
use by him) there shall be added "or by some other person".

Civic Government (Scotland) Act 1982 (c. 45)

A–60   3 —(1) Part V of the Civic Government (Scotland) Act 1982 (public processions) shall be   **A–60**
amended in accordance with this paragraph.
    (2) In section 62 (notification of processions)—

        (*a*) in subsection (1)—
           (i) after "below" there shall be inserted "(*a*)"; and
           (ii) at the end there shall be inserted—"; and
           (*b*) to the chief constable.";
        (*b*) in subsection (2)—
           (i) in paragraph (*a*), after "council" there shall be inserted "and to the office of
              the chief constable";
           (ii) in paragraph (*b*), for "that office" there shall be substituted "those offices";
        (*c*) in subsection (4)—
           (i) after "area" there shall be inserted "(*a*)"; and
           (ii) after "them" there shall be inserted—"; and
           (*b*) intimated to the chief constable," and
        (*d*) in subsection (12), in the definition of "public place", for "the Public Order Act
           1936" there shall be substituted "Part II of the Public Order Act 1986".

    (3) In section 63 (functions of regional and islands councils in relation to processions)—

        (*a*) after subsection (1) there shall be inserted—
        "(1A) Where notice of a proposal to hold a procession has been given or falls to be
        treated as having been given in accordance with section 62(1) of this Act—
           (*a*) if a regional or islands council have made an order under subsection (1) above
               they may at any time thereafter, after consulting the chief constable, vary or
               revoke the order and, where they revoke it, make any order which they were
               empowered to make under that subsection;
           (*b*) if they have decided not to make an order they may at any time thereafter,
               after consulting the chief constable, make any order which they were empow-
               ered to make under that subsection.";
        (*b*) in subsection (2) after "(1)" there shall be inserted "or (1A)";

(*c*) in subsection (3)—
    (i) in paragraph (*a*)(i), after "(1)" there shall be inserted or (1A) above";
    (ii) in paragraph (*a*)(ii), for "such an order" there shall be substituted "an order under subsection (1) above or to revoke an order already made under subsection (1) or (1A) above";
    (iii) at the end of paragraph (*a*)(ii), for "and" there shall be substituted—
        "(iii) where they have, under subsection (1A) above, varied such an order, a copy of the order as varied and a written statement of the reasons for the variation; and";
    (iv) in paragraph (*b*), after "(1)" there shall be inserted "or (1A)", and after "made" where third occurring there shall be inserted "and, if the order has been varied under subsection (1A) above, that it has been so varied"; and
    (v) at the end of paragraph (*b*) there shall be inserted—"; and
        (*c*) where they have revoked an order made under subsection (1) or (1A) above in relation to a proposal to hold a procession, make such arrangements as will ensure that persons who might take or are taking part in that procession are made aware of the fact that the order has been revoked.".

(4) In section 64 (appeals against orders under section 63)—

    (*a*) in subsection (1) for the words from "against" to the end there shall be substituted—
    "against—
        (*a*) an order made under section 63(1) or (1A) of this Act; or
        (*b*) a variation under section 63(1A) of this Act of an order made under section 63(1) or (1A),

    in relation to the procession.";

    (*b*) in subsection (4) after "make" there shall be inserted "or, as the case may be, to vary"; and
    (*c*) in subsection (7) after "order" there shall be inserted "or, as the case may be, the variation of whose order".

(5) In section 65 (offences and enforcement)—

    (*a*) in paragraphs (*b*) and (*c*) of subsection (1), after "(1)" there shall be inserted "or (1A)"; and
    (*b*) in paragraphs (*b*) and (*c*) of subsection (2), after "(1)" there shall be inserted "or (1A)".

(6) In section 66 (relationship with Public Order Act 1936)—

    (*a*) for "the Public Order Act 1936" there shall be substituted "Part II of the Public Order Act 1986";
    (*b*) in paragraph (*a*), for "or order made under section 3" there shall be substituted "under section 12", and "or that order" shall be omitted; and
    (*c*) in paragraph (*b*), "or order under the said section 3" shall be omitted.

Criminal Justice Act 1982 (c. 48)

A–61   4. The following shall be inserted at the end of Part II of Schedule 1 to the Criminal Justice   **A–61**
Act 1982 (statutory offences excluded from provisions for early release of prisoners)—

PUBLIC ORDER ACT 1986

27. Section 1 (riot).
28. Section 2 (violent disorder).
29. Section 3 (affray).".

Cable and Broadcasting Act 1984 (c.46)

A–62   5.— (1) The Cable and Broadcasting Act 1984 as it extends to England and Wales and Scot-   **A–62**
land is amended as follows.

(2) Omit section 27 (inclusion of programme in cable programme service likely to stir up racial hatred).

(3) In section 28 (amendment of the law of defamation), at the end add—

"(6) In this section "words" includes pictures, visual images, gestures and other methods of signifying meaning.".

(4) In section 33(2), in the definition of "relevant offence" omit "an offence under section 27 above or".

A–63   6.—(1) Section 27 of the Cable and Broadcasting Act 1984 as it extends to Northern Ireland   **A–63**
is amended as follows.

(2) For subsections (1) to (5) substitute—

"(1) If a programme involving threatening, abusive or insulting visual images or sounds is included in a cable programme service, each of the persons mentioned in subsection (2) below is guilty of an offence if—

     (*a*) he intends thereby to stir up racial hatred, or

     (*b*) having regard to all the circumstances racial hatred is likely to be stirred up thereby.

(2) The persons are—

     (*a*) the person providing the cable programme service,

     (*b*) any person by whom the programme is produced or directed, and

     (*c*) any person by whom offending words or behaviour are used.

(3) If the person providing the service, or a person by whom the programme was produced or directed, is not shown to have intended to stir up racial hatred, it is a defence for him to prove that—

     (*a*) he did not know and had no reason to suspect that the programme would involve the offending material, and

     (*b*) having regard to the circumstances in which the programme was included in a cable programme service, it was not reasonably practicable for him to secure the removal of the material.

(4) It is a defence for a person by whom the programme was produced or directed who is not shown to have intended to stir up racial hatred to prove that he did not know and had no reason to suspect—

     (*a*) that the programme would be included in a cable programme service, or

     (*b*) that the circumstances in which the programme would be so included would be such that racial hatred would be likely to be stirred up.

(5) It is a defence for a person by whom offending words or behaviour were used and who is not shown to have intended to stir up racial hatred to prove that he did not know and had no reason to suspect—

     (*a*) that a programme involving the use of the offending material would be included in a cable programme service, or

     (*b*) that the circumstances in which a programme involving the use of the offending material would be so included, or in which a programme so included would involve the use of the offending material, would be such that racial hatred would be likely to be stirred up.

(5A) A person who is not shown to have intended to stir up racial hatred is not guilty of an offence under this section if he did not know, and had no reason to suspect, that the offending material was threatening, abusive or insulting.

(5B) A person guilty of an offence under this section is liable—

     (*a*) on conviction on indictment to imprisonment for a term not exceeding two years or a fine or both;

     (*b*) on summary conviction to imprisonment for a term not exceeding six months or a fine not exceeding the statutory maximum or both.".

(3) In subsection (8) (consents to prosecutions), for the words from "shall not be instituted" to the end substitute "shall not be instituted except by or with the consent of the Attorney General for Northern Ireland.".

(4) In subsection (9) (interpretation) for " 'racial group' means a group of persons" substitute " 'racial hatred' means hatred against a group of persons in Northern Ireland".
(5) After subsection (10) insert—
"(11) This section extends to Northern Ireland only.".

Police and Criminal Evidence Act 1984 (c. 60)

A–64   7. In section 17(1)(*c*) of the Police and Criminal Evidence Act 1984 (entry for purpose of   **A–64**
arrest for certain offences) in sub-paragraph (i) the words from "4" to "peace)" shall be omitted and after sub-paragraph (ii) there shall be inserted—
"(iii) section 4 of the Public Order Act 1986 (fear or provocation of violence);".

SCHEDULE 3

REPEALS

Chapter	Short title	Extent of repeal
13 Chas. 2. Stat. 1. c. 5.	Tumultuous Petitioning Act 1661.	The whole Act.
33 Geo. 3. c. 67.	Shipping Offences Act 1793.	The whole Act.
57 Geo. 3. c. 19.	Seditious Meetings Act 1817.	The whole Act.
5 Geo. 4. c. 83.	Vagrancy Act 1824.	In section 4, the words from "every person being armed" to "arrestable offence" and from "and every such gun" to the end.
2 & 3 Vict. c. 47.	Metropolitan Police Act 1839.	In section 54, paragraph 13.
2 & 3 Vict. c. xciv.	City of London Police Act 1839.	In section 35, paragraph 13.
3 Edw. 7. c. ccl.	Erith Tramways and Improvement Act 1903.	Section 171.
1 Edw. 8 & 1 Geo. 6. c. 6.	Public Order Act 1936.	Section 3. Section 4. Section 5. Section 5A. In section 7, in subsection (2) the words "or section 5 or 5A" and in subsection (3) the words ", four or five". Section 8(6). In section 9, in subsection (1) the definition of "public procession" and in subsection (3) the words "by the council of any borough or district or".
7 & 8 Geo. 6. c. xxi.	Middlesex County Council Act 1944.	Section 309.
1967 c. 58.	Criminal Law Act 1967.	Section 11(3). In Schedule 2, paragraph 2(1)(*b*).
1968 c. 54.	Theatres Act 1968.	Section 5. In sections 7(2), 8, 9(1), 10(1)(*a*) and (*b*), 15(1)(*a*) and 18(2), the references to section 5.

Chapter	Short title	Extent of repeal
1976 c. 74.	Race Relations Act 1976.	Section 70. Section 79(6).
1976 c. xxxv.	County of South Glamorgan Act 1976.	Section 25. In Part I of Schedule 3, the entry relating to section 25.
1980 c. 62.	Criminal Justice (Scotland) Act 1980.	In section 75(e)(i), the word "or" at the end.
1980 c. x.	County of Merseyside Act 1980.	In section 30(2), paragraph (b), the word "and" preceding that paragrpah and the words from "and may make" to the end. In section 30(5), the words "in the said section 31 or". Section 31. In section 137(2), the reference to section 131.
1980 c. xi.	West Midlands County Council Act 1980.	Section 38, except subsection (4). In section 116(2), the reference to section 38.
1980 c. xiii.	Cheshire County Council Act 1980.	Section 28, except subsection (4). In section 108(2), the reference to section 28.
1980 c. xv.	Isle of Wight Act 1980.	Section 26, except subsection (4). In section 63(2), the reference to section 26.
1981 c. xi.	Greater Manchester Act 1981.	Section 56, except subsection (4). In section 179(2), the reference to section 56.
1981 c. xxv.	East Sussex Act 1981.	Section 29. In section 102(2), the reference to section 29.
1982 c. 45.	Civic Government (Scotland) Act 1982.	Section 62(10). In section 63(3)(a)(i), the word "or" at the end. In section 66, in paragraph (a), the words "or that order", and in paragraph (b) the words "or order under the said section 3".
1982 c. 48.	Criminal Justice Act 1982.	In Part I of Schedule 1, the entries relaing to riot and affray.
1984 c. 46.	Cable and Broadcasting Act 1984.	Section 27. In section 33(2), the words "an offence under section 27 above or".
1984 c. 60.	Police and Criminal Evidence Act 1984.	In section 17(1)(c)(i) the words from "4" to "peace)".
1985 c. 57.	Sporting Events (Control of Alcohol etc.) Act 1985.	In section 8, the word "and" at the end of paragraph (b).

APPENDIX 2

Sporting Events (Control of Alcohol etc.) Act 1985[1]

(1985 c.57)

ARRANGEMENT OF SECTIONS

An Act to make provision for punishing those who cause or permit intoxicating liquor to be carried on public service vehicles and railway passenger vehicles carrying passengers to or from designated sporting events or who possess intoxicating liquor on such vehicles and those who possess intoxicating liquor or certain articles capable of causing injury at designated sports grounds during the period of designated sporting events, for punishing drunkenness on such vehicles and, during the period of designated sporting events, at such grounds and, where licensed premises or premises in respect of which a club is registered (for the purposes of the Licensing Act 1964) are within designated sports grounds, to make provision for regulating the sale or supply of intoxicating liquor and for the closure of bars.

[25th July 1985]

Offences in connection with alcohol on coaches and trains

A2–01   1.—(1) This section applies to a vehicle which—   A2–01

 (a) is a public service vehicle or railway passenger vehicle, and
 (b) is being used for the principal purpose of carrying passengers for the whole or part of a journey to or from a designated sporting event.

(2) A person who knowingly causes or permits intoxicating liquor to be carried on a vehicle to which this section applies is guilty of an offence—

 (a) if the vehicle is a public service vehicle and he is the operator of the vehicle or the servant or agent of the operator, or

---

[1] The Act is set out as amended by the Public Order Act 1986, Sched. 1. Insertions and amendments are set out in square brackets.

(*b*) if the vehicle is a hired vehicle and he is the person to whom it is hired or the servant or agent of that person.

(3) A person who has intoxicating liquor in his possession while on a vehicle to which this section applies is guilty of an offence.

(4) A person who is drunk on a vehicle to which this section applies is guilty of an offence.

(5) In this section "public service vehicle" and "operator" have the same meaning as in the Public Passenger Vehicles Act 1981.

[Alcohol on certain other vehicles[2]

A2–02   **1A.**—(1) This section applies to a motor vehicle which—   **A2–02**

(*a*) is not a public service vehicle but is adapted to carry more than 8 passengers, and

(*b*) is being used for the principal purpose of carrying two or more passengers for the whole or part of a journey to or from a designated sporting event.

(2) A person who knowingly causes or permits intoxicating liquor to be carried on a motor vehicle to which this section applies is guilty of an offence—

(*a*) if he is its driver, or

(*b*) if he is not its driver but is its keeper, the servant or agent of its keeper, a person to whom it is made available (by hire, loan or otherwise) by its keeper or the keeper's servant or agent, or the servant or agent of a person to whom it is so made available.

(3) A person who has intoxicating liquor in his possession while on a motor vehicle to which this section applies is guilty of an offence.

(4) A person who is drunk on a motor vehicle to which this section applies is guilty of an offence.

(5) In this section—

"keeper", in relation to a vehicle, means the person having the duty to take out a licence for it under section 1(1) of the Vehicles (Excise) Act 1971,

"motor vehicle" means a mechanically propelled vehicle intended or adapted for use on roads, and

"public service vehicle" has the same meaning as in the Public Passenger Vehicles Act 1981.".]

Offences in connection with alcohol, containers etc. at sports grounds

A2–03   **2.**—(1) A person who has intoxicating liquor or an article to which this   **A2–03** section applies in his possession—

(*a*) at any time during the period of a designated sporting event when

---

[2] Inserted by Public Order Act 1986, Sched. 1, para. 2.

he is in any area of a designated sports ground from which the event may be directly viewed, or

(*b*) while entering or trying to enter a designated sports ground at any time during the period of a designated sporting event at that ground,

is guilty of an offence.

[(1A) Subsection (1)(*a*) above has effect subject to section 5A(1) of this Act.]³

(2) A person who is drunk in a designated sports ground at any time during the period of a designated sporting event at that ground or is drunk while entering or trying to enter such a ground at any time during the period of a designated sporting event at that ground is guilty of an offence.

(3) This section applies to any article capable of causing injury to a person struck by it, being—

(*a*) a bottle, can or other portable container (including such an article when crushed or broken) which—
(i) is for holding any drink, and
(ii) is of a kind which, when empty, is normally discarded or returned to, or left to be recovered by, the supplier, or
(*b*) part of an article falling within paragraph (*a*) above;

but does not apply to anything that is for holding any medicinal product (within the meaning of the Medicines Act 1968).

[Fireworks, etc.

A2–04   **2A.**—(1) A person is guilty of an offence if he has an article or substance to which this section applies in his possession—   **A2–(**

(*a*) at any time during the period of a designated sporting event when he is in any area of a designated sports ground from which the event may be directly viewed, or
(*b*) while entering or trying to enter a designated sports ground at any time during the period of a designated sporting event at the ground.

(2) It is a defence for the accused to prove that he had possession with lawful authority.

(3) This section applies to any article or substance whose main purpose is the emission of a flare for purposes of illuminating or signalling (as opposed to igniting or heating) or the emission of smoke or a visible gas; and in particular it applies to distress flares, fog signals, and pellets and capsules intended to be used as fumigators or for testing pipes, but not to matches, cigarette lighters or heaters.

(4) This section also applies to any article which is a firework.]⁴

---

³ Inserted by Public Order Act 1986, Sched. 1, para. 5.
⁴ Inserted by Public Order Act 1986, Sched. 1, para. 5.

Licensing hours within sports grounds

–05   **3.**—(1) Where licensed premises or registered club premises are situated   **A2–05**
within the area of a designated sports ground—

(a) the permitted hours in those premises for the purposes of Part III
of the Licensing Act 1964 (hours during which intoxicating liquor
may be sold or supplied in the premises or consumed in or taken
from the premises) shall not, subject to the provisions of any
order under this section in respect of the premises, include any
part of the period of any designated sporting event at the designated sports ground, and

(b) section 63(2)(b) of that Act (intoxicating liquor ordered for consumption off the premises) shall not apply during any part of that
period.

[(1A) Subsection (1)(a) above has effect subject to section 5A(1) of this
Act.][5]

(2) Where licensed premises or registered club premises are so situated,
a magistrates' court may by an order under this section provide—

(a) that the permitted hours in the premises or any part of them shall,
during so much of the period of any designated sporting event at
the designated sports ground as would (apart from this section) be
included in the permitted hours, include such period as may be
determined under the order, and

(b) that during the period so determined such conditions as may be
specified in the order (including conditions modifying or excluding any existing conditions of the justices' licence or, as the case
may be, the registration certificate) shall apply in respect of the
sale or supply of intoxicating liquor in the premises;

and the justices' licence or, as the case may be, registration certificate shall
have effect accordingly.

(3) An order under this section shall not apply to any part of the premises from which designated sporting events at the designated sports ground
may be directly viewed.

(4) It shall be a condition of any order under this section that there shall
be in attendance at the designated sports ground throughout the period of
any designated sporting event a person—

(a) who is responsible for securing compliance with this section,
being the holder of the justices' licence or a person designated by
him or, in the case of registered club premises, a person designated by the club, and

(b) written notice of whose name and current address has been given
to the chief officer of police.

(5) A magistrates' court may—

(a) vary an order under this section, either generally or in respect of a

[5] Inserted by Public Order Act 1986, Sched. 1, para. 5.

307

particular designated sporting event and, in the latter case, may in particular provide that the order shall not have effect in respect of that event, or

(b) revoke the order.

(6) A magistrates' court shall not in respect of any sports ground make an order under this section in any terms, or vary the terms of such an order (otherwise than by providing for it not to have effect in respect of a particular event), unless satisfied that, having regard in particular to the arrangements made for the admission of spectators and for regulating their conduct, an order in the terms proposed is not likely to be detrimental to the orderly conduct or safety of spectators.

(7) Where an order under this section is in force in respect of any sports ground and a police officer of rank not less than inspector is of the opinion—

(a) that the sale or supply of intoxicating liquor in pursuance of the order during the period of a particular designated sporting event is likely to be detrimental to the orderly conduct or safety of spectators at that event, and

(b) that it is impracticable for an application to be made to a magistrates' court for the variation of the order in respect of that event,

he may give written notice to the person whose name has been given to the chief officer of police in accordance with subsection (4) above.

(8) A notice is to be treated as given to a person under subsection (7) above if it is left at—

(a) the licensed premises or, as the case may be, the registered club premises, or

(b) the address notified under subsection (4)(b) above.

(9) [An order]⁶ under subsection (7) above may state that, with effect from the time when the notice is given, the order under this section shall, in respect of the sporting event concerned—

(a) cease to have effect, or

(b) have effect subject to such modifications as may be specified in the order;

and the order shall apply accordingly.

(10) A person who sells or supplies or authorises the sale or supply of intoxicating liquor at any time that is excluded from the permitted hours by virtue of this section or in contravention of conditions imposed under this section is not guilty of an offence under section 59(1)(a) of the Licensing Act 1964 (prohibition of sale etc. outside permitted hours) but shall be guilty of an offence under this subsection if—

(a) he is the holder of the justices' licence or, as the case may be, an officer of the club, or

---

⁶ Inserted by Public Order Act 1986, Sched. 1, para. 8.

(*b*) he knows or has reasonable cause to believe the sale or supply to be such a contravention.

(11) A person is not guilty of an offence under section 59(1)(*b*) of that Act (prohibition of consumption etc. outside permitted hours) in respect of any time which by virtue of a notice under subsection (7) above is not part of the permitted hours unless he knows or has reasonable cause to believe that the time is not part of those hours.

Supplementary provisions about orders under section 3

06   **4.**—(1) Subject to the provisions of this section, an order under section 3   **A2–06** of this Act in respect of any premises shall (unless sooner revoked) cease to have effect—

(*a*) on the coming into effect of a further order under that section in respect of those premises, or

(*b*) on the expiration of the period of five months beginning with the day on which it comes into effect,

whichever is the sooner.

(2) An order under that section in respect of licensed premises shall cease to have effect on the transfer of the justices' licence or on the premises ceasing to be licensed premises.

(3) An order under that section in respect of registered club premises shall cease to have effect if the club ceases to be registered.

(4) Where an order under that section is in force in respect of any premises and application is made not less than twenty-eight days before the order is due to expire for renewal of the order or for a further order in respect of the premises, the first-mentioned order shall not cease to have effect by virtue of subsection (1)(*b*) above until the application is disposed of by the magistrates' court.

(5) Applications for or relating to orders under that section shall be made to the magistrates' court acting for the petty sessions area in which the premises are situated.

(6) There may be charged by justices' clerks—

(*a*) in respect of the making (including the renewal) of an order under that section, a fee of £12.50, and

(*b*) in respect of the variation of such an order where application for the variation is made by the holder of the justices' licence or, as the case may be, the club, a fee of £4,

notwithstanding anything in section 137(1) of the Magistrates' Courts Act 1980 (Fees).

(7) An order under section 29 of the Licensing Act 1964 (fees chargeable in licensing matters) may provide that subsection (6) above shall have effect as if, for either or both of the amounts mentioned in that subsection, there were substituted such other amounts or amounts as may be specified in the order.

(8) Section 197 of the Licensing Act 1964 (Service of notices) applies for the purposes of this Act as it applies for the purposes of that Act.

(9) The Schedule to this Act shall have effect, but subject to any provision that may be made by rules of court.

Appeals

A2–07　　　**5.**—(1) Any party to the proceedings who is aggrieved by a decision of a　　A2–
magistrates' court on an application for or in respect of an order under section 3 of this Act, other than an application in respect of a particular designated sporting event or particular designated sporting events, may appeal to the Crown Court on such grounds as may be specified in his notice of appeal.

(2) In the event of such an appeal, any other party to the proceedings shall be party to the appeal.

(3) The judgment of the Crown Court on any such appeal shall be final.

[Private facilities for viewing events

A2–08　　　**5A.**—(1) In relation to a room in a designated sports ground—　　　　A2–

(*a*) from which designated sporting events may be directly viewed, and

(*b*) to which the general public are not admitted,

sections 2(1)(*a*) and 3(1)(*a*) of this Act have effect with the substitution for the reference to the period of a designated sporting event of a reference to the restricted period defined below.

(2) Subject to any order under subsection (3) below, the restricted period of a designated sporting event for the purposes of this section is the period beginning 15 minutes before the start of the event or (if earlier) 15 minutes before the time at which it is advertised to start and ending 15 minutes after the end of the event, but—

(*a*) where an event advertised to start at a particular time on a particular day is postponed to a later day, the restricted period includes the period in the day on which it is advertised to take place beginning 15 minutes before and ending 15 minutes after that time, and

(*b*) where an event advertised to start at a particular time on a particular day does not take place, the period is the period referred to in paragraph (*a*) above.

(3) The Secretary of State may by order provide, in relation to all designated sporting events or in relation to such descriptions of event as are specified in the order—

(*a*) that the restricted period shall be such period, shorter than that mentioned in subsection (2) above, as may be specified in the order, or

(*b*) that there shall be no restricted period.

(4) An order under this section shall be made by statutory instrument which shall be subject to annulment in pursuance of a resolution of either House of Parliament.

Occasional licences

2–09   **5B.**—(1) An occasional licence which is in force for any place situated in   A2–09
the area of a designated sports ground, and which would (apart from this section) authorise the sale of intoxicating liquor at the place during the whole or part of the period of a designated sporting event at the ground, shall not authorise such sale.

(2) Where the sale of intoxicating liquor would (apart from this section) be authorised by an occasional licence, its holder is guilty of an offence if he sells or authorises the sale of such liquor and by virtue of this section the licence does not authorise the sale.

(3) A person is guilty of an offence if he consumes intoxicating liquor at a place, or takes such liquor from a place, at a time when an occasional licence which would (apart from this section) authorise the sale of the liquor at the place does not do so by virtue of this section.

Clubs

2–10   **5C.**—(1) Subsections (3) and (5) of section 39 of the Licensing Act 1964   A2–10
(clubs), and subsection (4) of that section as it applies to subsection (3), shall not apply as regards the supply of intoxicating liquor in the area of a designated sports ground during the period of a designated sporting event at the ground or as regards the keeping of intoxicating liquor for such supply; but subsections (2) to (5) below shall apply.

(2) During the period of such an event at the ground, intoxicating liquor shall not be supplied by or on behalf of a registered club to a member or guest in the area of the ground except at premises in respect of which the club is registered.

(3) A person supplying or authorising the supply of intoxicating liquor in contravention of subsection (2) above is guilty of an offence.

(4) A person who, during the period of such an event, obtains or consumes intoxicating liquor supplied in contravention of subsection (2) above is guilty of an offence.

(5) If intoxicating liquor is kept in any premises or place by or on behalf of a club for supply to members or their guests in contravention of subsection (2) above, every officer of the club is guilty of an offence unless he shows that it was so kept without his knowledge or consent.

Non-retail sales

2–11   **5D.**—(1) During the period of a designated sporting event at a desig-   A2–11
nated sports ground, intoxicating liquor shall not be sold in the area of the ground except by sale by retail.

(2) A person selling or authorising the sale of intoxicating liquor in contravention of subsection (1) above is guilty of an offence.

(3) A person who, during the period of such an event, obtains or con-

sumes intoxicating liquor sold in contravention of subsection (1) above is
guilty of an offence.][7]

Closure of bars

A2–12   **6.**—(1) If at any time during the period of a designated sporting event at   A2–12
any designated sports ground it appears to a constable in uniform that the
sale or supply of intoxicating liquor at any bar within the ground is detrimental to the orderly conduct or safety of spectators at that event, he may
require any person having control of the bar to close it and keep it closed
until the end of that period.

(2) A person who fails to comply with a requirement imposed under subsection (1) above is guilty of an offence, unless he shows that he took all
reasonable steps to comply with it.

Powers of enforcement

A2–13   **7.**—(1) A constable may, at any time during the period of a designated   A2–13
sporting event at any designated sports ground, enter any part of the
ground for the purpose of enforcing the provisions of this Act.

(2) A constable may search a person he has reasonable grounds to suspect is committing or has committed an offence under this Act, and may
arrest such a person.

(3) A constable may stop a public service vehicle (within the meaning of
section 1 of this Act) [or a motor vehicle to which section 1A of this Act
applies][8] and may search such a vehicle or a railway passenger vehicle if he
has reasonable grounds to suspect that an offence under that section is
being or has been committed in respect of the vehicle.

Penalties for offences

A2–14   **8.** A person guilty of an offence under this Act shall be liable on sum-   A2–14
mary conviction—

> (*a*) in the case of an offence under section 1(2) [or 1A(2)][9]
> (*b*) in the case of an offence under section 1(3), [1A(3)],[10] 2(1),
>   [2A(1)],[11] 3(10), [5B(2), 5C(3), 5D(2)][12] or 6(2) to a fine not
>   exceeding level 3 on the standard scale or to imprisonment for a
>   term not exceeding three months or both, and
> (*c*) in the case of an offence under section 1(4), [1A(4)][13] or 2(2), to a
>   fine not exceeding level 2 on the standard scale.
> [(*d*) in the case of an offence under section 5B(3), 5C(4) or 5D(3), to a
>   fine not exceeding level 3 on the standard scale, and

[7] Inserted by Public Order Act 1986, Sched. 1, para. 4.
[8] Inserted by Public Order Act 1986, Sched. 1, para. 6.
[9] Inserted by Public Order Act 1986, Sched. 1, para. 7(2).
[10] Inserted by Public Order Act 1986, Sched. 1, para. 7(3).
[11] Inserted by Public Order Act 1986, Sched. 1, para. 7(3).
[12] Inserted by Public Order Act 1986, Sched. 1, para. 7(3).
[13] Inserted by Public Order Act 1986, Sched. 1, para. 7(4).

(*e*) in the case of an offence under section 5C(5), to a fine not exceeding level 1 on the standard scale.]¹⁴

Interpretation

A2–15   **9.**—(1) The following provisions shall have effect for the interpretation   **A2–15** of this Act.

(2) "Designated sports ground" means any place—

(*a*) used (wholly or partly) for sporting events where accommodation is provided for spectators, and

(*b*) for the time being designated, or of a class designated, by order made by the Secretary of State;

and an order under this subsection may include provision for determining for the purposes of this Act the outer limit of any designated sports ground.

(3) "Designated sporting event"—

(*a*) means a sporting event or proposed sporting event for the time being designated, or of a class designated, by order made by the Secretary of State, and

(*b*) includes a designated sporting event within the meaning of Part V of the Criminal Justice (Scotland) Act 1980;

and an order under this subsection may apply to events or proposed events outside Great Britain as well as those in England and Wales.

(4) The period of a designated sporting event is the period beginning two hours before the start of the event or (if earlier) two hours before the time at which it is advertised to start and ending one hour after the end of the event, but—

(*a*) where an event advertised to start at a particular time on a particular day is postponed to a later day, the period includes the period in the day on which it is advertised to take place beginning two hours before and ending one hour after that time, and

(*b*) where an event advertised to start at a particular time on a particular day does not take place, the period is the period referred to in paragraph (*a*) above.

(5) "Registered club premises" means premises in respect of which a club is registered.

(6) This Act does not apply to any sporting event or proposed sporting event—

(*a*) where all competitors are to take part otherwise than for reward, and

(*b*) to which all spectators are to be admitted free of charge.

(7) Expressions used in this Act and in the Licensing Act 1964 have the same meaning as in that Act, and section 58(2) of that Act (meaning of chief officer of police) applies for the purposes of this Act as it applies for the purposes of Part II of that Act.

---

¹⁴ Inserted by Public Order Act 1986, Sched. 1, para. 7(5).

(8) Any power to make an order under this section shall be exercisable by statutory instrument subject to annulment in pursuance of a resolution of either House of Parliament.

Amendment of Criminal Justice (Scotland) Act (1980)

A2–16   **10.** Part V of the Criminal Justice (Scotland) Act 1980 shall be amended   A2–16
as follows—

 (*a*) in section 68(1), after paragraph (*b*) there shall be inserted—
"(*c*) a sporting event, or a class of sporting event, taking place outside Great Britain:";

 (*b*) in section 69, after the words "public service vehicle" there shall be inserted the words "or railway passenger vehicle" and after the word "passengers" there shall be inserted the words "for the whole or part of a journey";

 (*c*) in section 77, at the end of the definition of "designated" there shall be added the words "and 'designated sporting event' includes a sporting event designated, or of a class designated, under section 9(3)(*a*) of the Sporting Events (Control of Alcohol etc.) Act 1985"; and

 (*d*) in section 77, after the definition of "public service vehicle" there shall be inserted the following definition—
" 'railway passenger vehicle' has the same meaning as in the Licensing (Scotland) Act 1976".

Short titlement and extent

A2–17   **11.**—(1) This Act may be cited as the Sporting Events (Control of Alco-   A2–17
hol etc.) Act 1985.

(2) Sections 1 to 9 of and the Schedule to this Act extend to England and Wales only.

(3) This Act does not extend to Northern Ireland.

Section 4

SCHEDULE

PROCEDURE

A2–18   1. An application for or in respect of an order under section 3 of this Act shall be made by   A2–18
complaint to a justice of the peace acting for the petty sessions area for which the magistrates'
court having jurisdiction in the matter acts.

2.—(1) A complaint for the making or variation of such an order may be made—

 (*a*) in respect of licensed premises, by the holder of the justices' licence, and
 (*b*) in respect of registered club premises, by the chairman or secretary of the club.

(2) The justice of the peace to whom the complaint is so made shall issue—

 (*a*) a summons directed to the chief officer of police, and
 (*b*) a summons directed to the local authority,

and each summons shall require the person to whom it is directed to appear before the magistrates' court to show why the order should not be made or, as the case may be, varied.

(3) A summons directed to a local authority under this paragraph shall not have effect (and accordingly the local authority shall not be party to the proceedings) unless there is in force in respect of the sports ground concerned a certificate under the Safety of Sports Grounds Act 1975.

(4) A copy of any order made on a complaint made by any of the persons mentioned in sub-paragraph (1) above shall be sent to the chief officer of police and (where the local authority are party to the proceedings) to the local authority.

3.—(1) A complaint for the variation or revocation of such an order may be made—

> (a) by the chief officer of police, or
> (b) where such a certificate is in force in respect of the sports ground concerned, by the local authority.

(2) The justice of the peace to whom the complaint is so made shall issue a summons directed to the holder of the justices' licence or, in the case of registered club premises, to the chairman or secretary of the club requiring him to appear before the magistrates' court to show cause why the order should not be varied or revoked.

(3) A copy of any order made on a complaint made by any of the persons mentioned in sub-paragraph (1) above shall be sent to the holder of the justices' licence or, as the case may be, to the chairman or secretary of the club.

4. Where a complaint is made for a new order under section 3 of this Act—

> (a) there shall be delivered to the justice of the peace at the time the complaint is made a plan of the sports ground showing the premises within that ground where intoxicating liquor would be sold or supplied in pursuance of the proposed order, and
> (b) the hearing shall not take place before the end of the period of 28 days beginning with the day on which the complaint is made.

5. On any complaint made to a magistrates' court for or in respect of an order under section 3 of this Act, or appeal to the Crown Court in respect of such a complaint, to which a club is a party, the club, if not represented by counsel or a solicitor, shall be heard by the chairman or secretary, by any member of the committee having the general management of the affairs of the club or by any officer of the club duly authorised.

6. In this Schedule, "local authority" has the same meaning as in the Safety of Sports Grounds Act 1975.

INDEX